When the Stars
Went to War

Roy Hoopes

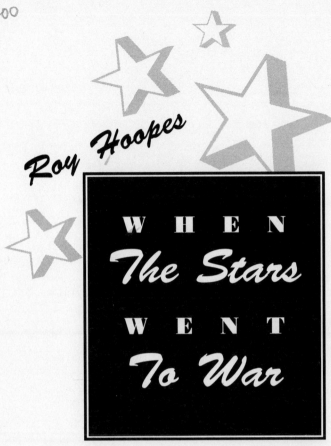

WHEN
The Stars
WENT
To War

Hollywood and World War II

RANDOM HOUSE

NEW YORK

Library of Congress Cataloging-in-Publication Data
Hoopes, Roy.
When the stars went to war: Hollywood and World War II / by Roy Hoopes.
p. cm.
Includes bibliographical references.
ISBN 0-679-41423-1
1. Motion-picture actors and actresses—United States—Anecdotes.
2. World War, 1939–1945—Motion pictures and the war. I. Title.
PN1998.2.H67 1994 791.43'028'092273—dc20 93-44733

Manufactured in the United States of America on acid-free paper
Book design by J. K. Lambert
2 4 6 8 9 7 5 3
First Edition

*To all the biographers, autobiographers, memoirists,
encyclopedists, reporters, film chroniclers, and photographers
who made this book possible*

Acknowledgments

I wish to extend thanks first to my editor, Robert Loomis, who had faith in the project from the beginning, stuck with it, and contributed the kind of assistance that confirms one's faith in the editorial process; to my wife, Cora, who (once again) not only typed a few chapters, but patiently read and helped get into shape a large manuscript; and to Marguerite Rhodes for typing most of it.

Contents

Howard Strickling, Ralph Mannix, Spencer Tracy, Lucille Ball, Joan Crawford, Al Menasco, General Hap Arnold, Wesley Ruggles, Melvyn Douglas, James M. Landis, Representative John Tabor, Harry Cohn, John Huston, Humphrey Bogart, Sydney Greenstreet, Vincent Sherman, Mary Astor, Veronica Lake, Ingrid Bergman, Shirley Temple, Ronald Colman, Al Weingand, Gloria Swanson, Cary Grant, Lucille Ball, Cecil B. De Mille, James M. Cain, Tyrone Power, Watson Webb, Linda Christian, Annabella, Edgar Bergen and Charlie McCarthy, Kitty Carlisle, Betty Grable, Myrna Loy, Mae West, John Steinbeck, Bob Hope, Frances Langford, Evelyn Keyes, Betty Grable, Frank Powolny, Marilyn Monroe, Susan Hayward, Yvonne De Carlo, Rita Hayworth, Lena Horne, Jane Russell, Howard Hughes, Noah Dietrich, Russell Birdwell, George Hurrell, Jack Benny, Mel Blanc, Joan Benny, Anita Loos, Paulette Goddard.

6. **Hollywood Really Goes to War—On Screen 99**
Cast of Characters, in Order of Appearance, Cameos, and Reappearance:
Peter Lawford, William Wyler, Greer Garson, Walter Pidgeon, Norma Shearer, Bob Hope, Richard Ney, Helmut Dantine, Louis B. Mayer, Henry Wilcoxon, Franklin D. Roosevelt, Winston Churchill, Michael Curtiz, James Cagney, Julius and Philip Epstein, Rosemary DeCamp, Humphrey Bogart, Leslie Howard, Hal Wallis, Julius and Philip Epstein, George Raft, Ingrid Bergman, Paul Henreid, Dooley Wilson, Murray Burnett, Frank Capra, Howard Koch, Casey Robinson, Mayo Methot, Claude Rains, Max Steiner, Franklin D. Roosevelt, Winston Churchill, Jack L. Warner, General Douglas MacArthur, Lieutenant Colonel James Doolittle, General Erwin Rommel, Humphrey Bogart, Raymond Massey, Lloyd Bacon, Alan Hale, J. M. Kerrigan.

7. **Bonding—Hollywood Style 110**
Cast of Characters, in Order of Appearance, Cameos, and Reappearance:
Bette Davis, Merle Oberon, Dorothy Lamour, Desi Arnaz, Joan Bennett, Joan Blondell, Charles Boyer, James Cagney, Claudette Colbert, Bing Crosby, Olivia De Havilland, Cary Grant, Charlotte Greenwood, Bert Lahr, Stan Laurel, Oliver Hardy, Groucho Marx, Frank McHugh, Merle Oberon, Pat O'Brien, Eleanor Powell, Risë Stevens, Spencer Tracy, Bob Hope, Frances Langford, Jerry Colonna, Eleanor Roosevelt, Mark Sandrich, John Huston, Harpo Marx, Greer Garson, Hedy Lamarr, Joan Leslie, Adolphe Menjou, Walter Pidgeon, Myrna Loy, John Garfield, Bette Davis, Jack L. Warner, Charles Laughton, Bud Abbott, Lou Costello, Franklin D.

Roosevelt, Fred Astaire, James Cagney, Judy Garland, Mickey Rooney, Greer Garson, Harpo Marx, Kathryn Grayson, Betty Hutton, José Iturbi, Paul Henreid, Dick Powell, Kay Kyser, Lena Horne, Judy Garland, David Rose, Lana Turner, Howard Hughes, Veronica Lake, Gary Cooper, Gene Tierney, Jeanette MacDonald, Hedy Lamarr, Marlene Dietrich, Frank Sinatra, Jimmy Durante, Paulette Goddard, Lana Turner, Pietro Badoglio, Charles Boyer.

Introduction

The call went out to all of us to get busy, to roll up our shirtsleeves and get things moving. —JOHN WAYNE, after Pearl Harbor

The sneak attack awoke the John Wayne in all of us. —BOB HOPE

John Wayne turned World War II into the greatest gunfight of them all. —HENRY FONDA

Judging by the above remarks, you would think that John Wayne practically won World War II by himself. And if he didn't, Errol Flynn did—or at least he retook Burma single-handed (in *Objective, Burma!*), which naturally infuriated the British. The fact is, neither Wayne nor Flynn ever put on a real uniform during World War II or fired a real bullet. Yet, with dozens of other Hollywood macho men, they helped America get ready for, enter, win, and pay for World War II.

Most Americans who were drafted or enlisted in the service during World War II went where they were told, did what they were told to do, and served their time without ever hearing or firing a shot in anger or going anywhere near combat. More often than not, they ended up in work at which they were skilled. Some liked being in the armed forces and wanted to serve their country; others were reluctant; still others hated the military; but they did their duty, and most, when it was all over, felt a little better about themselves.

Most male Hollywood actors did the same: They put on real uniforms, issued not by the MGM wardrobe department but by the government. Several went into combat and conducted themselves heroically, but more often than not their experience was a little different from that of other soldiers. This was especially true of big stars like Mickey Rooney, Robert Taylor, Alan Ladd, and Ronald Reagan. Wherever the stars went, the spotlight was on them, and top sergeants seemed dedicated to letting people know that these big egos from Hollywood were not getting any breaks in their outfits—unless, of course, they were making films in the Signal Corps, where they were among friends and were expected to know something about how a movie was made.

At the same time, many stars—men and women—entertained the troops at home and abroad, some experiencing wartime hardships and giving performances dangerously close to the front. At least one actress, Marlene Dietrich, virtually joined the Army—which, if nothing else, made Generals George Patton and James Gavin very happy indeed.

But most stars stayed home, selling war bonds and performing at fund-raisers, which made President Franklin D. Roosevelt and Prime Minister Winston Churchill happy, because they knew the stars could sell bonds and were aware of the value of films in educating, entertaining, and motivating the troops and the public.

"The principal battleground of this war," said Archibald MacLeish, head of the Office of Facts and Figures at the beginning of World War II, "is not the South Pacific. It is not the Middle East. It is not England, or Norway, or the Russian Steppes. It is American Opinion." Stars, of course, played a major role in making the movies and documentaries that helped shape American opinion.

However, although both FDR and his draft administrator, General Lewis B. Hershey, confirmed the importance of films to a nation at war, the mothers and fathers who had sons dying in battle would not permit open and official exemption of star actors. But, at times, studio heads were able to obtain a temporary exemption from the draft for an actor to make or finish a movie.

The films Hollywood made during the war years were probably the industry's most important contribution to the conflict that began in Europe in September 1939. As Russell Baker said after fifteen years of watching TV at midnight: "Neither Berlin nor Tokyo ever clearly saw the importance of destroying such vital elements of the Allied force as Errol Flynn, Humphrey Bogart, Gregory Peck, Cary Grant, Robert Taylor and James Cagney. This miscalculation cost them dearly."

That story of the films made by the "battalion of leading men who could never be wounded except inconsequentially in the shoulder," as Baker put it, has been well told elsewhere, especially in two books—*The Star-Spangled Screen*, by Bernard F. Dick (1985), and *Hollywood Goes to War*, by Clayton R. Koppes and Gregory D. Black (1987).

This, however, is the story—the many stories—of what the American actors and actresses themselves did during the war. The question might be asked: Who cares what the stars did during the war? They were no different from anyone else; everyone in America pitched in and tried to contribute to the war effort.

True enough; everyone did. But for some reason, for better or worse, people are interested in stars, as role models or envied success stories, who lead, at least when seen from afar, glamorous, exciting lives unlike their own. When Gregory Peck arrived in Hollywood during World War II to make his first film, *Days of Glory*, he became fascinated by the people in the movies. "They're not stars for no reason," he said. "They're stars because they are interesting people."

More than interesting, they were, as Katharine Hepburn says, "familiar." And by "familiar," she meant known by 150 million people: "I'm like the Statue of Liberty to a lot of people. . . . People identify their whole lives with you."

As a result, the stars developed an unusual power over the public. As Lionel Barrymore told Jimmy Stewart after Stewart came out of the Air Force in 1945 and they were making *It's a Wonderful Life* together: "Jimmy, don't ever forget that . . . when you act you move millions of people, shape their lives, give them a sense of exaltation. No other profession has that power"—except maybe politics.

But few politicians have aroused the public as much as some of Hollywood's stars. One example: During World War II, Betty Grable attended a New York opening of her movie with Tyrone Power, *A Yank in the RAF.* As novelist Richard Condon, then a Hollywood movie publicist, recalled the scene: "Despite police protection, a crowd of hysterical thousands . . . surged forward and succeeded in ripping all the clothes off Miss Grable down to her underwear."

People wanted to know everything about the Hollywood stars, who were perhaps America's first real celebrities. Veronica Lake said, "The public wanted to read of your latest beau, your latest escapade in which you threw your mink coat into a pool of perfume, lost a million dollars on one roll of the dice and tickled your leading man's thigh under the table at the Brown Derby."

And this power reached all the way to the marketplace. In 1934, when Clark Gable took off his shirt in *It Happened One Night* to reveal that he did *not* wear an undershirt, sales of undershirts plummeted. In *Road to Utopia,* made near the end of the war by Bob Hope, Bing Crosby, and Dorothy Lamour, Hope goes into a tough saloon and orders a "glass of lemonade"—but then, realizing his mistake and to show how tough he is, he adds: "In a dirty glass!" Soon, in bars all over the country, young men—including yours truly—were ordering drinks "in a dirty glass."

Gore Vidal says that the movies "changed our world forever," one result being, as he said, that when he worked from memory, it was quite possible that he "saw the world in movie terms, as who did not, or indeed, who does not?" We remember that Clark Gable, Jimmy Stewart, David Niven, Douglas Fairbanks, Jr., Wayne Morris, Tyrone Power, Sterling Hayden, and Robert Montgomery saw action in World War II. But if memory serves us, so did John Wayne, Peter Lawford, Humphrey Bogart, Jimmy Cagney, Errol Flynn, and Gary Cooper—or was that just in some movie?

Ask a G.I. what he remembers best about the war and likely as not he will say Veronica Lake's hair or Betty Grable's fanny, Jane Russell's breasts, Marlene Dietrich's legs, June Allyson's girl-next-door personality, Rita Hayworth kneeling in bed, Dorothy Lamour's sarong, or Lana Turner's sweater. Even the German troops had pinups of Marlene Dietrich, although it was well known that she was on Hitler's death list and hated the Nazis. At times it seemed as if the whole business of who or what we were fighting the war for was mixed up with the movies and the people who made them. One G.I. said: "Somehow it is better to be fighting for Lana Turner than it is to be fighting the Greater Reich . . . because she is all our girls rolled into one." And when a *New York Times* columnist wondered, "Are we going to fight a war to save the kind of characters who inhabit the books of James M. Cain and James T. Farrell?" Farrell responded: "What the hell are we supposed to fight and die for? Tyrone Power?"

Well, why not? In the 1940s, Power was the kind of man thousands of American boys wanted to be like: handsome, married to a glamorous

Ask any veteran what he remembers most about World War II and it's likely he'll recall the girls pinned up over his bunk or appearing onstage in a USO show—as exemplified here by Paulette Goddard, Dorothy Lamour, and Veronica Lake singing "A Sweater, a Sarong, and a Peek-a-Boo Bang" in the 1942 movie Star-Spangled Rhythm.

movie star (Annabella), and idolized by millions of women around the world. He was also a Marine pilot in the South Pacific.

It was the big-screen stars who captivated people. Writers, producers, and directors played an equally important role in the evolution of a movie and the birth of a star, but the public had—and still has—little interest in most of them. Which is why few of their war stories are told here, although many directors, producers, studio heads, and writers had interesting and significant experiences during that time.

Also absent from this book are British stars, except for a brief account of the experiences of the Britishers who were in Hollywood at the beginning of the war, but quickly went home to serve crown and country. Their stories must be told elsewhere.

"The war," said Mary Astor, "changed everyone's life, even my insulated and well-protected one." Hollywood's insulated actors and actresses were brought out of their comfortable lives by the Second World War, and considering the reverence and awe in which the American people held Gregory Peck's "interesting people," when a couple of hundred of them went to war some interesting stories were likely to result. In fact, the war produced dozens of them.

When the Stars
Went to War

Prelude

In 1937, there was a Spanish Civil War going, the Japanese were fighting in China, and Hitler repudiated the Versailles Treaty—but I wasn't mad at anybody. . . . I would don my shining armor and journey to Hollywood. —RONALD REAGAN

When RKO hired Orson Welles in 1939 to do a screen adaptation of Joseph Conrad's *Heart of Darkness,* many thought Welles was the first real genius to arrive in Hollywood since Charlie Chaplin. He was twenty-four, a former child prodigy who had shown talent in poetry, painting, cartooning, acting, piano playing, magic, and, of course, radio producing. The year before, with Americans glued to their radios listening to Hitler swallow Austria, Welles had decided that his Mercury Theatre radio program in New York would do an updated version of H. G. Wells's *The War of the Worlds,* describing the invasion of Earth by Martians. At eight P.M. on the evening of October 30, after an announcer introduced "Orson Welles and the Mercury Theatre on the

Air," the script went immediately to the fictitious "Ramon Raquellor and His Orchestra" playing in the Meridien Room of the fictitious "Hotel Park Plaza." Many listeners tuned in a little late—and suddenly the East Coast of the United States and much of the rest of the country thought America was being invaded by Martians—or maybe by Germans, who were on everybody's mind. The seeming authenticity of the attack was enhanced by the fact that Kenny Delmar (who would later play Senator Claghorn on Fred Allen's radio show), playing a fictional secretary of the interior, read his attempts to quell rioting in the streets in the voice of President Roosevelt, as the original script had called for him to do until the CBS censors decided it would be too risky.

The broadcast caused a panic, even scaring the hell out of its scriptwriter, Howard Koch. Koch listened to the program Sunday night, then went to bed exhausted, which prevented him from receiving an informative telephone call from the program's producer, John Houseman. The next morning, at a barbershop on Manhattan's Seventy-second Street, Koch heard snatches of conversations about "invasion" and "panic" and immediately "jumped to the conclusion that Hitler had invaded some new territory and the war we all dreaded had finally broken out."

For about twenty-four hours after the broadcast, everyone involved was walking on eggshells. The public and critics could not make up their minds whether the Mercury players had achieved something remarkable or were guilty of irresponsibly exciting the nation, as if they'd cried "Fire" in a crowded theater. Then the political columnist Dorothy Thompson decided that the program had done the nation a service by pointing out how vulnerable the country was to panic in case of an enemy attack—an insight that Southern California would confirm in three years.

Except for activists like Myrna Loy, Melvyn and Helen Gahagan Douglas, Edward G. Robinson, and the sensitive ones, like Greta Garbo, most members of movieland had not paid much attention to the storm gathering in Europe since Adolf Hitler had become Germany's chancellor. In October 1933, he had withdrawn Germany from the League of Nations; in 1935, he decreed universal military service for German men; that same year, Mussolini invaded Ethiopia. In 1936, Germany reoccupied the Rhineland, Mussolini annexed Ethiopia, and a civil war broke out in Spain, which quickly became a testing ground for the great powers. In 1938, Germany took over Austria, and Britain's

Dorothy Thompson finally decided that Orson Welles's radio program The War of the Worlds *did the country a service by helping to wake it up.* National Archives

prime minister, Sir Neville Chamberlain, went to Munich, toting his famous umbrella, to negotiate "peace in our time" by agreeing to let Germany occupy Czechoslovakia's Sudetenland.

The following year Hitler took over all of Czechoslovakia and prepared to invade Poland. Britain, finally announcing an end to appeasement, said it would defend Poland. But it was too late to stop German aggression. After Hitler signed a nonaggression pact on August 23 with Soviet dictator Joseph Stalin, war was inevitable.

Mae West, after whom the RAF named one of its most useful tools of war, a lifejacket, said: "I knew the world was burning on the edges as 1939 printed itself on history. Neville Chamberlain . . . was running about nervously with a rolled-up umbrella and Adolf Hitler was stamping his feet . . . in the German Chancellery. To show-people, he was a ham actor and a talented local murderer. But he kept us all off balance."

Harpo Marx, one of the four—later, three—performing Marx Brothers, was in Europe in 1933, the same year the Marxes' *Duck Soup* was released. In Hamburg, he would recall in his autobiography,

> I saw the most frightening, most depressing sight I had ever seen—a row of stores with Stars of David and the word *Jude* painted on them, and inside, behind half-empty counters, people in a daze, cringing like they didn't know what hit them and didn't know where the next blow would come from. Hitler had been in power only six months, and his boycott was already in full effect. I hadn't been so wholly conscious of being a Jew since my bar mitzvah. It was the first time since I'd had the measles that I was too sick to eat.

No one had to tell Marlene Dietrich, who was born in Berlin in 1901, what was going on in her native Germany. Her father, who died when she was a child, was in the Royal Prussian Police; her stepfather, a cavalry lieutenant, was killed on the Russian front in World War I. After making *The Blue Angel* in Germany, Dietrich came to America, where Josef von Sternberg converted her into a glamorous woman of mystery. Over the next six years, she starred in a number of movies, including *The Devil Is a Woman* and *The Garden of Allah,* then went to England to make *Knight Without Armour*—and to begin her affair with its author, Erich Maria Remarque, the pacifist who wrote *All Quiet on the Western Front.* Remarque had become a well-informed, intense anti-Nazi, which put him on Hitler's Most Wanted List as early as 1933.

While Dietrich was in England, Nazi propaganda chief Joseph Goebbels sent the German ambassador, Joachim von Ribbentrop, to try to persuade the actress to return to Germany and make pictures. He even promised that Hitler would greet her arrival in Berlin. But Dietrich had been watching what was happening to Germany since 1933; she rejected the invitation, even refusing to have dinner with Ribbentrop. She would soon join Remarque and many others on Hitler's death list, although apparently Hitler wanted her to do more than make pictures for him. According to one biographer, Dietrich once said, "Hitler wanted me to be his mistress. I turned him down. Maybe I should have gone to him. I might have saved the lives of six million Jews."

Instead of going to Germany, Dietrich returned to America to make *Angel* (with Melvyn Douglas) and apply for U.S. citizenship. And a Nazi party paper in Berlin let the world know what Hitler now thought of Germany's most famous actress; it ran a photograph of her taking her citizenship oath before a Jewish judge with this caption:

> The German-born film actress Marlene Dietrich spent so many years among Hollywood's film Jews that she has now become an American citizen. Here we have a picture in which she is receiving her papers in Los Angeles. What the Jewish judge thinks of the formula can be seen from his attitude as he stands in his shirtsleeves. He is taking from Dietrich the oath in which she betrayed her Fatherland.

Both *Knight Without Armour* and *Angel* were flops; Dietrich was beginning to acquire a reputation as box-office poison. When her contract was canceled she left for France, but she had not been there long when producer Joe Pasternak called her at the Hôtel du Cap at Eden Roc in the south of France. He was hoping to persuade Dietrich to play in a western in which the sheriff (Jimmy Stewart) would not wear a gun: *Destry Rides Again.* She finally agreed to do it—and it changed her career. Pasternak, incidentally, did not hide from her—or anyone else—how mad he was to go to bed with her. However, according to Broderick Crawford (who played in a Dietrich-Pasternak film, *Seven Sinners,* the following year, 1940), Dietrich finally said to Pasternak: "I'll go to bed with you when Hitler is dead."

In early 1939, Ray Milland, who had been born Reginald Truscott-Jones in 1905, accidentally sliced off part of his thumb with a circular saw in his do-it-yourself tool shop. He thereby eliminated himself from military duty, although he had served in the British army. While he was still recovering from surgery on the thumb, Y. Frank Freeman, then head of Paramount, called and told him he was going to England to make a picture, *French Without Tears.* So with little thought to the gathering storm, Milland insisted that his wife, Mal, and her mother go with him. They were off on the *Aquitania.*

The two women had a wonderful time that last summer of the old Europe, sightseeing in England and France. But Milland was becoming edgy: The laughter "was a touch hysterical. . . . People were being fitted for gas masks, air raid drills were being carried out at odd hours, all seemingly being treated as a big joke, a joke I failed to see."

But he really knew things were happening when he visited his old cavalry regiment. "Two thirds of the regiment had been dismounted and sent for tank training!" Well, they simply could not do that to the Blues Regiment of the Household Cavalry. Then Milland heard there were plans to evacuate civilians, and that no leaves longer than a weekend were to be granted. "That and Hitler's increased ranting painted, I thought, a pretty clear picture." He put Mal and her mother on the *Georgic,* and when he finished *French Without Tears,* Milland came back on the *Normandie.* It was to be her last voyage.

Comedian Eddie Cantor also went to Europe in the mid-1930s, between *Kid Millions* and *Strike Me Pink.* He had emerged as a Broadway star in the late 1920s and especially after the 1930 hit *Whoopee!,* which he also made into a movie. It was *Whoopee!* that helped make Cantor's meeting with Winston Churchill at the Savoy a memorable one. Churchill asked him how many choruses of "Making Whoopee" he remembered, and before Cantor could answer, Churchill said, "I know all the choruses, my boy," and began to sing: "Take Peggy Joyce, with little voice . . ."

Cantor also met Benito Mussolini. The comedian was then president of the Screen Actors Guild and had a business proposition to discuss with the Italian dictator. He describes his meeting in his autobiography, *Take My Life:*

> Mussolini had a trick. His office was probably the longest office in the world; it took minutes to walk the length of it, and at the far end Mussolini would sit at a desk on a raised platform. The only furniture in the room was this desk and the chair he sat on and one other chair. Therefore, as one walked toward him down this long empty room, the dictator could size you up and under his gaze you were to feel smaller and smaller.

But Cantor had a trick of his own: "The minute I come in I start to talk. Talk, talk, talk, whatever comes into my mind. Now he tries to hear what I'm saying and it isn't easy at that distance. He even strains a little forward to listen and he doesn't stare me down after all. He stands up and shakes hands. Then he pulls a handkerchief out of his pocket and starts waving it. 'El Toro!' he says. 'Cantor, El Toro!' He'd just seen *The Kid from Spain.*"

Cantor's proposition was to suggest that Mussolini allow American actors, actresses, and film crews to come into Italy and make movies, using Italy's historic monuments as backdrops. "Good tourist propaganda" for Italy, Cantor suggested, and it would give American actors a change of scenery.

Mussolini liked the idea and said Cantor should talk to his son-in-law, Count Galeazzo Ciano. Cantor thought they probably would have worked something out except for the gathering war clouds. He also remembered asking the count: "What is this unholy alliance between Mussolini and Hitler?"

"When the time comes," Ciano replied, "Mussolini will take Hitler and . . ." Using his finger, Ciano indicated that the Führer's throat would be cut.

One young actor who would not have believed that was Helmut Dantine, perhaps the only Hollywood actor who actually spent time in one of Hitler's concentration camps. Dantine was born in Vienna in 1917. When he graduated from the University of Vienna, he and four friends made one of those bets about where everyone would be in five years. Dantine knew where three of them were after five years—all dead either fleeing from or fighting for or against the Nazis. And Dantine was in perhaps the last place he had ever expected to be: Hollywood, fighting Nazis by playing them in anti-Nazi films.

His first job was with the Austrian consul in London. Dantine was called home to help organize Austrian resistance to the Nazis, but before the resistance could do anything the Nazis had taken over. Dantine was put in a concentration camp, where every day was spent in one small room with fifty men.

Finally, after three months, Dantine's uncle, a vice president of Consolidated Aircraft, obtained his release, and Dantine was put on a boat for America. With his uncle encouraging a business career, Dantine enrolled in the University of California–Los Angeles, but said he felt he had to do something that would help America awaken to the threat of Nazism. He could not write and he could not lecture, so he decided the theater would offer the best opportunity to spread the word. He started with the Pasadena Community Players, then was given a test by Warner Bros. and a small part in *International Squadron,* and would soon emerge as George Sanders's rival in portraying despicable Nazis.

Errol Flynn was the model swashbuckling hero, a prototype of the British gentleman from the days of piracy through the Crimean War and both world wars, who would gladly die, if not for country, at least for the beautiful women who were loyal to king and empire. But one Flynn biographer, Charles Higham, did extensive research to prove that Flynn was an anti-Semite, a Nazi sympathizer, even a spy. Higham devoted a whole book, *The Untold Story,* to this theory—and a journalist, Tony Thomas, devoted another (*The Spy Who Never Was*) to refuting the charge.

If Flynn was a Nazi sympathizer, he started early. Higham found someone who knew him in Australia in 1932 who said that "Errol was excited by the whole German mystique, by the sexual fascination of Nazism." In 1933, Flynn met Dr. Hermann Frederick Erben, who would eventually become a Nazi agent. Higham documents Erben's activities rather conclusively. In his 1959 autobiography, *My Wicked, Wicked Ways,* Flynn confirmed meeting Erben, although he called him Dr. Gerrit H. Koets (not an attempt to cover up, says Thomas; it was just that Erben could not be found in 1959 and the publisher was afraid to name him without permission). "He wore a broad Dutch grin," wrote

Was Robin Hood (i.e., Errol Flynn) really a Nazi spy?

Flynn, "showing enormous teeth parted. Everything about him was broad. His ears were monsters that stood [at] about the angle of an enraged elephant about to charge. His face was covered with blond hair, though he wasn't exactly bearded. . . . He looked like a blond, amiable orangutan in a mink coat."

Perhaps it was a case of opposites attracting: Flynn, at that point in his life, was one of the most handsome, graceful men in the world. For whatever reason, Flynn and Erben became close friends and remained so through the war years, although Erben had trouble coming and going in the United States because he was considered a Nazi agent by the authorities.

In 1934, according to Higham, Flynn had shown Nazi sympathies at a Mayfair party. British intelligence assigned an unnamed but prominent actress to watch him on his voyage back to America, and Higham, in his biography of Merle Oberon, says that Oberon, who would have had links to MI-6 through her husband, Alexander Korda, was probably that actress. Oberon remembered meeting Lili Damita (who would later become Flynn's first wife) and was present at the captain's table when Flynn, crashing the ballroom from second class, was introduced to them.

Flynn was still an Australian citizen; the following year, 1935, while he was making *Captain Blood,* he was nearly deported from the United States because of his connections to Erben.

In 1937, at a time when Hollywood was making every effort to stay neutral on the Spanish Civil War, Flynn took a trip to Spain with Erben. Flynn was to visit hospitals, write about the war for Hearst's *Cosmopolitan* magazine, and, he hinted, deliver $500,000 to the Loyalists from sympathizers in Hollywood. Erben was to be Flynn's photographer. But, according to Higham, Erben also planned to obtain the names of Germans fighting for the Loyalists and turn their names over to the Gestapo. The trip was highly publicized at the time because the two men had a narrow escape and the press thought they were dead, which produced headlines abroad that ERROL FLYNN EST MORT. Also, Flynn and Erben angered the Loyalists when they revealed that they did not have the money. Erben said he had used Flynn and the money to get into Spain.

Whether Flynn was actually pro-Nazi at this time or just having swashbuckling fun in Spain is not clear. But there is little doubt that in the period before Pearl Harbor, Flynn continued to associate with and defend Erben, helping him out of numerous confrontations with MI-6 and immigration authorities. Higham found so much firm evidence of

Erben's activities that he finally concluded Flynn "was the only individual on earth who did not know Erben was a Nazi."

=

From the point of view of Hollywood's subsequent war effort, one of
the most significant pre-war trips to Europe was taken by a virtually
unknown young man who, at the time, had absolutely nothing to do
with the film industry. Murray Burnett was a high school teacher in
New York City. In 1938, he went to Vienna with his wife, hoping to
help his stepfather's family escape from Austria. As *American Heritage*
reported, while in Europe the Burnetts learned all about letters of transit and the refugee escape route through the Italian Alps, across France
to Marseilles, then to Casablanca and Lisbon. They also discovered a
small café called La Belle Aurore on the French Mediterranean, packed
with refugees from all countries, German and French officials, and a
black piano player. Burnett decided that La Belle Aurore was the perfect setting for a play. Two years later, after the fall of France, he and a
collaborator, Joan Allison, wrote the play, calling the nightclub Rick's
Café Américain and placing it in Casablanca. The title of the play,
before the several transformations that turned it into a Hollywood classic, was *Everybody Comes to Rick's*.

Then there was the country's future President. Although the day in
1933 when Ronald Reagan joined the Fourteenth Cavalry Reserve, stationed in Fort Dodge, Iowa, may have been one of the momentous
dates in the history of filmland, it did not have a significant impact on
the spread of fascism. "I had no particular desire to be an officer," he
said. "Like everyone else [well, not everyone] I thought we had already
fought the last war; still, doing correspondence courses and going to
once-a-week classes wasn't too high a price to pay for getting astride a
horse." One early friend recalled that Dutch Reagan showed up at Des
Moines's Club Belvedere with many girls, but that "all he ever wanted
to talk about was horses."

One of the most interesting aspects of Reagan's early years was his
ability to fantasize. In his autobiography, Reagan wrote that when he
was in high school, he attended a performance of the play *Journey's End*,
and completely identified with the hero, a British captain in World
War I who visibly suffers the horrors of war. "For two and a half hours,
I was in the dugout on the eastern front, but in some strange way, I was
also on stage."

Later, when he was working as a radio announcer for the Chicago
Cubs, Reagan learned that he could create his own fantasy. His reports

relied on information telegraphed from the ballpark to his radio-station booth. During one game, the telegraph wire went dead while Cub out-fielder Augie Galan was at bat. So Reagan had Galan repeatedly foul off balls until the wire was fixed.

Finally, deciding that if he was good at radio fantasy, with his good looks he might be even better on the silver screen, young Reagan went West.

=

Today, Hollywood historians look back on 1939 as the most glittering of Hollywood's golden years. This assessment is based primarily on seventeen movies,* capped by *Gone With the Wind,* that have become classics and another dozen or so that are still noteworthy. Although *Ninotchka* poked fun at the Soviet Communists, and *Gunga Din,* accord-ing to Douglas Fairbanks, Jr., was a thinly disguised attack on Hitler's regime, only one of the year's noteworthy films—*Confessions of a Nazi Spy*—directly dealt with the Hitler menace.

The star of *Ninotchka* was Greta Garbo. It was her next-to-last film, but many thought this mocking satire was the apex of her career. In 1938, she had a warning. Her onetime lover Mauritz Stiller, the direc-tor who had discovered her in Stockholm (and who had died in 1928), told her from his grave (which she visited regularly to discuss things with her mentor) that "a whirlwind is approaching; they are calling me." Garbo knew that Mauritz meant that he was off to war; "he was occupied with something more important than me." She visited several mind-readers and fortune-tellers in Hollywood, trying to make contact with Stiller again, but she could not. She also heard people at MGM whispering, "She is crazy."

Maybe, but perhaps no more than Joan of Arc or others who have communicated with ethereal voices. And on the night of August 31, 1939, Garbo went to bed knowing something was going to happen, as she subsequently reported:

I tossed from side to side, racked by anxiety mixed with vague, unde-fined premonitions. I tried to collect my thoughts, but I was unable to. I was gripped by fear—fear that many people, including me, were

Gunga Din; Stagecoach; Love Affair; Midnight; Wuthering Heights; Dark Victory; Only Angels Have Wings; Goodbye, Mr. Chips; Young Mr. Lincoln; The Old Maid; The Wizard of Oz; The Women; Babes in Arms; Mr. Smith Goes to Washington; Ninotchka; Destry Rides Again; Gone With the Wind.

Greta Garbo went to bed on the night of August 31, 1939, "gripped by fear—fear that many people, including me, were facing disaster." She was right.

facing disaster. Finally I succumbed, or I thought I did, to sleep. Suddenly I woke up, perspiring and shivering. Dawn was breaking. Ugly dreams from my childhood were lurking in my head. . . . So I reached for the radio and turned it on to hear these words: "Today at dawn the German army crossed the Polish border and engaged the Polish army in a fierce fight . . ."

TWO

Quasimodo and the Bells of War

It was a wonderful place, full of friendliness, generosity, excitement, sadness, despair, and no smog in that long-ago Hollywood . . . when World War II shattered the calm. —DAVID NIVEN

The war came earlier to Hollywood than it did to most of the country, in part because of the film colony's sizable "British contingent." September 1, 1939, was the start of Labor Day weekend, and David Niven and Robert Coote, both members in good standing of the British contingent, had been invited to a yachting party at Catalina given by Douglas Fairbanks, Jr., a virtual card-carrying Britisher, although he was American-born. Niven, who was making *Raffles,* and his good friend and drinking buddy, Coote, a character actor working on *Vigil in the Night* (starring Carole Lombard), were supposed to sail over on a small sloop, *Huralu,* to join Fairbanks. But, as Niven would recall, he and Coote "drank an immense amount of rum at a party in the Balboa Yacht Club and did not quite make the tide."

Fairbanks's guests included Laurence Olivier, then shooting *Rebecca,* and his lover, Vivien Leigh, who had just finished *Gone With the Wind* (and who was furious with David O. Selznick for not giving her the female lead in *Rebecca*). Olivier and Leigh were convinced there would not be a war. "We talked about the situation in Europe," Jerry Dale, a young United Artists press agent, said, reporting on an earlier conversation. "The Nazis had made their pact with Russia, and somebody present—Nigel Bruce, I think it was—said: 'Well, that means war for sure.' Everyone else jumped him, saying 'No war, no war, Hitler would never dare. He doesn't have the resources,' and so on. Larry and Vivien were particularly vehement about it." This was probably a matter of wishful thinking.

Anyway, they were going to have a fine party at Catalina. They anchored near the *Dragoon,* a ketch belonging to Ronald Colman, who had just finished *The Light That Failed,* and his dark-haired British wife, Benita Hume, whose latest film, *Peck's Bad Boy with the Circus,* had been released that January. Also aboard, as mentioned earlier, was Nigel Bruce, who, with *The Hound of the Baskervilles,* had just launched a career of playing Dr. Watson.

At four A.M. on September 1, Niven and Coote, sleeping in the *Huralu* back in port, were awakened by a man in a dinghy, banging on the side of their boat. "You guys English?" the man asked.

"Yes," came the answer from Niven and Coote, leaning over the side, and the man said: "Well, lotsa luck. You've just declared war on Germany."

"We never spoke a word," recalled Niven, "just went below and filled two teacups with warm gin. I don't believe it was a toast to anything in particular." When Niven and Coote finally reached the Fairbanks party they found a somber—but not sober—group. Niven said it was beginning to dawn on all of them that they were "pawns in a game that had got out of control. . . . Nobody knew quite what to do."

Nobody except Olivier, who, according to Fairbanks, had "quietly and unobtrusively proceeded to get as smashed as a hoot-owl." Still, Olivier managed to board a dinghy, in which he started rowing around the harbor, stopping at each yacht and yelling at the occupants: "This is the end. You're all washed up. Finished. Enjoy your last moments. You're done for. . . . Relics, that's what you are now, relics."

However, Olivier and Niven, like most of the other British actors in Hollywood, would respond immediately to every loyal Englishman's and Englishwoman's instinct to defend king and country. In fact, Charles Laughton, who just a little over a month before had urged his wife, Elsa Lanchester, to return from England, did his best to literally sound the bells of war. He was making *The Hunchback of Notre Dame* when war was declared, and according to the director, William Dieterle, the tension on the soundstage was unbearable. Laughton was already exhausted from day after day of a five-hour makeup session for Quasimodo and then a long day of shooting. The scene in which Quasimodo rings the bells for Esmeralda, one of the most important moments because it was really a love scene between the two, had developed into something so moving that Dieterle forgot to call "cut" when the scene was over. "Laughton went on ringing the bells," Dieterle recalled. "Finally, completely exhausted, he stopped. Nobody was able to speak, nobody moved. It was an unforgettable thing. . . . In his dressing room, Charles could only say: 'I couldn't think of Esmeralda in that scene at all. I could only think of the poor people out there going to fight that bloody, bloody war. To arouse the world, to stop the terrible butchery! Awake! Awake! That's what I felt when I was ringing the bells.' "

And it was almost as if the British contingent in Hollywood heard them. Olivier's costar in *Rebecca,* Joan Fontaine—she and her sister, Olivia De Havilland, had British parents—said: "That autumn morning when Britain declared war on Adolf Hitler's Germany . . . calls to the British consul were placed from every bedside phone before the morning tea could steep. Should every male and female born under the British flag take the next plane home?"

Some, like Niven, went almost immediately; some, like Olivier and Leigh, could not make up their minds at first; others, like Laughton and George Sanders, never went; and some already had—Merle Oberon, for one, and Leslie Howard, who left Hollywood in August 1939 after creating the role for which he will ever be remembered: Ashley Wilkes, Scarlett's exasperating non-lover in *Gone With the Wind.*

There is apparently some disagreement in the Howard family as to just why Leslie Howard returned to England then. His daughter, also called Leslie, who published a biography of her father in 1959, wrote that Howard had rushed to complete his work in *Gone With the Wind* so he could return to England before the outbreak of war, which he felt sure was coming; he was convinced that only armed intervention would stop Hitler. In a press release announcing Howard's departure, agent Mike Levee said Howard's decision was "typically English, blind unswerving duty to King and Country, unquestioning response, that's the attitude of every true Britisher"—emphasizing, of course, that the real Howard was every bit as loyal to his country as Ashley Wilkes was loyal to the Confederacy. (Actually, Howard hated the role of Ashley

Wilkes. "Yesterday," his daughter quoted him as saying, "I put on my Confederate uniform for the first time and looked like a fairy doorman at the Beverly Wilshire—a fine thing at my age" [which was forty-six].)

On the other hand, Howard's son, Ronald, in *his* biography of his father, stressed that the elder Howard was on his way home to direct and act in a film, *The Man Who Lost Himself,* and that, in fact, he probably did not think there would be war, or, at least, had argued that point of view with his British friends in Hollywood.

However, Ronald said that whatever happened, going back on the *Aquitania* in late August his father "was looking forward to it—glad, if there was war, to be going towards it. . . . He only prayed there would be time for the film." (There wasn't: England stopped making commercial films after the war began.) When England declared war, Howard had to say good-bye to his son, who was off to join the Royal Navy. He waved to Ronald as he disappeared down the road, and later wrote: "We are now facing a challenge greater than any civilized people in history has ever known—a challenge that puts that first world war in the shade. And our children have had to take up that challenge—all our vows on their behalf have gone for nothing. . . . For they are now as we were then, and we were then as our fathers were before us in the Napoleonic wars and in the centuries before that."

It was England and her sons against the evil of the world—and it is little wonder that Leslie Howard would soon be chosen to broadcast weekly on the radio to America, reporting on the war from London.

=

Merle Oberon was born Estelle Merle O'Brien Thompson in Tasmania, started her career in London cafés as "Queenie" O'Brien, and later was a hostess at London's famous but ill-fated Café de Paris, which was destroyed during the Blitz. She married British producer-director Alexander Korda in 1939, after he had seen his own Galatea develop from her role in *The Private Life of Henry VIII* to costar with Olivier in *Wuthering Heights.* After *Wuthering Heights,* Oberon returned to England; she knew the storm was gathering. She had started a column for the *Daily Mail* while working on her next picture, her husband's *The Lion Has Wings,* and in August she wrote: "What with the weather and the airplanes, locations are becoming very difficult in Britain. At one time you could ask the local airport people not to fly over the studios when you were shooting outside, and your request was courteously respected. Now it's a matter of national emergency. And as soon as the rain stops, up out of the clouds come the planes."

In addition to the British contingent, Hollywood had a sprinkling of stars from other European nations whose lives and careers were changed forever by the war. Ingrid Bergman had just returned to Stockholm with her husband, Peter Lindstrom, and daughter, Pia, hoping to settle down and bring her little family together again. She had been in Hollywood for several months making her first American film, *Intermezzo*, with Leslie Howard. When she heard over the radio in their home in Djurgarden Park near Stockholm that Hitler had invaded Poland, she was stunned: "I knew the Nazis were evil people," she wrote later, "but I did not think they would involve us all in another European war. I'd been so excited, coming back from Hollywood and picking up the old threads again and then going straight into my next Swedish film, *A Night in June*, that I just hadn't seen the war coming."

She rushed through *A Night in June* and within three months, at the urging of David Selznick, she and Pia were on the way back to Hollywood. Peter, who was a dentist and of military age, stayed in Sweden, so Ingrid Bergman became perhaps the first movie wife to have a marriage upset by the war. On her way back to America, Peter accompanied Ingrid and Pia as far as Genoa, where they spent New Year's Eve 1939. And in *My Story*, which she wrote with Alan Burgess, she remembered that New Year's:

> Everybody was dancing and screaming, aware that the war was right outside their door, and trying to shut that out because who knew what would happen before the next New Year? And we danced and we were very sad, and we too tried to pretend that we didn't know there was a blackout and bombers flying in the night . . . but we did know. And I thought, I'm leaving the next morning with Pia, and maybe I'll never see Peter again. I was leaving with his child and he might get involved with the war and not survive . . . oh, those were terrible moments.

=

In the late summer of 1939, Charles Boyer was in France to shoot a movie, *Le Corsaire*. Boyer, who had been born in the little farming village of Figeac in southwestern France, was an intelligent and informed anti-Nazi from the early 1930s. He did not hide his feelings about the *Anschluss*, Munich, and the German occupation of the Sudetenland. In Hollywood, he was one of the leading opponents of the isolationists, and the only thing that kept him from being more vocal was that he was still a French citizen, although he had lived in Hollywood for years and

was the star of many major movies (including, most recently, *Tovarich,*
Algiers, and *When Tomorrow Comes*).

Hitler's invasion of Poland did not surprise Boyer. He returned to
Paris to spend a few days shooting *Le Corsaire,* but the film was abandoned as soon as it was evident that Hitler would not be stopped and
that, in Paris at least, it would be a long time before anyone had the
peace and tranquillity to make movies. So Boyer put his wife on a plane
for London and, at the age of forty, joined the French army.

Soon Boyer was manning a switchboard on the southern end of the
Maginot Line. And, oddly, no one knew he was there—not the French
public, or the army, or his studio in Hollywood, which was undertaking
the pre-production work on what was to be his next film, *All This and*
Heaven Too.

Boyer's tour of duty in the French army lasted eleven weeks. He was
silent about both his reasons for joining and how he was released.
Rumor had it that someone in Hollywood pulled strings, although
Boyer denied knowing anything about that. It was an agent of Edouard
Daladier (whom Boyer hated for his role in the Munich appeasement)
who not only obtained the actor's release, but convinced him that he
could be of inestimable value as an emissary of French goodwill in
America. In December 1939, the Boyers returned to America to find
Hollywood much more concerned about the launching of *Gone With the*
Wind than about the beginning of the war in Europe. But despite his
gloom, Boyer was determined to serve his country—or, rather, both of
them. (His main contribution came in the fall of 1940, when he
founded the French Research Foundation in Los Angeles. It began with
a mission to collect documents about France and its people. Eventually,
the foundation's primary goal became the documentation of France's
World War II history.)

Back in Hollywood, Boyer, now a veteran of World War II, found the
British contingent trying to decide whether it really wanted a part in a
show that involved real bullets and real blood. The media in both
Hollywood and London would soon join the debate, the question being:
"Would the British contingent 'do the right thing' for king and country,
or were they the 'Gone With the Wind Up . . . Regiment'?"

=

In the days after England's declaration of war, three groups of Hollywood
Britishers emerged: those who regretted what was happening but made
no immediate plans to leave, those who had no plans to leave, and those
who wanted to do the right thing and return home as soon as possible.

And for those who were not sure what the right thing was, Sherlock Holmes's companion and defender of the faith and empire would remind them. Nigel Bruce would sneak up on some young British actor and whisper: "Going back to do your bit? Jolly good show. You'll join the RAF, I suppose—or the RN [Royal Navy]. . . . By the way, here's your ticket to London. . . . It's the least we old-timers can do. What about the picture you're making now? Not to worry, old boy. We've organized an immediate release for you."

One magazine, *Picturegoer,* published an article suggesting that all British writers, actors, and directors be forcibly repatriated regardless of their age, to work in British studios for Army pay. The British contingent did not think this was a good idea—and who could blame them? No one in his right mind wants to give up a glamorous, exciting, well-paid career to risk his life for his country. But when one's career is based on one's image as a man of character—perhaps even a hero—as it was in the case of many stars, one has no choice.

Then there were those, like the Oliviers, who had family and loved ones back in England. In those dark and gloomy days of late 1939 and early 1940, it seemed that those back home quite possibly faced extinction. The decision to leave was not easy—although some had it made for them. Basil Rathbone wrote immediately to the War Office in London and received "a letter of interminable length," he said, which finally said politely but firmly: "You are too old." Sir Cedric Hardwicke tried to revive his captain's commission but was told: "Your reserve status has been cancelled by the War Office for reasons of your age."

Hardwicke said that when he went to the consulate, he found the clerk completely flustered: "I hope I'll never see a day like this again," she told him.

"War doesn't break out every day," he said, but she replied: "It isn't the war, but the dress show at Adrian's [a popular Beverly Hills fashion shop]. Those buyers are driving me crazy."

Olivier and the others were also told by the consulate that except in the case of an emergency, no one could go back to England at that time; the consulate was awaiting further instructions from the embassy in Washington.

To try to force the issue, Hardwicke, Olivier, producer-director Herbert Wilcox, and Cary Grant flew to Washington to talk directly to the British ambassador, Lord Lothian. Wilcox remembers the "nightmare flight through continuous thunder and lightning storms. Larry Olivier slept through it all, not bothered in the least by Cary Grant trying to calm my terror by singing old musical ditties." Lothian's instructions were to keep Hollywood turning out pro-British films, but he sympathized with his compatriots' plight—in fact, later he would cable the Home Office saying it was a mistake for British actors of military age "with all the limelight on them . . . not to go home." At one point, he asked each of the men his age and was not very amused at Grant's response: "For years I've been stepping it down," Grant said, laughing. "Now I'd better step it up." He was thirty-five.

However, as Hardwicke recalled, Lothian did not encourage them to do anything dramatic or precipitous. "You are here in America on legitimate business," Lothian told them. "What would Germany give to have such a corner as you actors have in the making of American pictures for the world market? And if the Englishmen are to be portrayed in those pictures, how much better that real Englishmen act the parts, rather than have them appear on the screen portrayed by American actors with monocles or spats."

The British quartet returned to Hollywood. Wilcox directed and produced *Irene* and *No, No, Nanette*; Hardwicke played Frollo in *The Hunchback of Notre Dame*; Grant made *His Girl Friday*; and Olivier finished *Rebecca* and then starred with Vivien Leigh in a Broadway production of *Romeo and Juliet*. (Before long, however, Olivier and Leigh would be appearing in precisely the kind of film Lothian had in mind.) At the same time, Olivier took flying lessons at a small airport near Hollywood, preparing for the day when he would return to England and join the RAF.

The set of *Rebecca*, with its largely British cast, was tense and gloomy. Director Alfred Hitchcock was worried about his family in England; Olivier had similar concerns and was unhappy that Joan Fontaine, not Vivien Leigh, was playing opposite him. And producer David O. Selznick was concerned about what might happen if Laurence Olivier and George Sanders, his two British male stars in *Rebecca*, returned home immediately to help Britain keep from falling into the hands of the Nazis. "We would be in a pickle," Selznick said, "if they walked out in the middle—not so much of a pickle as Poland, I grant you," he added, trying to keep everything in perspective, "but still in a pickle."

Selznick needn't have worried. Olivier would be around for a couple of years, making *Pride and Prejudice* and *That Hamilton Woman*; Sanders, who was not only the ultimate cynic but quite possibly pro-fascist (which might explain his convincing screen portrayals of Nazi officers), chose to follow instructions from the British ambassador and never left America.

Sanders was born in Russia of British parents and grew up in

England. He was, in his way, a pacifist, but it is hard not to think that he leaned toward the fascists. He told Douglas Fairbanks, Jr., "I couldn't care less if Hitler took over everything," and although this was said "laughingly," Fairbanks said he did not think it was very funny when Sanders said "he agreed with Errol Flynn in that he was not going to lift a finger to stop the Germans."

In a "Confidential Journal" Sanders kept between 1937 and 1938, he made this curious entry: "Let's make friends with those who would seek to overthrow our world so as to insure the reservation of ring-side seats for ourselves in the New World they create—and employ such skill as we may possess to consolidate friendships already made in case the Reformists score a miss. In short, let's run with the hare and hunt with the hounds." (Note that he called the creators of the New [fascist] World "Reformists.")

One reason for the tension on the set of *Rebecca* was the presence of the scriptwriter Robert E. Sherwood, one of Hollywood's most perceptive students of national and international affairs. In 1939, Sherwood was more involved in the government's information program than he was in films. He knew what was going on in Europe and did his best to alert Hollywood to the oncoming crisis. The author of several plays that had been turned into movies, including *The Petrified Forest, Idiot's Delight,* and *Abe Lincoln in Illinois,* he was in Hollywood polishing the *Abe Lincoln* script when he was asked to do a quick rewrite of *Rebecca.* He hated being in Hollywood in those tense days, mainly because the only news about Europe came on the radio. The New York papers were a day late and the Los Angeles papers carried very little foreign news. Sherwood had predicted in his diary that war would soon follow the Hitler-Stalin pact. When he heard the news that Hitler had invaded Poland he was at the Trocadero. He wrote in his diary:

> So it has come. Idiot's Delight. And what a setting in which to receive such sickening news. The dance floor was packed with Joe Schencks and L. B. Mayers and agents dancing La Conga with blonde, fake-breasted cuties. At one ringside table a group were huddled over a little portable radio, listening to a maniac who had just condemned millions of decent, helpless people to death.

At first, the war had settled into a lull during which Hitler digested Poland and prepared to assault the one hundred French divisions on the other side of the Maginot Line. The British accepted that strategy, not eager to risk the nine divisions of the British Expeditionary Force positioned along the Belgian border for an all-out attack against the Germans. So the journalists came up with phrases such as "Phony War," "twilight war," "Sitzkrieg," and "Bore War" to describe this eight-month hiatus in the fighting. During this period, the RAF's primary role was "dropping leaflets on the Germans suggesting politely that it would be much wiser for them to quit before they got hurt," as Niven put it.

Britain was helpless to do anything for Finland, which was invaded by Russia on November 30, 1939; nor could she do anything for the Low Countries when Hitler invaded them in May 1940. This forced the resignation of Prime Minister Chamberlain, who was replaced by Winston Churchill. The Germans now breached French lines, splitting the Allied armies in two. Belgium surrendered on May 28, the French army collapsed on June 1, and the BEF, with French and Belgian units, retreated to Dunkirk to perform the famous "miracle" in which, from May 26 to June 4, nearly 340,000 British, French, and Belgian troops were evacuated to England. Norway, having been invaded in April, surrendered on June 9. On June 22, France surrendered at Réthondes and Hitler danced his famous little jig at the surrender ceremonies.

Despite the fall of France, Britain refused to capitulate. And for leadership her people looked to Winston Churchill, who offered them nothing but "blood, toil, tears, and sweat" and said Britain would "fight on the beaches, . . . on the landing grounds, . . . in the fields and in the streets, . . . in the hills": "We shall never surrender." Whether or not Hitler ever intended to invade England, he gave every indication of doing so. On "Eagle Day," August 13, 1940, Hermann Göring's Luftwaffe launched a devastating and prolonged series of daylight bombing raids against RAF bases. Then, after a flight of German bombers mistakenly attacked London, and Britain retaliated with a raid on Berlin (which Hitler had said could never happen), Germany launched massive air attacks against London, partly in retaliation but primarily to try to bring Britain to her knees with airpower alone. In what Churchill called Britain's "finest hour," these raids were resisted, though with a horrible loss of civilians and RAF pilots, inspiring another immortal Churchillian phrase: "Never in the field of human conflict was so much owed by so many to so few."

Hitler and Göring did not know how close the RAF was to extinction, whereas the British, thanks to a very unsophisticated but efficient radar system and to the fact that they had broken Germany's Enigma encoding system, knew where German planes were heading and were able to concentrate their dwindling roster of Spitfires in defense of the targets. By the end of September 1940, the Battle of Britain was over, and Hitler now concentrated on nighttime raids on London designed primarily to break British morale. But the Blitz was suspended in May 1941, as Hitler prepared to launch one of his major blunders of the war: the invasion of Russia.

At the time David Niven returned to England to try to join the RAF,* the Battle of Britain had not begun. For the time being, the RAF had plenty of young pilots and trainees—more than it could handle at that stage of the war. In fact, hundreds of romantic young Englishmen, determined that they would not die the kind of squalid, unrecognized death their fathers and uncles had in the trenches of World War I, were rushing to join the RAF. And no one, perhaps, typified these young men more than a young poet named Richard Hillary, who deserves mention here because before long he would be having a dramatic and romantic love affair with one of Hollywood's most glamorous stars.

Hillary was born in 1918, at the end of the first World War. When World War II started he was a student at Trinity College, Oxford, and a member of the University Air Squadron. When the Battle of Britain began, in August 1940, Hillary, a pilot with the RAF's 306th Squadron, became one of those few to whom so many would owe so much. In his book, *The Last Enemy*, which he wrote while recovering from the flaming crash of his plane (less than a month after going into action), he recounted all his reasons for going to war, and for joining the RAF:

> I am fighting this war because I believe that in war one can swiftly develop all one's faculties to a degree it would normally take a lifetime to achieve. And to do this, you must be as free from outside interference as possible. That's why I'm in the Air Force. For in a Spitfire we're back to war as it ought to be—if you can talk about war as it ought to be. Back to individual combat, to self reliance, to responsibility for one's own fate. One either kills or is killed and it's damned exciting. . . . I shan't be sitting behind a long-range gun working out how to kill people sixty miles away. I shan't get maimed; either I shall get killed or I shall get a few putty medals and enjoy being stared at in nightclubs.

But he did get maimed, so badly that people would turn away from him in restaurants and on the street.

---

*Niven was rejected by the RAF, but joined the army and had a distinguished wartime career.

George Sanders (left) *not only made a convincing movie Nazi, he apparently did not care whether the reformers, as he called the Nazis, won or lost. Leslie Howard (below) wondered what would have happened to him if Hitler had never been born.*

Meanwhile, as the Battle of Britain intensified, Merle Oberon—the Hollywood star who would take pity on the disfigured RAF pilot—and her Hungarian-born British husband, producer Alexander Korda, returned to America. Many critics charged that they did so to escape the bombing. But biographers of both Korda and Oberon suggest that the real reason was to enable Korda (who was known to be active in British intelligence) to carry out an assignment, possibly one given him by Churchill himself. Although the British Official Secrets Act will probably prevent us from ever knowing precisely what he did do, Korda is believed to have been part of the Intrepid operation. His assignment was to help assess the American attitude toward Britain and the war, and influence that attitude with pro-British films. He had a perfect cover after it was decided that his still-unfinished *The Thief of Bagdad* could not be completed at the Denham studio in London or, as planned, in Egypt and Arabia. Hollywood, the Mojave Desert, and the Grand Canyon were chosen instead. Korda made repeated trips back to London (presumably to report to MI-6 and Churchill), but his main assignment in the United States was to make a pro-British film that would not reek of propaganda.

Leslie Howard, who remained in England, also made some propaganda films, including *Pimpernel Smith, 49th Parallel,* and *The First of the Few* (released in the United States as *Spitfire*). But he was mostly unhappy during the war because he could not get directly involved. In fact, there were times, he wrote in his diary, when he would have preferred to be somewhere else—even Hollywood.

What I would have been doing if Hitler had never been born—curse him! I would have been in my nice little house in Beverly Hills sitting by the swimming pool dressed in a pair of shorts, the hot California sun streaming down on me, but just pleasantly broken by the leaves of my favourite lemon tree. I would be humming happily to myself and cogitating somewhat thus: Metropolitan Colossal Pictures have just overpaid me atrociously for my last picture, and I gather from my agent that they are going to pay me even more for my next . . . upon which my young daughter would probably have turned up in a fetching Palm Beach bathing suit and dragged me into the pool. Then, I think, a nice drive through the palm trees, lunch with some friends, a game of tennis with my son.

THREE

A Few Good Men and Women

While I was kissing Deanna Durbin, Hitler was starting a war. —ROBERT STACK

Rosalind Russell would never forget the beginning of the war in Europe, but for her the key date was not September 1, 1939, but September 4. That was the date on the cover of *Life* magazine that reported the beginning of the war. However, instead of a photograph of the fighting in Poland, such as its sister publication, *Time*, carried, *Life* bore a picture of Rosalind Russell.

The actress was on *Life*'s cover because of her appearance in *The Women*, one of the films that helped make 1939 Hollywood's golden year. The movie was Hollywood's version of the hit Broadway play written by Clare Boothe Luce, wife of the publisher of *Life*. The idea of a *Life* cover devoted to a movie based on a play by the boss's wife seemed like a good one—until Hitler invaded Poland, and then the editors wanted a war-related photograph. Rosalind's sister, Mary Jane, was working at *Time* as a researcher; she reported to her illustrious sister in Hollywood that "you've never been called so many terrible things. They were screaming, 'Get that cover changed. Get that actress off!' I heard them all over the building."

But it was too late. *Life*'s cover of September 4, 1939, had gone to press. Russell would never forget the date: It is "burned in my brain," she would comment.

=

Bob Hope and his wife, Dolores, were on the *Queen Mary* coming home from Europe when the radio announced Hitler's invasion of Poland; two days later, war was declared and Dolores woke her husband to tell him that "they've issued black-out instructions and people are crying—and scared." Hope went immediately into action, seeking out the ship's captain and offering to give a show. The captain thought it was a good idea, so Hope did his first wartime show, telling jokes and singing "Thanks for the Memory," perhaps for the first time since he and Shirley Ross had introduced it in *The Big Broadcast of 1938*. He has been singing it ever since, although not with the lyrics he included that night for an audience that appeared to think itself already in the crosshairs of some U-boat's periscope:

> Thanks for the memory.
> Some folks slept on the floor,
> Some in the corridor,
> But I was more exclusive,
> My room had "Gentlemen" above the door.
> Ah! Thank you so much.

The Hopes returned to a Hollywood in which at least one actress was following the war: "The Germans," said Eve Arden, "were marching through all the countries I was hoping to travel to someday. Each night became more depressing. Frightening as it was, one had to listen." Although most of Hollywood, as Myrna Loy said, was reluctant to face the reality of war, there were several actors and actresses, like Loy, who found it as difficult as many officials in Washington did to maintain their neutrality. In the first place, the large British contingent could no longer hide its hostility to Hitler. In addition, most of the Hollywood studio heads—moguls, as they were called—were Jewish and could not maintain a convincing neutrality, although some tried to hide their Jewishness, and all of them were concerned about losing the lucrative

Axis markets for their films. But how could Hollywood convincingly maintain neutrality when the Nazis had replaced gangsters as the bad guys in their films, and wholesome young American boys were dying— in reality and on the screen—fighting the Nazis in the Royal Air Force?

Although there were a few actors at least sympathetic to the Nazis, they were completely overshadowed by the handful of pro-British and pro-French activists who did not hesitate to voice their opposition to Hitler. Most of the latter were included in a photograph (below) in Helen Gahagan Douglas's autobiography. They were members of the Non-Partisan Committee for Peace Through the Revision of the Neutrality Law [of 1935], later known as the Committee to Defend America by Aiding the Allies or as the William Allen White Committee, after its founder. Melvyn Douglas, Helen Gahagan Douglas's husband, was active in forming the Southern California branch of the committee, which was headed by Douglas Fairbanks, Jr. The photograph just mentioned showed the Hollywood members of the committee signing a petition to impose an economic boycott of Germany. There are some familiar faces: Claude Rains, Paul Muni, Edward G. Robinson, Helen Gahagan Douglas, John Garfield, Gloria Stuart (then filming *The Three Musketeers*, in which she played the queen), James Cagney, Groucho Marx, Aline MacMahon (filming *Back Door to Heaven*), Henry Fonda, Gale Sondergaard, Myrna Loy, Melvyn Douglas, and Universal's head, Carl Laemmle.

Although he was not in the photograph, perhaps the most active and effective member of the committee was Douglas Fairbanks, Jr., whose father was one of Hollywood's legends. Born at the pinnacle of his father's success, Fairbanks Junior was raised by his mother after his father went off with another Hollywood legend—Mary Pickford. The son became an actor himself in the 1920s but was not particularly well known until he married Joan Crawford, who had already achieved stardom as the personification of the Jazz Age flapper. His lifelong pro-British feelings were kindled in the 1930s, when he made several movies in England and became friendly with members of the royal family. (Another friend from those days was John Buchan, author of *The 39 Steps*.) As Hitler emerged as a serious threat to the survival of Britain, Fairbanks became the first American actor to speak out in an effort to bring the United States into the war.

One reason he was effective as an activist was his relationship with Franklin Roosevelt. He had come to know the President quite well through his friendship with Franklin, Jr., who'd been his playmate in Central Park when they were growing up. Roosevelt gradually became

Members of the William Allen White Committee signing a petition to impose an economic boycott on Nazi Germany. Standing, from left to right: *Claude Rains, Paul Muni, Arthur Hornblow, Jr.* (obscured), *Edward G. Robinson, Helen Gahagan Douglas, John Garfield, Gloria Stuart, James Cagney, Groucho Marx, Aline MacMahon, Henry Fonda, and Gale Sondergaard.* Seated: *Myrna Loy, Melvyn Douglas, and Carl Laemmle.*

fond of Fairbanks, particularly after he demonstrated his usefulness and effectiveness in pro-intervention organizing. Fairbanks recalled a White House meeting when the President explained to the representatives of the committee that "a leader in a democracy must never let himself get too far ahead of his constituents, or else he loses contact with them." Hence it was the committee's job to get the American people to demand support for the Allies. "Now go out there and get the public to push me," Roosevelt told them.

The President was aware of the power of films to influence public opinion and the power of movie idols to persuade. And Fairbanks did not let him down. He did everything possible to see that his own films contained a pro-British or internationalist flavor: no heavy propaganda, just making sure the audience knew who the bad guys were. These low-key anti-fascist films included *Gunga Din, The Sun Never Sets, Rulers of the Sea,* and *Safari.* As a result, Mussolini banned Fairbanks's films, and Hollywood isolationists began attacking him with remarks such as "Young Fairbanks is doing his best to get us in this goddamn thing. . . . Why doesn't he stick to acting?"

He also accepted every opportunity to mount a speaker's platform; as an actor, he was naturally good at public speaking. One of his favorite topics was the Nazi threat in Latin America. The threat was, in fact, a serious one: There were nearly two million German immigrants in

Latin America, among whom, naturally, some were pro-Hitler. In January 1941, Fairbanks undertook a mission, instigated by Undersecretary of State Sumner Welles and approved by FDR. In a letter to the actor, Welles set out the goals. "The mission would ostensibly be a mission to investigate in a broad way the effects on public opinion in Latin American Republics of American motion pictures. In reality, your mission would be directed principally toward getting in touch with certain national groups in some of the larger countries to the south which are now believed to be veering toward Nazi ideology."

While he was on his Latin American tour, Fairbanks's commission as a lieutenant (junior grade) in the Navy came through, but he was allowed to continue his State Department tour of Latin America, where he had authority to discuss such delicate subjects as the granting of military bases for use by U.S. forces and to suggest that steps be taken to counteract Nazi propaganda and the Nazi-controlled press. The State Department was ready to cut Fairbanks off immediately and disown him if the two-and-a-half-month mission got out of hand. But it never did. Fairbanks's reports to Welles were intelligent and useful, and he impressed everyone wherever he went. Norman Armour, the U.S. ambassador to Argentina, wrote Secretary of State Cordell Hull that despite early misgivings, Armour thought Fairbanks's visit was an "unqualified success." This, he said, was "due in a very great measure to his personality, his evident sincerity, his modesty, his quick intelligence, and above all, his truly remarkable talent as a public speaker."

Edward G. Robinson, born Emmanuel Goldenberg in Romania, grew up on the Lower East Side of New York and did not attempt to hide his Jewishness or anti-Nazism, especially after he received death threats while playing the FBI agent who licked the new villains of the screen in *Confessions of a Nazi Spy.*

Robinson became one of the most intense anti-Nazis in Hollywood, joining one group after another: the Anti-Nazi League, Bundles for Britain, Committee to Defend America by Aiding the Allies, Fight for Freedom. For a while, he carried a portable radio around with him to keep up with the war, but abandoned it when the news became "consistently appalling." He kept a secretary on the set of *Brother Orchid* and *A Dispatch from Reuters* so he could answer "appeals for help from all over the country; any committee with a title that seemed to me to suggest help for England and France against the Nazis which contained on its letterhead the name of a recognized figure, I responded to—usually with a check. Later I responded by making speeches."

Many of the organizations Robinson and other Hollywood activists joined (such as the Anti-Nazi League) included Communists and fellow travelers, who often dominated the meetings. But Robinson said that at the time, he didn't much care who else belonged to such organizations. "Let me tell you that if they were pacifists, warmongers, Trotskyites, Stalinists, Quakers, Holy Rollers, D.A.R.'s, anarchists or Republicans, I would have joined them in some small way to fight against the black horror that was beginning to sweep Europe."

=

Melvyn Douglas was also openly active in his pro-Allied and anti-fascist activities, so much so that he would land in hot water with the studios. In addition to his work on the William Allen White Committee, he was also active in the Anti-Nazi League. Many such organizations were thrown into confusion when Hitler and Stalin negotiated their nonaggression pact in August 1939; as chairman of the Motion Picture Democratic Committee, Douglas presented a resolution denouncing both the Nazis and the Communists. The resolution was ignored, so he resigned from the committee. Although he was attacked for his position, he continued his pro-British, anti-Hitler speeches, which finally produced a confrontation with his boss, MGM head Louis B. Mayer. One day, while Douglas was making Garbo laugh in *Ninotchka*, Mayer summoned Douglas to his office for what the actor called a "friendly little chat" about Douglas's political views and activities. "Of course it's all right," Mayer said, "for you to think what you please, but surely you see that you don't do yourself any good at the studio when you offend a lot of people. Consider what happens to our pictures in certain parts of the world because of your activities."

Douglas replied that his feelings about what was occurring in Europe were so strong that in good conscience he could not stop, even if to continue was not helpful to the studio or his career.

"Your wife's an actress, isn't she?" Mayer asked, shifting tactics.

"Yes," said Douglas. Helen Gahagan Douglas was a well-known Broadway actress and opera singer who, in 1935, appeared in her only movie, *She*, giving a remarkable portrayal of the eternally youthful queen of a lost kingdom.

"Do you think she'd like a nice contract at MGM?" Mayer asked Douglas.

"I think *my* contract should be terminated, since it's causing the studio discomfort."

Mayer paused a few moments and then said: "We'll see what happens at the box office." *Ninotchka* was a smash, and Douglas stayed on at MGM to do several more films before he went to work in Washington for the Office of Civilian Defense in 1942.

One thing Mayer apparently did not know was that Helen Gahagan Douglas was even more anti-Nazi than her husband, and just as outspoken. In the presidential campaign of 1940, in which both she and her husband were involved, she crossed the country several times, giving a total of 168 speeches—and making a significant discovery about the difference between public speaking and other appearances onstage: "After a play or a concert, people who approached me always talked about my performance—how well I did, how lovely I looked, and so on. But after a campaign speech, the embarrassing preoccupation with me didn't happen. Talk afterward was about the issues I had raised." By Pearl Harbor, she was a full-time Democrat, campaigning for the California Democratic slate in the 1942 congressional elections—and on the road that would eventually take her to Washington. In 1950, after two terms in the House, she ran for the U.S. Senate against Richard Nixon. He defeated her, in part by spreading the word that she was a Communist.

=

Myrna Loy, who had captured the public's attention as Nora Charles to William Powell's Nick in the *Thin Man* series, was another actress who followed events in Europe closely, supported the right causes, and—after Pearl Harbor—would become a full-time, active supporter of the war effort. For one thing, she may have been the only member of filmland who could say that she'd read *Mein Kampf,* and before 1938 she tried to convince the stars she worked with that Hitler meant what he said about swallowing up Austria, Czechoslovakia, and Poland. Like Melvyn and Helen Gahagan Douglas, she would soon learn that MGM did not like its stars to get involved in things that did not concern them. When she returned to Hollywood to begin work on *Another Thin Man* (the third in the series), she received a letter from Arthur Loew, who handled foreign distribution for MGM. He said she should be careful about mixing politics with her career; years later, the letter still enraged her: "Here I was fighting for the Jews and they're telling me to lay off because there's still money to be made in Germany. Loew and many of the company executives were Jewish, but they still condoned this horror. I know it's incredible but it happened." She grieved when Hitler invaded the Low Countries and said frankly that she became "a war-monger."

=

Another very active member of the William Allen White Committee was Tallulah Bankhead, the irrepressible daughter of William Brockman Bankhead, the speaker of the U.S. House of Representatives from 1936 until his death in 1940. Tallulah, one of the country's most popular stage actresses, had made a handful of films between 1928 and 1932 and would make more during and after the war. Having been the toast of London when she worked there in the late 1920s, she had a special fondness for the British.

Bankhead's greatest triumphs took place onstage. In fact, she was playing in Lillian Hellman's *The Little Foxes* in Chicago at the time of Dunkirk—which, she said, produced "my most notable attack of sobriety."

> That night in my bedroom, I dropped to my knees and prayed that through some miracle the British might escape annihilation. On the theory that their deliverance might be effected through the French artillery, I came into my living room at the Ambassador Hotel, nudged Room Service, and ordered up three French 75s. This drink, served in a tall highball glass, is a blend of champagne, gin, a spot of sugar, a squirt of lemon juice, the whole topped off with a brandy float. Consumed in quantity they can flatten a longshoreman. I drained all three, then weaved to my feet and announced: "As of now I'm on the wagon! And I'm staying on the wagon until the British are back in Dunkirk!"

As the war in Europe progressed, Tallulah became increasingly active in the effort to bring the United States in. Part of her anger was personal. In October 1940, she lost her father, who had been a strong supporter of FDR and preparedness. After the funeral, a friend said: "Tallulah, you need a drink." But she replied, "I'm not going to break it [her vow of sobriety], darling. Of all times now."* A month later, an early love, Napier George Henry Stuart Alington, the third Baron Alington, who was an RAF pilot, was killed in action. In any case,

---

*She kept her promise—well, almost: She went off the wagon briefly while working on *Lifeboat*.

Bankhead loathed Hitler. "God," she often said when she heard his name, "if I were only a man."

At the very least, Bankhead could do what she thought a man had to do. As a member of the William Allen White Committee, she spent many weeks going around the country giving speeches. These appearances made her nervous, one of her biographers reported, so occasionally she would take a little brandy (for medicinal purposes) out of the paregoric bottle she carried with her. When she was relaxed, she could work up a fine pitch of pro-war anti-Nazism:

> I don't pretend to understand world politics, but I can understand that if Hitler were to win this struggle our own situation would be in a pretty serious way. That is why I favor giving all we can to Britain. . . . You can't take away people's freedom of thought and religion without going back to the Dark Ages, and the world won't stand for that.

Of course, for the young actors who followed events in Europe and realized what was happening, making speeches and signing petitions were not enough. On the screen, actors were joining up to fight alongside the British; in real life, the draft board was keeping an eye on them once Congress narrowly passed the Selective Training and Service Act in 1940. In the first peacetime draft in U.S. history, men between the ages of twenty-one and thirty-six were subject to military service, and being out of uniform made many of the young single actors in Hollywood uncomfortable. Several chose to enlist before the draft called them. Robert Montgomery had been preoccupied with national and international affairs for some time. He was in London playing Lord Peter Wimsey in a movie eventually titled *Haunted Honeymoon* when England declared war. His costar, Maureen O'Sullivan, returned immediately to the States and was replaced by Constance Cummings. Montgomery's wife, Elizabeth, also returned to be with their children in Hollywood, but Montgomery stayed on to complete the film, which was not easy. Lord Haw Haw, broadcasting to England on Joseph Goebbels's behalf, said that Denham Studios, where *Honeymoon* was being made, would be bombed in retaliation for its film *The Lion Has Wings*. And shooting days were interrupted whenever *Honeymoon*'s director, Arthur B. Woods, also an RAF pilot, had to report for flight duty. After the film was finally finished, Montgomery returned to Hollywood to shoot *The Earl of Chicago*. Then he quit Hollywood and went to Paris for what he thought would be six months' ambulance duty with the American Field

Service. One film-magazine writer was assigned to write a piece about "Why Bob Montgomery Went to War" but he was unable to get Montgomery, always reluctant to talk to the press (especially about his wartime duty), to explain his motivation. But the writer did persuade Montgomery's friend Robert Sherwood to help answer the question. Sherwood wrote:

> Bob Montgomery is a typical American. He has the healthy skepticism which causes Americans to use those two devastating expressions, "Oh yeah?" and "So what!" But he has also the indomitable idealism, the devotion to the basic principles of freedom and justice, which enabled this country to be discovered and settled, which drove the embattled farmers into action at Concord and Lexington, which inspired both sides at Gettysburg, which sent the covered wagons rolling over the plains and mountains.

Because of the fall of France, Montgomery returned to the United States sooner than he expected and, *Time* said sarcastically, "became Hollywood's foremost authority on World War II."

Montgomery may not have been a World War II authority, but he did know that the Germans had bombed a French ambulance. He wrote about the episode in a letter to *Collier's* magazine:

> There were big Red Crosses painted on both sides and on top of the ambulances, so you had a good target. The driver was the only one saved. He had been carried off, wounded, just a few minutes before we got there. The Captain seemed to have been killed by the bomb in front. The stretcher cases were killed by the machine-gun bullets. We could see that for ourselves.

Collier's noted that "payment for this 'letter' has been made, at Mr. Montgomery's request, to the American Field Service." (Montgomery obviously did not need the money; the Treasury Department reported that in 1940 his income was $211,416.) Back in Hollywood, he told an industry forum: "I am convinced that the weakness of leadership under which, to my knowledge, this industry has been struggling is directly responsible for the poor quality of its average product in the past and will make it impossible for the industry to perform its function in national defense in the present crisis with any appreciable degree of success."

And just to make sure there was no doubt how he felt, he added:

"Any resemblance between the motion picture industry and creative art is purely coincidental."

Montgomery always seemed to be at the center of action and controversy. In 1939, risking both his career and his life, Montgomery helped create the Screen Actors Guild and expose labor racketeering in the film industry. He didn't like the mob—and he didn't like columnists either, especially Jimmy Fidler. When Fidler sent him a watch as a reward for his "Americanism," Montgomery returned it, saying to the press, "Fidler has the effrontery to appoint himself the giver of what he calls 'The Jimmy Fidler Award for Americanism.' He had the further gall to award it to me. Before I could send it back with a rude suggestion as to how he could best dispose of it, a number of my friends had called on the phone to rib me as 'you great big wonderful American, you!' "

In 1940, Montgomery was appointed chairman of the Hollywood Republican Committee to Elect Wendell Willkie. The following year, he applied for a commission in the Navy—and then, no doubt aware that his income would be reduced when he became a naval officer, made four quick movies before he was called up, all released in 1941: *Mr. and Mrs. Smith* (with Carole Lombard), *Here Comes Mr. Jordan, Unfinished Business,* and *Rage in Heaven* (with Ingrid Bergman and George Sanders). It was said that MGM put Montgomery in the last film (in which he played a psychotic villain rather than his usual debonair leading man) as punishment for all the trouble he gave them.

His commission came through on August 1, 1941, and his first assignment was as an assistant naval attaché in the American embassy in London, an assignment Douglas Fairbanks, Jr., would have loved. When Montgomery boarded his plane for Europe, he told reporters: "I'm washed up with Hollywood for the duration."

Montgomery's job in London was to run the embassy's naval operations room, which meant he had to keep track of all British and American ships. On December 7, 1941, he was ordered back to Washington to set up a similar operation in the White House.

As we have seen, Douglas Fairbanks, Jr., received his commission in the Navy while he was on his Latin American mission. As soon as that was finished, he was given a leave to make a film—*The Corsican Brothers,* a swashbuckling Alexandre Dumas tale of separated twins that did not afford many propaganda possibilities. Fairbanks said he felt foolish in front of the cameras with the world going to hell.

He was relieved to receive orders from the Navy to report for active duty as soon as *The Corsican Brothers* was completed. Fairbanks had suggested to both Sumner Welles and FDR that he be assigned to Colonel William Donovan's new information and intelligence operation, arguing that he had a great many contacts around the globe and he "might be of some use in helping to present a solid propaganda front between the democracies of the world." The Navy shot the proposal down. One senior naval officer noted on the request: "This is just an idea for a junketing trip. The young man in question would do more harm than good. The best thing for Fairbanks would be to get in some service in order to make a naval officer out of him."

When he reported for duty in Washington, Fairbanks was told by a lieutenant commander in the Bureau of Naval Personnel that he was being sent immediately to sea to avoid the kind of publicity Robert Montgomery—"an old sidekick of yours, I guess"—had been getting in London. "The brass has decided the quickest way for you to be a seagoing 'deck officer' is to go to sea and learn on the job."

The Navy may have put Fairbanks in his place, but he did not exactly go slinking out of the capital. The President of the United States gave Fairbanks his farewell party—in the White House. Roosevelt, an old Navy man, made a bad martini, said Fairbanks, "but you had to drink it anyway." The President's jokes weren't much better: FDR said Fairbanks would soon be promoted to "captain of the head." The President also warned the actor that "U-boat sinkings this week are higher than ever" and said "we never know when the [German battleship] *Tirpitz* is coming out."

On their last night in New York, Fairbanks and his wife, Mary Lee Hartford, saw the musical *Lady in the Dark,* starring Gertrude Lawrence and a newcomer, Danny Kaye. They both applauded the future star, while Mary Lee chided her husband about his earlier romance with Lawrence.

Fairbanks left Boston on an old supply ship headed for Iceland, where he would board the battleship *Mississippi.* Despite his gallant efforts to be "stiff-upper-lipped," Fairbanks said, as the supply ship put out to sea, "I could still see the tiny figure of Mary Lee waving on the quayside. I damned near blubbered. What the hell had I got myself into?"

He would find out when he finally reported to the *Mississippi* at Reykjavik. The press took pictures, and newspapers all across the United States let it be known that Douglas Fairbanks, Jr., had joined the Navy. "Have you hired yourself a press agent?" one angry senior officer asked him.

As a result, Fairbanks began his first regular assignment with a hostile group of regular Navy officers who did not like publicity-seeking movie stars coming aboard to win the war. He was made the butt of jokes and given inferior quarters and the worst watches. However, Fairbanks weathered his hazing period, and when he left the *Mississippi* the executive officer, Captain Jerauld Wright, wrote in his fitness report: "I believe that Lt. Fairbanks would make an excellent naval officer."

It is curious that these first actors to go into the service seemed to share a love of or experience with the sea. Montgomery had been a deckhand on an oil tanker in the 1920s after his father's death left the family broke; Fairbanks had always loved the "lore of the sea," he said, "adventure stories of the bounding main and almost everything to do with ships."

=

Another actor who shared an early love of the sea was Sterling Hayden. Hayden was a high school dropout who went to sea at sixteen and was captain of a schooner by his early twenties. He was also ruggedly handsome and tall, and to get money to buy his own boat he took modeling jobs, which eventually drew him to Hollywood. Later he would tell a British intelligence officer that it was Colonel Bill Donovan of the Office of Strategic Services (OSS) who had suggested "I go out to the West Coast and become an actor. . . . I guess it had something to do with my being able to use the acting thing as a cover in case we got into war." Hayden had a screen test with Paramount in 1940 and by that summer was costarring with Madeleine Carroll in "a melange of pap called *Virginia*," as he put it. Carroll had by now made several pictures in the United States (including *The General Died at Dawn* and *The Prisoner of Zenda*) after playing the lead in two Alfred Hitchcock films made in England, *The 39 Steps* and *Secret Agent*. Although *Virginia* was Hayden's first picture, the studio PR machines were now playing him as "the Beautiful Blond Viking God," and "the greatest find since Gable."

Naturally two of the most beautiful people in the world, Hayden and Carroll, were drawn to each other. But they had their differences: All he wanted was to raise money to buy a ship; all she wanted was "money enough to throw herself into the war"—specifically, to help orphaned children in Paris.

When the "melange of pap" was finished, he planned to be on his way: "What I'll do is buy me a typewriter and a good camera and be a war correspondent," he told a friend, who replied: "You've been reading

Hemingway. . . . You're so goofy over this dream upstairs [Carroll] that you got to go get your ass shot off."

Suddenly Hayden leaped up and shouted: "I'll get me a ship and haul cargo with her, maybe run the blockade into England and back. What do you say about that?"

His friend yawned.

Yvonne De Carlo, an aspiring young starlet with a bit part in *Harvard Here I Come!*, confirmed Hayden's infatuation with Carroll. De Carlo had a few dates with him at about this time: "I can remember never feeling so in awe of a man." On their dates he spoke of his love of the sea, of sailing, of the fact that the United States would have to go to war, of his abhorrence of material things, and of the fact that he had set Madeleine Carroll straight on such matters. "Her name came up far too frequently to please me," said De Carlo. "I pined for him for more than a year." But when she saw him in Hollywood after the war he had become a different person.

Hayden finally obtained his boat with a bit of blackmail inspired by a fit of jealousy. He and Carroll were making *Bahama Passage*. One day she was sitting in the corner on soundstage 31 with a lean, tall man in uniform who, Hayden learned, ferried bombers across the North Atlantic. "The greatest find since Gable" was sitting in a corner, sulking. "Suddenly, for the first time," he wrote in his autobiography, *Wanderer*, "I knew what jealousy meant."

For one thing, it meant he had no desire for dinner, so he drove all the way to Capistrano and back to Los Angeles Harbor—and by then he knew he had to buy his boat. He threatened to quit Paramount before *Bahama Passage* was completed unless they bought him a boat—the *Oretha F. Spinney*, a big one docked in L.A. harbor. It was owned by MGM. So Y. Frank Freeman at Paramount called Eddie Mannix at MGM and offered him "eighteen five" for the *Spinney*. Hayden would get a half interest—"as a bonus"—when he finished the picture.

Madeleine Carroll decided to return to England—to "rendezvous with her bomber man," Hayden was sure. The *Spinney* needed much work before she could put to sea, and Hayden could not wait. So he made a decision that he felt was so dramatic in prewar Hollywood that someday they might make a movie about it: He decided to turn his back on Hollywood's effort to make him a star! And his exit did play like a classic tale of a man doing what a man's got to do. But first Hayden had to deal with his agent, who said he had it on good authority that the studio was going to offer him the lead in *For Whom the Bell Tolls* and write him a new contract for three films a year, at $30,000 a picture. Hayden said no.

Then he had to see Henry Ginsberg, the studio hatchet man, who gave him a lecture: "Hayden, I am supposed to convince you not to quit. I'm not going to bother. I haven't the slightest sympathy with you. You are not an actor. You never have been. I doubt you ever could be an actor. You are what we call a Personality.

"We have brought you along until you are what is known as a hot property. You might go a long way in this business. If you would like my opinion, I would say the odds are against it. You have to care in this business, and you don't give a damn. If you walk out on us, you will never work in pictures again. It will be the biggest mistake in your life, and from what I heard, you've made your share."

Ginsberg also suggested that the actor could probably expect a breach-of-contract suit, then paused and said: "Does what I have said make sense to you, Hayden?"

Hayden said yes—but he was still leaving. So Ginsberg said he should talk to Freeman, the man who bought him the *Spinney*. Freeman used an avunculur approach, asking Hayden to level with him. What was really bothering him? "I'm your friend and it won't go beyond this room."

"Well, sir," said Hayden, "it's just I don't feel right as an actor. I wasn't cut out for it. I'm the first to admit I may be fouled up, but with the war going on and all I feel I have got to get out and get out right now."

Freeman didn't buy that: "This war thing is nonsense. Our country isn't in the war yet—if it was, then I'd be the first to understand. You know and I know that you're leaving something out. I know what it is and you know I know and you know I'm fond of you both. This thing that's eating your heart out will pass."

Hayden admitted that Madeleine Carroll was a big part of the trouble, but then he made a remark reflecting what in one way or another would soon be haunting many of Hollywood's leading men: "I don't want to go on imitating men and that's just all there is to it."

Freeman knew he was licked. He stood up from his chair, sighed, and escorted Hayden to the door, wishing him luck.

Hayden had tears in his eyes during his speech to Freeman. But by the time he reached Boston (he drove straight through—sleeping only an hour at a time, scrunched up in the back of his car—hoping to reach Madeleine before she left for England), he said he felt like a man again. For the benefit of the press boys, he threw his California license plates into Boston Harbor. The reporters asked him what he was going to do next. He said he didn't know—but he was lying. First, he would "intervene between Madeleine and that man from the bomber command"; then he would go off to war.

Hayden went to England, joined the British commandos, and broke his leg on his eleventh parachute-training jump.

=

If ever there was someone who did not suggest a Hayden-like man of action, that someone was James Stewart. In such films as *You Can't Take It with You, It's a Wonderful World, Mr. Smith Goes to Washington,* and *Destry Rides Again,* he had established himself as the prototype of the shy, mumbling, unassuming man of integrity. Although he held an architecture degree from Princeton (he was persuaded into acting by a classmate, director-to-be Joshua Logan), his favorite reading was "Flash Gordon" comics.

But Stewart did have one thing in common with Hayden: He was very attractive to women. When Marlene Dietrich first saw him on the set at Universal where they would make *Destry,* she felt just like Yvonne De Carlo first meeting Hayden. The movie's producer, Joe Pasternak, said: "She took one look at Jimmy Stewart and she began to rub her hands. She had to have him at once." To break the ice, Dietrich locked Stewart in his dressing room, then let him out and presented him with a life-size doll of Flash Gordon.

Jimmy Stewart was not the kind of young man you would expect to turn his back on a $2,000-(or more)-a-week career and go off to fight a war that his country was not in yet. But he did go, right after finishing *Ziegfeld Girl.* He had his pilot's license and had flown many hours, so in November of 1940, when he began thinking about joining the Army, he naturally thought of the Air Corps. However, he was ten pounds too light. He went on a diet to gain weight, came back four months later, and made it by a single ounce. Bill Grady, an MGM casting director who went with Stewart when he took the physical, remembers him racing out of the medical office screaming: "I'm in! I'm in!" And the medico told Grady: "That fellow sure is an oddball. Didn't even complain when he found out that he'd been accepted."

Louis B. Mayer, who tried to talk Stewart out of joining up, didn't understand him either. "You've got to remember that this was nine months before Pearl Harbor. That bullhead really wanted to go into the service and no amount of talking helped."

As did most Hollywood stars, Stewart found that life in the Army for a movie celebrity was not the same as it was for the average G.I.

"Dozens of fans would wait outside the wire gate," said one man who went to Moffett Field, the Army Air Corps training camp, at the same time Stewart did,

> to catch a glimpse of him as he walked by. Even in the rain. Reporters and newsreel cameras singled him out.
>
> At the beginning he would get several dozen phone calls a day. Most of them were from admirers—young female admirers. I understand several made some pretty bawdy and outright proposals. Things got to be so confusing and embarrassing that Jimmy started refusing overnight passes. What's more, the scuttlebutt was they he had turned down a thousand dollars a week his studio wanted to send him regularly. He settled to get along like his buddies on a lousy twenty-one dollars a month. Who does that voluntarily? We felt the poor bastard should be given a section eight [a mental-illness discharge]. I don't mind telling you we were damn jealous. But after a couple of weeks, we realized Jimmy was really okay.

Shortly after Pearl Harbor, Stewart graduated from flight school and received a second lieutenant's commission: "I don't think there ever was a prouder pilot than I was when those wings were pinned on me."

=

Mickey Rooney said that as early as 1939, when he was nineteen, "I wanted to join the fight then and there!" But, he said, Louis Mayer

> wasn't about to lose his biggest star. He squeezed the draft board in Culver City, persuading them that I could help the war effort more by going out with the MGM stock company and selling war bonds coast to coast. I put up no objections, and I did get out and sell.
>
> In 1940, Judy Garland and I and a gaggle of other actors and actresses started crisscrossing the nation on something called "The Metro Bond Train." We'd entertain and we'd sell bonds. Judy would sing, I would tell jokes or do imitations, and both of us would dance together. Sometimes we'd do ten shows a day, then get on the train, and move on to the next city. It was absolutely exhausting.

At nineteen, Rooney was indeed one of MGM's biggest stars. He began his film career at six and had already appeared in fifty-three movies (including several of the Andy Hardy series). He and his usual costar, Judy Garland, were idolized by millions of teenage movie fans. Most American movie stars were also idolized in Latin America—

where, before Pearl Harbor, public opinion favored the Nazis and ran against the United States. Nelson Rockefeller, the State Department's coordinator of the Office of Inter-American Affairs, was aware of the Hollywood stars' popularity south of the border; hoping they could win people's hearts, in 1940 he sent Rooney and a group of movie stars to Latin America on a goodwill tour. Included on the trip were Norma Shearer, Robert Taylor, Lana Turner, Tyrone Power, James Cagney, Bing Crosby, and Desi Arnaz and his band.

The trip was a lark, full of high jinks and hanky-panky. According to Arnaz, the "big romance" of the tour was between Mickey Rooney and Norma Shearer, star of *Marie Antoinette, Idiot's Delight,* and *The Women.* By now, Shearer had recovered from the death of her husband, the legendary Irving Thalberg, and had had affairs with Jimmy Stewart and George Raft. She was also seeing Rooney. In his very candid and amusing autobiography, Rooney says he became friends with her on a dinner-and-theater date in New York when Shearer was staying at the Waldorf. After the revue, *Streets of Paris* (with Abbott and Costello), she invited him up to her room "for a nightcap." He said he was so young and inexperienced at the time that he almost said: "I don't wear one."

But young Rooney had learned that women found him—or at least Andy Hardy—attractive. On a 1940 bond drive with Judy Garland, he said, women were "hurling themselves at the window of our limousine crying out 'Mickey! Mickey!' " He knew he was no Clark Gable or Tyrone Power, "But women seemed to want me anyhow. It was the war, I guess."

Whatever it was, Shearer apparently wanted him, too, and when Rooney finally figured it out, he wondered, "How can I put a move on Marie Antoinette?"

Back in Hollywood in the French dressing room that had been made especially for Shearer during the filming of *Marie Antoinette,* Rooney must have made all the right moves, because his relationship with Shearer, which he candidly describes, would probably fulfill every nineteen-year-old boy's fantasies on the subject of making love to a movie star, appropriately "French style," he says, in Marie Antoinette's dressing room, "with me sitting on the couch, my pants at my ankles, and her on her knees." Later, MGM gave the dressing room to Rooney and he said he never went in it without "thinking of Norma and the recollected warmth of her lips."

According to Arnaz, the affair continued into Latin America: "They looked kind of funny together," he says, "Miss Shearer always elegant in long organdy dresses with a parasol, and Mickey trotting alongside

Norma Shearer and Mickey Rooney: Rooney would always remember Shearer's Marie Antoinette *dressing room and her warm lips.* Courtesy of the Academy of Motion Picture Arts and Sciences

her through the Presidential Gardens of Chapultepec Park. When they stopped to talk and faced each other, if you weren't close, it looked as though Mickey was talking to her knockers."

As for Arnaz, his own movie career was just getting started with *Too Many Girls.* Unquestionably it was aided and abetted when he married his already arrived costar in *Girls,* Lucille Ball. The trip to Latin America did not help Desi with his new wife, who was learning that Desi could never have too many girls. She was furious when she was not invited on the Latin American tour (Arnaz was invited primarily because he was Hispanic) and grew enraged when she read in columns such as Earl Wilson's that in Mexico City, "Desi and Mickey Rooney seemed to be in a contest to see who could score the most."

Arnaz said that in Mexico City the stars drew large crowds and were royally treated—except that every time one of them stepped out on a balcony, the crowds disappeared "because [they thought] the crazy goddamn Americans are going to piss on us." A few years earlier, Lee Tracy had gone to Mexico City, got drunk, and done just that—as a parade was going by.*

When Arnaz returned and the State Department people asked him what Mexicans thought of Americans, he said they were "suspicious," though not because of what American men might do on a balcony. Lucille Ball's husband is not known as an expert on hemisphere affairs, but his summation of Latin American feelings about the United States on the eve of World War II is probably as good as any assessment the State Department ever received from a South American embassy:

> They don't get this, all of a sudden Good Neighbor policy deal. . . . One Mexican put it to me, because I think he put it very well, when I asked him why he was suspicious of this policy. I said to him, exactly the following, "I know that President Roosevelt means it, I know he wants to strengthen the relations between the United States and Latin America. So why are you suspicious?" He said, "Well, that might be all true and that's fine and dandy, but let me tell you something, Desi. If you lived next door to somebody for twenty years, and he never said good morning to you, never invited you for a drink, never remembers your wife's birthday, Christmas, or anything and he's been your neighbor for twenty years, but never had anything to do with you at all; then all of a sudden one day he says good morning, sends your wife flowers and asks you over for dinner. What's your reaction? It's got to be 'What the hell does the sonofabitch want?' "

The Selective Training and Service Act of 1940 made stars like Rooney and Arnaz uncomfortable being out of uniform, but they would soon be in the Army. At the same time, the draft gave many Hollywood stars, male and female, a way to make a contribution to national defense by doing something they were good at: entertaining. The government knew that all those young men being sent to training camps across the country needed to be entertained—and who could do the job better than the country's stage and screen actors? The result was the United Service Organizations (USO), through which Hollywood and Broadway stars would eventually make a contribution to the war perhaps even more important than selling bonds to pay for it.

---

*A Mexican general reportedly had his cape dampened by Tracy's contribution to the parade. The story goes that when the comedian Fred Allen heard of the incident, he quipped: "The general dried at dawn."

In its official history, the USO traces the tradition of civilian support of the military back to the Revolution, when General George Washington said: "When we assumed the soldier, we did not lay aside the citizen." Several private organizations had assumed responsibility for providing recreation and some entertainment for troops in World War I, and as Americans began to mobilize in 1940, some of these groups met to discuss what should be done to help comfort the tide of new troops coming into boot camps. The organizations included the YMCA, the YWCA, National Catholic Community Service, the National Jewish Welfare Board, the National Traveler's Aid Association, and the Salvation Army. They decided to form a new organization (the USO). Army officials, however, felt that the military should control troop recreation and entertainment. Roosevelt preferred to see a civilian organization control the entertainment of troops, although he agreed that the government would erect the buildings.

The USO's first national chairman was Thomas E. Dewey, who resigned to run for governor of New York in 1942. He was replaced by Prescott Bush, then a partner in Brown Brothers Harriman (and later a U.S. senator from Connecticut), the father of George Bush. However, the person most associated with the USO today is Bob "Don't Shoot, It's Only Me" Hope.

Hope was born in England but grew up in Cleveland, Ohio, and spent his early career in vaudeville, musical comedy, and radio. As a result of his success in *The Big Broadcast of 1938,* he was offered a new radio show, "The Bob Hope Pepsodent Show," to be sponsored by the toothpaste company, and a movie contract with Paramount. His first Pepsodent show, featuring Constance Bennett, Jerry Colonna, and Skinnay Ennis and his band, showed little concern for the imminent war. "We were no different from the rest of the American people, pretending not to hear the distant thunder. We went on with the business of being funny, because that was our life."

Then came the fall of France and Dunkirk. "Still we weren't too concerned over here," said Hope. Singing "Thanks for the Memory" in *The Big Broadcast* had already given Hope a touch of immortality. Then, in early 1940, came *Road to Singapore,* with Bing Crosby and Dorothy Lamour, the first of the seven famous *Road* pictures. Hope says the main reason for these movies' success was that they took America's mind off the war in Europe.

Even after the fall of France, Hope said, "on the 'Pepsodent Show' we tried to continue as if it didn't matter. It can't happen here, America told itself. Other things were of much more importance," like the fact that "The Bob Hope Pepsodent Show" had become the number one radio show in the nation.

Then, in 1940, came Selective Service. Soon Hope would entertain at his first military base. From then on, for the rest of his career he would rarely be without a captive audience of U.S. troops.

Hope's first camp show was on May 6, 1941, at March Field in Southern California. And he knew immediately that the rules of his game were changing: "We represented everything those new recruits didn't have: home cooking, Mother, and soft roommates. Their real enemies, even after war broke out, were never just the Germans or the Japanese. The enemies were boredom, mud, officers, and abstinence. Any joke that touched those nerves was a sure thing."

The jokes didn't have to be good. All they had to do was remind the kids of home, to help them remember how great it was to sit around the radio with their family and listen to bad jokes. Hope opened his first show with the line "Good evening, ladies and gentlemen. This is Bob 'March Field' Hope telling all aviators, while we can't advise you on how to protect your 'chutes, there's nothing like Pepsodent to protect your toots."

The laughter was so loud, he said, he had to look down to see if his pants had fallen. But he also told some good jokes and as the war went on—and some great ones.

The next week the show was broadcast from the studio in Hollywood and Hope said the civilian audience was "tough and unreasonable." They had no gratitude for getting in free and, worst of all, they wouldn't laugh at bad jokes! "I had to get back to the military before my option came up," said Hope. The following week, he did the show from the naval base in San Diego—and more laughs, especially when the Navy, mistaking the musicians in Skinnay Ennis's band for a bunch of new recruits, shaved off their hair. The band members, thinking everyone on a naval base had to have their hair shaved, didn't resist. And Hope felt he helped create the term "G.I." by referring to one Marine as having a G.I. (government-issue) haircut. However, the biggest laugh of the night came when Vera Vague responded to some insult from Hope by saying: "If you get fresh with me, I'm going to the head—"

She was supposed to say "of the Navy—he's a dear friend of mine," but no one heard that part of the line because at the word "head," thousands of sailors let out a roar that almost brought the roof down.

With the laughter came a sudden jump in the show's ratings. Pepsodent told Hope it would pay for any trip he wanted to make, at least in the United States. But as America began to build up bases abroad, the

USO was ready to send Hope anywhere overseas he wanted to go. That was all Hope needed to virtually join the Army—and the Navy, Marines, and Air Corps.

Although Bob Hope would soon become synonymous with the USO and troop entertainment, a group known as the Flying Showboat, under the direction of the Friends of New York Sailors and Soldiers, had the distinction of being the first troupe to entertain U.S. troops abroad. It consisted of Stan Laurel, Oliver Hardy, Ray Bolger, Chico Marx, Mitzi Mayfair, and John Garfield; they began at Fort Dix, New Jersey, in October 1941, then continued for two weeks in the Caribbean. It was a significant experience for Garfield, whose own career was just emerging with *They Made Me a Criminal* and *Dust Be My Destiny*, among other movies. He learned, as Hope would, that no matter how bad the jokes or how mundane the material, the G.I.'s loved the performers. "How many are from the South?" Garfield would shout, and a roar would come back: "Yeah! Yeah!" Then he would add, "I mean from south Brooklyn," and get another roar. "A surefire stunt," he said, "was to pick out some feature of the camp and improvise a verse about it to the tune of a popular song. Something like, 'The Last Time I Saw Trinidad,' with a lot of crap about the camp at Trinidad. They'd love it. Or in Puerto Rico, where we had this Boca Chica drink, we'd make up something like, 'It will make you mucho seeck-a if you drink a Boca Chica when you're in Puerto Rico.' "

The Celluloid War

Nobody obviously was going to outdo G-man Edward G. Robinson and by no stretch of the imagination would the Nazis win. —EDWARD G. ROBINSON, commenting on his role in *Confessions of a Nazi Spy*

As the war in Europe intensified, the question of whether America should go to the aid of the Allies became a burning issue. In the Hollywood studios, as in the rest of the country, opinion was divided. There were those, like Darryl F. Zanuck, head of 20th Century–Fox, who supported intervention. In January 1941, he was commissioned a lieutenant colonel in the Army Reserve and began immediately to pre-pare Hollywood to produce training films. Before he left his studio he produced *The Man I Married,* in which Lloyd Nolan, playing an American correspondent in Germany, said that "perhaps war was the only way to make an end to these lunatics who spread fear and hatred over the world." Off the screen Zanuck made no effort to hide his feelings. Three months before Pearl Harbor, he told an American Legion convention: "If you charge us with being anti-Nazi you are right and if you accuse us of producing films in the interest of preparedness and national defense, again you are right."

On the other hand, MGM's vice president and general manager, Louis B. Mayer, typified the more conservative, neutral approach to the war. The studio had big investments and markets in Europe. Mayer hoped to preserve these markets, and Greta Garbo would recall a conversation she had with Mayer just after the beginning of the war in Europe when Mayer said: "I think it will be a long war. In Europe, there is no more market for us. It is very bad to lose such a profitable market for your pictures. . . . Right away, we have to begin work on a new picture. You will play a glamorous girl. American. Fun-loving."

Garbo was enraged: "A typical American businessman," she thought, "not worried that because of Hitler many people will die. All he can think about is his film market."

Mayer said: "Think it over. . . . We have to stick to our contract. You've got to play, war or no war." (She played—in *Two-Faced Woman,* her last film, and it was a disaster.) As Mayer walked her to the door, he said: "The Nazis will fight the Communists. They will end up destroying each other, and we will have peace. Democracy will come to Europe once more. Then we have the whole European market in our hands. European pictures will be no more."

There was no question that after September 1939, the public wanted war movies and although anti-fascist or pro-British movies may have alienated some movie audiences, their acceptance at the box office suggested that most Americans liked them. In his study of pre–Pearl Harbor Hollywood films, Bernard F. Dick found fourteen movies to be "unequivocally anti-Nazi," and he identified nearly fifty additional films that encouraged military preparedness or aiding England: World War II spy thrillers (with the spies appearing to be fascists), patriotic comedies, and movies whose villains resembled the Nazis.

It was perhaps inevitable that Charlie Chaplin would eventually direct and star in Hollywood's most devastating satire on Adolf Hitler. In the first place, Chaplin's perceptions about national and international events were uncanny. His films had made him a millionaire by the early twenties, but as the decade neared its end, he was so convinced something was wrong on Wall Street that he took his money out of the stock market and put it in Canadian gold—before the crash. He was also one of the first in Hollywood to see the impact of the industrial age on the individual, which led to his great 1936 film *Modern Times* (costarring his young wife, Paulette Goddard). Inevitably he would oppose the spreading fascism of the 1930s.

Then there was the similarity—in appearance—between Chaplin the clown and Hitler the dictator. In his autobiography Chaplin said that "Alexander Korda in 1937 had suggested that I should do a Hitler story based on mistaken identity—Hitler having the same moustache as the tramp, I could play both characters."*

Hitler fascinated Chaplin. He told one of his writers, "This guy is one of the greatest actors I've ever seen," and watching the newsreel of Hitler dancing his little jig after the surrender of France, he said: "Oh you bastard, you son-of-a-bitch, you swine, I know what's in your mind."

He began to develop the story, about a little Jewish barber who was mistaken for the dictator, and he agonized over whether to take "such a risk," as he put it. What if Hitler died or was assassinated? According to Garson Kanin, Chaplin even thought of going to Washington, telling the story to FDR, and letting him decide. But then he thought: "What if he said no?"

When Chaplin finally decided to make the film, it took two years and $2 million of his own money—$500,000 was spent before the first scene was shot. And it was one of the most difficult times in Chaplin's life. His marriage to Paulette Goddard was beginning to come apart and it did not help that she was his costar in the film. She said he was harsh to her on the set and embarrassed her in front of the crew. At the same time, he was furious when she and her agent appeared in his office to demand that she be "featured seventy-five percent on all posters." He yelled at them, "Don't tell me what billing she's to get. I have her interests at heart more than you have."

During the making of the film, he received calls from people threatening to make it impossible for the film to be shown in any theater, and United Artists doubted the film could be shown in England, where people saw Hitler not as a clown but as a monster. Chaplin appreciated the British attitude, but, he said, "Hitler must be laughed at." (Later, he said that had he known the full extent of the Nazi atrocities in the concentration camps, he would not have made the film.)

---

*A writer named Konrad Bercovici said he had suggested the idea to Chaplin even earlier, and he had a witness to prove it—Melvyn Douglas. Douglas confirmed Bercovici's claim, not only in his autobiography but in court, when Bercovici sued Chaplin for plagiarism and won.

When Germany invaded Poland, and England declared war, the worried letters from the studio stopped. Now, said Chaplin, the New York office was wiring frantically, HURRY UP WITH YOUR FILM. EVERYONE IS WAITING FOR IT.

Chaplin himself was unusually tense while making the film. During the scenes in which he played the little Jewish barber, he was warm and sentimental; during the scenes in which he played Hitler ("Hynkel"), he was more dictatorial than usual on the set—and off, as long as he was in uniform. Reginald Gardiner, who played the pilot in the film's classic upside-down-airplane scene, said that he was driving with Chaplin in uniform to a new location when Chaplin became very abusive toward the driver of a car that was in their way. Suddenly Chaplin realized what was happening: "Just because I'm dressed up in this darned thing," he told Gardiner, "I go and do a thing like that."

On the set, Chaplin and Jack Oakie, who played Mussolini ("Napaloni"), would have contests to see who could be funnier than the other, with Chaplin invariably winning. One day, according to Chaplin biographer David Robinson, Oakie had tried everything, until finally Chaplin stopped the cameras and said: "If you really want to steal a scene from me, you son of a bitch, just look straight in the camera. That'll do it every time."

By the time they were shooting the last scenes, Hitler had evolved from the fanatical leader of a German political party into a dictator who had absorbed Austria, Czechoslovakia, and Poland, a madman poised and ready to march through Western Europe. So Chaplin decided to include a message at the end of the film. He worked on it for three months while Hitler was invading the Low Countries and forcing France to her knees. His two screenwriters opposed the final speech and one film salesman said it would cost the film $1 million. "I don't care if it's five million, I'm going to do it," said Chaplin. His writers argued that it was uncharacteristic of a Chaplin film, that critics would object to it—and would probably be right—but the final six-minute speech he gave as the little barber masquerading as the German dictator was a measure of the hatred Hitler had aroused in Chaplin—and in most of the world.

With the Chaplin-Goddard marriage disintegrating, the Hollywood columnists speculated as to whether Paulette would even attend the New York premiere. She did, although, as the columnists noted, it was probably not coincidental that director Anatole Litvak (Goddard's latest lover) flew to New York at the same time. Chaplin introduced Paulette on stage after the show, saying: "My wife and I hope you enjoyed the picture." The next day, columnist Dorothy Kilgallen noted that Litvak had been "casting sheep eyes at Paulette" and that he was "there last night kissing her hand." Chaplin and Goddard would soon break up, becoming, said Goddard's biographer, one of the few Hollywood couples to part in the wake of a success. "Usually Hollywood marriages split up in the wake of a failure."

==

To Be or Not to Be was another film that satirized the Nazis, although it did not create as much excitement when it was released in early 1942. Still, it attracted its share of controversy and eventually became something of a classic. Everyone who played in it seemed to remember it with great fondness. Jack Benny, who took the role of a Polish actor (who also impersonated a Nazi colonel) after Maurice Chevalier turned it down, said it was the "best picture I ever made."

Carole Lombard, who was also a second choice (after Miriam Hopkins had withdrawn), said *To Be or Not to Be* was the happiest experience of her career, "the one time," according to her biographer Larry Swindell, "when everything began right, stayed right and ended right." Lombard had already emerged not only as one of Hollywood's most personally popular stars, but as a first-rate comedienne in such classics as *My Man Godfrey* and *Nothing Sacred*. In *To Be or Not to Be*, she played Maria Tura, a Polish actress married to Jack Benny's character. The role came at the peak of her career and resulted in one of her most memorable films; tragically, it was to be her last.

Young Robert Stack, playing a Polish aviator, had to make advances to his real-life childhood idol Carole Lombard in her dressing room while her husband was onstage. He called his participation in the movie "one of my greatest thrills," and not just because *To Be or Not to Be* was an anti-Nazi film being made on the eve of America's entry into the war. It was also something of a breakthrough for the former skeet-shooting champion. In his earlier films, Stack had played dead-serious roles, but now, with Carole Lombard loosening him up ("You're supposed to have ants in your pants for me," she would hiss at him when he froze up in a love scene), he demonstrated that he could relax and even play comedy.

And there was no denying that young Stack had his fans—all over the world. At about the time he was making *To Be or Not to Be*, young Anne Frank was writing her diary in Nazi-occupied Holland. In it she had a picture of herself, inscribed "This is a photo as I should wish myself to look all of the time. Then maybe I would have a chance to come to Hollywood." Later, it was discovered that she also had a picture of Robert Stack.

Helmut Dantine relished spoofing the Nazis by playing one. He had only a small part in *To Be or Not to Be,* but he was, in a sense, grooming himself for the villainous Nazi who would soon appear in Mrs. Miniver's backyard. Also reveling in *To Be or Not to Be* was the veteran German actor Sig Ruman. He had not been exiled by the Nazis, having left Berlin long before Hitler came to power, but he hated them every bit as much as Dantine did. He had recently had a triumph as one of the bumbling Communists in *Ninotchka,* and now he would have even more fun spoofing a Nazi general.

Lombard's biographer Larry Swindell says that just about the only person who did not enjoy the making of *To Be or Not to Be* was Lombard's husband, Clark Gable. He did not like Jack Benny or the director, Ernst Lubitsch, and he did not share his wife's interest in international affairs. He had ignored the Spanish Civil War, while she had supported the Loyalists; he was indifferent to the plight of England, while she did volunteer work for Bundles for Britain. Listening to Ruman, on the set of *To Be or Not to Be,* tell stories about the horrors of Germany under Hitler, Lombard became an intense anti-Nazi; Gable maintained his indifference.

Lubitsch was pleased when the film's eventual success justified his decision to go through with it at a time when the wise men in filmland were saying he had better not. *The Great Dictator* had been criticized for spoofing Hitler with Europe at war; Lubitsch had difficulty raising the money for his film and had casting problems as well. Jack Benny, for example, while enjoying his time on the set, was puzzled as to why Lubitsch had picked him to play an actor when he considered himself a comedian.

"Jack," Lubitsch said, "I'll tell you. In the first place, you are known as an entertainer and not as an actor. Consequently, if in this film you give a fine dramatic performance—I, Lubitsch, will get all the credit.

"That, Jack, is number one. Now I tell you number two. You think you are a comedian. You are not a comedian. You are not even a clown. You are fooling the public for thirty years. You are fooling even yourself. A clown—he is a performer what is doing funny things. A comedian—he is a performer what is saying funny things. But you, Jack, you are an actor, you are an actor playing the part of a comedian and this you are doing very well. But do not worry, I keep your secret to myself."

Jack Benny's father was convalescing in a Florida nursing home when he first saw the movie. He had the nurse take him from the theater before the comedy was over and would not speak or write to his son for weeks. Finally, when Jack could reach his father to find out what was wrong, he said, "You're no son of mine."

"Why?" asked Jack.

"You gave the salute to Hitler is what you did."

Jack had to explain that if his father had stayed to the end he would have seen that his character was actually fighting against the Nazis. His father went back—forty-six times.

=

If Chaplin, Oakie, Lombard, and Benny had demonstrated how effective it was to spoof the Nazis, Bud Abbott and Lou Costello, a couple of slapstick vaudeville comedians, demonstrated how therapeutic a spoof of your own military organizations could be. And like Bob Hope, Abbott and Costello could credit the launching of their career to the passage of the Selective Training and Service Act as much as anything.

Although they had already had a small role in the film *One Night in the Tropics,* in 1940 they were invited to Hollywood to star in a film that would burlesque the draft; the result was *Buck Privates,* which made Universal Pictures $10 million and Abbott and Costello stars. It didn't hurt that the film included the Andrews Sisters, also just starting their film careers; they sang three hits, including one of the best songs to come out of World War II: "Boogie Woogie Bugle Boy."

Buck Privates, an $180,000 "B" picture, was not only beating the anti-Nazi, pro-British films at the box office, it was outdrawing the major films of the day, such as *Citizen Kane, Sergeant York,* and *Here Comes Mr. Jordan.* The film was built on a formula that would sustain the comedians for sixteen years: four or five Abbott and Costello skits held together by a loosely scripted plot. It is hard to imagine a nation of young men going into the service finding anything more enjoyable than seeing straight man Abbott and Costello the clown trying to do close-order drill, a routine they made famous in *Buck Privates.* And Universal and the Treasury Department got the message: Abbott and Costello's stint in the Army was quickly followed by *In the Navy* and *Keep 'Em Flying,* with *Hold That Ghost* in between. The former burlesque stars were on their way to becoming two of the country's most successful war-bond salesmen.

=

Of course, if you're going to help keep the men in uniform happy you have to do a lot more than make jokes about drill sergeants and girl-crazy sailors. You have to let them know why they're in uniform, ready to die for their country. And who could deliver this message with more conviction than Gary Cooper—with the help of Sergeant Alvin York, the World War I pacifist who was drafted, went to France, and showed the Germans how people could shoot in the mountains of Tennessee.

To no one's surprise, *Sergeant York* was a huge success when it was released in July 1941. The timing was perfect, and *York* was one of those films that made just about everybody happy. It also won Gary Cooper his first Oscar, and when James Stewart, in uniform, presented it to him in an emotional ceremony at the Academy Awards dinner, Cooper said, "It was Alvin York who won this award."

=

A Yank in the RAF, starring Tyrone Power and Betty Grable, and *International Squadron,* with Ronald Reagan, appeared in American theaters about the same time as *Sergeant York.* And Power and Reagan reinforced Gary Cooper's message that democracy was worth fighting for. Not only did the two RAF movies help bring American public opinion closer to readiness for war, they were also milestones in the careers of Power, Reagan, and Grable, who played Power's girlfriend. Like him, she was a star in 1941, but mostly in musicals—*Moon over Miami, Tin Pan Alley, Down Argentine Way.* But now her new studio, 20th Century–Fox, thought Grable was ready for a breakthrough. Zanuck insisted that she sing a few songs in *A Yank in the RAF,* but she did get a chance to prove she could handle a dramatic part. She was encouraged by Zanuck, who, not aware of the contribution Grable's derriere would soon be making to the war effort, told her, "Act your pretty ass off for Britain."

One of Power's biographers says that as they were making *A Yank in the RAF,* the participants seemed to take on the attitude of "real warriors going into battle." The movie's director, Henry King, said Power spent so much time in the cockpit of his studio Spitfire that he could have qualified for a license—which, in fact, he did, ultimately joining the Marines as a pilot. *A Yank in the RAF* also earned Power an invitation to Buckingham Palace—and drinks with Winston Churchill—when he was in London during the war.

At the same time, *International Squadron* enhanced Reagan's screen image as a soldier, although one scene from the movie might have given the studio executives a turn. Reagan's character was supposed to take a mop soaked in oil, light it inside the cockpit, then open the hood and hang the burning mop outside to make German pilots think he was

Gary Cooper receives his Oscar for Sergeant York *from pilot Jimmy Stewart.*
National Archives

Veronica Lake's hair became a threat to the war effort.
National Archives

in trouble. But the first time Reagan tried the maneuver, the cockpit hood stuck and he was overcome by smoke before the movie crew could get it open.

=

Perhaps the most frankly anti-Nazi film made before the United States entered the war was *Confessions of a Nazi Spy,* a story based on a series of *Saturday Evening Post* articles by Leon Turrou, an FBI agent best known for the work he had done on the Lindbergh kidnapping case. Turrou had uncovered a Nazi spy ring in the United States and was fired by the FBI for selling his story to the *Post,* a fact that did not deter Warner Bros. from buying the movie rights in 1938. Hollywood came up with an excellent cast, even if the story it developed was not quite as good as the real one. Edward G. Robinson played an FBI agent (not Turrou) who broke the German-American Bund. The Nazis were played by Francis Lederer, Paul Lukas, and George Sanders.

The film was commercially successful in the United States, but not abroad: It was banned in eighteen countries. It also played an important role in turning George Sanders into Hollywood's favorite Nazi. The process had actually begun with *Lancer Spy,* a World War I melodrama in which Sanders played both a Royal Navy officer and a look-alike German officer captured by the British. Sanders, who spoke perfect German, said his eventual success as a Nazi was due to the fact that nobody "could enunciate the word *Schweinehund* quite as feelingly as I."

Sanders's next role as a German clinched his being drafted, for a while at least, as Hollywood's resident *Schweinehund. Man Hunt* was based on Geoffrey Household's best-selling novel *Rogue Male,* in which Captain Alan Thorndike, a British big-game hunter, just for sport stalks Hitler to Berchtesgaden, aligns the Führer in his telescopic sight, and is then captured by the Nazis, led by George Sanders. Thorndike escapes to London, where he learns he has been followed by Sanders and another Nazi, John Carradine. The movie's real star, of course, was Walter Pidgeon, who played Thorndike. In the final scene, one of the most dramatic in Hollywood's pre-war movies, Thorndike, after joining the RAF, is on a reconnaissance flight over Germany when he suddenly parachutes out of his plane. As he drifts to earth, a narrator says: "Today, somewhere in Germany, is a man with a precision rifle and the high degree of intelligence and training that is required to use it. It may be days, months, or even years, but this time he clearly knows his purpose. . . ." This being, of course, to get Adolf Hitler in his telescopic sight again and pull the trigger.

=

While portraying the British and the RAF as good guys in the fight against the Nazis, Hollywood was not ignoring our own heroic pilots. *I Wanted Wings,* for example, not only portrayed the hardships young men endured to win their Army Air Corps wings, but introduced a young lady who would play a prominent part in the war effort: Veronica Lake, whose long, straight blond hair kept slipping down over her eye.

In 1940, Connie Ockelman, who had taken the stage name of Constance Keane, was a twenty-year-old girl with long hair who had had bit parts in four films when she auditioned for a role in *I Wanted Wings.* One of the films was *Forty Little Mothers,* starring Eddie Cantor as a teacher. Constance was one of the little mothers. "And here begins the incredible, stranger-than fiction saga of the world famous peek-a-boo bad-girl hair style," Constance wrote in her autobiography. It was all the fault of the *Forty Little Mothers* director, Busby Berkeley, who felt he knew when a female had something special the camera would catch— like long blond hair that kept falling in her eye. "I spent my whole life trying to keep it from falling in my eyes," said Constance. "It's annoying to walk around half blind. And dangerous."

But apparently she never thought of cutting it. When it kept falling over her eye in the filming of *Forty Little Mothers,* Cantor became annoyed. But Berkeley said, "If I were you, Eddie, I'd let it fall."

"She looks like some damn sheepdog. It's a mess," said Cantor.

"I still say let it fall," replied Berkeley. "It distinguishes her from the rest."

She kept her long hair; but, she said, "no one noticed." So she put her hair up behind her ears, at least for a while.

In the *I Wanted Wings* audition, she was supposed to be a tipsy woman in a nightclub. Of course, when her arm slipped off the table once, the long blond hair slipped over her eye. "I spent the next several minutes trying to continue with the scene as I kept shaking my head to get the hair out of my eyes." She became madder and madder, storming off the set when the take was finished: "God, how I cried in my dressing room." Staring at her image in the mirror, she exclaimed, "This god-damn hair!"

She would not even go to the screening room when the test was run, she was so convinced she had failed. But two days later, producer Arthur Hornblow, Jr., called and asked her to come to his office. She was stunned when Hornblow said: "Constance, I'm going to cast you as Sally Vaughn in *I Wanted Wings!*" And her hair? It was a smash.

The screen test had also revealed that Constance had another essential ingredient for stardom: "some sort of magnetism," she said, "the kind that stars emit on the screen." She had the magnetism and she had the gimmick. But she still needed something else. "The name you begin your career with is very crucial," Hornblow said. "It has to be something that associates in the fan's mind the person attached to the name. . . . It has to do with images."

Though he liked "Constance Keane" all right, he had been sitting in his office all night thinking about the matter and had seen something in the filmed audition he wanted to exploit: "I believe that when people look into those navy blue eyes of yours [color was just becoming a serious consideration in films], they'll see a calm coolness—the calm coolness of a lake."

So Constance thought she was going to be named "Lake something or other." When Hornblow started talking about her classic features and how they suggested the name "Veronica," Constance had it: "Lake Veronica."

No. Veronica Lake. So young Veronica Lake went unhappily off to Texas to shoot *I Wanted Wings*—unhappily, because she was very much in love with John Detlie, a thirty-three-year-old art director at MGM: "I suppose you could say I'd fallen in love with him if that's what a twenty-year-old girl does. I do know I had hot pants."

And the nation would soon see them in a photograph that Veronica called "not a bad break." One day she was standing next to a B-17 having a publicity photo made. She was stooping over, at the photographer's request, when the B-17 pilot started his engines and Veronica's dress flew up above her thighs. Paramount used that shot in its advance publicity, and suddenly fans were writing the studio wanting to know more about that newcomer Veronica Lake.

I Wanted Wings was shot with the full cooperation of the Army Air Corps, which probably wanted this picture more than Paramount did. But even the Air Corps could take only so much from a temperamental Hollywood director. One day a squadron of planes flew by, ruining the sound track of a scene being shot. Director Ted Weeks shouted to a general: "Get those planes out of the air." A couple of days later, Weeks was replaced by Mitchell Leisen.

With the possible exception of *They Were Expendable*, which would be filmed near the end of the war, *I Wanted Wings* probably had more genuinely macho actors than any other movie to come out of Hollywood during the war years: Ray Milland was a good pilot who would later train pilots during the war; at seventeen, Brian Donlevy had played the bugle with General Jack Pershing's expedition against the Mexican rebel Pancho Villa; William Holden would serve as an Army lieutenant in the coming war; and Wayne Morris would become a Navy fighter pilot, winning four Distinguished Flying Crosses. In flying scenes, Milland and Donlevy often flew their planes themselves—although a military pilot always came along, just in case. The movie won an Oscar for its special effects.

Lake's contribution to the success of the picture was unquestionable. Because of her provocativeness, the Legion of Decency would give it only a Class B rating—objectionable in part. This was almost as good assurance of success as being banned in Boston. And Cecilia Ager, in *PM*, explained why: "Miss Lake was supposed to be a *femme fatale* and to that end it was arranged that her truly splendid bosom be unconfined and draped ever so slightly in a manner to make the current crop of sweater girls prigs by comparison." Another critic said Veronica Lake "made Lana Turner look like a schoolgirl."

All this inspired the spoiled little schoolgirl (Veronica, not Lana) to demand a $925-a-week raise for her next picture, *Hold Back the Dawn*. (She had been paid $75 a week for *I Wanted Wings*.)

After the release of *I Wanted Wings*, Veronica Lake's hair joined the national culture. Beauty shops promoted it; *Life* ran an article about it; the studio called Lake the "Peeping Pompadour"; *The Harvard Lampoon* called her the worst actress of the year; comedians Bob Hope and Fred Allen made jokes, topped perhaps, by Groucho Marx's "I opened up my mop closet the other day and I thought Veronica Lake fell out." People saw her dancing with her husband and said: "Look at that dame. Who does she think she is, Veronica Lake?" Others, who did not know how short she was, said, "That must be Veronica Lake, Jr."

===

Aviators were much on Hollywood's collective mind. *Dive Bomber*, a story about the problems the Navy had with pilots blacking out after pulling out of a steep dive, starred Errol Flynn and had a strong supporting cast, including Alexis Smith, Fred MacMurray, Ralph Bellamy, and Robert Armstrong. It was filmed at the naval air base at San Diego and on board the carrier *Enterprise*. The director was Michael Curtiz, a Hungarian whose very thick accent was assumed by most of the Navy personnel to be German—especially after Curtiz began treating them, no matter what their rank, like extras.

The Navy didn't like Flynn either, although he could usually outcharm anyone in a direct confrontation. Perhaps the Navy's suspicions were justified: biographer Charles Higham is convinced that Flynn was actually a Nazi spy while on the set. Flynn urged that film he had taken of Pearl Harbor be included in a special documentary insert in *Dive Bomber,* which was shipped to Japan. Few people besides Higham, though, seem to think Flynn was a spy. David Niven, for example, who was one of the actor's closest friends in pre-war Hollywood, said the idea was "ludicrous." (However, Flynn's decision to become an American citizen and stay in Hollywood after England went to war did strain his friendship with Niven.)

Niven believed that in general "all this talk about movie stars being used as spies is just a lot of bloody nonsense." The only celebrities he knew who had actually worked for British intelligence were Noël Coward and Leslie Howard. Niven, who played William Stephenson in *A Man Called Intrepid,* also said that despite rumors, he had never worked for British intelligence. Stephenson himself, late in the master spy's life, said that the idea that Flynn was a Nazi spy "appears nonsensical on the face of it." Stephenson should have been in an excellent position to know. Not only was he head of the British Security Coordination in America (a front for British Intelligence) and the direct link between Churchill and Roosevelt, but he set up a worldwide intelligence network dedicated to the defeat of the Axis powers.

=

The war not only shaped the content of the films coming out of Hollywood, but also at times affected life on the sets: Unlike gangsters, Indians, and cattle rustlers, the new villains aroused real passion. During the filming of *The Mortal Storm,* a film about the impact of Nazism on a German family (starring Margaret Sullavan, James Stewart, and Robert Young), the ferocity and sadism of a Nazi storm trooper (played by the young actor Dan Dailey, making his film debut) were so realistic that a woman from Austria who happened to be visiting the set fainted and had to be taken to the hospital.

At the same time, Germany was letting it be known that everyone associated with *The Mortal Storm* would be "taken care of" after the war. Robert Stack, who also appeared in the movie, said that about two weeks into shooting, after this word reached the set, he saw Robert Young pacing back and forth, his hands behind his back, mumbling, "My children, what about my children?" Those who made *Confessions of a Nazi Spy* would also be subject to vengeance, it was said. The family of *Confessions'* star, Edward G. Robinson, had to be placed under guard because of death threats; later, in London, Scotland Yard had to give Robinson constant protection.

The war also had an impact on the set of the Alfred Hitchcock film *Foreign Correspondent.* Walter Wanger, its producer, had hoped to make a documentary warning America of the coming cataclysm. Wanger was a sophisticated, Dartmouth-educated liberal who had worked on Woodrow Wilson's staff during the Paris Peace Conference after World War I. While at the American Embassy in Rome, he produced a film about the Allied war effort; the result impressed him with the power of films. He also decided that making movies would be his niche after the war. This brought him to Hollywood, where he worked for Paramount, Columbia, and MGM before becoming an independent producer with United Artists. In 1936, he bought the film rights to Vincent Sheean's *Personal History,* one of the first and best of a stream of books by correspondents who reported from Europe during Hitler's rise to power.

Events in Europe accelerated; by 1938, the Spanish Civil War and Germany's demands on Austria and Czechoslovakia were included in various scripts for *Personal History* written by new writers, including Budd Schulberg. As Hitler marched on, so did Wanger and *Personal History,* with John Lay and John Meehan, writers from the "March of Time" newsreel. New scripts continued to be developed; it soon became obvious that a final version could probably never be written, because Wanger kept insisting that the story stay up-to-date to reflect Hitler's every aggression. All told, Wanger put $140,000 into the script before he finally worked out a deal with MGM to have it directed by Alfred Hitchcock. Hitchcock, scriptwriter Charles Bennett, and producer Joan Harrison worked out a new script that had little resemblance to Vincent Sheean's account of his reporting from Europe. *Foreign Correspondent* was shot between March 18 and May 29, 1940, a period marking the end of the Phony War and the beginning of Hitler's march into the Low Countries and France. Almost every day, Wanger would call Hitchcock to ask him if Hitler's most recent outrage could be incorporated in the script. According to Hitchcock biographer Donald Spoto, Hitchcock totally ignored Wanger—until the end of the film.

Foreign Correspondent focuses on the love affair of a crime reporter (Joel McCrea) sent to Europe to find out what the hell is going on. He meets the daughter (Laraine Day) of the head of a pacifist organization who turns out to be a Nazi spy. Day's father is played by Herbert Marshall, despite the fact that George Sanders was also in the cast.

Sanders this time plays a jolly English friend of McCrea's, Scott ffolliott ("double *f* at the beginning, old boy, and they're both small *f*s"). Laraine Day was convinced that Sanders was really a nasty Nazi at heart. He was rude and vulgar, she said, especially in what was intended as the last scene—a plane crash in which McCrea, Day, and Sanders struggled to get out of the windows of a plane sinking in the ocean. "Mr. Sanders continually tried to get his hands under my dress," said Day, although Sanders's biographer, Richard Vanderbeets, thought surely Sanders must have been joking. Day apparently did not.

Comic relief was furnished by Algonquin wit Robert Benchley (now well into his Hollywood career) as a London newspaperman who upholds the journalistic tradition of a fondness for strong drink. And the message at the end of the film was inspired by the rush of events. As the final scenes were being shot, Wanger and Hitchcock heard that the bombing of England was about to begin. So at Wanger's insistence, a scene between Sanders and McCrea—set on an ocean liner after the characters' rescue from the sea—was scrapped, and Ben Hecht was brought in to write a new ending.

The movie is set in the period from August 20 to September 3, 1939, when England declared war, but Hecht's final scene depicted McCrea in a London studio, broadcasting a radio message to America as bombs fall all around:

> I can't read the rest of the speech I have because all the lights have gone out, so I'll just have to talk off the cuff. All that noise you hear isn't static. It's death coming to London. It's too late now to do any-thing except stand in the dark and let them come. It feels as if the lights are all out everywhere—except in America.
> [The American national anthem is played in the background.]
> Keep those lights burning! Cover them with steel, ring them with guns! Build a canopy of battleships and bombing planes around them. Hello, America. Hang on to your lights! They're the only lights left in the world.

It may not have been art, but life would soon be imitating it. The scene was not shot until July 5, 1940; the bombs had not started falling. But they did fall, less than a week later.

A somewhat subtler pro-interventionist film was *That Hamilton Woman,* although it had nothing overtly to do with World War II. There is some disagreement as to who originated the idea. In his family biography, *Charmed Lives,* Michael Korda says Churchill had the idea;

Alexander Korda's biographer, Karol Kulik, says it came to Korda on the train between New York and Hollywood while he was reading a book on naval history by Admiral Alfred Mahan. The subject would be the Napoleonic wars; Lord Nelson and the archvillain, Napoleon, would be the perfect historical characters to suggest Churchill and Hitler and Britain's heroic fights against Continental despots. But as Korda would tell his proposed hero and heroine, "Propaganda needs sugar coating"—in this case, the love affair between Lord Nelson and Lady Emma Hamilton. *That Hamilton Woman* would be the title of his film; Laurence Olivier and Vivien Leigh would play Nelson and Lady Hamilton. And, well aware that Olivier and Leigh would soon be free to marry, Korda had the perfect publicity ploy for the two lovers.

About this time, Olivier and Leigh were in something of a dither. Their *Romeo and Juliet* had opened to horrible reviews ("Laurence Olivier talked as if he were brushing his teeth"; "the worst *Romeo* ever") and closed after thirty-five performances. Having put most of their money into the play, they were broke, and Olivier was beginning to receive more flak from the press reminding him that real Englishmen were engaged in the Battle of Britain, not playing Shakespearean children onstage.

After Dunkirk, attacks on the British actors in America had understandably intensified. Olivier, more determined than ever to do the right and heroic thing and join the RAF, resumed his flying lessons— the best way, he thought, to overcome his fear of flying. Among his many British friends was Alfred Duff Cooper, recently appointed minister of information by Churchill. So deciding, as he put it in his autobiography, "this deed I'll do before this purpose cool," Olivier called Duff Cooper from New York and offered his services. Duff Cooper promised to reply soon; obviously he was aware of Korda's instructions, because a few days later he wired Olivier: THINK BETTER WHERE YOU ARE STOP KORDA GOING THERE.

Not long after that, Olivier would recall, Korda called him and asked: "Larry, you know Lady Hamilton?"

"Wasn't she Admiral Nelson's piece?" Olivier replied.

Soon Olivier and Leigh were meeting with Korda and two writers, R. C. Sherriff and Walter Reisch, to discuss the film, although Olivier was reluctant, still thinking that the right thing would be to return to England. Korda assured him, however, that Churchill not only "wants this done, he wants you and Vivien in it." Besides, Korda argued, the movie would earn them the money they needed to get home; in fact, he gave them half their salaries in advance.

That Hamilton Woman was shot in six weeks on a modest budget, something of a record for Korda, and it achieved its propaganda goals. In one scene, Sir William Hamilton (played by Alan Mowbray) explains to his wife that "we must fight those who want to dictate to the world," and in another, Nelson warns the Neapolitan court: "We can't protect all Europe." But the clincher was Nelson's speech to the Admiralty, which some suspected the prime minister himself had written.

Lord Spencer, gentlemen—you're celebrating a peace with Napoleon Bonaparte—peace is a very beautiful word as long as the impulse of peace is behind it. But gentlemen, you will never make peace with Napoleon. He doesn't mean peace today. He just wants to gain a little time to re-arm himself at sea and to make new alliances with Italy and Spain—all to one purpose. To destroy our Empire! Years ago I said the same thing at Naples. I begged them, I entreated them not to give way but they wouldn't listen to me, and they paid the price. But that was a little Kingdom miles away in the Mediterranean. But now it is England, our own land. Napoleon can never be master of the world until he has smashed us up—and believe me, gentlemen, he means to be master of the world. You cannot make peace with dictators. You have to destroy them. Wipe them out! Gentlemen, I implore you—speak to the Prime Minister before it is too late. Do not ratify this peace!

Even if he did not write it, the speech must have made Churchill happy; in fact, *That Hamilton Woman* became his favorite movie and played a big part in the knighting of Alexander Korda the following year. Churchill said *Lady Hamilton* (an alternate title) was worth four divisions—and U.S. isolationists apparently agreed, because they were very unhappy with the film.*

The film was released in April 1941. By September, Washington had

---

*In December 1940, with mounting hostility in England toward British actors who had remained in Hollywood, Olivier felt the time had come for him and Leigh to return home. Olivier immediately tried to enlist in the RAF. At thirty-three, he was too old to be a fighter pilot, and the medical exam revealed a damaged ear nerve that made him unfit for combat duty. But with help from his friend Ralph Richardson he was admitted to the Fleet Air Arm as a training pilot.

Olivier was miserable in the service, where he acquired a reputation, in the words of one biographer, as "among the worst fliers in history." However, the government eventually put him to good use, releasing him to make one of Britain's greatest patriotic films, *Henry V*.

become so suspicious of Hollywood that the Senate launched an investigation by a subcommittee under the chairmanship of Idaho senator D. Worth Clark to determine whether Hollywood was, in fact, guilty of "inciting war."

According to Lowell Mellet, who would soon become the Office of War Information's coordinator of motion pictures, as early as December 1940 the U.S. ambassador to England, Joseph P. Kennedy (who knew his way around Hollywood, or at least around Gloria Swanson's dressing room), had tried to put "the fear of God" into filmland's executives and producers, many of whom were Jewish. In a meeting with several of them in Hollywood, he warned that anti-Semitism was growing in England and that the Jews were being blamed for the war. He also said the Catholic church, to which he belonged, wanted peace at any price. Hence Hollywood should stop making anti-Nazi films.

But the films kept coming, until the isolationists in Congress felt something had to be done. On August 1, 1941, Senator Gerald P. Nye of North Dakota spoke at a rally in St. Louis sponsored by the America First Committee: "At least twenty pictures have been produced in the last years," he said, "all designed to drug the reason of the American people, set aflame their emotions, turn their hatred into a blaze, fill them with fear that Hitler will come over here and capture them, that he will steal their trade.... [The movies] have become the most gigan-

Charlie Chaplin in The Great Dictator, *which satirized Adolf Hitler, whom Chaplin called "one of the greatest actors of the century."*

Vivien Leigh and Laurence Olivier in That Hamilton Woman, *a film "worth four Army divisions," said Winston Churchill (who was said to have written one of Lord Nelson's speeches for the film).*

tic engines of propaganda in existence to rouse war fever in America and plunge the Nation to her destruction."

Nye listed the names of several studio chiefs, many of whom were Jewish; the crowd booed even the name of Darryl F. Zanuck, who was a non-Jewish World War I combat veteran from Wahoo, Nebraska. "In each of these companies," said Nye, "there are a number of production directors, many of whom have come from Russia, Hungary, Germany, and the Balkan countries. . . . Why do they do this? Well, because they are interested in foreign causes. . . . Go to Hollywood. It is a raging volcano of war fever. The place swarms with refugees. It also swarms with British actors."

Not only the Jews, but British actors! That was it. The British contingent was really a nest of spies, slowly but surely rallying the gullible American public to rise up and go to war against Germany.

That same day, Senator Champ Clark of Missouri had introduced Senate Resolution 152, calling for "a thorough and complete investigation of any propaganda disseminated by motion pictures and radio or any other activity of the motion picture industry to influence public sentiment in the direction of participation of the United States in the present European war."

For almost three weeks in September, Clark's subcommittee held hearings. Defending the industry on freedom-of-speech grounds was Wendell Willkie, who had challenged Roosevelt for the presidency in 1940. One of the most eloquent refutations of the subcommittee's charges was given by Jack L. Warner, whose studio was accused of producing four films for the purpose of "inciting the United States to war":* "If Warner Brothers had produced no pictures concerning the Nazi movement, our public would have had good reason to criticize. We would have been living in a dream world. Today seventy percent of the nonfiction books published deal with the Nazi menace."

In October the Clark hearings were suspended. At the same time, the Senate Foreign Relations Committee expanded its ongoing investigation of "foreign agents" in America to include the British contingent in Hollywood. Perhaps the investigators had learned that Basil Rathbone, who was born of British parents in South Africa, had already enlisted A. Conan Doyle's immortal Sherlock Holmes in the anti-Nazi cause. At about the time the Senate Foreign Relations Committee was going into action, Rathbone and Nigel Bruce were making their third Sherlock Holmes movie, *Sherlock Holmes and the Voice of Terror.* And any Senate investigator snooping around the Universal lot could have told that the game was afoot, because Holmes and Watson were not in gaslit London, sleuthing in horse-drawn carriages, but in war-torn England, fighting the threat of a Nazi invasion. As he defeats the Nazis, Holmes tells the good doctor that there is a gathering storm. But the stubborn, always optimistic doctor says: "No, I don't think so. Looks like another warm day."

Holmes's reply would not have fooled any Senate investigator: "Good old Watson, the one fixed point in a changing age. There's an east wind coming all the same, such a wind as never blew in England yet. It will be cold and bitter, Watson, and a good many of us may wither before its blast. But it's God's own wind, nonetheless. And a greener, better, stronger land will be in the sunshine when the storm has cleared."

Lines like that were enough to cause any isolationist in Congress concern, but *That Hamilton Woman* was even worse. Isolationists were especially disturbed by Lord Nelson's speech to the Admiralty, which,

---

*International Squadron, Underground, Sergeant York, and *Confessions of a Nazi Spy.*

of course, everyone in Washington now assumed had been written by Winston Churchill. Alexander Korda was subpoenaed to appear before the Senate Foreign Relations Committee on December 12, 1941, but before that happened, the Japanese intervened and the Senate dropped its investigation of Hollywood.

What the Japanese did should have come as no surprise to Errol Flynn, though not because of his presumed connections with the Nazis. According to Charles Higham, in late 1938 Flynn was in Hawaii worrying about an Oahu land deal. One night he had a dream in which he was looking at Pearl Harbor when a squadron of planes appeared and began bombing the naval installation. The dream was so vivid that when he awoke the next morning, he drove out to Pearl Harbor, only to find everything peaceful and calm. When he told his business partner in California, the partner said: "Don't buy that land. Something's going to happen."

What eventually did happen did not surprise Mae West, either. In the fall of 1941, "satiated with success," as she put it, West decided to look for God, or at least a hereafter. This led her into a number of churches and finally to a psychic, the Reverend Jack Kelly of Buffalo, who happened to be in Los Angeles holding seances. West attended one; her first question was "Will there be a war?"

The Japanese would completely surprise the Navy, the Army, the White House, and Hollywood, but the medium from Buffalo knew what was coming. "We will have a surprise attack on Honolulu within three months, by Japan," he told West.

FIVE

Hollywood Goes to War

The day after Pearl Harbor, I was up at City Hall rolling bandages. —ROSALIND RUSSELL

At three A.M. on December 7, 1941, Lieutenant Commander Kanjiro Ono "was listening to Bing Crosby sing 'Sweet Leilani.'" Ono was in the radio room of the Japanese aircraft carrier *Okagi*, the command ship of a task force headed for Pearl Harbor. And he was not really a fan of Der Bingle. He was listening to the all-night music program from KGMB Honolulu, primarily for the weather report. And when he heard it—"partly cloudy, ceiling thirty-five hundred feet, visibility good"—he knew the weather was perfect for what the task force planned to do.

In 125 minutes, the Japanese destroyed or damaged 18 ships and 188 planes, and killed 2,400 American sailors and soldiers. But when actress Eve Arden heard the news, she did not take it very seriously: "I was running the vacuum over our sublet carpet and could catch only an occasional phrase from the radio I had. 'Attacking in waves,' I heard. 'Battleships already sunk,' and the words 'Pearl Harbor' and 'Japanese planes.' Well, I thought, Orson's done it again."

Bob Hope did not take the report seriously, either. He was going over his monologue for his Pepsodent radio show when his wife, Dolores, rushed into the room. "The Japanese have attacked Pearl Harbor," she said. Hope's first reaction was to laugh: "This sounded like a [Jerry] Colonna line, like the one when [he] hurried in during a war sketch and shouted: 'Hope, I've just delivered an ultimatum to the enemy.' 'Are you sure they got it, professor?' 'How could they miss it; I put it in an ultimatum can.' "

But Alexander Korda was not joking when he said that he and Winston Churchill could take credit for Pearl Harbor. "He gave a little credit to the Japanese," a friend of Korda's told Laurence Olivier's biographer Thomas Kiernan. "But he assured everyone that because of himself and Churchill, Roosevelt was persuaded to bring the U.S. in and that FDR precipitated the attack . . . so as to give the U.S. an excuse to go in as quickly as possible."

One thing's for sure: There was a future President of the United States who had absolutely nothing to do with Pearl Harbor. Ronald Reagan was literally caught napping. It was around eleven-thirty A.M. California time when the news went out across the nation; in his autobiography, *Where's the Rest of Me?*, Reagan wrote: "I have no intention of doing a chapter on 'Where was I on December 7.' I was in bed asleep."

Lana Turner was going to have a party that Sunday afternoon, she recorded in her autobiography: "The guests included Tommy Dorsey, Buddy Rich, and Frank Sinatra, along with two of my favorite girl friends, Linda Darnell and Susan Hayward. The party began in the early afternoon and was still going strong that evening when my mother returned from a visit with some friends in San Francisco. She seemed astonished at all the noise."

"It's just a party, Mother," Turner said.

"You mean you haven't heard? Pearl Harbor has been bombed. Turn on the radio, for heaven's sake."

"During that whole fun-filled afternoon," said Turner, "we hadn't an inkling that the country was about to go to war. I got the musicians quieted down and turned on the news. As we listened I looked around at the stunned young men in my living room and thought how drastically our lives were going to change."

Another young actress on the way up, but never to such Hollywood heights as Lana, was Evelyn Keyes. She vividly remembered December

7: "I was at [director] Charles Vidor's house. He was later my husband; he wasn't then. It was quiet. I remember the sunshine, of all things, because it seemed incongruous that the sun was shining when we heard this news. Someone telephoned. They said: 'Did you hear? The Japanese have attacked Pearl Harbor!' I was sick. All the young men were going to get themselves killed. I looked at Charles and thought: 'Oh, thank God, he's too old.' Immediately I was ashamed. We clung to the radio until all the stations went off the air with the frightening announcement that Japanese planes were approaching San Francisco. Then we clung to each other."

Edward G. Robinson: "Who in my age bracket does *not* remember where he was that Sunday?" Robinson had a special reason to remember Pearl Harbor. His wife, Gladys Lloyd, was suffering from depression at the time; her "reaction to Pearl Harbor was manic. . . . She was prepared to go out and die for her country. She raged against the Japanese, predicted a squad of Marines would destroy them in a few days. She was prepared to fight the war single-handed. . . . Not only she, but I could win the war."

But then came her depression: "I'd started it all. It was my fault," Robinson said. He was Jewish, and maybe, she implied, "if it hadn't've been for the Jews there would have been no Hitler, and hence no Pearl Harbor."

Milton Berle had just arrived at Lake Arrowhead on his honeymoon with his new wife, Joyce, his mother, his brother Frank, and his good friends Jimmy and Ruth Ritz. "It wasn't much of a honeymoon," said Berle, "but I can't take all the blame. The day after we got to Arrowhead, Joyce and I were sitting around the lawn with Jimmy and Ruthie, just soaking up the sun and talking. The portable radio I had brought along was on the grass beside me. Suddenly, the music stopped and we got the announcement of the Japanese attack on Pearl Harbor.

"No one knew what the war was going to do to Hollywood," he said, "what material would be available, who would still be in civilian clothes. I left my bride behind at Arrowhead with Mama and Frank's wife."

Gene Tierney was on Catalina Island that Sunday, shooting her first comedy, *Rings on Her Fingers,* with Henry Fonda. "We had just started our cameras when an assistant came racing down the beach." He told them about the attack and said, "We've got to clear out for the mainland right away." In her autobiography, she recounts their panic:

We wrapped up at once and were soon sailing toward San Pedro. The radio reports of the Japanese attack were shrill and disconnected, and led to wild speculation aboard our boat. Some of the cast thought that they might hit the California coast next. For all anyone knew, the waters we were now churning through might have been mined.

Another work in progress affected by the bombing of Pearl Harbor was the adaptation of the hit play *Arsenic and Old Lace,* which was to be Frank Capra's last movie before he entered the Army.* He had agreed to direct the film only in order to bank enough money to take care of his family during his lean military years, and was under constant pressure from the Army to finish the film and report for duty. The star, Cary Grant, was also under pressure; four days before Pearl Harbor, he had announced his engagement to socialite Barbara Hutton, who was having trouble obtaining a divorce from her German husband, Count Reventlow. The count was under constant surveillance by the FBI, which thought he was a Nazi sympathizer. Grant completed the shooting of his role five days after Pearl Harbor, but the new bombing so affected the cast (which included Raymond Massey, Peter Lorre, and Josephine Hull) that according to one Grant biographer, "it is possible that the strained mood of much of the film is due to the fact that everyone who made it was depressed, concerned and fretful over the future."

But of all the stars stunned by Pearl Harbor, the ones making *Across the Pacific* had to be the most distressed. John Huston, Mary Astor, Sydney Greenstreet, and Humphrey Bogart were hoping to take advantage of their recent success, *The Maltese Falcon;* their new film was about thwarting a Japanese plan to destroy Pearl Harbor. They began filming at the end of November but had to shut down production when Japan actually did it. "It was a creepy feeling," Mary Astor said in her memoir, *A Life on Film,* "to have been talking about 'the plans of the Japanese' in the picture and then have them practically blueprint our script."

According to Mickey Rooney, he and Norma Shearer heard President Roosevelt declare war while they were in Shearer's dressing room. Rooney did not mention the intimacies they had shared earlier: "I was yacking with her," he reported, "about the pros and cons of her next [and last] picture [*Her Cardboard Lover*]."

It had been only two months since Red Skelton's radio show, *The Scrapbook of Satire,* had been introduced on NBC Tuesday nights, right after Bob Hope's show, but already the trademark phrase of his "Mean

---

*Although completed a few weeks after Pearl Harbor, the movie was not released until 1944, because of a contract that specified it could not be shown until the play completed its Broadway run.

Widdle Kid" character, "I dood it," was mouthed in every American household. That Sunday, Skelton happened to be at the home of Gene Fowler, where he had gone to have Fowler sign a copy of his book *Good Night, Sweet Prince,* a biography of John Barrymore. Skelton rushed home to tell his wife, Edna, that he was going to join the Marines, although he was twenty-eight and had a little daughter. Edna—and Louis B. Mayer—managed to talk him out of it.

At the time of Pearl Harbor, Alan Ladd was in a hospital, recovering from pneumonia after collapsing on the set of *This Gun for Hire.* According-ing to one columnist, "though weak as a fly and still burning with fever, Alan jumped out of bed yelling, 'Got to get out of here, they'll be need-ing guys like me.' " However, it would take the Army nearly two years to catch up with him.

There were also the usual jokes making the rounds: RKO did not have to worry about air strikes "because they haven't had a hit for years." Jack L. Warner had a large sign painted for the roof of one of his studios—LOCKHEED THATAWAY, accompanied by a large arrow pointing to the aircraft factory. But, he soon decided, "this gag does not seem so funny."

And Bob "Don't You Know There's a War On" Hope said he met a man at the top of a hill looking down at the blacked-out city of Los Angeles and laughing. "What's so funny?" asked Hope. "At last, I'm not alone," the man replied. "Look, this month *nobody* paid their bills." "I've been digging a bomb shelter under my cellar and I can't quit now," Hope quipped. "The tunnel almost reaches Hedy Lamarr's house. . . . And the shortage of everything is worrying me. This morning when the bank sent back my check, it was marked 'Insufficient Rubber.' "

One reason the movie people came a little unhinged in their initial response to Pearl Harbor was that Hollywood, on the shores of the Pacific, seemed more vulnerable to attack. And it was surrounded by four major aircraft factories—Douglas, Lockheed, North American, and Vultee. On December 9, the *Los Angeles Times* carried the headline ENEMY PLANES SIGHTED OVER THE CALIFORNIA COAST. The story reported that two squadrons of Japanese planes had been sighted near San Jose and then returned to sea. Reporters asked why they had not dropped any bombs; Lieutenant General John L. DeWitt said he did not know but was sure they were enemy planes.

About this time, Walt Disney received a call from his studio man-ager, who said: "The Army is moving in on us."

When Disney asked for clarification, the manager said, "Five hun-dred soldiers. They told me they're moving in."

"What did you tell them?" asked Disney.

"I said I'd have to call you."

"What did they say to that?"

" 'Go ahead and call him—we're moving in anyway.' " The Army had decided the Disney studio was perfectly located and constructed to serve as a support to the anti-aircraft unit being set up in the mountains above Los Angeles.

Warner Bros. built an air-raid shelter. Jack Warner remembered "sitting in this rough underground haven playing checkers with [producer] Jesse Lasky, [producer-director] Mervyn LeRoy and others, expecting to have the game broken up any moment by Japanese bombs."

Evelyn Keyes had to face the bombs alone in her apartment when she was not at Charles Vidor's house. She remembers awaking one night: "Outside it was like a newsreel at the opening of a movie, with big searchlights—and I thought, 'Oh, my God, the Japs are coming.' I was seeing what I thought were parachutes hanging in the air; they turned out to be puffs of smoke. They were shooting something, so I grabbed a poker and I was ready."

Fading star Marion Davies always had her lover, newspaper tycoon William Randolph Hearst, with her. They had three houses in California—their castle on the coast at San Simeon, a beach house at Malibu, and an estate at Wyntoon, 250 miles north of San Francisco. One night at Malibu, they saw what they were sure was a Japanese plane shot down near Santa Monica. Hearst, who had been warning of the "Yellow Peril" for years, climbed to the top balcony to watch the Peril in action, while Davies, said her biographer, "shivered under a table." Hearst decided to move, for the duration, to Wyntoon, which made Davies very unhappy. She hated the place and called it Spittoon.

Hearst could at least be grateful to the Japanese for one thing: Pearl Harbor managed to take Hollywood and the nation's mind off the most-talked-about film playing that December: Orson Welles's *Citizen Kane,* a devastating portrait *à clef* of Hearst.

Of course, Californians soon discovered that the "Yellow Peril" was not just out there over the horizon, it was right here in River City, everywhere! The day after Pearl Harbor, the Japanese-American sculptor Isamu Noguchi began work on a bust of Ginger Rogers but was delayed when he was sent to a Japanese internment camp. Charlie Chaplin's house was viewed with suspicion, not because of his own left-wing sympathies, which would later cause him trouble, but because of his servants. They were Japanese, and they too were soon interned. Shortly after Pearl Harbor, the FBI searched Joan Fontaine's house for hidden arms: After all, she and her sister, Olivia De Havilland, had both been born in Tokyo.

A group of stars formed the California Evacuation Corps, primarily, said one Corps member (Rudy Vallee) because another member (Lewis Stone) "always had a secret yen to be in uniform." The Corps included Robert Young, Cesar Romero, Cliff Arquette (Charley Weaver), Buster Keaton, and Victor Borge, all picked primarily, said Vallee, because they had station wagons. They drilled two nights a week at the Warner Bros. studio on Sunset Boulevard. Their primary mission was to know the shortest routes to the hospitals so they would be in a position to evacuate the wounded when the Japanese bombed the coast. Some Corps members were convinced that the Japanese Americans in California amounted to one huge fifth column and should be put safely away in concentration camps, which they tried to convince Wendell Willkie (who happened to be in town for a speech) the government should do. Vallee even thought their efforts at persuading Willkie had something to do with the eventual internments.*

Although most Californians and others throughout the country eventually admitted the mistake, the conviction that the Japanese Americans in California were either spies or potential supporters of an invasion was widespread in Hollywood and elsewhere. "Before the war," said scriptwriter and novelist James M. Cain, "if they weren't a nation of spies, they were giving a hell of an imitation of it. . . . Whether this was imaginary I don't know . . . but I remember having the feeling out there that the Japanese were reporting an awful lot to somebody who was smuggling a lot of information back to Japan. . . . After Pearl Harbor it could not be assumed that an invasion of California was a far-fetched, idiotic idea. Pearl Harbor was a far-fetched, idiotic idea."

=

When Sam Goldwyn entered his office Monday morning, December 8, 1941, he found on his desk a letter from advertising executive Albert Lasker that summed up the mood in Hollywood: "Since yesterday afternoon we lived in another world. What it will bring forth no man knows." That evening, Orson Welles, at Washington's request, talked

---

*Vallee later regretted the internments. One of his servants, Fumo Ito, and her parents were put in an internment camp; Fumo's husband, Johnny, also a Vallee servant, had served in the Army, so he was not detained. To try to atone for what he called this "dastardly and cruel action," Vallee helped put Johnny through college and became godfather to his and Fumo's two children.

about the war on his radio program: "This is the time for energetic and unashamed patriotism." MGM boss Louis B. Mayer agreed: "This is a sad time," he told his staff. "Many of our young men will be going to war and some will die. But we who stay at home must help all we can. Please join now in a toast to our president—Nicholas Schenck [president of Loew's, Inc.]." As John Wayne said: "The call went out to all of us."

And with equal measures of patriotism and egotism, they answered the call: Katharine Hepburn, who had just completed *Woman of the Year,* wired FDR to say she would do anything to support the war effort, in either Hollywood or the East; Bette Davis, who was shooting *In This Our Life,* wrote FDR, offering to do whatever she could do to support a nation now at war. The day after Pearl Harbor, Dorothy Lamour let Secretary of the Treasury Henry Morgenthau, Jr., know that she was ready to go on a bond tour.

At the time of Pearl Harbor, Melvyn Douglas and Burgess Meredith were in Fresno attending a conference on children. They sat up all that night in their hotel room discussing what show-business people could do to support the nation. By dawn, Douglas would recall in his autobiography, they had devised a plan for a temporary government agency that might harness the creative people needed to disseminate information and develop propaganda. It was essential that this agency bypass the motion-picture studios, radio networks, advertising agencies, and agents who controlled show business, and work directly with actors and actresses. So enthusiastic were Douglas and Meredith that they decided to fly immediately to Washington and confer with Archibald MacLeish, the Librarian of Congress, who was also in charge of government information and propaganda. MacLeish liked the idea and said it would be put into the right hands.

Lieutenant Colonel Darryl F. Zanuck (U.S. Army Reserve) also flew to Washington immediately after Pearl Harbor to discuss with General George C. Marshall a plan similar to Douglas and Meredith's, except that he also wanted to make training films. He suggested incorporating Hollywood actors and technicians into a Signal Corps group that he would head. His plan approved, he returned to Hollywood and called a meeting of all eligible males at 20th Century–Fox, urging them to join his unit.

America's favorite couple, Clark Gable and Carole Lombard, had heard the news at Gilmore Field, watching the Hollywood Stars pro football team beat the Columbus Bulls, 21–9. They went to their ranch and turned on the radio; while Gable sat in shock, Lombard cursed the Japanese with every obscenity in her arsenal, which was formidable. Gable immediately wrote the White House to offer his services as well as his wife's. The President wrote back urging them to stay in Hollywood, because, he said, films were essential to the war effort.

In mid-January, Gable was scheduled to start working on *Somewhere I'll Find You,* with Lana Turner. Even before his role as Rhett Butler, Gable had been crowned king of Hollywood (Myrna Loy was the queen); Turner had recently become Hollywood's first "sex kitten." They had recently appeared in *Honky Tonk,* "a talky marathon," as one critic put it, but enhanced by the heat radiated by the king and the kitten. Naturally, the columnists began linking them romantically. Everyone knew that Gable was madly in love with his wife, but Lombard had made frequent visits to the set of *Honky Tonk* and warned MGM boss Louis B. Mayer that her husband was off-limits to Turner.

Soon after Pearl Harbor, Lombard and Gable were asked by MGM's publicity head, Howard Dietz, to launch a bond-selling drive to begin in the heartland of America. But Gable did not want to go: "I'll help in any way I can," he said, "other than personal appearances. I hate crowds and I don't know how to act when I'm in one. Besides, I'm not a salesman."

He did, however, approve Lombard's participation, and Washington thought she was the perfect choice to kick off the first big bond drive. She had met both FDR and his envoy Harry Hopkins and was one of the President's favorite movie stars. Hopkins felt women were "much better than men at arousing patriotic instinct." Besides, Lombard was from Indiana—a good place to begin the tour, since Indianapolis was very near the United States' population center in 1941. Lombard, her mother, and Otto Winkler (Gable's personal PR man, who said he was along "to take care of [Gable's] old lady") left Los Angeles by train on January 12, 1942, with Lombard's mother, Bess Peters, joking that she would catch a millionaire while selling bonds, and Carole calling people to "look after Pappy" (Gable, who was in Washington inquiring about an Army commission). When Gable came home, he found in his bed a blond dummy, with a note from "Ma": "So you won't be lonely." The next day, when he started working on *Somewhere I'll Find You,* he asked his stand-in and friend, Lew Smith, to make Carole a male dummy for her bed.

From Chicago, Bess Peters took the train to Indianapolis, while Lombard and Winkler attended some business meetings at which the

Carole Lombard and husband Clark Gable: Did she hurry back from her 1942 bond-selling tour because she was worried about her husband making Somewhere I'll Find You *with Lana Turner?* Courtesy of the Academy of Motion Picture Arts and Sciences

actress promised to enlist every star "with any glitter at all" in the bond-selling campaign. On the fourteenth, they flew to Indianapolis, from where she tried to call Gable but could not reach him.

Thursday the fifteenth was an absolute triumph for the star. At first, although she was drawing a large and excited crowd, she sold very few bonds. Then she decided not to give an autograph until someone purchased a bond. This brought the crowd to life. When an order for a bond came to her, she signed the receipt "Carole Lombard Gable." That evening, before twelve thousand fans and dozens of Indiana dignitaries (including Wendell Willkie) in the Cadle auditorium, Carole made her final sales pitch in a stunning strapless black velvet gown. At the end of the program, she sang "The Star-Spangled Banner." In one day she had sold two million dollars' worth of war bonds.

The next day, she wanted to go home as quickly as possible and asked Winkler to inquire about planes going to California that night—which disturbed her mother, who was afraid to fly and did not mind saying so. Winkler reported that the scheduled flights to California were booked solid, but Lombard kept calling the airline offices until she found a cancellation on a TWA flight. Her mother still objected, and Winkler remained neutral—so they tossed a coin to see whether they would go by plane or train. Lombard called it "tails." Tails it was, and Winkler wired Gable and MGM that they were on their way. Carole wired, "Pappy, you'd better get in this man's army." Some Indiana friends who saw them board the twenty-one-passenger Douglas "Skyclub" said that even at the last moment, Bess Peters was trying to talk her daughter out of flying home.

But Carole insisted, and inevitably the rumors started—they persist to this day—that she was rushing home because she was worried about what her husband was doing with Lana Turner. According to Gable biographer Lyn Tornabene, however, what Gable was doing was planning a welcome-home dinner for "Ma," to include Winkler's wife, Jill, and Carole's brothers, Fred and Stuart Peters. The house was filled with flowers and the big surprise was to be the male dummy, with a rather large erect penis, that Lew Smith had made. As he was leaving the set, Gable asked Robert Sterling, his male costar in *Somewhere I'll Find You,* to help him to the car with the heavy dummy. As he was driving away Gable winked at Sterling and said, "Don't hurry to work tomorrow. I'm goin' to be late."

Carole Lombard's flight left Indianapolis at four A.M., Friday, January 16. Flying time to Los Angeles was seventeen hours; with time changes the expected arrival at the Burbank airport was six P.M. on Friday.

Most of the passengers were members of the Army Ferrying Command. When they made a scheduled stop in Albuquerque, they found nine officers waiting with military orders enabling them to bump any civilian or Ferrying Command pilots on the plane. But Lombard argued that having just sold two million dollars' worth of war bonds, she must have some "rank." She could be very charming and amusing in this kind of situation, as anyone knows who has seen her on the screen. The Army officials gave in, permitting Lombard, her mother, and Winkler to continue on the flight. Winkler wired MGM that they would be an hour late arriving at Burbank, and the studio made arrangements to have Larry Barbier, an MGM public relations man, meet the plane.

The plane made an unscheduled stop in Las Vegas and at 6:50 P.M. proceeded west. The pilot, Wayne Williams, seemed unconcerned when he reported at 7:07 P.M. that he was slightly off course, about thirty-five miles west of Las Vegas. Eyewitnesses later reported that it was just about that time that the plane burst into flames. Some thought it happened just before the plane hit Olcott Mountain (also called Table Rock and Double U Peak); there was speculation that the absence of beacons—blacked out for fear of Japanese air raids—was responsible for Williams's losing course. (Later investigations revealed that the pilot, who had been reprimanded several times for not following flight instructions, was taking a shortcut through a restricted area to make up for lost time.)

Barbier, waiting at Burbank, was the first to hear that there had been a plane crash. He immediately called Howard Strickling, another MGM publicity man and close friend of Gable's. Strickling told Barbier to charter a plane; then he called Gable, who immediately left for the airport with MGM executive Ralph Wheelright. Jill Winkler, Lombard's brothers Stuart and Fred Peters, and Fred's wife left for Las Vegas by car. MGM executive Eddie Mannix took a scheduled flight.

On the chartered flight to Vegas, Strickling would recall, Gable was tense "because he sensed what had happened. . . . You knew you shouldn't talk to him. You knew not to say, 'It's going to be all right,' or 'I'm sorry.' "

When Gable and his group finally reached the base of the mountain, he wanted to go with the second search group, which included stretcher-bearers and medical supplies, but was persuaded to stay behind. Mannix and Wheelright went, however; years later, Mannix said Lombard was burned and headless—and that Gable had been told.

Gable rode on the train that carried the bodies back to Los Angeles and then purchased three crypts at Forest Lawn cemetery, one for Carole, one for her mother, and one for himself. The Army offered to give Carole a military funeral, and the Hollywood Victory Committee wanted to build a monument honoring the first star to give her life for her country. But Gable refused both suggestions, explicitly carrying out his wife's funeral instruction:

> I request that no person other than my immediate family and the persons who shall prepare my remains for interment be permitted to view my remains after death has been pronounced. I further request a private funeral and that I be clothed in white and placed in a modestly priced crypt in Forest Lawn Memorial Park, Glendale, California.

The death of Carole Lombard was Hollywood's first wartime tragedy. Those who were close to her, like Spencer Tracy, went into deep depression; Lucille Ball said she never really lost touch with her friend, that Carole visited her in her dreams for years, often advising her on important decisions. Joan Crawford immediately offered to replace Lombard in *They All Kissed the Bride* and donate her salary to the Red Cross. (When her agent insisted on taking his cut, she fired him.)

Gable was inconsolable. "The boyishness he had . . . was gone," said Strickling. What replaced the boy was a guilt-ridden, unapproachable middle-aged man. Gable left the care of his ranch to his secretary, Jean Garceau, and stopped work on *Somewhere I'll Find You.* For some reason he felt responsible for Lombard's death, but at the same time he was gracious in absolving Howard Dietz, who wrote Gable a letter taking the blame for sending Carole on the tour. He ate alone and tried to escape. "He'd get into his car," said Strickling, "and drive up to Oregon, all by himself. He'd drive out in the valley, just drive and drive to all kinds of places, sometimes not knowing where he was going." Then he bought a motorcycle with Al Menasco (a close friend since the film *Test Pilot,* for which Menasco, a pilot, was a consultant), and he would roar around the canyons. Some days he wouldn't talk to anyone, and when he did it was usually about "Ma": "Anytime he'd run into you," said Andy Devine, "it would make him think of Carole."

Because of the memories it held, Gable put up for sale the ranch he had bought with Carole. This prompted rumors that he was getting ready to go into the service, which, in turn, inspired a telegram from General Hap Arnold offering him a "Specific and Highly Important Assignment" in the Army Air Corps. But the studio intercepted the telegram, and replied that it was not advisable to discuss such a move with Gable at the present time. The implication was that Gable was still in mourning, but the truth appeared to be that MGM had no intention of letting its top star go into the Army.

A little over a month after Carole Lombard's death, Gable went back to work on *Somewhere I'll Find You.* Director Wesley Ruggles told everyone on the set not to baby him. He was drinking too much and had completely lost his sense of humor, a loss that is quite noticeable in *Somewhere I'll Find You.* He was also beginning to feel uncomfortable being in civilian clothes. The situation was especially tough for the nation's symbol of virility, whose wife—just before she died in service to her country—had urged him to "get in this man's army." On August 11, he arrived by motorcycle at Jill Winkler's house with an engraved gold bracelet as a gift. "I'm going in and I don't expect to come back and I don't really give a hoot whether I do or not," he told her.

There were rumors that he had been offered an officer's commission, which he could easily have had. Instead, he enlisted in the Army Air Corps as a private—and was sent to officer candidate school in Miami Beach.

Douglas and Meredith had a quick response from Washington from their offer to help. Within weeks, James M. Landis, who had been picked to run the Office of Civilian Defense, invited Douglas, without Meredith, to the capital. After questioning Douglas extensively on how his plan would work, Landis finally said: "Okay. I'm convinced. Will you run it?"

Douglas could hardly say no, so he became the first head of the Arts Council of the OCD. He also became "the target of some of the country's most virulent and powerful anti–New Deal forces." One of the first attacks came from Representative John Tabor (R–N.Y.), who said Douglas had been hired to teach the OCD how to dance. The Hearst papers picked up the attack, reprinting the ludicrous charges and launching what Douglas said was "a new kind of newspaper humor—Melvyn Douglas jokes." (Sample: "When Eleanor [Roosevelt, who was the OCD's assistant director] appointed Melvyn Douglas to the OCD the little lady was leading with her left.")

The attacks on Douglas receded somewhat when he gave a well-received speech at the National Press Club. But they were enough to make Mrs. Roosevelt announce that she was going to resign. Douglas offered to resign as well, but Mrs. Roosevelt supported him in a radio address in which she said: "It is apparently all right for businessmen to come to Washington to give their services on an expense basis, but not for an actor; we should be equally grateful to men like Mr. Melvyn Douglas . . . because people have fought and stood for liberal causes, they need not be branded as Communists in this country."

She also wrote Douglas a note urging him not to resign and saying that the attacks were directed at her, not at him: "To know me is a terrible thing." Douglas said in his autobiography that those who were lucky enough to be her friends knew "that to *be* Mrs. Roosevelt also could be a terrible thing."

However, before Douglas could really become active at the OCD, he had to return to Hollywood to fulfill his contract. James Landis had naïvely announced that he had asked Columbia Pictures to release Douglas, assuming that a public request would put pressure on the studio to respond as airlines and rubber and steel companies had responded, by letting their executives come to Washington to help win the war as "dollar-a-year men." But he reckoned without Columbia's head, Harry "White Fang" Cohn, who wired Douglas that he was "utterly amazed" at the request. Cohn said that Douglas's next film,

They All Kissed the Bride, could not be made without him, in part because his costar, Joan Crawford, had agreed to do the picture only if Douglas was her leading man (Douglas was one of the most popular leading men of the late 1930s and early 1940s, having appeared with Greta Garbo, Claudette Colbert, Marlene Dietrich, Myrna Loy, and Irene Dunne).

Douglas returned to Hollywood, but commuted to Washington while shooting the film. He also set up a Los Angeles Arts Division, which worked with government agencies that needed talent to provide music, graphics, acting, and writing. And when the film was nearly completed, he wrote Mrs. Roosevelt: "At the end of my current picture assignment I intend to finish with movies for the duration, provided that I can continue to do a war job. I cannot, with a clear conscience, face the mother whose son has been killed in Bataan nor the young man who is doing his 'hitch in hell' with the desert tank-corps unless I too am doing my utmost." Douglas said he had had some tentative offers of a commission but he also knew he had been investigated as a security risk by the FBI:

> This leaves the alternative of enlisting as a private. I would jump at this if I thought I would be assigned to combat duty, but in view of my age (41) I might end up at a desk job. On the other hand, my enlistment might have excellent political repercussions. . . . Believe me I would not burden you if I did not think that, whatever I do from here out is apt to have certain implications to yourself, the President and the Administration effort in general.

Mrs. Roosevelt wrote back saying he would be "in an impregnable position" if he joined the Army, which he soon did.

Meredith would soon be in the Army, but before he was drafted he became involved in a controversial radio project. As co-chairman of a radio series, *The Free Company,* he had to develop a program that he says in his memoir, *So Far So Good,* was "no more and no less than defending the Bill of Rights." He had an all-star cast of writers, one of them being the current boy genius Orson Welles, who contributed a one-act play called *His Honor, the Mayor,* depicting democracy in action at the grass roots. The problem was that Welles's *Citizen Kane* was about to be released, which most everyone at that time presumed was an attack on William Randolph Hearst. The Hearst press had not paid much attention to *The Free Company* until Hearst heard that Welles was involved in one of the plays—after which the Hearst papers attacked the radio program on the grounds that many of the actors and actresses involved were Marxists. Meredith now recalls the fear that was "everywhere" then but notes philosophically that the war is over and Hitler, Welles, Hearst, and William Paley, who took most of the heat at CBS, are dead. But *Citizen Kane* "seems to improve with time."

=

Another Hollywood personality to leave for the service early was director John Huston. While finishing *Across the Pacific* (which now concerned a Japanese plot to blow up the Panama Canal instead of Pearl Harbor), he received a phone call from Washington summoning him into the Signal Corps, which he had joined shortly after the Japanese attack. When Huston left the set, Humphrey Bogart, who played an Army officer involved in thwarting the Japanese plot, was being held prisoner by master spy Sydney Greenstreet. Huston decided to make things as difficult as possible for Vincent Sherman, whom Warner Bros. had chosen to replace him. "I had Bogie tied to a chair," Huston says in his memoirs, "and installed about three times as many Japanese soldiers as were needed to keep him prisoner. There were guards at every window brandishing machine guns. I made it so there was no way in God's green world that Bogart could logically escape. I shot the scene and then called Jack Warner and said Bogie will know how to get out." He did, with the help of Sherman, who had one of the Japanese guards throw a fit for some reason. In the ensuing confusion, Bogart's character escaped with the comment: "I'm not easily trapped, you know."

For those left behind in Hollywood, as in the rest of the country, the war would soon be having its impact. Mary Astor, who was also working on *Across the Pacific,* said that "for the first time I heard the phrase 'Don't you know there's a war on?'" Veronica Lake was forced to change her peek-a-boo haircut when it was estimated that 20,000 women working in defense plants were wearing their hair similarly; some of it was getting caught in the machinery. Changing her hair was all right with Veronica, who said: "I wanted to pull my hair back, to prove I could act and that I wasn't a sex symbol." Still, the boys in the barracks preferred the old Veronica in their pinups. The machinery be damned!

Meanwhile, another hairdo was on the way. As Maria in *For Whom the Bell Tolls,* Ingrid Bergman wore her hair short, and soon the Maria haircut was the style of the nation. But according to Bergman, it was a terrible mistake for the Rosie the Riveters to copy her. "They didn't know I had a hairdresser who followed me around like a shadow and rolled my

The stars not only did their bit but publicized their efforts so others would do the same: Veronica Lake (above) *and Ingrid Bergman* (above right) *trimmed their locks so as to help keep defense plant workers' hair out of the machinery; Rita Hayworth* (below right) *helped find metal.*

All photos National Archives

PLEASE DRIVE CAREFULLY.
MY BUMPERS ARE ON THE SCRAP HEAP

hair up every minute of the day. . . . But of course the poor women who had their heads done in the Maria cut in the morning found that after two hours it fell down again and they looked like little rats."

The list of hardships goes on and on. Shirley Temple said: "My doll-house was provisioned with extra bottled water and canned goods against probable enemy invasion." And she lost her radio program based on the *New Yorker* series "Junior Miss." The program was sponsored by Ivory Snow washing powder, but the tallow used in the manufacture of soap was needed to make nitroglycerin, so soap was soon in such short supply it was no longer in need of advertising. "Lard has gone to war," Miss Temple said in her last broadcast.

Before the war, Ronald Colman and his friend hotel manager Al Weingand opened the Harbor, a restaurant in an abandoned yacht club on the Santa Barbara wharf. Shortly after Pearl Harbor, the Army insisted that people provide identification before being allowed on the wharf. Fifteen days later, the restaurant was forced to close. On the other hand, for a while it looked as if Gloria Swanson's company, Multiprises, which made buttons, would profit from the war. But then business dropped off and her two partners went into government war work developing industrial diamonds. But what really dismayed her was the war's impact on her comeback film—*Father Takes a Wife*, with Adolphe Menjou. It was shot in the summer of 1941 and RKO prepared a big promotion campaign with ads proclaiming "There's Glamour on the Screen Again Because Gloria's Back" and "You'll Swoon Over Her Trunkful of Stunning Fashions." But nobody was interested in Miss Swanson or her stunning fashions after Pearl Harbor. The comeback had to wait until after the war was over, when Swanson and William Holden made the classic *Sunset Boulevard*.

Cary Grant had a different sort of problem: What to do about his citizenship? He wanted to marry heiress Barbara Hutton, who had a large fortune in London banks. If he married Hutton while he was an Englishman, her money would be frozen in England. If he married her as an American, the money could be transferred to America—where, among other things, Hutton could give donations to her favorite charities, especially the Red Cross. Shortly after Pearl Harbor, Grant applied for U.S. citizenship papers, defying the critics who questioned his patriotism. After he became a citizen he married Hutton.

═

The stars' contributions to the war were many and varied: According to one biographer, Lucille Ball was coming home from the dentist one day when she heard noises in her new filling. She was convinced they were code and she reported them to the F.B.I., which immediately searched the Coldwater Canyon area where Lucy had heard them. The F.B.I. found a hidden transmitter belonging to a gardener who was, indeed, part of a Japanese spy ring. Lucy, in fact, was having an inconvenient time with the war. Cars were especially hard to get; once, when Desi had a hot one delivered to their home, Lucy returned it, not because it was hot but because it was red. "It screamed when it saw my pink hair," she said.

Many Hollywoodians, including Cecil B. De Mille, James M. Cain, and Tyrone Power, acted as air-raid wardens. Power spent two nights a week sitting in a blacked-out building at the corner of Sunset Boulevard and Thurston Avenue, often with close friend Watson Webb, a New York socialite trying to work his way up in the movie business. They became even closer "after our nights on watch together," as Power put it in a letter to Webb. In fact, during this period as an air-raid warden, Power developed a closer friendship than any he had ever shared with a man, and Annabella, to whom Power was married from 1939 to 1948, loved Webb and welcomed him into the family.

Hospital visits helped wounded servicemen forget their troubles and, if the hospital was abroad, the stars reminded them of home; they made some men laugh, others cry. Edgar Bergen and his wooden dummy, Charlie McCarthy, aroused one young man who had not said a word for eight days to sit up and say "Hi." And Kitty Carlisle remembered sitting with one young boy who was badly burned: "I couldn't find anything to say, but I couldn't leave him. I just sat there for a long, long time and all at once I knew that he had died." One young actress was asked by a young wounded soldier to sing "Abide with Me." When she started to sing, he stopped her and said, "Not now, at the funeral." A few days later, she sang it for him.

Hospital duty proved especially difficult for Betty Grable when she ran into a life-size cardboard cutout of herself as she did at the Halloran Hospital in New York. Myrna Loy was with her and remembers how disturbed she was; she wanted to leave. "Don't be upset," Loy told her. "They love you. They're just happy to see you." So, according to Loy, Grable swallowed her indignation and stayed, "putting her lip-prints on plaster casts as the men moved joyfully around her, some on crutches, some legless in wheelchairs, some excitedly clapping their good hands against their legs, in lieu of a hand that was gone."

Hospital visits were so emotional for Mae West that she could not sleep or work for days afterward. When she was in Washington, D.C., appearing in her show *Catherine Was Great,* she found a substitute for the visits. She asked that as many wounded soldiers as possible be brought to the National Theatre for a special performance. The theater was packed.

According to John Steinbeck, who was reporting for the *New York Tribune,* when Bob Hope and his troupe were comforting wounded men in a hospital overseas, Frances Langford began to sing "As Time Goes By" but had to quit—from her own exhaustion and emotion—when some of the boys began to sob. When she left the ward, there was dead silence, until Hope walked down the row of beds and said: "Fellows, the folks at home are having a terrible time about eggs. They can't get any powdered eggs at all. They've got to use the old-fashioned kind you break open."

The wounded soldiers began to laugh. Wrote Steinbeck: "There's a man for you. There's really a man."

But it was not Bob Hope's jokes that the men who fought World War II remember most about Hollywood's entertainers. Years later, *South Pacific* got it right: There was nothing like a dame. But if they couldn't have the real thing, a pinup would do, the bigger the better. Pinups were plastered everywhere, but mostly on the walls around bunks. If a man couldn't get a pinup poster, a photograph would do, or the cover of a magazine; the Robert Landry photograph of Rita Hayworth on her knees in bed, first seen on the cover of *Life,* would appear in barracks all around the world. Pinups were "presumably to encourage masturbation," said pinup Evelyn Keyes in her candid autobiography. "It was our patriotic duty to answer the gallant servicemen . . . with pin-up pictures—the nakedest the Hays Office would allow."

The most famous pinup to come out of World War II was the one of Betty Grable with her fanny to the camera. In fact, the day photographer Frank Powolny took that photo was a momentous occasion. Powolny had already made one of the most notorious never-used publicity shots in Hollywood history: Carmen Miranda twirling in her flared skirt and revealing the fact that she was not wearing panties. Now he was about to make perhaps the most famous, widely used publicity shot ever snapped in a town that snaps publicity shots all day long, every day of the year: "It was 1941, during the summertime, before Pearl Harbor," said Powolny. "That's when we shot the picture. I only made two. I didn't shoot it in color. It was the early days before color. As we finished the poses, I asked Betty: 'How about some shots?'

" 'Like this?' said Betty, turning around.

" 'That's what I want, that's exactly what I want.' "

Pinups for the boys overseas. Top to bottom, left to right: *Betty Grable, Yvonne De Carlo, Jane Russell, Rita Hayworth, Evelyn Keyes, Marie McDonald, Ginger Rogers, Marie Wilson, Veronica Lake.*

According to Grable's biographer, Powolny decided that the first shot did not have the body swinging hard toward the camera the way he wanted it, so he requested another. "That's all it was," said Powolny, "just a posed shot."

But what a shot! It has been said by some G.I.'s that pinups won the war, and because Grable's routine posed shot would become the most famous pinup in World War II, the contribution of her fanny cannot be overlooked.

"There we were," one World War II veteran told Grable, "out in those damn dirty trenches. Machine guns firing. Bombs dropping all around us. We would be exhausted, frightened, confused and sometimes hopeless about our situation, when suddenly someone would pull your picture out of his wallet. Or we'd see a decal of you on a plane and then we'd *know* what we were fighting for."

The Grable pinup was probably the first and certainly the best known, but there were dozens of other stars and starlets ready and eager to send posters and photos of their scantily clad bodies overseas: "We females spent hours posing in bathing suits, negligees and shorts, jumping out of candy boxes for Valentine's Day," said Keyes. "Posing with turkeys for Thanksgiving, sleighs for Christmas. We donned our sexiest threads and visited army camps, always with a photographer present who had elected us 'girl of the week—month—year.' 'The one-to-be-with-on-a-deserted-island.' (I was elected 'Miss Tastiest Dish.')" Marilyn Monroe, still several years away from her first movie, was designated "The Girl We Would Most Like to Examine" by the medical corps of the Seventh Division.

"Our careers were built on war camp walls," says Keyes. Susan Hayward thought she was getting more publicity buildup than time in front of the cameras and complained about having to pose for " 'Miss Everything' except 'Miss Take.' " Pinups could get confusing. At one New York luncheon, Susan Hayward was introduced as "Rita Hayward" and was photographed kissing a Marine Corps hero of the 1942 Battle of Guadalcanal, Sergeant Carl Hickman. (The Marine Corps killed the photograph, deeming it undignified, although one copy did make its way to the London *Daily Mirror*.)

Paramount starlet Yvonne De Carlo, who did not appear in her first picture until 1945, spent most of the war "striking cheesecake photos for sex-starved G.I.'s." She was the "Sweetheart of the U.S. Mechanized Forces," and her pinups were plastered inside the walls of many tanks. And one tank, operating in the Burma campaign, went into battle with a five-foot cutout of Ginger Rogers (which would not fit in the tank) wired to its front.

"Ginger Rogers" was also scrawled on the front of one World War II B-17 bomber, which pleased the original very much. But Rita Hayworth was furious when she learned that her pinup was attached to an atom bomb tested at the Bikini atoll after the war. The men had named it "Gilda," for what was probably her sexiest movie and which had established her, even more than her famous *Life* photo had, as a sex goddess. "Men go to bed with Gilda," she lamented, "but wake up with me"—which was all right with the thousands of GIs who had her *Life* photo pinned up to their bunkside walls.

Another entertainer who did not like her status as a pinup girl was Lena Horne. Horne was aware that she was probably the most popular black pinup girl, and she knew why: "If the officers [of a Negro unit] were white," she said, "it was hardly safe for a Negro soldier to put up any of the fifty or so white lovelies, ranging from Grable to Lamarr. They did not have fifty or so Negro lovelies to choose from. They only had little ol' me. I therefore chose not to accept my status as a pinup queen as a compliment. It was, rather, an afterthought, as if someone had suddenly turned to the Negro G.I.'s and said: 'Oh yes, here, fellows, here's a pinup girl for you, too.' "

Jane Russell was built up by Howard Hughes during the war years. With *The Outlaw*—a saga ostensibly about Billy the Kid—Jane Russell's breasts joined Betty Grable's fanny and Veronica Lake's hair as a major element of Hollywood's war effort. Russell's career began when Howard Hughes excitedly told his assistant, Noah Dietrich: "Today, I saw the most beautiful pair of knockers I've ever seen in my life." And by 1940, Howard Hughes had seen plenty of them.

Hughes was rightfully one of Hollywood's greatest legends—before, during, and after the war. He had inherited the Hughes Tool Company in 1924, when he was eighteen. The company made oil-drilling equipment, but by the time he was twenty the handsome young Hughes was ready to try making films—primarily, it is said, because he was attracted to Hollywood's beautiful women. By the early 1930s, he had produced several successful movies, including *Hell's Angels* (which made Jean Harlow a star), *The Front Page*, and *Scarface*.

Then, suddenly, Hughes disappeared from Sunset Boulevard, turning up as an American Airways copilot named Charles Howard, intent on learning everything he needed to know for his next venture—as a designer, test pilot, and builder of airplanes.

In 1939, however, after breaking several world records (for flying planes around the world) and bones (in various accidents), he suddenly decided to go back into the movie business. And, he told Noah Dietrich, he had found the perfect story, that of the legendary Billy the Kid. He also told Dietrich he could make it for $250,000 and he wanted an attractive but completely unknown female he could turn into another star, as he had done for Harlow. He had seen Miss Russell at his dentist's office, where she worked as a receptionist.* She was given a screen test, with which she apparently had no trouble: "They gave me this peasant blouse to wear and it was 'Janie, bend down and pick up those pails.' I did it and the next thing I know they're aiming the camera down my navel." When she complained to Hughes, he said: "That's the way to sell a picture."

It was also the way to get into trouble with the Hays Office. Hughes had a long fight over *The Outlaw* with the Motion Picture Association, which he finally convinced (with photographs and film clips) that breasts had always played a prominent part in Hollywood films and their promotion. *The Outlaw* was approved by the Hays Office in the spring of 1941. But instead of releasing the film immediately, Hughes put it on the shelf and instructed his publicity agent, the legendary Russell Birdwell, who, among other things, had conducted the much-ballyhooed (by him) talent search for Scarlett O'Hara, to promote Jane Russell's breasts into a national icon. Birdwell had Hollywood photographer George Hurrell take dozens of pictures of Russell in all manner of activities and poses. The most famous one depicts a sultry-looking Russell in her peasant blouse, the right shoulder strap slipped to her elbow, sitting in a bale of hay that looked as if it had been recently rolled in. And who among us who were in the service in the 1940s does not remember seeing that poster sometime, somewhere, pinned up on some barracks wall? I myself saw it many times in the South Pacific.

And if Jane Russell's breasts, Veronica Lake's hair, and Betty Grable's fanny went to war, could Jack Benny's Maxwell be far behind? In perhaps one of the cleverest publicity stunts of the war, Benny's PR men decided that Jack had better give up his old Maxwell to the scrap metal drive. As Benny's biographer said, "It was like asking Groucho Marx to give up his mustache." And it was all the more difficult because, like Groucho's mustache, Benny's old car didn't really exist. It was a figment of radio imagination created by the voice of Mel Blanc,

*Another Hughes biographer, Tony Thomas, says Hughes picked Russell from a pile of photos submitted by agents.

Paulette Goddard knitting for the men overseas, especially the ones in a cold climate.
Courtesy of the Academy of Motion Picture Arts and Sciences

who was more famous for the voices of Bugs Bunny and Porky Pig. But Benny convinced the nation that his old car had gone to war. "I had a dream about my Maxwell. I dreamed that it became a B-29. You hear the ear-splitting roar of bomber after bomber, winging across the Pacific. The roar becomes louder and louder. Suddenly there is a discordant grinding, clunking of bolts, a wheezing and a groaning. . . . I didn't have to explain what that bomber had formerly been."

Benny also converted his badminton court into a victory garden. His daughter, Joan, only remembered "the radishes and carrots, because they grew the fastest." She recalled, more vividly, knitting with her friends for the soldiers overseas:

We knitted—only knitted, none of us was clever enough to purl. Someone else did the assembly. Can you imagine this spoiled group of six-to-ten-year-old Hollywood brats with nannies in attendance to pick up all the dropped stitches sitting by the pool or in the living room of one of our grand homes, or in some cases, estates? . . . I was being served tea from a Georgian tea service and pastries on a silver salver covered with a lace doily by the butler and waitress. As they say, "Only in Hollywood!" I still feel sorry for the men who received those pathetic misshapen blankets.

On the other hand, screenwriter and novelist Anita Loos remembered knitting, under quite different circumstances, with Paulette Goddard. One day, needles flying, they began to sing a ballad popular at the Hollywood Canteen:

> Hitler has only got one ball
> Göring has two but they are small
> Himmler has something similar
> But Goebbels has no balls at all.

One thing led to another and soon they were knitting what Loos called peter heaters, which were sent abroad, presumably to the colder fronts.

SIX

Hollywood Really Goes to War—On Screen

National Archives

The Germans are coming. —PETER LAWFORD'S sole line in *Mrs. Miniver*

If ever there was a film that confirmed President Roosevelt's conviction that films were essential to the war effort, it was *Mrs. Miniver,* which was just going into production at the time of Pearl Harbor. The movie was based on a series of newspaper essays (and then a book) by the English novelist Jan Struther about the trials and tribulations of a middle-class English family during the Blitz. The director was William Wyler, who had made such hits as *The Little Foxes, The Letter,* and *The Westerner.* And Wyler understood propaganda as well as Alexander Korda did: "To make propaganda," Wyler said, "your film must be successful. The most satisfaction I get out of a film, aside from its critical and financial success, is its contribution to the thinking of people. In this sense, every film is propaganda. But of course propaganda must not *look* like propaganda."

For Wyler, Struther's novel was "perfect as propaganda for the British because it was a story about a family, about the kind of people audiences would care about." The film family was headed by Greer Garson and Walter Pidgeon, neither of whom had wanted to appear in the movie. The Canadian-born Pidgeon, at forty-four, was not only debonair and mature—the model of a British family man (on screen, at least)—but ineligible for the draft. However, because of "Ninety-Take Wyler"'s reputation for shooting scenes over and over again, Pidgeon tried desperately to get out of the film.

Garson had shown enough character in *Pride and Prejudice* and *Blossoms in the Dust* to convince *Mrs. Miniver*'s producers that she was ideal as the perfect wife who could endure any hardship for England and her family. But she did not want to play *Mrs. Miniver* for the same reason Norma Shearer turned the part down: She would be playing a woman with a son old enough to go off to war. However, as Mr. and Mrs. Miniver, Garson and Pidgeon, said Bob Hope, "saved [the British] from going under."

The cast also included Teresa Wright and Richard Ney. Ney, playing the Minivers' son, would become involved in what, excluding the Cary Grant–Barbara Hutton merger, you might call Hollywood's first "wartime romance." After agreeing to play mother to Ney's young-man-old-enough-to-go-to-war, Garson decided that Ney was old enough to be her husband—in real life. They eventually married, but, at MGM's request, not until after the movie's release.

The young Austrian Helmut Dantine was also in *Mrs. Miniver.* Now, instead of spoofing the Nazis as he had in *To Be or Not to Be,* he would play a real, cold-blooded killer—at least, he thought he would. Before Pearl Harbor, Louis B. Mayer, who had seen the rushes, called director Wyler to his office and warned: "Look, maybe you don't understand, we're not at war with anybody. This picture just shows people having a hard time and it's very sympathetic to them, but it's not directed toward Germany."

Wyler could only respond by asking: "Mr. Mayer, you know what's going on, don't you?"

"This is a big corporation," replied Mayer. "I'm responsible to my stockholders. We have theaters all over the world, including a couple in Berlin [which, incidentally, had not been showing American films for years]. We don't make hate pictures. We don't hate anybody. We're not at war."

Wyler argued that if he had several Germans in the picture, he could be more balanced in his treatment: "But I've got only one German [a pilot who comes down in Mrs. Miniver's backyard] and as long as I have only one, he's going to be one of Göring's little monsters. That's the way he's been brought up."

Mayer surrendered: "I can always have another director shoot it over if I don't like it." But after Pearl Harbor, the mogul called Wyler back to his office and said he could have Dantine portray the German "as a typical Nazi son-of-a-bitch."

Wyler also strengthened the final sermon in the bombed-out church. The minister (Henry Wilcoxon), in Churchillian prose, tries to explain the deaths of a choirboy, the stationmaster, and Mrs. Miniver's daughter-in-law: "This is not only a war of soldiers in uniform. It is a war of the people—of all the people—and it must be fought not only on the battlefield but in the cities and in the villages, in the factories, on the

Greer Garson and Walter Pidgeon in Mrs. Miniver. *Neither of them wanted to appear in the film that Winston Churchill said was "worth one hundred battleships."*

farms and in the homes, and in the heart of every man, woman, and child who loves freedom."

President Roosevelt urged that the movie be rushed to the theaters and had Wilcoxon's message reprinted and dropped on German-occupied countries. The Voice of America broadcast it, *PM* and *Look* reprinted it, and the President told Wyler that the movie had been significant in establishing in America the ideas of self-sacrifice and of coming to the aid of England. Winston Churchill wired Mayer: MRS MINIVER IS PROPAGANDA WORTH 100 BATTLESHIPS.

Some months later, when Wyler was in London in uniform preparing to shoot a documentary on the Eighth Air Force (the movie eventually became *Memphis Belle*), he was invited to a screening of *Mrs. Miniver* for the top military brass in England. He was anxious because of the contrast between the Hollywood sets used for the film and war-torn England; he was sure the movie would not ring true with "an audience like this." He had to be threatened with a court-martial before he agreed to attend. But near the end of the movie he noticed that half the audience was pulling out handkerchiefs to wipe the tears. Among the weeping was Wyler himself: "Christ, what a tearjerker," he told his commanding officer.

Mrs. Miniver was released in June 1942; in the first ten weeks nearly 1.5 million people saw it at Radio City Music Hall in New York. The critics loved it; one even suggested it was "one of the greatest motion pictures ever made." It won seven Oscars. The Office of War Information had not opened its Hollywood office yet, but if all Hollywood films had been like *Mrs. Miniver,* it wouldn't have needed to. The theme of a British family enduring Dunkirk, the Battle of Britain, and the Blitz in order to maintain an island of civilization in Europe until the rest of the world (i.e., America) woke up was pure OWI gospel.

OWI must also have loved *Yankee Doodle Dandy.* It was scheduled to go into production the day after Pearl Harbor; and it did start, immediately after President Roosevelt's announcement of the declaration of war, which the cast and crew heard on a radio on the set. The director was the Hungarian-born Michael Curtiz, and the star was James Cagney, who played George M. Cohan. The cast included Walter Huston, Rosemary DeCamp, Joan Leslie, and Eddie Foy, Jr. As a price for doing the film, Cagney had insisted that his favorite screenwriting team, Julius J. and Philip Epstein, rewrite the script. He liked what they did and so did Cohan, who also approved Cagney as his alter ego. Cagney especially wanted to do the film—not only because, as he said in his autobiography, "once a song and dance man, always a song and dance man" (which was Cohan's credo also), but because he felt a nice patriotic role would be good for him at a time when he had to appear before the House Committee on Un-American Activities to defend what he called his New Deal liberalism. After hearing Roosevelt declare war, Cagney said: "I think a prayer goes in here . . . turn that thing off."

Then Curtiz addressed the cast: "Boys and girls, we have work to do. That was bad news, but we have a wonderful story to tell the world. So let's put away sad things and begin." They did, with what Rosemary DeCamp called a "patriotic frenzy," as if we were "sending a last message to the free world."

Yankee Doodle Dandy was finished at the end of May 1942; the premiere was held in New York and the film made $5.7 million. It also won Cagney his first Oscar (he beat Bogart in *Casablanca*) and, with its warm mixture of nostalgia ("part of an America that people liked to look back on," Cagney said) and unabashed patriotism, it continued to be popular throughout the war years.

It seems appropriate that it was December 8, 1941, when a story reader at Warner Bros. appraised *Everybody Comes to Rick's*, the play by Murray Burnett and Joan Allison about the refugees from Nazi Europe who gathered at Rick Blaine's café in Casablanca. The reader called it "sophisticated hokum," but a "box office natural for Bogart."

When the war began, World War I veteran Humphrey Bogart was nearly forty-three years old. (He had been a seaman on board the U.S.S. *Leviathan* when it was shelled by the Germans. The attack was reputed to have given Bogart a scarred and partly paralyzed upper lip, which caused the slight lisp that would later terrorize police, thugs, and, eventually, Nazis on the big screen. Actually, Bogart acquired his scar when he was transferring a naval prisoner from one base to another. The prisoner hit him in the face, cutting his lip severely. Bogart shot him as he was trying to escape.)

His screen career began to take off with his twelfth movie, *The Petrified Forest,* in which he played Duke Mantee. His costar, Leslie Howard, had insisted that Bogart be given the part. In the thirty-odd films between *Forest* and *Casablanca,* Bogart mostly played tough gangsters and tough private eyes.

Before Pearl Harbor, Hal Wallis, the studio producer who first saw *Everybody Comes to Rick's,* probably would have turned it down. But after the Japanese attack, Warner Bros. bought the play for $20,000 and assigned it to Julius and Philip Epstein. The Epsteins were told that Dennis Morgan would play the role of Rick, Ann Sheridan his long-lost

American lover (who later became the Norwegian Ilsa Lund), and Ronald Reagan the Czech patriot Victor Laszlo. George Raft (contrary to rumors that he rejected the role) had asked for the part of Rick, but was rejected; Dennis Morgan was replaced by Bogart.

Then Ingrid Bergman, who was in Europe, was asked to take the role of Ilsa. At first she refused, because she was more interested in *For Whom the Bell Tolls.* But when she heard that Vera Zorina had been offered the role of Maria in that film, she agreed to do *Casablanca*, because she was anxious to return to Hollywood with her daughter. Paul Henreid eventually was picked to play Laszlo but was also unhappy with the role because he did not "want to be the second lover in a film, second to Humphrey Bogart." He was promised the role would be built up in later revisions.

The movie also included the veteran actor Claude Rains and two *Maltese Falcon* alumni, Sydney Greenstreet and Peter Lorre. The outstanding supporting players were also remarkable in that most of them, like the leading lady and Henreid, were born in Europe and were refugees from Nazism or the war. Bergman was born in Stockholm; Henreid in Trieste; Helmut Dantine in Vienna; Conrad Veidt in Potsdam; Marcel Dalio in Paris; S. Z. Sakall in Budapest; Ludwig Stossel in Lockenhaus, Austria; Madeleine Lebeau in Italy; and Curt Bois in Berlin.

It was director Michael Curtiz, a Hungarian veteran of more than sixty films, who decided the script needed a real villain. He asked the Epstein brothers to develop the role of the Nazi Strasser (Veidt), which not only added tension to the film but increased its propaganda value. Curtiz also agreed to strengthen Rick's part, primarily because Bogart was unhappy with it. He did not like the way the first scripts had him spend so much time crying in his bourbon about a lost love, when all the young Americans who looked to Bogart as a tough guy were getting ready to go to war.

In the real French Mediterranean café, La Belle Aurore, that had served as Burnett's model for Rick's, there had been a black pianist; the film's corresponding role of Sam went to Dooley Wilson, a supporting actor and onetime drummer who could not play the piano. "As Time Goes By," the 1931 song Rick does not want to hear (though he finally orders Sam, "You played it for her, you can play it for me"), was actually Burnett's favorite record from his fraternity-house days at Cornell. And of course, nobody in the film ever says, "Play it again, Sam"— although Ilsa does say, "Play it, Sam. . . . Play 'As Time Goes By.' "

As all *Casablanca* buffs know, the shooting script for the film was a mess. After the Epstein brothers completed a draft, they left Hollywood to write the Army's propaganda film series *Why We Fight*, directed by Frank Capra, who was now an Army major in Washington. Producer Wallis and director Curtiz began working on the script and then brought in future director and producer Howard Koch (who wrote Orson Welles's *War of the Worlds* script) and veteran writer Casey Robinson (who had recently worked on *Kings Row*). Because of Bergman's schedule, shooting had to start on May 25, at which point only half a script was ready.

Most *Casablanca* buffs also know that the shooting of the film was marked by the deterioration of Bogart's marriage and his wife's intense jealousy of Ingrid Bergman. Mayo Methot was sure her husband was having an affair with the beautiful Swede. There was also tension between the hard-driving Curtiz and just about everybody in the cast. Bogart, Rains, and Henreid walked off the set when Curtiz cussed out a bit player and would not return until he apologized. There was also tension between Curtiz and Howard Koch: Curtiz wanted to play up the romance, but the more idealistic Koch wanted to emphasize the struggle against fascism.

Bergman recalled that "from the very start, Wallis was arguing with the writers ... and every lunchtime Mike Curtiz argued with Wallis.... Every day we were shooting off the cuff. Every day they were handing out the dialogue and we were trying to make some sense of it. No one knew where the picture was going and no one knew how it was going to end. ... It was ridiculous, just awful. Michael Curtiz didn't know what he was doing because he didn't know the story either. Bogart was mad because he didn't know what was going on, so he retired to his trailer"—alone, or at least not with Bergman.

The entire film was shot in the Warner Bros. studio at Burbank or at the Van Nuys airport. The fog was phony and the airplanes were models. When the film was in its final week of shooting, there was still no ending. Would Rick get Ilsa? Would Laszlo get her? Would Rick die? Would Ilsa and/or Laszlo get away? Would Strasser prevail (highly unlikely)? At about this time, according to legend, the Epstein brothers returned and wrote two endings, one in which Rick ends up with Ilsa and one in which Rick enables Ilsa and Laszlo to escape by shooting Strasser. When Police Chief Renault (Rains) hears of this, he utters a line that has become even more repeated than the mythical "Play it again, Sam": "Round up the usual suspects." They shot this ending first and decided that was it.

By the time Bogart and Rains are photographed walking off into the phony fog and declaring the beginning of their beautiful friendship, Bergman had left the set to play Maria in *For Whom the Bell Tolls*. She had finally won her cherished role, after Zorina proved unsatisfactory.

After the picture was completed, serious thought was given to jettisoning "As Time Goes By" and having an original tune written for Sam to play, as Max Steiner (who had previously composed the music for *Gone With the Wind*) was miffed at having to build his score around an old Tin Pan Alley tune. However, "As Time Goes By" was saved for eternity when it was learned that Bergman had already cut her hair short for the part of Maria. Reshooting her "Play it, Sam" scenes would be impossible.

But there were other, larger forces at work, propelling *Casablanca* toward its rendezvous with destiny. On November 8, 1942, the Allies landed at various sites on the coast of North Africa, including Casablanca. Less than three weeks later, the movie premiered in New York; by the time of its general release in January 1943, Roosevelt and Churchill were holding their Casablanca Conference (although this could not be made public at the time)—and pundits would soon begin writing about the similarity between Rick and FDR, "the uncommitted American," as Nathaniel Benchley, author of the biography *Humphrey Bogart*, wrote, "who stands by while others do the fighting, and then at the proper time steps in and turns the tide."

After the landings in North Africa, some Warner executives in New York urged Jack L. Warner to include an epilogue linking the movie to the latest events. But Warner refused: WILL DEFINITELY NOT TOUCH PICTURE, he wired New York, PREVIEWED IT AGAIN LAST NIGHT AND AUDIENCE REACTION BEYOND BELIEF. FROM MAIN TITLE TO THE END THERE WAS APPLAUSE AND ANXIETY.

The landings on the coast of North Africa were about the only encouraging news in a very discouraging first year of the war. Within a few days of Pearl Harbor, the Japanese sank the HMS *Prince of Wales* and *Repulse*, took Guam, landed on Luzon in the Philippines, and invaded Borneo; by Christmas they had captured Wake Island and Hong Kong. Early in 1942, Japan began the siege of Bataan, attacked the Netherlands East Indies, and captured Tavoy in Burma. The British withdrew from the Malay Peninsula to Singapore, which surrendered to Japan in February. General MacArthur was ordered to leave the Philippines, and the Japanese invaded New Guinea.

Then, just after the surrender of Bataan, came the April 18 raid on Tokyo by Lieutenant Colonel James Doolittle, who took off from the carrier *Hornet* with sixteen B-25s and bombed Tokyo and four other

Japanese cities. This was followed in early May by the Battle of the Coral Sea, the first naval engagement in history in which the two forces engaged never came in sight of each other. Although the United States lost the carrier *Lexington* and suffered damage to the *Yorktown,* it won a strategic victory by preventing the Japanese task force from landing at Port Moresby in New Guinea. U.S. planes also damaged two Japanese carriers, *Shokaku* and *Zuikaku,* preventing them from taking part in the critical Battle of Midway, which came the following month and was considered by many to be the turning point in the Pacific naval war. The battle cost the Japanese four of their six main carriers and they suffered a serious loss of trained pilots. The attempt to take the Midway atoll, a thousand miles west of Pearl Harbor, was thwarted.

In late May, Germany defeated the Russians at Kharkov after a vicious eleven-day battle, and in the first week and a half of June, after Midway, the Japanese invaded the Aleutian Islands and completed their conquest of the Philippines. The British withdrew from Libya, leaving Tobruk isolated; it soon fell to General Erwin Rommel's forces. In late June, the Germans started a major offensive against Russia; in less than three months they would be in the suburbs of Stalingrad. The Allies were also suffering heavy losses in the North Atlantic convoys and, for a while at least, at Guadalcanal in the South Pacific, where the Marines landed virtually unopposed but were then met by stiff resistance in a battle for the island that went on for over six months.

However, as 1942 came to an end, there were signs that the Germans and Japanese were losing momentum and were not invincible: The Germans were defeated at El Alamein; in Operation Torch, Allied troops landed on the coast of North Africa; the British retook Tobruk; the Russians counterattacked at Stalingrad; and the United States was on the way to a decisive victory at Guadalcanal.

As a result, by the time Roosevelt and Churchill met at Casablanca in January 1943 (where they had hoped Joseph Stalin would join them; he didn't, saying he was preoccupied with Stalingrad), the Allies could talk about future plans with a confidence based on military victories.

=

With the United States taking such heavy losses on the Murmansk run in the North Atlantic, it was inevitable that sooner or later someone in Hollywood would say: "Let's make a movie about the merchant marine," which according to Raymond Massey was exactly the way Jack L. Warner conceived *Action in the North Atlantic.* Warner knew that any film glorifying the valor of the merchant marine sailors and their

Humphrey Bogart and Raymond Massey (standing) *in* Action in the North Atlantic. *After a four-martini lunch, Massey said to Bogart, "My double is braver than your double." Bogart replied, "I'm braver than you." Then they went back to the set and did the lifeboat action scene themselves.* Courtesy of the Academy of Motion Picture Arts and Sciences

regular Navy gun crews would be welcomed by the government and the public.

The movie would costar Humphrey Bogart and Raymond Massey, two very macho actors concerned about their images as tough guys since they were out of uniform. Massey, who was born in Toronto, served in a World War I Canadian field artillery unit, part of the Canadian Expeditionary Force sent to Siberia. After the war, he went into acting and in 1932 made his first film, playing Sherlock Holmes in *The Speckled Band.*

Action in the North Atlantic was shot entirely on the Warner Bros. lot; the freighter sunk in the early part of the film and the Victory ship on which most of the action took place were both constructed on the lot. Most of the horrifying scenes of sailors running through a burning ship or diving into water covered with burning oil were done on the set with fire created by a "smoke bum." Massey and Bogart had battle-scarred stuntmen taking their risks for them.

One day when the director, Lloyd Bacon, said Massey and Bogart could take the afternoon off because the stuntmen were going to shoot a scene in a lifeboat surrounded by burning oil, they went to the club to have lunch and play golf. But before lunch, after they had had some martinis—four to be exact—someone from the studio appeared and said they were needed back at the set for the lifeboat scene. There were two versions of what happened—Massey's and Bogart biographer Nathaniel Benchley's—so we will take what we need from both to make the best story. Massey said, "My double is braver than your double," to which Bogart replied, "He is like hell. My double is the bravest double there is." Then he paused and said, "Come to think of it, I guess I'm braver than you."

Massey replied, "Maybe so. Are we going to let two men risk their lives to make us look good?"

"Are we men or mice?" said Bogart.

So they went back to the set, insisting that they replace their stuntmen in the lifeboat scene. "Okay," said Bacon, "but if either of you gets fried, it'll be your fault and we'll have to alter the script."

And from Massey's autobiography, we have this description of World War II action on a Hollywood set:

We could not see well. There was a lot of smoke on the deck as well as flames. Each of us had to follow a coloured line from the bridge down a companionway to the boat deck by the davits. The flames parted like the Red Sea as we staggered on. It was damned hot.

The camera on the big crane followed us pretty closely. There was no sound being recorded so we could shout whatever we wanted. Bogie got to the taffrail first and as he climbed over to grab a line his pants caught on a cleat. As he slid down the falls to the boat, one leg of his pants was torn off.

"All right, Bacon," he barked. "You can fix my pants in the script!"

I slid down unscathed and shouted, "Lower away." Alan Hale started paying out the stern lines. But the rope slipped. Before he could hold it, the boat was forty-five degrees down by the stern. J. M. (Joe) Kerrigan, playing the cook in his dirty whites, was thrown at my feet. This former member of the Abbey Theatre in Dublin inquired philosophically, "Do you ultimately affect the legitimate theatre?"

"Don't split infinitives, you Hibernian savage!" yelled Bogie from the bows.

We hit the studio sea.

Lloyd Bacon shouted, "Cut! Perfect! Print it! You're not actors— you're all bums. I love you!"

SEVEN

Bonding—
Hollywood Style

Courtesy of the Academy
of Motion Picture Arts and Sciences

I think it is outrageous that movie stars have to wheedle and beg people into buying bonds to help their country. But if that's the way it is, I'm going to squeeze all I can out of everyone. —BETTE DAVIS, boarding a train for a 1942 bond-selling tour

With Carole Lombard's death in January 1942, a little over a month after Pearl Harbor, Hollywood's entry into the war came quickly. And despite all the mumbling about easy commissions and deferments to make pictures, many actors and directors went on active duty and saw action. Those who did not nevertheless made substantial contributions selling bonds and entertaining the troops in camps at home and abroad. In fact, it might be debatable who, in the long run, contributed most—those who went into uniform or the actors and actresses who helped raise money to finance the war or kept up troop morale. There was no doubt how Washington felt; it wanted the stars to help sell war bonds.

Since early in 1941, the Treasury Department had been making plans to finance the war. There were still plenty of Treasury aides around who remembered how effective Mary Pickford, Douglas Fairbanks, Sr., and Charlie Chaplin (all partners later in United Artists) were at selling war bonds in 1918. Pickford's World War I experience must have been memorable: It was during a Liberty Bond drive that the affair between "America's Sweetheart" and Fairbanks, Sr. (who was married and had a young son, Douglas junior), became public.

After Carole Lombard's death, one of the first stars to sell war bonds in 1942 was her close friend Merle Oberon. On February 5, 1942, the New York Stock Exchange opened its doors to Oberon, the first time a woman had ever been on the floor of the exchange before three P.M. She spent several hours with George Jessel and Robert L. Stott, president of the exchange, raising money for the Navy relief show to be staged at Madison Square Garden. The following day, Oberon was given a tour of a new battleship, and after hearing everything her tour guides had to say, she went immediately to her husband, Alexander Korda, and told him she felt she had been told far more than she needed to know, or should know, about the ship—even if she was connected to intelligence (which many people thought she was).

Twelve days later she participated in a new fund-raising gimmick, involving the sale of posters that carried the message "Loose Talk Can Cost Lives." Oberon stressed the danger of talking about military affairs to anyone and reminded her audience of the possibility that leaked intelligence might have been responsible for the sinking of the *Normandie* in New York Harbor. "Be smart, act dumb," she told them.

Dorothy Lamour said in her autobiography: "The Japanese attack on Pearl Harbor left me in a state of shock. . . . I had to do something—but what? . . . Could I use my name to sell bonds?"

Indeed she could. Lamour remembered her first bond-selling tour very well because a sulfa drug she had taken for a touch of the flu caused her to break out in a rash on her arms and legs. As a result, for her initial meeting with a group of bankers she chose a "ladylike, long-sleeved black dress with high neckline, a very conservative hat and gloves." One banker, a dignified gentleman, rose to comment on her attire: "Miss Lamour, I cannot tell you how happy I am to see you dressed that way. We were afraid you might not remember that you are now working for the United States of America and that you might be wearing one of those sarongs." She assured the banker that her mother had raised her to be a lady.

Then Lamour went to New York's City College, where, again wearing her long black dress, she read a speech that had been prepared by one of FDR's writers. She had wanted to give her own speech but was talked out of it. On stage, she sensed immediately that the students knew she was reading something that had been written for her. Suddenly, from the back of the hall, came: "Hey Dottie, take it off." She threw away the speech, began to talk from her heart, and sold $10,000 worth of war bonds without even having to remove her gloves.

After New York, she went to New England, where, she later said: "In most places there were as many as twelve to fifteen thousand people lined up on the streets. I had set up where I would sell the bonds and had someone with me to count the money. I made a deal with the Treasury Department that I would not take pledges, only cash. That way I got the money before they got the autograph. I was extremely proud that in the first four days, I brought in $30 million."

Then she went back on the "road" again—*Road to Morocco*.

In the spring of 1942, the Army-Navy Relief Fund organized a gigantic extravaganza, which it called the Hollywood Victory Caravan, to raise money for the families of men killed overseas. It was the largest collection of Hollywood celebrities ever assembled up to that time, and they were scheduled to tour the country in a seventeen-car train. The stars included Desi Arnaz, Joan Bennett, Joan Blondell, Charles Boyer, James Cagney, Claudette Colbert, Bing Crosby, Olivia De Havilland, Cary Grant, Charlotte Greenwood, Bert Lahr, Stan Laurel and Oliver Hardy, Groucho Marx, Frank McHugh, Merle Oberon, Pat O'Brien, Eleanor Powell, mezzo-soprano Risë Stevens, Spencer Tracy—and of course, Bob Hope and his two faithful lieutenants, Frances Langford and Jerry Colonna. "If that train had been wrecked," said Arnaz, "Hollywood would have been out of business."

In fact, the group was so large that Frank McHugh, a supporting actor known for his high-pitched voice and nervous laugh, said that "someone like Marlene Dietrich could join us for a few days in Washington and you wouldn't know she was there."

For some, like Bert Lahr, *The Wizard of Oz*'s Cowardly Lion, who was only getting parts in B pictures, it was an honor to be included in such an array. For others, like Groucho Marx, who was in the middle of an unpleasant divorce while the Marx Brothers team was also disintegrating, it was a chance to get away from troubles at home. For established stars like Cary Grant and Olivia De Havilland, it was a time to do something different; De Havilland played in a comedy sketch with Groucho Marx while Grant acted as part-time emcee and played straight man in an act with Bert Lahr.

Most of the actors and actresses lived in their own closed circle in Hollywood and never mingled with other stars, except at large affairs like an Academy Awards dinner. But now they were brought together on a train and stayed in hotel rooms for several weeks. This may have meant camaraderie for someone like Lahr; for others, no doubt, it meant time away from home to pursue the gorgeous starlets. In fact, Bob Hope biographer Arthur Marx says that one reason Hope liked to travel was the freedom it gave him to pursue the starlets.

Accounts of what happened on the Caravan vary considerably. For example, in his autobiographical *Don't Shoot, It's Only Me,* Bob Hope says that most of the stars went by train from Los Angeles, a trip he remembers well because Arnaz drove everyone nuts playing "Babalu" on his bongo drums, until finally Pat O'Brien took Arnaz by the throat and said: "Listen, you Cuban so-and-so, we beat your brains out in '98 and we can do it again." Hope also says that when Groucho Marx saw the screaming mob of fans at Union Station in Washington, D.C., he said, "If this is the American public, we ought to surrender right now."

However, Hope biographer William Robert Faith wrote that Hope (who shared the emceeing duties with Cary Grant), Langford, and Colonna flew to Washington and caught up with the Caravan just in time to join the others at the White House party given by Eleanor Roosevelt. The acrobatic comedienne Charlotte Greenwood greeted her by kicking a high one, and Groucho told the First Lady: "You could do that if you put your mind to it." When Groucho was introduced to Mrs. Roosevelt, he said, "Are we late for dinner?"

Arnaz remembers that when he went through the receiving line, Mrs. Roosevelt amazed him by saying, "Hello, Desi. How is Lucille?" (Lucille was home, furious that she had not been invited on the Caravan, if for no other reason than to chaperone Desi.) Arnaz, who had just completed his third B picture, *The Navy Comes Through,* says: "I was really nobody in those days. So I was thinking: 'How the hell can she do this?' " He noted that she made a personal comment to almost everyone who came through the line.

But he finally figured it out: "I spotted a fellow standing behind her. Let's suppose that Cagney was in front of me and she was shaking hands with him. The guy behind Mrs. Roosevelt would whisper: 'Desi Arnaz, married to Lucille Ball; he's a Cuban.' "

The President was unable to attend the dinner, and his absence did

Members of the 1942 Victory Caravan visit the White House. Bottom row, left to right: *Oliver Hardy, Joan Blondell, Charlotte Greenwood, Charles Boyer, Risë Stevens, Desi Arnaz, Frank McHugh, an unidentified man, James Cagney, Pat O'Brien, Juanita Stark (behind O'Brien), and Alma Carroll.* Standing, left to right: *Merle Oberon, Eleanor Powell, Arleen Whelan, Marie McDonald, Faye*

McKenzie, an unidentified woman, Mrs. Roosevelt, Frances Gifford, Frances Langford, another unidentified woman, Cary Grant, Claudette Colbert, Bob Hope, Ray Middleton, Joan Bennett, Bert Lahr, Joel Rose, an unidentified man, Stan Laurel, Jerry Colonna, and Groucho Marx. Gene Lester

not go unnoticed by Groucho. After the Marine band had performed a march that Lahr thought was "god-awful," Groucho turned to Mrs. Roosevelt and said, "No wonder the old man didn't come."

Or did he? James Cagney's biographer Ron Offen wrote that Cagney, who had just finished *Yankee Doodle Dandy*, met the President at the White House and that Roosevelt said: "I'd like to see you do something from that fine new picture of yours, Mr. Cagney," to which Cagney responded: "Your wish is my command."

At first, since Groucho Marx did not wear his greasepaint mustache and eyebrows, he looked more like a scholarly professor than the leering, slouching Groucho on screen. This made his outrageous, irreverent remarks all the more startling; when a beribboned general came up to him in the White House and asked where Mrs. Roosevelt was, Groucho replied: "She's upstairs filing her teeth." And as Lahr and Groucho were leaving, the chauffeur asked: "Where would you gentlemen like to go?"—to which Groucho responded: "Are there any cathouses in the area?"

After the White House affair, the troupe went to Constitution Hall to rehearse all night for the three-hour variety show that would open the next night at the Capitol Theater. The show had been developed by producer-director Mark Sandrich (veteran of several Astaire-Rogers musicals); it was written by Howard Lindsay and Russel Crouse, Moss Hart, George S. Kaufman, and others, and had music by Jerome Kern, Johnny Mercer, Frank Loesser, and Arthur Schwartz. It was a tough show, said emcee Hope. "You were lucky if you could mention your own picture every half hour."

At the rehearsal, Groucho was complaining about the size of his part and that Bob Hope "has seventeen guys writing jokes for him." When Sandrich said there were only six, Groucho said: "Only six? For Hope, that's practically ad-libbing." Groucho's fears were justified. Herb Colden, commenting on the opening show, called it "Bob Hope's Victory Caravan," saying that "only those performers, and fortunately there were a lot of them, who had the benefit of gagging with the Pepsodent peddler came out completely satisfactory on the comedy end. As long as Hope was on the stage the show had zest and lift."

After Washington, the Caravan headed back toward California, stopping at fourteen cities. Each actor and actress had his or her own compartment, and the chaperones stationed between the men's and ladies' cars were not always successful in keeping males and females apart. Groucho said he fell madly in love with Olivia De Havilland, his costar in the comedy skit they had worked up, "Who's Olive?," although she

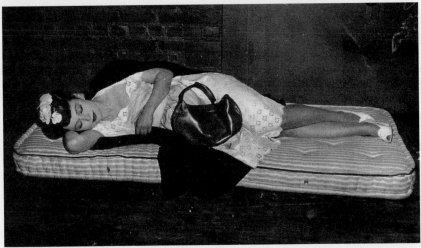

Above: *Stan Laurel (left) and Oliver Hardy reviewing the troops as they arrive in Union Station, Washington, D.C.* Below: *Olivia De Havilland catches a nap between performances of "Who's Olive?"* Gene Lester

said she did not learn this until thirty-five years later. She had interests of her own—a "certain officer," who apparently was John Huston, already in uniform. Huston said he would desert if De Havilland did not stay in his car, and what exactly happened we do not know except that she was twenty-five minutes late for the first meeting in Washington and everyone was asking, "Where's Olive?"

One night on the train, Cagney rounded up a bunch of actors who were reveling in the observation car and motioned them to follow him. "There's a maiden in distress," he announced, and led them to the compartment of an attractive young starlet, where they could hear the voice of a well-known screen Romeo whom Cagney, later recalling the story, preferred not to name: "Oh, my darling," they heard the actor say, "I was struck by you the moment I set eyes on you."

Then the group listening at the door heard the young actress giggle: "Hey, take it easy."

"But if you knew how much you mean to me . . ."

"Oh, Mr. ———, how can you say that? We only met a few days ago."

"What does it matter how long we've known each other?" they heard the actor say above the sound of a struggle. Finally, the young lady's voice could be heard: "But, Mr. ———, I want to sleep alone."

When Cagney heard that, he knocked on the door and said "Western Union for Mr. ———."

"You must have the wrong compartment, young man," came the response, with the actor trying to sound like an elderly gentleman.

"Well," replied Cagney, "the people at the end of the car told me they'd seen him *going* there," which brought an anguished plea from the young lady: "He hasn't been in here. Now please go away."

Cagney and his group began to laugh and beat a hasty retreat, satisfied that they had saved the maiden from a fate worse than having to be auditioned by Harry Cohn.

Claudette Colbert also had a visitor to her compartment: her husband, who was a Navy doctor. After they did not emerge for two days, Groucho put a note on her door: "Isn't this carrying naval relief too far?"

Merle Oberon had her own strategy for keeping the wolves away from her compartment door. She developed a close camaraderie with Cagney, Lahr, and McHugh. McHugh remembered dinners at Chicago's Ambassador Hotel: "She was beautiful—just beautiful. When we'd go to the Pump Room, this gorgeous creature would enter followed by Lahr, Cagney, and myself and you could see them saying to themselves: 'What's goin' on?' " Everyone called at their table, but Oberon did not ask anyone else to join them. One would-be pursuer stopped her in the hotel lobby and asked: "What are you doing with those three men all the time?"

"I guess I just love baggy-pants comedians," she replied.

But there really was a bond between Oberon and her baggy-pants friends. Once Lahr said to her, "Merle, you know why Jimmy, Frank, and I love you so much?"

"Why?" she asked, making a big mistake.

"Because you're hairy-assed," said Lahr.

Bob Hope with his writers may have gotten the most laughs on the Caravan, but Cagney thought that Bing Crosby was probably the biggest attraction. At Soldiers Field in Chicago, he said, he went on after Crosby, and he'd never appreciated that old vaudeville adage so much: "What an act to follow." Crosby had been casual and cool onstage; when he finished singing, the ovation gave Cagney goose-bumps. He was amazed to see Crosby come offstage perspiring and tense, showing how hard he worked at being casual.

At the Soldiers Field concert Harpo Marx recalled some praise he could have done without: "For my dough, you're the best one on the program," a hot-dog vendor told him. And when Marx said that he was flattered, the vendor replied: "Yes sir, Mr. Marx, when you played your harp I sold four times as many hot dogs as when anybody else was onstage."

It was on this trip that several of the film stars, who had little experience with live audiences or crowds, learned firsthand the mysterious attraction they had for their fans. Most of them reported being mobbed in every city: "You've never seen so many people," said Lahr. "They lined up—perhaps five feet from the cars. We'd round a corner and there would be a tremendous cheering. You'd hear 'Hurray'—every time a recognizable star came into view."

In Chicago, according to Lahr's biographer, Charles Boyer's car was approached by a man who yelled, "You've ruined my marriage. My wife's crazy about you." Boyer said he had never seen the man before. And one of Cary Grant's biographers insists that this happened to Grant in Topeka, Kansas.

On the other hand, Groucho proved that if you could not be recognized from your screen image, you were nobody. Without his false mustache and eyebrows, Groucho tried to join a group of Caravaners

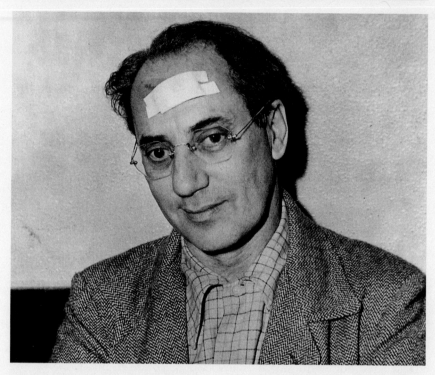

Groucho Marx: At first he went on bond-selling tours without his greasepaint mustache and eyebrows, but he soon found that no one recognized him. Courtesy of the Academy of Motion Picture Arts and Sciences

being photographed on a train platform: "Where are you going?" asked a policeman, stopping him at the gate.

"I'm Groucho Marx," the star said.

"Sure. And I'm Jimmy Durante," said the policeman. For the rest of the trip, Groucho wore his stage makeup in public.

Most of the stars agreed with Joan Bennett, who called the Caravan a "wild and wooly trip . . . I'll never forget." They swapped show-biz stories in the dressing rooms, where most of them gravitated to Laurel and Hardy, who always had a bottle of whiskey sitting between them. Even the cynical Groucho would say how much he enjoyed the tour and the all-night singing groups, which included "a million-dollar crooner straining his voice to top the sound of the train and trying hard to outdo an obscure baritone who insisted he was Bob Hope."

When the train came to its last stop, in Glendale, Lahr recalled seeing Oliver Hardy trying to look away, in tears, saying good-bye to his friends. "Don't let's lose this. Let's keep in touch," said Hardy to Lahr.

(Lahr called it "a caravan of love.") The next day, perhaps in recognition of the good times they had all had, every member of the group received a telegram from Joan Blondell and Joan Bennett that read: ARE YOU GETTING MUCH?

That spring, Congress passed a wartime budget of $154 billion. It seems like a piddling amount today, but Roosevelt said, "This is more money than has ever been spent by any nation at any time in the history of the world." To help raise the money, the Treasury Department and the White House continued to look to the stars, and as Bob Hope said, "Who in Hollywood had the guts to tell the IRS he was going to be out of town?"

With the help of Howard Dietz and the Hollywood War Activities Committee, the Treasury Department organized another extravaganza, called "Stars Over America," to sell war bonds. A Treasury Department month-by-month record shows the number of stars and the cities they visited from January through August of 1942,* culminating in a huge "Stars Over America" drive in September. For this drive, more than three dozen stars were organized in seven groups:

Group 1	Group 2	Group 3	Group 4
Joan Leslie	Ronald Colman	Edward Arnold	James Cagney
Walter Pidgeon	Lynn Bari	Frances Dee	Fred Astaire
Adolphe Menjou	Bette Davis	Gene Tierney	Hugh Herbert
Ralph Bellamy	Janet Gaynor	Chester Morris	Ilona Massey
Richard Arlen	Basil Rathbone	Laraine Day	Dorothy Lamour
Jean Parker	Nigel Bruce	Andy Devine	
Walter Abel	Ginger Rogers	Vera Zorina	

Group 5	Group 6	Group 7
Greer Garson	William Gargan	Ann Rutherford
John Payne	Hedy Lamarr	Charles Laughton
Jane Wyman	Irene Dunne	Virginia Gilmore
Veronica Lake	Lynne Overman	Constance Bennett
	Paulette Goddard	

*Month	Cities	Stars
January	10	25
February	28	37
March	23	61
April	21	36
May	65	81
June	66	79
July	86	78
August	49	20

Just about every star in town not committed to a film shooting schedule agreed to sell bonds, and most of those otherwise committed would go on a tour sooner or later. The new drive began on the steps of the Treasury Department on August 31, 1942, and the seven groups visited 353 cities and small towns in September. Greer Garson drew a crowd of twelve thousand in Huntington, West Virginia. Hedy Lamarr was the star in Philadelphia; and for two days in the San Francisco Bay area, Joan Leslie, Adolphe Menjou, and Walter Pidgeon attended civic luncheons and shipyard rallies. The drive culminated in a massive rally at Madison Square Garden in New York that featured most of the stars. That night alone brought in $86 million for the Treasury; the month-long tour had sold $775 million worth of bonds. A highlight of the Madison Square Garden rally was Myrna Loy doing a "mock striptease," as she put it: "My hat brought $30,000, and a pair of elbow-less crimson gloves $25,000."

=

Although he was not on the Treasury Department list, John Garfield also took part in the Madison Square Garden rally. In many ways his participation was one of the most significant events of the "Stars Over America" tour, because while in New York he also helped out at the Stage Door Canteen, a relaxation center for troops organized and operated by New York's actors and actresses. There he had the idea of starting a similar spot for servicemen in Hollywood.

=

By 1942, Bette Davis was already a legend. Her rebellious, bitchy screen personality had been established in a number of famous movies—*Jezebel, Of Human Bondage, Dangerous,* and *The Little Foxes.* She had just finished *In This Our Life* (with Olivia De Havilland and George Brent) when she did her stint with "Stars Over America." And perhaps to no one's surprise, she soon became the most-quoted star on the bond-selling circuit. She started in Iowa and then went on to Missouri and Oklahoma, where she danced in barns, visited private homes, and spoke at fairs, Rotary meetings, and schools.

In Oklahoma City, she told a group of factory workers that they should do everything they could at their "top level . . . or you're not my idea of an American." When she was cautioned to be a little more tactful, she continued: "It lights fires under their asses. It gets them reacting and acting. Somebody has got to wake these people up to the fact that they're fighting for their lives."

Finally Davis's boss, Jack L. Warner, called and told her to tone it down a little, to which she responded: "Jack, I know what I'm doing. You and your brother in New York just sit around and count the money I make for you. I'm the one who has to deal up front with the public, and I know what I'm doing!"

She must have, because in Tulsa, Oklahoma, she sold an autograph for $50,000, and at an aircraft factory she sold a picture of herself in *Jezebel* for $250,000 worth of bonds. In just two days, she sold $2 million worth of war bonds.

When Davis finished her trip with "Stars Over America," she returned to make one of her best pictures, *Now, Voyager,* with Paul Henreid, who started a nationwide craze of lighting cigarettes for women by putting two in his mouth, lighting them both, and then passing one to Davis.

=

Charles Laughton was another successful bond salesman. He sold $500,000 worth of bonds by reading the Bill of Rights on Wall Street and another $298,000 in a phone-in broadcast on the radio station WEAF from seven A.M. until midnight. "There were some bad moments on tour," he told a *New York Times* reporter.

> In Connecticut I experienced one of the worst things I have ever seen in my life. Eighteen thousand people had come to see me and other motion picture stars, while eight sailors who had been through blood and bullets at the battles of Midway and the Coral Sea remained in the background on the speakers' platform.
>
> Those fellows would rather go into battle than face an audience. They got up before the microphone all prettied up and they bumbled and fluffed and were miserable. Those men, who went through blood and filth to protect us, had to get up and appear foolish because people were buying war bonds.

The good moments came when Laughton found he could establish direct communication with his unsophisticated audiences across America simply by reading some poems and selections from the Bible, culminating, as he usually did, with Lincoln's Gettysburg Address. Then there was that supreme moment in a Times Square rally where the Treasury Department had assembled three coffins marked "Hitler," "Mussolini," and "Hirohito," and invited people to drive nails into them at the cost of one $18.75 bond (which would mature at $25) per nail. As a long line of nail drivers formed, Laughton drove the first one into

Counterclockwise from top left: *Selling bonds: Bette Davis sold a photograph of herself in* Jezebel *for $250,000 worth of bonds; Myrna Loy did a mock striptease, selling her hat and gloves for $55,000; Lana Turner puckered up for $50,000; Hedy Lamarr sold kisses for $25,000 apiece; Marlene Dietrich got only $1,025 per smooch (possibly because she had kissed so many GIs and generals for free). When they asked Dorothy Lamour to "take it off," she sold $10,000 worth of bonds without even having to remove her gloves.*

Hitler's coffin after proclaiming, "Who of these three men do I hate the most? Why, Hitler, of course! He started it and he bombed my house in London." Laughton sold $4,500 worth of bonds with this stunt. (It was noticed by at least one reporter that no one chose to drive nails into the Mussolini box—until finally a Greek couple decided the Italian dictator's coffin should not go unsealed. They drove two nails into it.)

For Laughton, who often felt great guilt for not serving his country at home and in uniform, the bond tour was an immensely rewarding experience. And at midnight, when he was signing off on the all-day WEAF radio marathon in a barely audible voice, he put his feelings into words. "It is," he said, "a duty and a privilege to buy bonds—the last chance to save the flickering flame of democracy. God help you and your children if that flame goes out."

Periodically the government would also arrange special bond-selling tours such as the one for Bud Abbott and Lou Costello, particular favorites of FDR. Once when they were at a White House dinner, the President asked them to come to his table. He said he watched their movies "in our little theater at the White House—and they're good for what ails me," although he confessed that Eleanor could not understand why he was laughing: "She doesn't get the jokes." The President also said, "Henry Morgenthau tells me that you two are the best salesmen for war bonds that he's got. I want you to know your country appreciates all the work you've done."

Then FDR asked one favor, that the comedians do their famous "Who's on First?" routine—which they naturally did. They got into it like this: "We've got a special request from the Prez," said Lou.

"Lou, I'm ashamed of you," Bud said.

"What'd I do now?" Lou asked.

"Honestly, referring to him as 'the Prez'!"

"That's better than what the Republicans call him."

"Now stop that!" Bud said. "You must show respect when you're invited to a gathering like this. Just look out there and what do you see?"

"A bunch of stuffed shirts," Lou replied.

"Don't talk like that. These newspapermen invited you to their banquet and you act like a guttersnipe. Have you no manners? Have you no sense of decorum? What have you got to say for yourself?"

Lou gazed at the audience, then stuck a finger in his mouth, and muttered, "I'm a ba-a-a-ad boy!"

"Now what were you trying to say?" Bud asked.

"I was trying to say that the Prez—I'm sorry, Abbott—that the Commander-in-Chief hasn't had time to go to the baseball park because he's too busy winning the war. So he'd like you to tell him who's playing for the Washington Senators these days."

"I'd be glad to. But you'll have to listen carefully. You see, a lot of the regular players are away in the service, and the new ones have strange names."

"Okay, tell me their names."

"Who's on first, What's on second, and I Don't Know is on third."

Needless to say, they brought down the (White) House.

In February 1943, they were sent on a whirlwind bond-selling tour, targeting eighty-five cities in thirty-six days with the troupe flying from city to city in a bomber and then being rushed to the auditorium or factory or school or theater where they were to appear. It was a difficult trip for both comedians. Abbott did not like to fly and said they were pushing their luck on this kind of trip (Costello once helped him out with his fear by putting a sleeping pill in his coffee at the airport and then betting $100 that Abbott would fall asleep "the minute he got on the plane"). And Lou had a hard time leaving Hollywood because two months before, his wife, Anne, had given birth to their first child, Lou Junior.

With audiences numbered in the thousands, Abbott and Costello would usually open their show with Lou yelling their trademark, "Heeeeeeeeeeeeeeeeey, Abbott." They told jokes, sang "God Bless America," and made their pitch for bond buying, often divvying up the audience, with Bud saying, "All right, Lou, I'll take this side over here. They're respectable people," and Lou would respond: "Okay, Bud. I'll take this side. They're a bunch of crapshooters. How 'bout it, crapshooters, can we beat those bankers? Who'll start with a thousand-dollar bond?"

The grueling tour ended in New York City, where they were greeted by Mayor Fiorello La Guardia. When they were done, they had sold $5 million worth of bonds, but it was a costly trip for Costello. He was running a fever and near collapse. A doctor said he might have influenza and should go to a hospital immediately. But Costello wanted to see his son, "Butch," so they headed for home.

He was still sick when he arrived. He saw Butch, was amazed at how much he had grown in a month and a half, then went to bed with a high fever, swelling in his joints, and an erratic heartbeat. The illness was finally diagnosed as rheumatic fever.

The government also organized another big bond tour, this one simply called the Cavalcade, involving several stars, including Fred Astaire, James Cagney, Judy Garland, Mickey Rooney, Greer Garson, Harpo Marx, Kathryn Grayson, Betty Hutton, the pianist José Iturbi, Paul Henreid, Dick Powell, and Kay Kyser and his band.

Astaire had just appeared in *You Were Never Lovelier* (his last picture with Rita Hayworth); he also completed *Holiday Inn* and *The Sky's the Limit* at about the time he went on his two bond trips. One of his biographers, Michael Freedland, says that for Astaire, these tours were "like the old Orpheum vaudeville circuit again—going from one tank town to another, singing a song one minute, dancing a number the next, and then a few minutes later holding out his hands and asking the audience to buy a bond for America."

The Cavalcade was similar to the Caravan, in that the whole group traveled together on the same train, with the stars hanging out in the observation car every night—Mickey Rooney playing the drums and singing with Judy Garland, José Iturbi accompanying Kathryn Grayson on the piano, and Cagney doing an occasional vaudeville routine.

Astaire remembered that Lena Horne joined the others in Washington but did *not* stay at the hotel where most of them were booked. Washington, of course, was still a segregated town then. Astaire was certain that Horne had declined to test the hotel's restrictions, even though she had arrived as a Hollywood star, with singing roles in recent movies—*Panama Hattie, Cabin in the Sky,* and *Stormy Weather.* (These last two were all-black films, but her other roles were usually carefully constructed so that they could be edited out for the southern market.) Horne was to have even more annoying experiences with World War II color barriers when she went on USO tours to entertain black troops.

Although most of the stars remembered the bond drives with fondness, for young Judy Garland it was a very difficult time. Her marriage had begun to come apart, her husband, David Rose, was now in the Army, and she had had an illegal abortion. She was also having problems on the set of *For Me and My Gal*—in which, ironically, she played a girl on a bond drive. The Cavalcade was a chance to get away and have some fun. She especially remembered one night when she went practically the whole length of the train at two A.M. waking people, saying: "I'm Judy Garland—would you possibly have a deck of cards?" (She eventually found one.) In fact, the fun and freedom she had on the 1942 Cavalcade inspired her successful "Judy's International Variety Show" on a nationwide tour in 1955.

Lana Turner said, "I appeared in so many cities that they're all blurred together in my mind. But I do remember a stopover in Chicago, where I ran into Johnny Meyer, a sort of right-hand man for Howard Hughes. He told me Hughes had enjoyed my pictures and was eager to meet me. Not long afterward Howard Hughes called me and asked me out to dinner."

Veronica Lake has her memories of Chicago too; they involved Gary Cooper and a night on the town. "There was Coop, myself . . . a few studio publicity types, and Rita Hayworth." When they arrived at a strip joint on State Street, "we were already bombed," she said, and up on the stage was "a flat-chested stripper wearing pasties, G-string, and a feather boa to cover an old appendectomy scar." As they got drunker, "Suddenly we were joined by a pasty-faced little girl wrapped in an oversize imitation of a fur coat." The girl stood around a few minutes and then said: "That's my sister up there."

Cooper, impressed, said, "I'll be damned," and asked her to have a seat. "Ain't that awful," the girl said, after she had joined the table and been offered a drink. "My sister having to take off all her clothes like that for all them guys to play with themselves under the table and like that."

Cooper was concerned: "Yeah, that's a terrible thing."

"Awful," Lake agreed.

"Sure is bad," the girl continued. "Guys all sit around lickin' their lips and all 'cause my sister lets 'em see her boobs."

Soon she was gone and Lake says she was certain the girl did not know who they were (although it's hard to imagine that you could find anyone in 1942 or 1943 who did not recognize either Cooper, Lake, or Hayworth).

The bond sellers continued their pilgrimage from strip joint to joint. In the last one, Cooper noticed the girl whose sister was condemned to letting the customers "see her boobs" sitting at a bar being fondled by a customer. Then she announced to the man at the bar: "Honey-pie, I gotta go dance now. Stay here and I'll give you a good time when I git back."

And, said Lake, "she blew a kiss in his ear, gave his bulging pants a squeeze, and left." Moments later she emerged on stage, announced as the Sensational Something-or-Other.

"I'll be damned," said Cooper. They decided to leave; as the party made its way to the door, the stripper snapped her G-string at one of the nation's all-time great screen lovers. "I've had it with bad whiskey," said Cooper. "Let's go back to the hotel and drink some good stuff."

According to Lake, they sat up all night drinking and listening to Cooper's off-color (but "never dirty") stories. By high noon the next day, the hard-partying bond seller would not be saving his town from a gunslinger but fighting off one of the great hangovers of World War II.

=

For the beautiful Gene Tierney, the bond tour was really "a learning time: about myself, my own insecurities, and a kind of show business I had never known." Tierney, the daughter of a New York stockbroker, attended boarding schools in Connecticut and Switzerland before cautiously and timidly going into the theater after her society debut. When Darryl Zanuck saw her in the play *The Male Animal,* he signed her to a 20th Century–Fox contract. By 1942, Tierney had appeared in a few films, including *Belle Starr* and *The Shanghai Gesture,* but had not yet made her two big movies, *Leave Her to Heaven* and *Laura.*

For beautiful actresses who did not sing or dance or comfortably strut around in a bathing suit (although Tierney could fill one out nicely) the problem on bond-selling tours was: What should they do? At the rehearsal for a show for servicemen emceed by Groucho Marx, Groucho suggested that at one point Tierney should do "a bump."

"A bump?" asked the future Laura.

"Yes, you know, like a bump and grind," replied Groucho.

"I don't think I'm the type."

"You can do it," Groucho assured her. "At least, give it a try."

"Well, anything for the boys," Tierney said gamely. As she later told the tale: "I went out and gave a bump and there was absolute, dead silence. No laugh, no reaction, nothing. The audience was as surprised as I was. A Marilyn Monroe could have done a bump and looked adorable. But not me. A bad judgment. I asked Groucho the next day if he wanted the bump again. 'No, no,' he said, 'leave it out!' He had decided I was no threat to Gypsy Rose Lee."

You can hardly imagine Jeanette MacDonald doing a bump and grind either. The performance she would remember most was given in September 1942 for the Army Relief Fund. MacDonald was backed by the 104th Cavalry Regimental Band and *not* accompanied by Nelson Eddy, her "singing sweetheart" in a number of syrupy musicals beginning with *Naughty Marietta* in 1935. She arrived on stage as the band played "The Star-Spangled Banner," and sang several Scottish ballads. Then, unabashedly, she told her audience that the encores would cost, say, five hundred dollars in contributions to the relief fund. There was no response, so she passed the hat herself while singing "Indian Love

Call." A man requested "One Dozen Roses"; she did not know the words to the song, but went backstage and quickly picked out a dozen roses from a bouquet an admirer had given her. She kept singing, but by the close of the evening had collected only a thousand dollars. So she sent girls out into the audience to collect and began singing songs on request in return for hundred-dollar donations. By the end of the evening she had raised $2,500, and over the course of eleven more concerts she raised a total of $94,681.87, including $169 for autographs. (One sailor declined an autograph even when she said it would be free. "You're a married lady," said the sailor, "and I don't think it would be right for me to be running around with your autograph in my pocket.")

On the other hand, Hedy Lamarr had no trouble at all selling kisses—at $25,000 each. She said she sold more than $17 million worth of bonds in one day. Lana Turner decided she would top that. She promised a kiss to anyone who would buy a $50,000 bond, "and I kept that promise—hundreds of times. I'm told I increased the defense budget by several million dollars." Marlene Dietrich also sold kisses for the Red Cross, but for some strange reason, she charged only $1,025 for the privilege of placing one's lips on that beautiful face. According to Kitty Kelley, Frank Sinatra sold his kisses for only $100.

In the early war years Sinatra had not reached the heights he would later attain as "Chairman of the Board." He'd appeared in two films (*Las Vegas Nights* and *Ship Ahoy*) as a vocalist in Tommy Dorsey's band; he had also become the darling of the adolescents who'd soon come to be called bobby-soxers. The scrawny young vocalist, who was making a thousand dollars or more per week in show business, was also "4-F"—unfit for service—and thoroughly hated by all the young men marching off to war. To compensate, Sinatra signed up for as many bond-selling tours as he could, which Myrna Loy said took real guts, "I thought, for a 4-F to go out there and go through all that. But he was willing to do it and they loved him. You could always count on Frank. All during the war he did broadcasts and rallies for President Roosevelt. Frank used to be a good Democrat."

Like MacDonald, Sinatra would also sell songs to the highest bidders—"Night and Day" once brought $500 and "The Song Is You" $10,000. Later, for WABC radio in New York, Sinatra also did a strip-tease, auctioning off his clothes for bonds—which must have made Hitler wonder just what kind of enemy he was up against.

Perhaps the most innovative bond-selling technique was recorded by Marlene Dietrich, who said that on one trip with Jimmy Durante, when nobody was buying, Durante finally said: "For all of you who will buy bonds, Marlene and me will wash all the windows in your house free of charge." For the next few weeks, Dietrich said many years later, "we did exactly what Jimmy had promised. I've still got a sore back to prove it."

But the most unusual war-bond sales pitch may have been made by Paulette Goddard to her ex-husband, Charlie Chaplin. This was at a time when the FBI was investigating Chaplin for what it considered questionable morals (and also looking into Goddard's contributions to left-wing causes). An FBI memo (which Chaplin learned about while trying to find out from highly placed friends why he was being investigated) revealed that, among other things, Goddard had advised Chaplin that considering the problems he was having with the government, "it would be a good idea for him to be first of all to buy a $1 million War Bond strictly for publicity." Good advice on several counts, but Chaplin did not follow it.

Meanwhile the stars kept selling bonds from those long trains "that rolled into cities where munitions plants were located," as Lana Turner put it. "At every stop, we were greeted by wildly cheering crowds, often mostly women. That sea of female faces—you knew that the men had gone to war."

=

By the end of July 1943, Mussolini had been replaced by Pietro Badoglio; and in September General Eisenhower announced Italy's surrender, although the Germans continued to fight Allied troops in Italy. In August, the Russians retook Kharkov, and the long battle to drive the Germans out of the Soviet Union was under way. In November, Allied leaders met at Tehran, where Stalin agreed to declare war on Japan after Germany was defeated. May 1944 was set as the target date for the Allied invasion of Europe, and the broad principles of a postwar United Nations were agreed upon.

In January 1944, the Allies landed easily at Anzio, near Rome, but met stiff resistance behind the beaches and could not break away from the coast until the end of May. Once out of the beachhead, however, they moved quickly, entering Rome on June 4. Two days later, the Allies hit the beaches of Normandy and launched the long drive to retake Paris and meet the advancing Russian armies in Germany. (Incidentally, Charles Boyer predicted the Normandy landings. On the evening of June 5, after hearing President Roosevelt speak on the radio announcing the fall of Rome and concluding with a prayer, Boyer startled his dinner guests by leaping up and shouting: "It's about to happen, I know it!" The next morning it did.)

EIGHT

Stars' War

National Archives

I made no bones about being terrified. . . . Others often thought me cool and calm and—sometimes—even funny. Usually only I knew my lighthearted banter was my particular form of hysteria. —DOUGLAS FAIRBANKS, JR.

Douglas Fairbanks, Jr., received his naval lieutenant's commission in April 1941, six months before Pearl Harbor, and was still in the Navy on V-E Day. The first volume of his memoirs, *Salad Days,* is devoted in part to his wartime experiences; the second volume, *A Hell of a War,* deals exclusively with them. In addition, several chapters of a biography by Brian Connell treat Fairbanks's war years. All this makes his war experience the most extensively described and best-documented of any of the Hollywood stars'.

Although in his memoirs Fairbanks stresses that he was no hero and was scared most of the time he was in action (and that some of his early assignments were primarily as an observer or trainee), he eventually carved out a significant role for himself as an expert on deception tactics and led some effective commando-like raids on several Mediterranean islands.

At the same time, no Hollywood star began the war more ignobly than Fairbanks. On December 7, he was assistant communications officer on the battleship *Mississippi* in the Atlantic. The *Mississippi* was in a convoy headed by a British flagship. On his watch, Fairbanks was mostly preoccupied with decoding routine messages when he received one that read "Air raid on Pearl Harbor this is not a drill." Fairbanks said, "It made no sense to me whatever; I tore it up and threw it in the wastebasket." Two messages later, he woke up: "What the hell was that?" he said, retrieving the message and running to the captain's office. In a few minutes, a message came blinking from the flagship: "Welcome to the party."

When the *Mississippi* returned to Norfolk to repair damage suffered during a storm at sea, the crew was not allowed ashore the first night. Everyone was ordered to attend the showing of a special film on the afterdeck. Fairbanks had "the duty" that night as officer-of-the-deck, more or less in charge of shipboard activities. He might have been exempt from watching the film, but was pressured by the top brass to put in an appearance. When the deck was darkened, Fairbanks gave "a huge gulp": The movie was *The Corsican Brothers,* which he'd made just before going on active duty. It was a swashbuckler, and soon the crew was yelling "Go get 'em, Doug," "Atta boy, loo-tenant," "Yoo-hoo, Dougie"—and worse when the love scenes came on.

As a result, "Dougie" was not unhappy when orders came transferring him to Washington—although the disrespectful "star treatment" continued. He was eventually transferred to the Office of Naval Intelligence, but soon the press reported that he was on duty in the capital; one congressman inquired of the secretary of the Navy whether Fairbanks's presence in Washington was due to "favoritism to a celebrity"?

Although the head of naval intelligence, Rear Admiral Alan Goodrich Kirk, had been quite friendly to and supportive of his star, he called Fairbanks into his office and accused him of seeking publicity. Fairbanks finally convinced Kirk that he did not have a press agent, preferred anonymity, and wanted to go to sea and experience some action—"That last a barefaced lie," he said, "but I made myself believe it."

Kirk said he was pleased to hear that. He was having Fairbanks assigned to sea duty because, frankly, his presence in Washington was an embarrassment to the Navy.

The "sea duty" turned out to be as executive officer (second in command) of the minesweeper U.S.S. *Goldcress,* operating out of Staten Island. The skipper must have been a big fan of Fairbanks, because after only a couple of months he gave him such a glowing fitness report that, as Fairbanks said, "not even the immortal [Admiral Horatio] Nelson could deserve such high marks."

The Navy decided that Lieutenant Fairbanks was now ready for real sea duty; soon after, he was transferred to the staff of Task Force 99. The force, headed by Rear Admiral Robert Giffen, was attached to the British fleet and operated out of Reykjavik and Scapa Flow. It consisted of a flagship, U.S.S. *Washington,* the carrier *Wasp,* two cruisers, *Wichita* and *Tuscaloosa,* and several destroyers. Before leaving for England, Fairbanks was invited to the White House to hear firsthand one of Roosevelt's fireside chats; the President, as he often did, greeted him with: "Well, Doug, have you made captain of the head yet?"

After serving on Admiral Giffen's staff for a few weeks with no fixed assignment, Fairbanks was made his flag lieutenant, responsible for the admiral's signals, messages, and general communications while at sea. In port, he was Giffen's social aide, keeping track of his visitors and ceremonial duties. Then one day, Giffen said that he had a "special duty" he was sure his flag lieutenant would enjoy. "I sensed by the way he spoke," said Fairbanks, "that I would not like it at all." The admiral also said: "If you come back safe—as I hope you will—and do well, I may send you on another job like this. I know you like lots of action and perhaps I'll send you on one of the Russian convoys. You'll enjoy that."

After he was dismissed, Fairbanks decided the admiral had seen too many old movies of him in action "and, damn it all, taken them seriously."

The "special duty" was aboard the *Wasp,* part of a convoy taking Spitfires and supplies to the besieged island of Malta in the Mediterranean. Fairbanks's assignment was as aide to Captain John Hall, representing Giffen, who could not go along on the mission. Giffen said Fairbanks would have some communication and gunnery duties. ("I know you don't know a helluva lot about either but Captain Hall will give you your cues.") But his most important mission was to write a detailed log of the operation.

The Malta trip was uneventful and Fairbanks had little to do, once even finding time, when the *Wasp* neared Trafalgar, to daydream about Admiral Nelson and his great victory. But Captain John W. Reeves brought him out of his reverie, shouting: "For Christ sake, Fairbanks, if you've got nothing to do, get the hell off the bridge."

The next mission—as part of a convoy of ships taking supplies to the Russians at Murmansk—was more exciting and dangerous. German submarines were regularly sinking ships headed for Murmansk, and the sailors hated the run—"hell below zero," they called it. Fairbanks was assigned to the *Wichita,* but before he left Scapa Flow, he experienced one of those incidents that would continually plague his naval career. When King George VI was paying Task Force 99 a formal visit on its flagship, the *Washington,* Fairbanks was lined up with Admiral Giffen's staff officers. As the king approached them, he recognized Fairbanks, seized his hand to shake, and said: "Well, what are *you* doing here? I haven't seen you since we played golf at Sunningdale's five years ago." The ship's photographer snapped a picture, which found its way to the press, and once again Fairbanks's shipmates jeered him—although more good-naturedly now, as he was gradually being accepted as one of them.

Fairbanks's assignment aboard the *Wichita* was described as "temporary additional duty," but despite this vagueness Fairbanks was accepted aboard in good spirits by the ship's crew. This was to be the largest convoy to Murmansk yet—thirty-five merchant ships accompanied by forty-seven British and U.S. naval vessels, including two battleships, one carrier, four cruisers, and twenty-four destroyers. Obviously, the Allies were expecting trouble, so they should have been ready for it. Oddly enough, it turned out that they weren't.

PQ-17, as the convoy was called, was continually attacked by German submarines and planes, as vividly recorded several times in Fairbanks's journal: "Reports of more enemy planes and U-boats are dogging the air," he wrote on July 4, 1942. "The radio room is bedlam. The bridge cannot keep up with reports. New flag signals are hoisted before the orders for previous ones can be executed. More enemy aircraft approach the convoy on its starboard side." Less than an hour later came a "shocking" message from the Admiralty: "Cruiser force must withdraw to westward at high speed."

Within fifteen minutes came another message: "Because of threats from main enemy surface forces, convoy PQ-17 is to disperse and proceed to Russian ports"—without any protection.

Two days later, Fairbanks wrote in his log: "We all feel we have run away. We cannot yet analyze the situation." When they finally did, the explanation was humiliating. The escorts accompanying the convoy had orders not to engage any German task force that included the battleship *Tirpitz.* When it, the heavy cruiser *Hipper,* and several destroyers, all supported by the Luftwaffe, were reported to be steaming along the Norwegian coast, naval intelligence assumed the Germans were forming a heavy task force that would have devastated the Allied ships accompanying convoy PQ-17. (However, it was later learned that the *Tirpitz* was not part of a big task force, and it soon returned to port.)

With the convoy's escort out of the way, German U-boats and torpedo bombers moved in for the kill. The result was a naval defeat that even Churchill conceded was "one of the most melancholy naval episodes in the whole history of the war." Of the thirty-five merchant ships in the convoy, only eleven made it to the Russian ports; the rest were lost at sea with cargoes of 430 tanks, 210 aircraft, and 100,000 tons of equipment. One hundred fifty-three men were lost on this run.

By July 12, the *Wichita* was safely back at Hafnarfjördhur, and when he reported to the flagship *Washington,* Fairbanks found that he had been ordered to London. Why, he did not know, but Admiral Giffen assured him that he had performed his duties "more than satisfactorily" and would be given a fine fitness report. Back in London, Fairbanks learned the reason for his transfer: Some time ago he had written his old friend Lord Louis "Dickie" Mountbatten, asking to serve on Mountbatten's Combined Operations staff, which was in charge of amphibious training for the eventual invasion of Europe. There were several Americans on the staff, which was charged with teaching American forces how the combined British and American Operations staff worked.

Fairbanks was assigned to the deception phase of the operation, designed to persuade the enemy that a planned amphibious assault was intended for somewhere other than its real target. He had been involved in this operation only a short time when he took part on the fringe of Operation Jubilee, a raid (August 19, 1942) on the French coastal town of Dieppe. He went out in a small boat with what he called the hocus-pocus group, but did very little in the operation. The press, however, learned that he was involved and someone reported that "Douglas Fairbanks, Jr., had been seen—face blackened, commando-style—on the beaches," which was unfortunate because, first, it was not true, and second, the Dieppe raid was soon deemed a colossal failure.

Fairbanks said that Mountbatten was "marvelous to me," and they maintained their friendship. But Mountbatten was finding that Fairbanks's celebrity status was not only embarrassing to the operation but threatened its security because so many people were aware of the star's comings and goings and curious as to what he was doing. Mountbatten said that although he eventually wanted Fairbanks to be his emissary on deception tactics to the American forces, he also wanted him to see some amphibious action to prepare him to take over an amphibious deception flotilla of small boats. Like Admiral Giffen, Mountbatten assumed that the swashbuckling Douglas Fairbanks, Jr., he knew from films was anxious to experience "the real thing at close quarters."

Fairbanks said he was "stunned." "My wits began to trip over themselves thinking of ways to 'beg out' of this proposal without seeming frightened, though I knew I was." He tried to get out of it by suggesting that British sailors would not want to take orders from him when they were in action, but Mountbatten simply replied: "Cross that bridge when you come to it."

He did, and soon found that he got along very well with the officers and men in the commando-training units. And after a few months of minor operations along the French coast, which Fairbanks survived (although some officers jealously said it would have been best for the Navy if he, or some celebrity like him, had become a casualty), he was ordered to report to Admiral Kent Hewitt, commander of the amphibious force of the U.S. Atlantic Fleet in Norfolk, Virginia. Fairbanks knew all about Operation Torch (the planned invasion of North Africa) and assumed that on Admiral Hewitt's staff, he would be part of it.

He was wrong. Although Admiral Hewitt accepted Fairbanks's ideas for deception teams operating in tandem with amphibious forces, Washington was cool. Hewitt nevertheless sent Fairbanks and another officer, an electronics expert, out to the universities to recruit "beach jumpers" to take part in Hewitt's deception plans for Operation Torch. Hewitt also tried to promote Fairbanks to lieutenant commander so that he could command the deception flotilla, but Washington disapproved. So a naval captain was put in charge of what Fairbanks felt were "his" beach jumpers—and Fairbanks was detached from Hewitt's staff and thus missed Operation Torch. He thought the explanation was simple: "I had wangled, conned and slid my way into official areas well beyond my real capabilities. . . . The official explanation . . . was that I just did not have the requisite rank to take over something this important."

The next Allied landing (it took place on July 10, 1943) was to be on Sicily. While that operation was being planned, Fairbanks rejoined Hewitt's staff, now headquartered in Algiers. Once again he was kept on the fringe of the invasion. This time the explanation was that a staff officer could not be in on the operation for fear that he might be captured and forced to tell what he knew about future plans. So Fairbanks saw the Sicily invasion from a distance on the headquarters ship, *Monrovia*.

He did have one interesting assignment, though. General George Patton, the commander of the American forces, was also stationed on the *Monrovia*; he asked Fairbanks to read and comment on his personal message to the men just before they embarked for the invasion: "I said I thought it was wonderful," Fairbanks says. "I suppose it was, in a rather corny, melodramatic way."

After the invasion started, the operations officer noticed that "Blue" beach was not being used. "Seeing me standing about on the bridge doing nothing," wrote Fairbanks, "he angrily ordered me to get the British staff liaison officer, go ashore and see why the hell nobody's using that beach." Fairbanks and the British officer landed and walked over the empty beach, looking for the officer in charge, the "beach master." When they found him, he said: "Thank God you're okay. You've just walked over a minefield"—which explained why the beach was not being used. As for the overall deception plan, Fairbanks maintained that it was successful: "The enemy was unable to decide whether Sicily, Sardinia or Greece was our principal objective until we were all well and truly landed."

After Sicily, Fairbanks and his small staff of technical experts in electronic deception had to prepare for a landing at Salerno. With the aid of a British army deception group (known as A Force), the strategic deception team in London (primarily concerned with providing deception for the forthcoming D-Day) worked out a plan to threaten the coast north of Naples, thereby pinning down German forces held in reserve there. This plan was unknown to Fairbanks's group.

The first phase of the plan called for a small task force, headed by the DD *Knight*, that would try to make the Italians defending the Pontine Islands (a communications center for the Germans) surrender without firing a shot. This was plausible because just before the invasion of Salerno the Allies had announced the surrender of Italy. But the deception task force could not be sure that the Italians defending the islands, prodded by the Germans who had not surrendered, would not put up a fight.

Under cover of darkness, the deception group convinced the forces defending a key island, Ventotene, to surrender. But after the three rockets signifying surrender went up, the commander of the operation, Captain Charley Andrews, decided that someone ought to go ashore and make sure the surrender was genuine. Fairbanks started to suggest how this might be done and Andrews misinterpreted his comments to mean he was volunteering.

Despite the navy's policy that staff officers should not be operational,

Fairbanks and three beach jumpers were sent ashore in a small boat. Fairbanks said he did not have the nerve to back out of the assignment—especially since the novelist John Steinbeck, covering the operation, had insisted on going along in another boat.

On shore, Fairbanks soon found himself in a confused situation, wandering around not knowing whether the rifle and machine-gun fire he heard was coming from the enemy or from his own men, who had gone in a different direction. What should he do? "Then in a silly ridiculous flash, I recalled Gary Cooper ducking a tough hombre's bullets in the night. Coop had flattened himself against a wall and slid quickly along it toward his target." Although, as he said, "none of my movies called for this sort of maneuver," he turned in a fine performance that might have won him an Oscar and did win him a Silver Star.

With not much searching, he found many Italians ready to surrender. However, when he regrouped with his own men, he also learned that on the northern tip of the island were about four hundred Germans, who were *not* ready to surrender. But apparently they had been fooled and did not know that the Allied "invasion force" on Ventotene consisted only of a few sailors, some OSS officers, a handful of beach-jumper experts in electronic deception, and one scared former movie star. After a one-day standoff during which they and the invaders exchanged sporadic fire, the Germans surrendered.

But Fairbanks's most unusual contribution to the Italian campaign was still to come. For some time, with official approval, he had been corresponding with one of his friends, the Duke of Aosta, nephew of Italy's King Victor Emmanuel III and first cousin to Italy's Crown Prince Umberto. As Fairbanks was returning to Hewitt's flagship with the victorious Ventotene "invasion force," his ship was approached by an Italian torpedo boat flying a large white flag. As it came closer, a voice came over a loudspeaker seeking "a U.S. Navy Lieutenant Fairbanks." The boat had a message from the duke: If the Allies came quickly they could take the Isle of Capri. The Germans were vacating it. Aosta also offered Fairbanks a fleet of torpedo boats to help in the operation. A small landing party, with the Italians leading the way through the minefield in the Bay of Naples, took Capri with little opposition.

Fairbanks was awarded the Silver Star for his participation in the planning and execution of the amphibious assault on Italy, especially at Ventotene, where he "courageously led an armed reconnaissance" under fire. Fairbanks says the language explaining the citation "was so damned exaggerated and embarrassing that if I had had a bit more integrity I would have declined it." Instead, he said, "I accepted it graciously." As for the Capri operation, Aosta's cousin, King Umberto II, later awarded him the Italian War Cross, which he also accepted graciously.

Fairbanks had a minor role in other operations along the Italian coast and then, after a bout with the flu and being promoted to lieutenant commander, he was given leave to return home for a while. In Washington, he was still unable to convince the brass that a special section in war planning devoted to deception was warranted. He also found that the "Chairborne Brigade" questioned whether Fairbanks the movie star had ever had any real sea duty or seen any real action.

On his return to the European theater, Fairbanks's next major operation was the Anzio landing. He went ashore a few times without incident, but the sight of dead bodies started him wondering why he was there at all. He knew he was a "closet coward. Would I not have better

Douglas Fairbanks, Jr., with Admiral Raymond Fenard, chairman of the French Naval Mission in the United States, after being made a chevalier of the French Legion of Honor and receiving the Croix de Guerre. National Archives

served the cause by being a supporting celebrity at home, speaking publicly and making movies?" And what possible difference did his service "make to any resolution of the worldwide conflicts? None!" he concluded.

But Fairbanks continued his curious career of repeatedly being reminded of his celebrity status and winning medals while admittedly scared. In preparation for a landing on Elba, he had had to fly to Corsica, but when British admiral Sir John Cunningham informed Corsica that he was coming, some wit wired headquarters: IS AIR COMMAND CARTING FAIRBANKS OVER TO LOOK FOR HIS CORSICAN BROTHER? Admiral Cunningham did not think this was funny and wired back: I KNOW OF NO MORE URGENT BUSINESS IN CORSICA THAN THAT WE HAVE COMMISSIONED LT CMD FAIRBANKS TO DO. Fairbanks's participation in the Elba operation, in which he led a small, diversionary landing party, earned him a French Croix de Guerre.

Next came Operation Anvil (also called Dragoon), aimed at southern France and designed to take pressure off the Allies at Normandy. Fairbanks's men had to make a parachute jump; in the tradition of commanding officers who would not ask their men to do anything they would not do, he signed up for parachute training. But when the moment came to jump, he said: "I just plain chickened out." However, he otherwise conducted himself honorably, taking part in a naval action for which he was awarded another French medal, becoming a chevalier of the Legion of Honor. He was also awarded the Royal Navy's Distinguished Service Cross for his Mediterranean operations. All this prompted Fairbanks to say that he was "greatly over-rewarded" for his wartime service, especially in view of "my really 'scaredy-cat' wish to run away."

But he stuck it out for the duration, spending the rest of the war mostly in the Mediterranean theater. Later, Admiral Hewitt would say that Fairbanks "was constantly trying to contribute the maximum toward winning the war and making good as a naval officer, while avoiding any appearance of capitalizing in any way on either his own or his father's reputation as an actor. . . . I was happy to have him with me."

LIEUTENANT ROBERT MONTGOMERY

I reached the limit of my endurance
standing idly by without doing something.

National Archives

After a brief tour of duty in the White House in late 1941, Montgomery volunteered for sea duty and was sent to the torpedo-boat school in Connecticut. But before he went, he narrated a half-hour nationwide radio broadcast, "This Is War"—the first in a series of thirteen programs that would help make America conscious of the war. "Take heart, resist much," he told his country and the world. "Fight how you can. We are building for you. We are on the move."

However, Douglas Fairbanks, Jr., and his friends were complaining that Montgomery had become "inexplicably pompous and indescribably stuffy." They wondered if his Washington duty had gone to his head.

When he finished the torpedo-boat course, Montgomery commanded PT boats in the Panama Canal area and then in the South Pacific, where he saw action at Guadalcanal and the Marshall Islands, made a lieutenant commander, came down with malaria, and lost twenty-two pounds.

In the summer of 1943, after a month's convalescence at home, he was given training in New England, where he learned how to be a deck officer on a destroyer. Then he was assigned to an Atlantic Fleet destroyer that took part in the Normandy invasion. Montgomery's ship was the first to enter Cherbourg harbor and he received a Bronze Star, for "meritorious achievement" during the operation.

After the invasion of Europe, Montgomery was sent back to the states and given his release so he could play Lieutenant John Bulkeley in Hollywood's version of *They Were Expendable*, which, as we will see, would cause John Wayne no end of anguish. There is very little information about Montgomery's war record because he was always reluctant to discuss it.

JAMES STEWART

*I had a lot of close calls. . . . The whole thing
was a close call. . . . But I was just doing my duty.*

After James Stewart won his wings, he thought he was headed overseas as a pilot. But the Air Corps decided to use him in a public relations job, doing a radio show. "My instructions were to make soldiers laugh," said Stewart, who had had very few comedy roles before he entered the service. "For three months I traded so many jokes with Edgar Bergen and Charlie McCarthy that I was beginning to feel that I, too, had been carved out of wood."

But he persisted in his efforts to see action and was finally sent to flight instructor school at Kirland Field, New Mexico. There he learned to fly four-engine bombers. "When I was transferred to heavy bombers," he said, "I had to work pretty hard at subjects I'd forgotten and was never any good at anyway. Math, for instance."

He must have satisfied his officers, though, because he was soon made a first lieutenant and a flight instructor. "A cushy job," said one officer. "Stewart could have been doing that until the war ended but he kept asking for European or Pacific assignments."

In July 1943, Stewart made captain; in November, his requests for overseas duty took him to England to join the 445th Bombing Group flying B-24 raids over Europe. Before leaving the United States he had a long talk with his father, asking him if he had ever been afraid while soldiering in the Spanish-American War and World War I. "Every man is, son," Stewart's father said, "but just remember you can't handle fear all by yourself. Give it to God. He'll carry it for you." And just to make sure God was walking with his son, Stewart's father gave him an envelope to take with him but not to be opened "until you're in transit." It contained a copy of the Ninety-first Psalm.

Just eleven days after arriving in England, Stewart went on his first bombing mission with the 703rd Bombing Squadron on a raid over the naval base at Kiel, Germany: "Stewart was a damned good commanding officer," said one of his navigators, "even if he went rigidly by the book. But I always had the feeling that he would never ask you to do something he would not do himself. Everything that man did seemed to go like clockwork."

An officer in the group's photography division said, "Stewart supplied us with some of the best pictures we had. And you could always count on his reports."

Stewart never had the trouble Fairbanks did with being a movie star, in part because of his inherent shyness and in part because of his zealous efforts to keep out of the limelight. He even went up in a plane whenever he heard that reporters and photographers would be visiting the base. Only once did it appear that Stewart was taking advantage of his star status. He was thought to have tried to communicate with the royal family without going through channels. It turned out that one of his fans had asked the queen mother to forward a message to him; the Army exonerated him, after a considerable stir in the press.

Figuring he was comfortable in front of a camera, the Air Corps did ask him to conduct some news briefings for newsreel photographers, but Stewart became so flustered they had to start over. "In Hollywood," he told reporters, "they let you do things over, but out here, the first take is what counts."

From November 1943, until he left England at the end of the summer of 1945, Stewart flew twenty combat missions, some extremely hazardous and some worthy of commendation. He received an Air Medal for a raid on Bremen, an Oak Leaf Cluster for a Berlin raid, and a Distinguished Flying Cross for a raid on a Braunschweig, Germany, aircraft factory in which Stewart displayed courage that was, according to the citation presented by General James Doolittle, "in large measure responsible for the success of the mission."

Did he experience fear during combat? Stewart, characteristically, never talked much about his Air Corps experience, but he told one reporter that although there were plenty of bombing runs when he did not think he would get back, there just wasn't time to think about it. "Afterwards, well, you thought for a few seconds and then before you knew it you were up there again."

His biggest fear when piloting his bomber over Europe, he said, was that "I'd make a mistake at the controls, make a wrong decision. A lot of guys depend on you when you're in charge. . . . Fear of mistake was stronger than fear for my personal safety.

"Our group had suffered heavy casualties during the day," he said, recalling one particular night, "and the next morning at dawn I would have to lead my squadron out again, deep into enemy territory. Imagination can become a soldier's worst enemy. Fear is an insidious and

Jimmy Stewart receiving one of his decorations. National Archives

deadly thing; it can warp judgment, freeze reflexes, breed mistakes. Worse, it's contagious. I knew my own fear, if not checked, could infect my crew members and I could feel it growing in me."

That's when he would remember his father and the Ninety-first Psalm, which reads: "I will say of the Lord, He is my refuge and my fortress. . . . his truth shall be thy shield and buckler. . . ."

Stewart reread it and "felt comforted, felt that I had done all I could."

STERLING HAYDEN

*The challenge now is to devise some way to dance
on the coals of war, to give an illusion of a stalwart
man of action on a constant quest of danger.*

National Archives

After giving up a Hollywood career to help England win the war (and pursue the woman he was desperately in love with), breaking his legs in training as a British commando, and returning to America to enlist in some branch of the service, Sterling Hayden discovered an alarming fact about himself.

Coming back to the States, the Norwegian freighter on which he was a passenger was attacked by a submarine. This was the real thing, thought Hayden, sitting in the mess. A steward said, "Now is the time I don't envy those engineers."

Suddenly, Hayden knew the truth: "A stroke of terror" stunned him, he wrote in his autobiography. "And all at once he knew that the thing he most feared was true. He was yellow."

He and Madeleine Carroll were married in Peterborough, New Hampshire, and settled down in their little house in Connecticut—where, Hayden said, he would gladly have stayed "until the war was finished and gone." But America was in it now; Hayden decided to become a torpedo boat officer. The Navy, however, said that despite all his sea experience, it could not give a lieutenant's commission to a man who had dropped out in the tenth grade. He turned down an ensign's commission, which would not have given him command of a PT boat.

Then he had another idea: "I was vastly intrigued by the thought of hauling freight in wartime." After Carroll put up the money to buy out Paramount's half of the *Spinney*, Hayden was given a draft deferment to haul ninety-five tons of explosives from Port Everglades in Florida to San Juan, Puerto Rico. But the Coast Guard said the *Spinney* wasn't built to haul explosives, so instead he took aboard 112 tons of general cargo for Curaçao in the Netherlands Antilles. The trip was a thirty-two-day disaster during which his crew nearly mutinied. When he arrived in Curaçao he found that the *Spinney* had leaked, damaging his cargo. He got drunk with a bunch of local marines and by the time he returned to New York, he had made another decision:

> It was four in the morning when I joined Madeleine in a room at the Beekman Towers Hotel. We had champagne with breakfast on a tiny terrace above the East River, with high-breasted tugs sweeping downstream and the sun rising over Brooklyn. At nine sharp I picked up the phone directory, got the address of the Marine Corps recruiting station, and within the hour I had enlisted for boot training at Parris Island in South Carolina. My image shone brighter than ever.

But at Parris Island, he experienced the same thing many stars would endure in the service—especially glamour boys like Sterling Hayden. "You! You big guy there in the middle. Take three steps forward," the Marine sergeant said on the occasion of their first meeting on the drill field. "So this is the big-shot actor from Hollywood. Well, Hayden, let me tell you if you think just because you're married to Madeleine Carroll, you're going to get special treatment down here, you got another think coming. . . . Because, Buster, let me tell you, and this goes for the rest of you slobs, beginning now I want you to know the shit's on good."

This was especially tough on a sensitive young man who had made a decision *not* to be a star. Wherever he went he got the star treatment anyway. He thought it might help to change his name, so he went to court and became John Hamilton for the duration. Despite the tough sergeants at boot camp, he made it to officer candidate school in Quantico, Virginia. Then he decided that maybe Bill Donovan would not mind the fact that he was a Hollywood star. He applied for OSS and became one of three men in his camp transferred to it; 80 percent of his fellow Marine officers went to the Pacific.

John Hamilton and a Navy enlisted man who spoke perfect Greek were sent to Cairo. Their instructions, in Hayden's words, were something about "getting together a group of escapees from Greece, fitting out a cargo ketch, and running her up through the Greek islands."

When they reported to Cairo and told the British officer who would be commanding them about their assignment, the officer said, "The British have that sewn up." Hayden asked what he thought they ought to do, and the officer replied: "Well, Hamilton, a report has just come in that there is a man named Tito up in Yugoslavia. They say he's a Communist, but apparently he's in control of quite a large guerrilla organization, so why don't you hop up to Bari, Italy, and locate our Major Huot and see whether you can be of some service."

Hayden was certain he detected an immense sigh of relief from the British officer when he produced the papers ordering him and the Navy enlisted man to Italy. And no sooner did he arrive in Bari than he experienced what he called the birth of John Hamilton ("He died, three years later . . . in West Hollywood"). As Hamilton, Hayden discovered: "Good Christ—I'm not a coward at that." He made this discovery out on the end of a dock at Bari; an air raid was in progress and, ignoring an instinct to run, he paused to offer a cigarette to a Yugoslav partisan who was blazing away at the German planes with a pistol. When he lit the man's cigarette, he noticed to his surprise that his hands were not shaking.

Now he was working with men whose spirit made anything he'd seen before seem sophomoric. They were Yugoslav Communists who had been fighting Nazis for years under a real, honest-to-God Communist named Tito. Hayden said that "if the U.S.A. hadn't even heard of Tito until a few weeks ago—they had better find out what was what in the world."

Three days after he arrived, Hayden/Hamilton was put in charge of four hundred Yugoslavs (fifty of them women) and ordered to establish a partisan base at Monopoli, about twenty-five miles east-southeast of Bari. They had twenty-two vessels of various sizes and their main job was to run supplies to the partisan island of Vis, off the Dalmatian coast. Hayden continued to be impressed by the intensity and dedication of the Communists.

He had his share of war stories to tell in his autobiography, *Wanderer*. Although pleased to have discovered he was not a coward, he also learned that he could not kill a man; once he raised his rifle barrel before he shot at an enemy who was in his gunsight. He also became fed up with the High Command when it held back supplies and armaments from the Communist partisans: "My dear chap," a British officer told one of Hayden's partisans, "there are such things as politics to be considered, you know."

After a few months of guerrilla warfare, Hayden learned still more about himself: He did not want to be buried in the middle of the night (as most partisan fighters were) in some lonely grave in the woods. And the emerging Sterling Hayden "was no selfless radical, no reckless humanitarian." He said he felt like a traitor the first night he had that thought.

Then he came down with jaundice and spent long periods at OSS headquarters in Bari talking with himself—or rather, with Lieutenant Hamilton. "Hamilton boy, you better wise up. You better . . . just take care you come out of this fucking war in one piece."

He would occasionally see Madeleine, who was stationed in Foggia, so when he was given a thirty-day leave, he went home to Connecticut to see his mother, and to Hollywood, where he made another discovery: "There's nothing wrong with being a movie star. You could go around the country in between films. You could talk to kids in schools, not about socialism, because you don't care that much about it, but about questions that have been troubling you." He made his decision: Once the war was over, he would "return to Hollywood, claw his way to the top, and become the only actor out there whose stardom was justified."

In February 1945, he went back to Paris, where he was told to report to the First Army, which was in the Ardennes Forest recovering from the Battle of the Bulge. Colonel B. A. Dixon, the G-2 (intelligence officer), asked him what the hell a Marine captain was doing there. Before Hayden/Hamilton could reply, Dixon said: "You're OSS! Ten thousand dollars says you're one of Donovan's beagles. Right?"

Colonel Dixon poured Hayden a drink and as the other officers in the room were laughing, he proceeded to let Donovan's beagle know what "real soldiers" thought of them: "The OSS is the most fantastic damned organization in all of our armed forces. Its people do incredible things. They seduce German spies; they parachute into Sicily one day and two days later they're dancing on the St. Regis roof. They dynamite aqueducts, urinate in Luftwaffe gas tanks, and play games with I. G. Farben and Krupp, but ninety percent of this has not a goddamned thing to do with the war."

The officers laughed and poured another drink and so did Hayden.

The colonel had closed his little speech by saying: "Hamilton, when you get tired of being mysterious we'll put you to work." Hayden accepted the invitation. His first (and only) major assignment before the war ended was to photograph bomb damage in fifty-three ports from Germany to Norway. When he asked why—"Are we getting ready for the third world war?"—the colonel did not laugh.

The final irony of Sterling Hayden's World War II adventure came in France, where he separated from the woman who was partly responsible for his romantic rush off to war. "We knew without knowing why, without much discussion, that the marriage had dissolved." It was agreed that he would get a divorce in Reno. Madeleine had an apartment in Paris and "spoke longingly of remaining in Europe for several years."

He had delivered some supplies to her apartment and was preparing to leave, trying to avoid her eyes, when Madeleine said: "Would you, before you leave—have just one glass of sherry."

Hayden was given a citation from Tito and awarded a Silver Star by the OSS. "Was there another man on earth," he asked in his autobiography, "who didn't know why he had it?"

CLARK GABLE

admitting to John Lee Mahin that he was scared in combat

Yes, it's murder up there. They're falling
like moths. Like dying moths.

National Archives

When the word went around that Clark Gable was coming to officer candidate school in Miami Beach, the men could not believe it. With his pull he should be going to officers' training school with a commission already in hand, rather than to OCS, where, as journalist A. E. Hotchner, who graduated in the class ahead of Gable's, said: "The object of the course was to crack you. . . . You were kept in a state of nervous and physical exhaustion."
Hotchner's view is probably an exaggeration; I went through a similar program in the Navy and it was just a routine four-month course. Any intelligent young man in good health could have passed it. On the other hand, Gable was forty-one.

The first days were tough. It didn't help when Gable was a day late reporting because there were so many people waiting to see him at the station in New Orleans, where he had to change trains, that he missed his connection to Miami. According to his biographer Lyn Tornabene, he also had the misfortune to report to OCS with a Hollywood photographer, who in the first few days virtually never left his side. "Gable is the only private in the history of the Army," one officer said, "who had his own orderly."

He was asked to pose for photographers when he shaved off his mustache (he later let it grow back). Women gathered in the streets of Miami Beach to see him marching to and from classes and mess— although without his mustache and with an overseas cap and wilted khaki shorts (the temperature was over a hundred degrees almost every day Gable was at OCS) he was practically anonymous, for the first time since he became a movie star.

Gradually, however, Gable was accepted by his fellow classmates not only as a regular guy, but as a natural-born officer—at least in appearance: "The day he walked in," said a Philadelphia radio executive who was in school with Gable, "he had more military bearing than most of the men had when they left, partly because of his natural posture and partly because he was an actor."

Being an actor also helped Gable in his classwork, which consisted mostly of learning mimeographed material given to the officer candidates: "Gable would sit through the class," said the radio executive, "looking like he was half-asleep and you'd wonder whether he was listening at all. Then he would get top grades in his exams. One day I asked him how he did it. He said, 'It's easy; I memorize everything on the sheet and give it back to them.' It was just like studying a script to him."

On watch at night, Gable also talked about the death of his wife; there were some who thought he had a death wish. But he passed the course and was popular enough with the 2,600 would-be officers he trained with that they asked him to speak for them at graduation: "The important thing, the proud thing, I've learned about us," said Gable, "is that we are men. . . . Soon we will wear the uniforms of officers. How we look in them is not very important. How we *wear* them is a lot more important."

Not long after graduation, Gable learned that General Hap Arnold wanted him to organize a team to shoot a film about aerial gunners. They had suffered so many casualties that they were becoming an endangered species; the Air Corps hoped a film would stimulate interest in aviation gunnery. So Gable's first assignments were in gunnery and photography schools at Tyndall Field, Florida, and Fort Wright in Spokane, Washington. Once again his fans started mobbing him, which prompted an Army press release: "Lieutenant Gable [he made first lieutenant when he graduated from gunnery school] will appreciate it if the public will not interfere with his training. He wishes to be treated like every other member of the Service."

After Fort Wright, Gable reported to Colonel William Hatcher's 351st Heavy Bombardment Group of the Eighth Air Force's First Air Division. His assignment: "making a training film showing the day-to-day activities of a typical heavy bombardment group" with special attention to the role of gunners in protecting the bombers. Gable chose as his writer a friend from Hollywood, John Lee Mahin, the scriptwriter on *Too Hot to Handle* and *Boom Town*. Mahin was in combat intelligence and at first did not want to work with Gable, finally saying he would "if I couldn't get a better job," a remark he would regret. Colonel Hatcher flew Gable to New Mexico to pick up Mahin, who told Gable's biographer that he was somewhat surprised at how serious Gable seemed on their first meeting in the service: "He looked a little stunned. He didn't know whether he was going to be any good at what he was committed to. I had that feeling. An actor worrying about his role, really. He had a role to play, damn it. He was America's hero going out to help, to be with the kids, none of whom believed he was going to do anything at all."

In fact, the "kids"—his fellow officers and crewmen of the 351st—did not think Gable was really going to go up there and get shot at when they got to Europe. They also resented what they all called "the Little Hollywood Group" that was flying around the country and spending a lot of time in Hollywood recruiting a film team. Now Gable had to prove all over again that he was just a regular guy. He was still the king—and as his biographer pointed out, "sometimes he didn't know when he behaved like one."

In April 1943, the 351st was assigned to Polebrook, an air base about eighty miles north of London, and at first even Mahin had trouble with Gable acting the star: "Suddenly, I found the Colonel and Clark going off to London or Clark going to parties" without asking him. Mahin finally said, "Wait a minute, bub. You and I are equals in this thing now. I don't want any of this stardom. I want to be in on the fun, too."

Gable then confessed that he was still smarting from Mahin's initial reluctance to join him, but said, "Okay. Come on, let's get drunk."

So there was no more stardom bit with Mahin, but the kids were still wary. When Gable exited the plane after his first combat mission, they said it must have been a milk run. "It wasn't, really. . . ." said Mahin. "He was damned near killed" by a twenty-millimeter shell that came through his cabin. His second mission was a tough one, too, and after that "the kids adored him. They couldn't stay away from him," said Mahin.

The movie fans in England couldn't stay away from him either. One woman jumped on his back in Blackpool; Mahin had to literally pull her off. British royalty invited him to dinner, and Hermann Göring offered any German pilot who could bring Gable back to the base for dinner a promotion, a leave, and a cash reward. But Gable refused to carry phony identification papers. "How could I hide a face like this?" he said. "If the plane goes down, I'll just go with the son of a bitch."

Mahin was very much aware that Gable still missed Carole Lombard, but he did quietly pursue other women, sometimes "strange-looking women," said Mahin, some so ugly that "the kids wouldn't have believed it." But he "seemed to think he got into less trouble with the ugly ones."

Although Gable probably did not have a death wish, the officers and men he worked with gradually came to realize that he was taking more chances than he had to. Frank Capra said that when he was in London working on a film, he asked one of Gable's commanding officers how the star was doing, and the general replied: "The damn fool insists on going on bombing missions and he wants to be a gunner yet. No officer mans a gun; the guy's crazy. You know what it would do to us if he gets himself shot? . . . He gives me the willies. He's trying to get himself killed."

The Air Corps was getting really worried—and after it had fifty thousand feet of film about aerial bombardment in the can, it decided to send Gable, Mahin, and their Little Hollywood Group home. Gable was awarded an Air Medal "for superior performance of duty" and other appropriate commendations, none of which, Gable insisted, were "hero's medals." He was going home with what he considered the most important thing: the respect of the officers and men he fought with: "Everybody thought he was great," said one sergeant who served with the 351st.

When Gable and Mahin returned to the States, they quickly learned how it was in the Army in war when General Arnold said: "Well, Clark, what was it I sent you to Europe for? I've forgotten."

"To make a film," Gable replied. "There was a gunner problem, sir."

The general replied: "Oh, we've licked that."

Gable was apparently dumbstruck, so Mahin replied, "Well, we've got all that footage, so we'll have to think of something else to do with it."

"Go out and do anything you want, any way you want to," the general replied—and Gable was assigned to Fort Roach in Culver City, where the Signal Corps had set up its Hollywood film studio. But since he was free to work anyplace he wanted to, he chose MGM, where he felt more at home.

In December 1943, he also signed a twelve-year contract with MGM for $7,500 a week, guaranteed only forty workweeks, to make two movies a year. The contract would go into effect the day he left the Signal Corps. And the next month he started to work with Mahin and editor Blanche Sewell trying to make something out of the film they had brought home from Europe. He also was asked to play the role of the returning hero for Air Corps promotion and bond-selling campaigns. His first assignment was one of the most difficult he had had since entering the Army: to preside over the launching of the Liberty ship *Carole Lombard*. Irene Dunne christened the ship and Gable wept when the champagne bottle hit the bow.

Nothing significant was ever made from Gable's Air Corps footage. In addition, he became tired of being used by such groups as the Motion Picture Alliance for the Preservation of American Ideals, which gradually developed into a red-baiting organization. In June 1944, after D-Day and with no real orders from the Army yet, Gable asked to be relieved of his duties.

His first film after returning to Hollywood was *Adventure*, with Greer Garson. "Gable's back and Garson's got him" was the theme of the movie's publicity campaign.

HENRY FONDA

*I don't want to sell war bonds or be photographed
with soldiers and sailors. I want to be a sailor.*

At thirty-seven, Henry Fonda had already had a phenomenal career in Hollywood. He had gone almost immediately from Broadway, where he had starred in the 1934 production of *The Farmer Takes a Wife*, to make the play into a movie. Then he followed it up with an incredible string of major movies, including *The Trail of the Lonesome Pine, You Only Live Once, Jezebel, Spawn of the North, Jesse James, Young Mr. Lincoln, Drums Along the Mohawk, The Grapes of Wrath, The Return of Frank James, The Lady Eve, The Male Animal,* and *The Big Street.*

He was also married to a charming socialite, the former Frances Seymour Brokaw, and had two lovely children, Jane and Peter, both of whom wanted to be movie stars like their famous father.

But Father wanted to be a sailor, an urge that hit when he was making *The Ox-Bow Incident.* As he explained to Frances: "The wives and mothers of a lot of soldiers and sailors'll see me on the screen and say: 'Why isn't he out there?' " Although he was thirty-seven, he said, "I still look like a baby."

But there was more: "Frances, this is my country and I want to be where it's happening. I don't want to be in a fake war in a studio or on location. I'm not crazy about the idea of getting hurt, but I want to be on a real ocean, not the back lot. I want to be with real sailors not extras."

So the day after he finished *The Ox-Bow Incident,* without telling any-one—especially 20th Century–Fox or its publicity department—Fonda enlisted in the Navy. As an enlistee, he was given a twenty-four-hour pass before having to report for duty—which was just long enough for 20th Century's boss, Darryl F. Zanuck (who was a lieutenant colonel in the Signal Corps), to go into action. In his autobi-ography, Fonda recounted what happened when he arrived at the Navy's San Diego boot camp: "The Shore Patrol picked me up and shipped me right back to where I came from. Why? Because Darryl F. Fuck-It-All Zanuck had pull in Washington and demanded, 'I want Henry Fonda for a picture I'm planning. It's for the war effort and I need him.' And he had enough weight to swing it. So there I was back in Imperial Valley, California, the hottest part of the desert, making a film called *The Immortal Sergeant.*"

Fonda said the plot of *The Immortal Sergeant* was a simple one: "I won World War II single-handed."

After he finished *Sergeant,* Zanuck let him go into the Navy to really help his country win the war. In boot camp, Fonda later said, "for the first time in my life I gained weight," despite the fact that by the end of camp he was jogging three miles a day. When he made ordinary sea-man third class, he wanted to be a gunnery mate, logically figuring that "we're in a shooting war and the gunners did the shooting."

But after he filled out the aptitude questionnaire, an old chief petty officer called him into company headquarters and said to him: "You know what the fucking gunners' mates do in this man's fucking Navy."

The chief did not elaborate but let Fonda know that "you're too smart to be some fucking gunner's mate. You're officer material."

Fonda did not want to be an officer: "I'll be stuck on some damn shore station doing public relations work for the rest of the war."

"You wanna go sailing on the pretty ocean?" was the chief's reply. "Okay, wise-ass, sixteen weeks in quartermasters' school." In the Navy, a quartermaster has to know how to keep the books and assist the navigation officer; quartermasters are also trained as signalmen. They are usually picked from the brightest kids in camp.

When Fonda became a quartermaster third class, he was assigned to a new destroyer, the USS *Satterlee*, about to be launched in Seattle. The *Satterlee*'s first port of call was San Diego, where he was given a week's liberty. Quartermaster Henry Fonda hitchhiked home. Then he returned to San Diego, where once again his superiors said they wanted to make him an officer. This time Fonda agreed, but said he would like to stick with the *Satterlee* on its trip through the Panama Canal to Norfolk, Virginia (it had been ordered to join two other destroyers as escorts for the British aircraft carrier *Victorious*).

When they arrived in Norfolk, Fonda and the signalman first were given shore leave; they did what most sailors away from home do— they tried to drink all the liquor in town.

The next morning, when Quartermaster Third Class Fonda went to the naval training station in Norfolk, en route to New York (where he was supposed to report to 90 Church Street), he was still drunk. Fortunately, someone recognized him and put him on the train to New York. Fonda did not remember much about the trip. But he did remember that at 90 Church Street they told him to report to Washington— where he was told he'd be making training films. He started "bellowing and bitching" to a full commander, who fortunately did not like being stuck behind a desk himself. So when Fonda told him he really wanted to be in air combat intelligence, the commander sent him to officer candidate school in Quonset, Rhode Island. And there he got from an old ACI officer, speaking in a lowered voice, some of the most important advice he would get before going overseas: "Take all the liquor you can carry. Now, it's a well-known fact that liquor is not allowed in the United States, not on any shore installation, not aboard any ship. But you will find that it is barter. Don't take it because you want a drink, but you might find yourself in a position where your admiral wants a jeep or a shore boat or whatever it is, and the only way you can get that jeep or that shore boat or whatever is with a jug of something."

Fonda graduated at the top of his class; like Gable, he found that learning classwork at OCS was mostly memorizing mimeographed workbooks. "That's one thing I've always had, the ability to memorize. If I read the theatrical page of the *Los Angeles Times* twice, I've got it down whole."

When he boarded the train for home leave, his luggage included a parachute bag that he would not let anyone touch because it contained fourteen bottles of bourbon. At home, he became so emotional, he decided "I didn't want to leave my family"—especially when Jane, who was at Brentwood School, sang "Anchors Aweigh" to him one night at bedtime, adding at the end:

> Heads up and shoulders back,
> That's the way to stand.
> Fill up your lungs
> And let them hear you shout to beat the band
> No matter where you are,
> Make people say:
> That child's a credit to
> The Brentwood Town and Country School. Hooray!

After spending a week with Frances in San Francisco at the Mark Hopkins Hotel, Fonda kissed her good-bye, saying, "Take care of the kids and take care of yourself." She squeezed his hand and said: "I'm not going to war, Hank, you are. Good luck."

In Hawaii, Fonda took a course in anti-submarine warfare, then was assigned to Admiral John H. Hoover's staff, which served under Fleet Admiral Chester Nimitz. In February 1944, after nearly a year in the Navy, he was flown to Kwajelein in the Marshall Islands to join Admiral Hoover's staff. Here he had his first look at the real fighting Navy: "It was an awesome sight. The lagoon was enormous and it was filled with battleships and carriers and cruisers and destroyers. The lagoon stretched so far that I could not see all the ships."

He also had a dispatch case he was supposed to deliver to Admiral Nimitz on the carrier *Essex* before reporting to Admiral Hoover. It was a long ride out to the *Essex* in a small boat, so he asked a chief petty officer in one of the Navy Quonset huts if he could store his luggage, including his parachute bag, under a counter. But when he returned to the hut after delivering the dispatch case, Fonda found that "some son-of-a-bitch had loaded my parachute bag onto a departing plane. Then someone else figured it didn't belong there and hurled it onto the steel-webbed runway."

Then it was chucked back under the counter—with its five changes of khaki and fourteen bottles of Old Taylor, several of which were broken. Fonda tried to control himself because he knew "it was wrong for enlisted men to see an officer crying."

Going out to the destroyer *Curtis,* where Admiral Hoover's staff was, he got soaking wet. It was so rough the bosun of the small boat had to stop and bail out four times.

As soon as he could put together a decent, dry uniform he reported to Admiral Hoover, who barely acknowledged his new officer, let alone recognized him as a movie star. Lieutenant Junior Grade Henry Fonda was now just another ACI officer trying to help win the war. He shared a cabin with another ACI officer, Lieutenant Commander John Dinkelspiel, formerly a San Francisco lawyer. Dinkelspiel has left us a nice description of Fonda on the *Curtis:* "He was a modest man at all times— a calm customer and a very competent naval officer. He stood his watches along with the other officers and did his chores to a point where one would not know he was a quote-unquote famous personage."

And incredibly enough, although the enlisted men knew who Fonda was, according to Howard Teichmann, who worked with Fonda on his autobiography, the senior officers he served with never "ever recognized him as anything but a lieutenant (junior grade)."

Fonda had to man a battle station only three or four times, during bombardments and air attacks; when he was not at a battle station during an attack, he would sometimes crawl onto the bag where the signal flags were stored. "Yes, in the beginning I was scared as hell, but I was so exhausted that after a while, the goddamn noise lulled me to sleep."

The *Curtis* slowly moved north with the Pacific Fleet as the United States retook key islands. Fonda had occasional shore leave, during which there wasn't much to do except go to one of the island officers' clubs, have a few drinks, and maybe sing songs around an old upright piano. He told a rather touching story about these shore leaves. Usually, after they had sung "Anchors Aweigh," Fonda would sing the "heads up and shoulders back" version Jane had sung to him. "Months afterward," said Fonda, "when I'd walk into an officers' club on Saipan or Tinian or Guam, I'd hear men singing about 'The Brentwood Town and Country School.' They didn't know what the school was or where it was, but it reminded them of kids, and they hadn't seen kids in months, maybe years."

Fonda was a good correspondent, writing Frances, Jane, and Peter often. Frances's letters to him were always cheerful as she reported how Jane and Peter were getting to know their father by seeing such movies as *Chad Hanna* and *Drums Along the Mohawk,* although Jane had to hide her face when the Indians were chasing her father in *Drums.* And when watching *Chad Hanna* (a film about the circus), Peter ran to the screen and started pounding on it when his father was about to be eaten by a lion. (Fonda never did receive a "Dear Hank" letter from Frances, although years later he learned that she had had some affairs while he was overseas.)

Under normal battle conditions, Fonda would be in the navigation room plotting on a thick piece of Plexiglas the position of a Japanese sub, which they had picked up by radar or from PBY search planes or because the United States had broken the Japanese code and knew the location of most Japanese ships and subs. For one excellent bit of detection—which resulted in the confirmed sinking of a Japanese submarine—Fonda received a presidential citation and a Bronze Star.

Fonda had only one close brush with death, an unusual one that occurred while he was on one of his shore leaves—probably singing "Anchors Aweigh." As the Pacific Fleet and the invading Marines and soldiers advanced closer to Japan, the Japanese became so desperate in their efforts to stop the Americans that they began sending out suicide pilots—kamikazes, who would pick out a ship and try to crash into it with their loads of bombs.

On one occasion Fonda and his bunkmate, Lieutenant Commander Dinkelspiel, were at the officers' club on Guam when the *Curtis* had to lift anchor and put to sea without the officers and men who were on shore leave. (This was probably because of a threatened air raid.) While at sea, the *Curtis* took a hit from a kamikaze, totally demolishing the photo lab and the cabin that Fonda and Dinkelspiel shared. When Fonda returned to the *Curtis* and saw the wreckage, he said, "Jeesus! If we had stayed aboard we'd have been killed."

After the kamikaze attack, the *Curtis* had to go into dry dock for repairs. Hoover transferred his staff to Guam, where Fonda heard the news of V-E Day. To Fonda and most every fighting man in the Pacific, it meant one thing: "that more men and more ships would be coming out to us for what we believed would be a hard fight to take Japan." Shortly after that, Fonda and another officer flew to Tinian, where they met the crew of a B-29 named *Enola Gay:* "I knew why we were there," Fonda said, "and I had a vague notion of what was going to happen the next day."

TYRONE POWER

commenting on Marine boot camp

They made me do everything twice.

National Archives

After he finished *The Black Swan* (a beautiful film that won an Oscar for its photography), in which he plays a dashing pirate who duels Anthony Quinn and George Sanders and rescues the gorgeous Maureen O'Hara, Tyrone Power became increasingly depressed. As the Japanese advanced in the Pacific, he felt he had to do something in the war effort, so he enlisted in the Naval Reserve. He thought he had been promised a chief petty officer rating in the morale and recreation section. When he heard nothing from them for a while, he went on an impulse to the naval recruiting station in New York to join up, telling them of his earlier enlistment in the Naval Reserve and inquiring why he had had no word.

In New York, Power was given the star treatment—from an old Navy hand who apparently did *not* like movie stars coming in to help win the war. Power told the recruiter he had a pilot's license, but that didn't impress the man much either. In fact, Power was classed as "unqualified" for any rank except that of ordinary seaman.

Power went back to Hollywood mad, but not mad enough to accept an offer from Darryl Zanuck to obtain a commission to work with him in the Signal Corps. "What do I know about being an officer?" Power said. Then, listening to radio accounts of the Marines fighting in the Solomon Islands and at Guadalcanal, he was impressed by what the Marine bomber scouts had done. He wanted to be one of them.

This was in August 1942. Power immediately enlisted in the Marine Corps, despite the fact that earlier that summer he had started work at the submarine naval base in New Haven, Connecticut, on *Crash Dive,* in which he played a submarine sailor in love with a girl (Anne Baxter) who is also in love with another submarine sailor (Dana Andrews). Power had already reported to Camp Pendleton when a Marine officer called him in to headquarters and told him that he was being given a four-month leave to complete a film. The innocuous *Crash Dive* was now being described as a "propaganda film" that would depict the hazardous life of the submarine sailors who guarded our coasts.

As the making of *Crash Dive* dragged on into the fall, Power became certain it was all part of a studio plot to keep him out of the service. He did not think *Crash Dive* had anything to contribute to the war effort. When it was released, Bosley Crowther, writing in *The New York Times,* agreed: "More of the Hollywood warfare, which looks like nothing at all but unbridled fancies of scriptwriters worked out through special effects [which, incidentally, won an Oscar].... no more sense of reality about this war than a popular song. . . . It leaves one wondering . . . whether Hollywood knows that we're at war."

When *Crash Dive* was in the can, Power was finally ready to go in the service and "the prettiest Marine I've ever seen," as someone in boot camp called him, would leave behind a very complicated love life. And yet, according to biographer Fred Lawrence Guilles, Power was not really promiscuous; it was just that he "was utterly unable to ever deny the gift of himself to any presentable and charming person who sought it, the only prerequisite being that the person pleased him. It would have shocked him had anyone ever called him promiscuous."

But there was more. Power was bisexual. In *The Secret Life of Tyrone Power,* Hector Arce quotes one of Power's male lovers as saying: "He was 70 percent work, 10 percent woman and 20 percent male." When he left Hollywood in 1942 he still loved his work more than anything, except that he agreed with Crowther that the studios did not really know what was going on in the world; the 10 percent of him that was "woman" was, according to Arce, involved with "a young actor who might someday replace him as 20th's male star"; and the "male" 20 percent was going through a cooling-off period with his lovely and witty French wife, Annabella, and had suddenly developed a passion for Judy Garland—the new, more mature Judy he saw on the screen in *For Me and My Gal.*

He told everyone, including Annabella, how impressed he was with the new Judy. When Annabella flew East to meet someone who said he could put her in contact with her mother, who was still in France, Power met Garland at a party and told her himself how much he admired the grown-up woman.

This was the period when Judy Garland's marriage to David Rose (who was in the Army and very unhappy about the high life Judy was leading while he was serving his country) was deteriorating. And despite her maturing looks, she was still an insecure little girl inside—

and very vulnerable to Power's flattery and attention. They quickly became lovers.

Power even pulled his old *Forever* ploy, giving her the Mildred Cram novel (which he had also given Annabella and many others) about two lovers who pledge eternal love, are killed in a car crash, and then discover they really did have eternal love. "We'll make this picture together," Power told Garland—and apparently she believed him, even after a friend asked her: "Do you have any idea how many copies of this book Tyrone has handed about to girls?"

According to several reports, Judy Garland was extraordinary in bed. And he "needed a relationship that was free, sensually," wrote Guilles. "Judy had caught on to that immediately. He was not a conventional lover. He wanted to do everything, try everything, and, if it was good, do it again and again."

When Power finished boot camp in California and headed east for Marine officers' training school in Quantico, Virginia, he was in the midst of one of the most emotional and unpleasant triangular wartime romances that any soldier ever had, all the more incredible and dramatic because it involved three movie stars. Annabella, who would make two pictures that year (*Tonight We Raid Calais* and *Bomber's Moon*), knew about her husband's affair with Judy Garland, but refused to give him a divorce, although she had decided her own romance with him was "dead" and she dated other men. Garland gave Power an ultimatum—divorce Annabella or lose Judy—wrote him fifteen-page letters declaring her love, and then, when she learned she was pregnant, threatened to have an abortion unless Power and Annabella were divorced.

Power was distraught; it is hard to imagine how he passed his classwork at OTC, except that, like Gable and Fonda, he must have been pretty good at memorizing mimeographed sheets. He wrote his friend Watson Webb: "God—sometimes I don't think I can stand it. I do love her [Judy] so." He told Annabella that he wanted the baby and the divorce (although, according to Guilles, Annabella insisted that she did not know of the pregnancy and that her husband did not ask for a divorce at this time), but she refused.

Judy, with time running out, was infuriated after a friend told her that Power had been showing her long letters to his Quantico bunkmate. She had a Mexican abortion and turned first to producer-director Joe Mankiewicz and then to her *Meet Me in St. Louis* director, Vincente Minnelli, for solace.

Power's affair with her was over by the time he was commissioned a second lieutenant in the Marine Corps and he decided to pay a surprise visit to Annabella in New York to show her his new uniform and gold bar. When he arrived at her apartment, he found a large party, including one of Annabella's serious suitors. He carried on brief conversations with some of the guests, then returned to Quantico to write his wife a letter declaring that he had been a fool and that "I only love you, my darling." Eventually they became lovers again.

While Annabella was on a cross-country bond-selling tour, Power was transferred to the Marine Corps air base at Corpus Christi, Texas, for flight training. He wrote Annabella that for companionship he had met "a very nice boy," a lieutenant from Florida. Although Power's biographers found no evidence that this "nice boy" was Power's lover, Arce says that before the actor went overseas, Power's "10 percent woman" did go into action. He met a male hustler named Smitty Hanson, who, Arce says, became Power's on-again-off-again lover for the rest of his life. Hanson told Arce he thought Power was essentially homosexual and contracted marriages as matters of convenience. But it is hard to imagine Power becoming involved in a triangle as horrendous as his wartime romance with Judy Garland and Annabella if he looked on marriage as just a cover-up. Tyrone Power was truly a complex man.

He was also a frustrated one. In April 1944, having been in the Marines for sixteen months, he was transferred to the naval air station at Atlanta. Now he was farther away from the fighting than he had been in Hollywood. Next he was transferred to the Marine Corps air base at Cherry Point, North Carolina; from there he wrote his friend Webb that "they haven't the slightest idea what to do with me." He also said he felt sorry for those actors who had not entered the service. "They really don't know what the hell they're missing. . . . I wouldn't take anything for what all this has taught me." Still, he was not fighting.

In late August 1944, Annabella was released from her part in Franz Werfel's play *Jacobowsky and the Colonel* so she could join the USO production of *Blithe Spirit,* which was headed for the Allied base in Caserta, Italy. Power was furious: "The whole thing seems more unbelievable every day—the life we all used to live before—and now this." "This" meant the fact that his wife had been sent into a battle zone before him.

But soon Power was on his way to the South Pacific to become a Marine transport pilot on Saipan. The main mission of his transport group was to fly supplies to forward Marine bases in the Pacific. His plane, which he named *Blithe Spirit*, had a few close calls and was eventually blown up (in a hangar) during an unusual kamikaze attack. A large Japanese transport plane landed at the Saipan airstrip; a dozen Japanese leaped out and raced for the hangar as Power and others fired on them with machine guns. The hangar went up in flames; according to one of Power's biographers, sixty-nine marines were killed in the raid.

But mostly the enemy was boredom. To occupy his time at the base, Power started an autobiographical novel, which he never finished. Another welcome distraction was his job as supervisor of the base's entertainment; this involved selecting the films and working with the USO entertainers, like Gertrude Lawrence and her troupe, who came to Saipan. One thing that disturbed him was seeing on the screen young men like Dana Andrews, Van Johnson, Frank Sinatra, and Peter Lawford who, with legitimate reasons for not joining up, were nevertheless advancing their careers in the absence of the stars who had.

All in all, the war years were a maturing time for Power: "There is something that has happened to me," he wrote Annabella. "I don't know quite how to explain it, nor really what it is. I felt old. I really felt that I was thirty."

Power did not know why, but as the war came to an end and he was preparing to come home, after logging 1,100 hours in the air, he had a dreaded feeling that there would be recriminations, perhaps a "Dear Ty" letter. As it turned out, he had nothing to fear.

WAYNE MORRIS

*Every time they showed a picture aboard
the* Essex *I was scared to death it would be
one of mine. That's something I could
never have lived down.*

National Archives

Wayne Morris's career as a naval pilot was much like Ted Williams's: It might very well have prevented us from knowing just how good he was at what he did. Morris had "great promise" written all over him from the day he entered the Pasadena Playhouse on scholarship after graduating from Los Angeles City College as a star football player. His first screen test with Warner Bros. led to bit parts in a number of 1936 and 1937 movies, including *China Clipper,* before the studio decided he was ready for a major role—*Kid Galahad,* with an incredible cast including Bette Davis, Edward G. Robinson, and Humphrey Bogart.

From then on the Kid was given the star treatment. The studio thought he was going to become a major star after fine performances in such films as *Valley of the Giants, Brother Rat,* and *The Kid from Kokomo.* In 1939 he made one of his most significant films, although it is little remembered today: *Flight Angels.* While shooting it, Morris decided to take flying lessons. His interest was intensified during the shooting of *I Wanted Wings,* which made Veronica Lake a star. Morris played an ex–college football hero who joins the Army Air Corps and dies in a plane crash. *I Wanted Wings* was Morris's thirty-fourth movie, but, although he had made some good films, he was still looked on as a promising young actor rather than a real star. After two more insignificant movies, *Bad Men of Missouri* and *The Smiling Ghost,* in the summer of 1941 he enlisted in the naval aviation service. The following February he married Patricia Ann O'Rourke, whose uncle Captain David McCampbell commanded Air Group 15 aboard the carrier *Essex.* "I started praying the day I was married," said Patricia; this was none too soon, because Morris was eventually assigned to Air Group 15 and anyone headed to the Pacific as a naval pilot on a carrier at the beginning of World War II would have had trouble buying an insurance policy. But Morris not only survived the war, he was one of Hollywood's genuine heroes. As many writers have said, his wartime experience was far more thrilling than anything he ever did on screen. His squadron undertook raids on Wake Island, Iwo Jima, and Okinawa, and he fought in both Philippine Sea battles. "I think the toughest session we had," Morris told Jon Bruce in an interview for *Silver Screen* magazine, "was in the second battle of the Philippine Sea. That was the day we took on the Jap fleet. When our flyers had finished, four Jap carriers were resting on the bottom."

Morris added:

Attacking Jap aircraft was comparatively easy, principally because the Yanks could always outfight the little yellow men. But strafing and bombing were different stories. In these jobs, you're so busy watching a hundred and one things about the attack that you find yourself forgetting the bullets that are flying all around you. But once you've done your job and are pulling out, you suddenly see those tracers coming at you and your stomach turns into jelly....

As to what a fellow thinks when he's scared, I guess it's the same with anyone. You get fleeting glimpses in your mind of your home, your wife, the baby you want to see. You see so clearly all the mistakes you made. You want another chance to correct those mistakes. You wonder how you could have attached so much importance to ridiculous, meaningless things in your life. But before you get to thinking too much, you're off into action and everything else is forgotten.

Morris flew fifty-seven missions and shot down down seven Japanese planes; three of the F6F Hellcats he flew had to be dropped into the ocean because they were so full of bullet holes. He was also credited with sinking a Japanese gunboat and two destroyers and taking part in the sinking of a submarine. For his heroics, he was awarded four Distinguished Flying Crosses and two Air Medals.*

While Morris was in the Pacific, he also became a father. After hearing the news, he wrote his wife: "Needless to say, I was elevated from a very morose young man to the happiest guy in the fleet and, really, secretly, I was just a little bit happy that it was a girl."

---

*This was almost as many citations as were won by Audie Murphy, who was, in a sense, just beginning his "movie career" in Europe.

NINE

The Canteen

THROUGH THESE PORTALS PASS THE MOST BEAUTIFUL UNIFORMS IN THE WORLD —sign over the Hollywood Canteen at 1415 Cahuenga Boulevard, a block off Sunset Boulevard

One rising Hollywood star who did not enter the armed forces was John Garfield. His failure to serve caused him considerable discomfort and embarrassment during the war years. Several other macho stars who never went into uniform felt much the same, but the situation was especially difficult for Garfield because he often played tough, cynical street kids who might overcome adversity and fight their way to success—as the actor did in real life.

The son of an immigrant Jewish tailor, he grew up on New York's Lower East Side, where he fought in many a street brawl and might have ended up a perennial mug except that he won a *New York Times* debating contest, which led to a drama school scholarship. During the Depression, riding the rails and playing small parts in Broadway productions, he ended up in Hollywood. Between 1938 and 1942 he appeared in fifteen movies, among them *Four Daughters, They Made Me a*

Criminal, Dust Be My Destiny, Saturday's Children, and *Tortilla Flat,* which he was making at the time of Pearl Harbor.

Garfield was quite outspoken about the much-discussed idea that actors should be given deferments to make morale-building and propaganda films: "We'll go when we're called," he said, "just like everyone else," a statement that inspired an invitation to the White House and special thanks from the President. But the Army found that he had a heart murmur, which earned him a 4-F classification and a good case of humiliation. He wrote an article for *Theater Arts* urging actors to become involved selling bonds and entertaining troops. Garfield did both. He persisted in trying to have his draft classification changed, and finally succeeded, being notified that he would be called within ninety days. But before he received his "Greetings" from the Army, he had a heart attack while working, appropriately, at the Hollywood Canteen.*

But Garfield did serve his country. "One day, just after the start of World War II," Bette Davis wrote in her book *This 'n' That,* "in the Green Room, our dining room at Warner Bros., Johnny Garfield sat down at my table during lunch. He had been thinking about the thousands of servicemen who were passing through Hollywood without seeing any movie stars. Garfield said something ought to be done about it. I agreed, and then and there the idea for the Hollywood Canteen was born."

The idea was inspired by Garfield's work at New York's Stage Door Canteen. But, as Swindell wrote, "he was better in coming up with an idea than in carrying one through." However, he knew who did have enough clout and initiative to get such a project started—Bette Davis.

Garfield had picked the right woman. Davis was an organizer, a catalyst, and an inspirer. Working with people like Bob Taplinger, who headed public relations at Columbia; Alfred Ybarra, an MGM art director; Jules Stein, head of the Music Corporation of America, and his wife; and a Hollywood chef named Milani; and assisted free of charge by members of the forty-two Hollywood unions, Davis found and in three weeks renovated an abandoned nightclub one block off Sunset Boulevard (today it is a four-story garage). The Canteen had bleachers on either side of the entrance. People paid $100 each to sit there on opening night and watch three thousand soldiers, sailors, and marines

---

*Six years later he suffered a life-ending attack—primarily, a friend said, because he had been blacklisted by the Hollywood studios, not because he was thought to be a Communist but because he had refused to cooperate with the House Committee on Un-American Activities.

enter. (Civilians, including the stars, entered by a separate side entrance.) Davis also persuaded the stars to contribute money. Some donated their salaries from such films as *Thank Your Lucky Stars* and *Hollywood Canteen.*

Davis even got her archrival, Joan Crawford, to work at the Canteen one night a week. The rivalry, of course, continued. On Crawford's first night, she was mobbed and signing autographs when Davis walked in. "Hello, Joan," Davis said. "We need you desperately in the kitchen. There are dishes to be washed."

Crawford agreed to appear in the film *Hollywood Canteen* only when she learned that the billing would be alphabetical. "C," of course, precedes "D." After shooting her brief scene, she was mobbed by extras and onlookers. Said Davis to the producer: "I'll bet you five bucks she paid them to rush her."

After the Canteen had been in action a few weeks and proved an overwhelming success, some in Hollywood were a little jealous. According to Davis, she was called in by the Hollywood Victory Committee, which was responsible for determining which stars could participate in which war-supporting events, and told she could no longer contact the stars directly but had to go through the committee.

In *This 'n' That*, Davis recorded her response:

What they were asking would make the Canteen impossible to run. We had to be able to call a Spencer Tracy or a Marlene Dietrich at the last minute and ask him or her to appear that evening. I reminded the committee that an understanding had been reached on this point before we opened. I suggested that they refer to the minutes of that meeting.

The chairman, James Cagney, said that "regrettably, the minutes of that meeting had been lost," so they no longer felt bound by whatever commitment they had made. I rose and said, "Mr. Cagney, ladies and gentlemen, I will give you until tomorrow morning to give me back your original permission. If not, I will have no choice but to close the Canteen. I will so advise the forty-two guilds and unions who are part of founding the Canteen. I will send a statement to the press if you have not changed your minds by tomorrow morning.*

The next morning she received a call: The committee had "met all night [and] agreed to let us continue as we had in the past."

---

*In his autobiography, Cagney does not mention this incident.

From old movie fan magazines and the biographies and autobiographies of the stars, it is clear that just about everyone in Hollywood put in an appearance at the Canteen at one time or another, performing, dancing with the soldiers, working in the kitchen, or acting as host or hostess. Harry James's orchestra appeared often and Kay Kyser and his band played Saturday nights. And every soldier who went through a Southern California port or air base en route to the Pacific probably remembers a night or nights at the Canteen. Johnny Carson, a young naval air cadet, never forgot dancing there—with Marlene Dietrich.

Davis set up the Canteen so that one person had responsibility for one night of the week. She picked people she knew to be good hostesses and organizers. One of Hollywood's most famous hostesses, responsible for Sundays, was Ouida Bergere Rathbone, wife of Sherlock Holmes's most famous portrayer. In his autobiography Basil Rathbone recounted not only how one Canteen hostess operated but what it was like for the stars at the Canteen:

> Every Monday for two years she started to work for the following Sunday. She somehow got gallons of ice cream donated and a birthday cake containing five-dollar bills! Any member of the armed forces present in the Canteen with a birthday on that particular Sunday could come up at "the cut the birthday cake ceremony" and try his luck at cutting a piece of cake containing five bucks, and kissing the hostess, whoever the star might be on that occasion. I remember one young kid who got a hold on Joan Crawford and virtually strangled her with his kisses. . . .
>
> Behind the coffee, cakes, and ice cream counter, which ran along one complete side of the Canteen, the waiters and waitresses were all stars or featured players, such as Ronald Colman and Walter Pidgeon, the Gabor sisters, Kay Francis, Greer Garson, etc., etc., etc., and the major studios supplied us with their beautiful little starlets to dance with the boys. I shared the MC spot every Sunday with Reggie Gardiner, and in between we went backstage and helped the unseen "heroes" and "heroines" wash up. There were hundreds upon hundreds of cups and saucers and plates and spoons and knives and forks to be washed and dried continuously. Sundays became a gala day and we were always "sold out" (metaphorically speaking—there was no charge for anything) and to our regret many had to be turned away. There was room in the canteen for about eight hundred, including a roped-off area for hospital cases.

Rathbone also said that during those years there were those who never said no to a request for work on Sunday night, but "there were some stars, a very few I am glad to say, who were unpleasant." The complaint was often "Don't you realize I am working on a picture and Sunday is my day off?" To this Mrs. Rathbone would reply, "Don't you realize that young America is fighting a war and for them there is no day off—they can be killed on Sunday, just as easily as on any other day of the week."

Sometimes studio heads volunteered to put together a show. According to comedian Phil Silvers, "Zanuck simply ordered his head of casting to call Betty Grable, Harry James's orchestra, and several performers under contract and put together an exciting show."

Columbia head Harry Cohn did it his way. Silvers said that during the filming of *Cover Girl,* he was called into Cohn's office several times to discuss a Canteen show he was preparing. "He had to prove that he knew show business," said Silvers, "that he knew talent and how to combine it in a live show. 'I started out as a song plugger,' he bragged, 'and I know more about stage shows than all these half-ass producers put together.' "

Silvers's favorite skit at the Canteen was a clarinet routine with Saul Chaplin, Columbia's assistant musical director. The bit revolved around Chaplin's elaborate flourishes on the piano, played every time he introduced Silvers. The flourishes prolonged the introduction so that it appeared Silvers would never get an opportunity to play. One night, Cohn, not recognizing Chaplin as his own music director, walked up to him, slapped him on the back of the neck, and roared: "Let him play."

More often than not, a request to help out at the Canteen came from Davis. And it was Davis who cautioned the hostesses how to treat wounded men. She passed out mimeographed instructions:

Forget the wounds, remember the man. Don't be over-solicitous, nor too controlled to the point of indifference. Learn to use the word "prosthetics" instead of "artificial limbs." Never say, "It could have been worse." And when he talks about his war experiences, *listen,* but don't ask for more details than he wants to give.

Of course, the big question everyone—especially the men—asked about Canteen-type entertainment was "Do the girls date the soldiers after closing time?" Apparently, some did and some didn't. Hedy Lamarr said she had a no-date rule; Yvonne De Carlo, who made her film debut in *Harvard, Here I Come!* the same year the Canteen opened, said: "I was forbidden to make dates after performing at the Canteen ... but most of us did anyway. My pal Pat Starling and I quickly accumulated a sizable collection of pilot's wings and other military insignia, which were given us as remembrances. . . . I've often wondered who among the many time-blurred faces made it through the war—but, more poignantly, who did not."

Of course, it would not be surprising if the young starlets were tempted to date the men coming through the Canteen on the way to the Pacific—many perhaps seeing their country for the last time. "Eat, drink, and be merry tonight, men, for tomorrow we may die" has always been a wartime theme of reveling and lovemaking. The war years were a romantic time, and Hollywood was the capital of romance and adventure. With their boss, Bette Davis, setting the example, how could the starlets resist attraction to the young men coming to the Canteen? Everyone in the know in Hollywood during the war was aware that Bette Davis liked men and was attracted to the servicemen who came through the Canteen. It is quite possible that the sexuality that helped make her a star also contributed to the incredible energy she threw into the Canteen. Vincent Sherman, the director of *Mr. Skeffington,* one of the films Davis made during her Canteen days, said of her that "the sexual suppression you see on the screen, her nervous hysterical energy, was not acting. That's the way she was in real life. The only way I could finish the picture was by having an affair with her."

Davis was especially tense during that period, only a year after her husband died (or was killed) in very unusual, maybe war-related, circumstances. She had met Arthur Farnsworth, a young socialite pilot, working in a New Hampshire inn where she took a six-month vacation after making *The Private Lives of Elizabeth and Essex,* her sixth major film in a row. "She plunged into the affair with Farney," says Davis's biographer Charles Higham, "with all the recklessness and optimism of one of her affairs on the screen."

They were married in 1940, surprising almost everyone in Hollywood, and the intensity of their relationship continued—for a while. During the war, Farnsworth went to work on top secret projects for the Honeywell Corporation in Minneapolis. Davis disliked the long separations her husband's work required, but the couple tried to keep their marriage intact. Then, less than a year after the Canteen opened, Farnsworth suddenly collapsed on the sidewalk in front of a tobacco store at 6249 Hollywood Boulevard. Witnesses in the store said they heard a scream, rushed out, and saw Farnsworth, carrying a briefcase and dispatch case, fall back and hit his head on the pavement. He was hemorrhaging with violent convulsions. A crowd quickly gathered. Farnsworth was rushed to the hospital but died the next day.

The papers in his dispatch case proved to be intact, but his briefcase disappeared, leading police to think he might have been involved in foul play in connection with his work for Honeywell. An autopsy showed a previous cranial injury (suffered, Davis said, when he fell down the stairs in New Hampshire shortly after they had met), which was presumed to have played a part in his death. However, medical officials also thought the fatal blow might have been caused by the butt of a gun or a similar blunt weapon. Despite this testimony, the inquest verdict was that the New Hampshire fall had been the primary culprit. Rumors persisted, however, that the culprit was really a jealous husband who had caught Farnsworth in bed with his wife the week before; and biographer James Spada uncovered some evidence that Davis may have been with her husband and pushed him that day in Hollywood.

After Davis began shooting *Mr. Skeffington,* a young boy appeared on the set insisting that it was a matter of life and death that he see her. He confessed that he had taken Farnsworth's briefcase and said he wanted to return it. Davis opened it to find several bottles of liquor, suggesting that her husband had been an alcoholic, which she had not realized, although she did know that he drank a lot. According to biographer Higham, Davis kept the contents of the briefcase secret for years.

The combined strain of her husband's death, the heavy filming schedule, and her work at the Canteen no doubt contributed to her tension during this period, even to her wandering eye. Actress Kay Francis, Delmer Daves, director of *Hollywood Canteen,* and actor Jack Carson discussed this last with Davis's biographer Lawrence J. Quirk. "Some of these kids were prize specimens," Daves said of the boys at the Canteen, "real catnip for the gals. I'm not saying she [Bette] disappeared with any of them, but I would not have blamed her if she had. She was in a real intense, uptight mood at times and some romantic quickies might . . . have calmed her down."

Carson, however, finally came to feel that Davis did "disappear with some of them": "There were some real lookers at the Canteen," he said, "knockouts like Dolores Moran and Julie Bishop and Dorothy Malone. But Bette was the one they clustered around." Carson remembered asking one marine what it was about Bette Davis that attracted such a crowd, and he said quite candidly: "I hear she screws like a mink."

Carson's first reaction was that this was a real "ungentlemanly remark," considering how hard Davis worked serving food, washing

Jack Carson (left), *Jane Wyman, and Hollywood Canteen founders John Garfield and Bette Davis in the movie* Hollywood Canteen.

dishes, and dancing with everyone. He was about to reprimand the marine for it when he decided: "Well, ain't it the truth?"

Apparently it was, and soon the whole country would know about it, or at least about one of her amours: Signal Corps Corporal Lewis A. Riley, who was stationed in Los Angeles. There were so many photos of them and stories about them in the press that Warner Bros. became worried. "He's a nobody," Ann Warner told her. "You are a famous woman. Why throw yourself away on a good-looking set of muscles in khaki?"

But Davis persisted in seeing Riley, and when the corporal was transferred (at Jack Warner's instigation, some said) to Fort Benning, Georgia, she rented a house for a month in nearby Phenix City, Alabama, not too far from FDR's getaway at Warm Springs, Georgia. (At the President's invitation, Davis spent an evening with him—strictly platonically, of course.)

In Phenix City, reporters and photographers gathered around Davis's house, much as the British press stalks the royals today. According to Pauline Swanson of *Photoplay* (for which, appropriately, Davis was writing an advice-to-the-lovelorn column), Davis had not lost her sense of humor. She answered autograph requests by sending a dog with an autograph attached to its collar.

For a while it appeared as if the affair would end in marriage, but Corporal Riley was transferred overseas (Quirk raises the possibility that Warner Bros. had something to do with it). His parting words were, in effect, that he would wait to marry until the war was over. Soon, however, Davis said she was "tired of living my life in a mailbox."

Back at the Canteen, she was not only keeping her eyes on the boys but engaging in comic skits that surprised the G.I.'s; in one she impersonated Groucho Marx, smoking a cigar and asking some soldiers to dance; in another, she took part in the oldest vaudeville gag there is, letting herself be hit in the face with a pie.

And not long after coming back from Georgia, she met an ex-marine and artist named William Grant at a Laguna Beach dinner party. They were married on November 29, 1945, one week after the Canteen closed. Davis was finally calmed down—at least for a while.

It is understandable why, when they were making the film *Hollywood Canteen,* insiders used to joke that a much better movie could have been made from Bette Davis's after-hours activities. But she insisted she never could have done such a film. Joan Leslie told Quirk that during one scene Davis kept blowing her lines until she finally said: "I just can't do this. . . . If you give me a gun, a cigarette, a wig, I can play an old bag, but I can't play myself."

Hollywood Canteen is one of the most fascinating films to come out of the war. Joan Crawford called it "a very pleasant pile of shit for wartime audiences"; although the critics didn't go that far, they did not like it. Neither did G.I.'s; one group of enlisted men wrote Warner Bros. that *Hollywood Canteen* was "a slur on the intelligence and acumen of every member of the armed services."

The movie is engaging today because of the number of World War II–vintage stars in it. In addition to the principals—Davis, Garfield, Robert Hutton, Dane Clark, and Joan Leslie—it included dozens of stars in cameo appearances or doing a song, dance, or musical number.* The story centers around the millionth G.I. to come through the Can-

*The full cast included Joan Leslie, Robert Hutton, Janis Paige, Dane Clark, Richard Erdman, James Flavin, Joan Winfield, Jonathan Hale, Rudolph Friml, Jr., Billing Manning, Larry Thompson, Mell Schubert, Walden Boyle, Steve Richards, the Andrews Sisters, Jack Benny, Joe E. Brown, Eddie Cantor, Kitty Carlisle, Jack Carson, Joan Crawford, Helmut Dantine, Bette Davis, Faye Emerson, Victor Francen, John Garfield, Sydney Greenstreet, Alan Hale, Paul Henreid, Andrea King, Peter Lorre, Ida Lupino, Irene Manning, Nora Martin, Joan McCracken, Dolores Moran, Dennis Morgan, Eleanor Parker, William Prince, Joyce Reynolds, John Ridgely, Roy Rogers and Trigger, S. Z. Sakall, Alexis Smith, Zachary Scott, Barbara Stanwyck, Craig Stevens, Joseph

teen.† He dances with hostess Joan Leslie, falling in love and wanting a date with her. The movie is recommended as a nostalgic trip down memory lane.

Another cameo-studded movie associated with the Canteen was the musical *Thank Your Lucky Stars,* starring Eddie Cantor and Joan Leslie, with appearances by several stars including Humphrey Bogart, Errol Flynn, Olivia De Havilland, and (again) Garfield and Davis. Each star contributed his or her $50,000 fee to the Canteen. Davis, playing a woman whose soldier boyfriend is overseas, went all-out for the war effort, agreeing to do a jitterbug number with a contest-winning jitter-bugger and even to sing a song, neither of which she had done before. She enters a club and dances with an old man, then the prize-winning young boy, before singing "They're Either Too Young or Too Old." The song stayed on the radio "Hit Parade" for over a year.

Naturally, some real romances—other than Davis's—came out of the Canteen. All were well publicized at the time. Betty Grable, who was divorced from former child star Jackie Coogan, met Harry James there one night when he was appearing with his band. They had to keep their affair secret for a while—not because James, although sepa-rated from his wife, was still married, but because Grable was afraid of her longtime boyfriend, George Raft. And Raft was someone to be afraid of: He was intensely jealous of Grable's other boyfriends, who included bandleader Artie Shaw; he had already beaten Grable once, and he had underworld connections, some of whom he used to spy on Grable. One night when Grable and James were making love in a back bedroom of her home, they were startled by a loud noise outside the window—caused by two of Raft's spies falling out of a tree.

Grable was five weeks pregnant when James's wife finally agreed to divorce; they were married on July 4, 1943, at the Frontier Hotel in Las Vegas—halfway, more or less, between New York, where James's band was playing, and Hollywood, where Grable was working on *Pin Up Girl.* (At least one critic would have recommended that Grable stay

---

Szigeti, Donald Woods, Jane Wyman, Jimmy Dorsey and His Band, Carmen Cavallaro and His Orchestra, Rosaria and Antonio, Sons of the Pioneers, Virginia Patton, Lynne Baggett, Betty Alexander, Julie Bishop, Robert Shayne, Johnny Mitchell, John Sheri-dan, Colleen Townsend, Angela Green, Paul Brooke, Marianne O'Brien, Dorothy Mal-one, and Bill Kennedy.

†The real millionth G.I. to come through the Canteen was one Sergeant Carl Boll, who was given a four-day tour of Hollywood and its nightspots during which he was accompanied by a series of starlets.

in Las Vegas: "During the making of *Pin Up Girl*," wrote James Agee, "Betty Grable was in the early stages of pregnancy; everyone else was in a late stage of paresis.")

Grable and James quickly became America's favorite wartime civilian couple, photographed doing everything and written about constantly in the fan magazines. According to Grable's biographer, Spero Pastos, they shared many things—baseball, bowling, horses, horse racing, gambling, and, most important, "a deep loathing for Hollywood."

Victoria—"Vickie"—Elizabeth James was born on March 4, 1944. Long before she could stand and look over her shoulder with her backside to the camera the press gave her the name "The Little Pin-Up." *Life* magazine photographed her in the classic baby pinup style: nude, lying on her stomach, with, if not million-dollar legs, at least a million-dollar smile.

After the war, James and Grable had another baby girl, Jessica; according to biographer Pastos, this was not a happy birth. James apparently was indifferent, probably because Jessie was not a boy. Jessie's sex also disappointed Grable, who said she would never have another child. Her mother scolded her for becoming pregnant: "Don't ever, *ever* do this to me again."

In the postwar years, problems began to develop in the marriage, primarily because Harry James was having trouble being Mr. Grable. For one thing, his band earnings, which rarely exceeded $50,000 a year, could not cover his drinking and gambling bills, which forced him into the humiliating position of having to take money from his wife. In addition, says Pastos, James was simply incapable of loving Grable—or anyone. There were also problems with Jessie when she reached the teenage years, and one thing led to another until finally the couple was divorced in 1965. The grounds: extreme cruelty. One friend said the marriage produced a "crack-up" in Betty.

Although the relationship did not last quite as long as Grable's, Hedy Lamarr also found love at the Canteen. According to her autobiography, *Ecstasy and Me:* "It was on Christmas Eve of 1942 at the Hollywood Canteen, amid the bedlam of several hundred G.I.'s trying desperately to have fun, that I realized John Loder was something more to me than a fellow dishwasher ... and George Montgomery something less than a fiancé."

George Montgomery was one of those unusually handsome Hollywood men who for some reason never quite made it as a star. The son of a Russian immigrant farmer, he went to the University of Montana for two years, majoring in interior decorating; he was also an outstanding boxer. Using his real name, George Letz, he worked in Hollywood as an extra and stunt man and then in some small parts. In the early forties, before his career was interrupted by the Army, he had leading roles in action films such as *The Cisco Kid and the Lady, The Cowboy and the Blonde, Riders of the Purple Sage,* and *Ten Gentlemen from West Point.* Although he resumed acting after the war, what brought him most attention was his love affairs, which included his engagement to Hedy Lamarr and later marriage to Dinah Shore. Lamarr sighed when "he went off to war in khaki . . . even more attractive than in any of his Hollywood roles."

It had been only four years since Hedy Lamarr had arrived in Hollywood from Austria, but her career was near its peak. She was incredibly beautiful, but not much of an actress; her fame on arriving in Hollywood centered on a ten-minute nude scene in the Czechoslovakian film *Ecstasy,* of which her first husband, the Austrian industrialist Fritz Mandl, had unsuccessfully tried to buy up all the copies so he could retire them. She was most typically cast in woman-of-mystery roles (meaning she didn't have to do or say much) in such films as *Algiers, Lady of the Tropics, Comrade X,* and *White Cargo.*

By the time Montgomery marched off to war in his khakis, one of the most beautiful women in the world was, incredibly enough, spending many a lonely night. "My home seemed more empty than ever," Lamarr wrote. "No amount of success could help keep me warm at night."

And then fate intervened to change her life, as you would expect in any Hollywood romance.

> One night [wrote Lamarr], after a rough day at the studio, I went right home and to bed. I was dozing off when Bette called. Several actresses who had promised to work that night, for one reason or another couldn't make it.
>
> I protested but Bette was insistent. I told her that the way I looked I'd do more harm than the enemy. But I dragged myself out of bed and went back to the Canteen. . . . I went to the kitchen and helped put some sandwiches together and then I saw about two hundred unwashed cups piled in the sink. Bette smiled and said, "I washed the last few hundred. Now it's someone else's turn."
>
> "Mine," I groaned.
>
> "Yes," said Bette, "but it isn't so bad. John will dry them for you." It was the first reference I had to the man with a dish towel standing at my elbow.
>
> He smiled. "John Loder." We shook hands.

Loder was in the second, Hollywood phase of his career, having appeared in a few movies before going back to England (where he was born) in the early 1930s to become a major star. When he returned to Hollywood on the eve of World War II, he usually played the lead in B pictures or supporting roles in major films, such as *How Green Was My Valley,* behind Walter Pidgeon, and *Now, Voyager,* in which Paul Henreid, not Loder, lit Davis's cigarette and his own at once.

Loder was forty-one by the time England went to war in 1939. The son of a general, he had been a second lieutenant in the British Expeditionary Force of 1914. He fought at Gallipoli, ending up as a prisoner and probably having seen enough of war to be cynical and uninterested in doing it again in his forties. Lamarr said that she and Loder had a strong physical attraction "right from the start," but there were the usual problems when stars marry stars and try to reconcile careers. Loder apparently did not think he would ever become a major star in the United States; as for Lamarr's career, she wrote, "I don't think John was ever quite with it." As an example she cited one night when her

Hedy Lamarr serving at the Hollywood Canteen, where she also met her eternal (for a while) love. National Archives

husband picked her up to go to the Canteen. Lamarr said, "John, remember the picture [*Crossroads,* costarring with William Powell] I was trying to get? I've got it!"

After a few moments, Loder replied: "You know, I don't think I'll stay at the Canteen tonight. I think I'll play some billiards with the boys."

So she repeated: "I am going to star in *Crossroads.*"

"Of course, darling," he replied, "and I am going to play billiards."

Lamarr said that Loder simply was not interested in movie careers, his *or* hers. In fact, at least two things interested him more: "his brisk early morning walks and his naps after dinner." Not only that, Lamarr said, he wore his shorts under his pajamas and thought that she was much sexier clothed.

When she played Tondelayo in *White Cargo,* Loder thought she was just plain funny, but critic George Jean Nathan was even funnier. When he went to the movie, in which Lamarr delivers the line "Me Tondelayo. Me stay," he said: "Me George Jean Nathan. Me go."

Lamarr was in a period in which the studios were offering her out-and-out sexy roles, which she said confused her and eventually led to her seeing a psychiatrist whose name she can't remember despite the fact that she fell in love with him. And now she was really confused: "I was in love with George Montgomery, John Loder and Harry [the name she gave the doctor]." Her big problem, she wrote in her autobiography, was that although the whole world thought she was beautiful, she did not.

Hedy Lamarr and John Loder, by now veterans at the Canteen, were married on May 27, 1943. The decision came about one night after they went to a garden party given by a Broadway director to celebrate his parents' golden wedding anniversary. There was much bantering as to what produced the longevity in the marriage; when Lamarr and Loder cornered the old gentleman, he confessed that the essence of the relationship was good sex—for the first thirty years they'd made love every conceivable night, and they had had sex nineteen times on their two-day honeymoon.

Driving home that night, Lamarr and Loder were talking about this, Loder saying he thought nineteen times on a weekend was conceivable and Lamarr saying that on the basis of her experience with men, she doubted it. Suddenly Loder said, "Will you marry me now?"

She was offended: "You are just interested in beating a sex record." But she agreed. The newlyweds went on a three-day honeymoon, but after making love eight times in one day, they decided not to try for nine times because, she says, "we felt we were cheapening our marriage." Nonetheless, John was proud of his eight performances in a day, Lamarr wrote in *Ecstasy and Me*. "I wouldn't be surprised if he passed it along to his billiards friends."

After *White Cargo*, Lamarr made *The Heavenly Body*; she said she was now a "homebody." Loder adopted her son, James, and they had a daughter, Denise. But the pain and trauma of motherhood sent her to another psychiatrist, with whom she also promptly fell in love ("A woman always falls in love with her analyst"). Then she decided to have a second child: "I had to seduce John, and it wasn't easy anymore. But one lost weekend did it." She also wanted a divorce because, as she told Louis B. Mayer during contract negotiations, "John and I have not been getting along."

Lamarr's confrontation of Loder was worthy of any movie she had ever been in: She simply said, "I am pregnant and I want a divorce. . . . I'm not going to ask for alimony or child support because I can handle that." (Her contract negotiations with Mayer had been successful.)

Loder said it was quite a scene, although "you should put more emotion in it." But he agreed to the divorce and then "went back to his reading."

After the divorce was announced in the press, said Lamarr, "the wolves came running"—and they were much more difficult to fend off than anyone she had met at the Hollywood Canteen.

=

Another Canteen romance was the Hayward-Barker affair, which also led to a wedding, two children, and divorce—although it did last longer than the Lamarr-Loder marriage. Edythe Marrener was a fiery redhead from Brooklyn who migrated to Hollywood with the regiment of ambitious young ladies who tried out for the role of Scarlett O'Hara. She did not win it, of course, but she was offered a short-term contract with Warner Bros., then Paramount, changed her name to Susan Hayward, and eventually emerged as a star *Time* called "Hollywood's ablest bitch-player."

She could also be something of a bitch offstage; her drama coach at Warner Bros. (whom she needed badly because at first she could not really act) told her agent, Benny Medford, "This is not a very nice girl." Early in the war, she had a brief romance with another young Hollywood aspirant, John Carroll, an MGM contract player who liked to date fast women (including Virginia Hill, the ex-girlfriend of gangster Bugsy Siegel). But the Hayward-Carroll affair (which, biographer Beverly Linet assures us, left Hayward's virginity intact) ended when Carroll joined the Army and Hayward went to the jewelry store to pick out an engagement ring—the biggest, most expensive one she could find. "If he really wants to marry me, he'll buy me that ring," she told her brother, Wally. When Carroll called from his Army base that night, Hayward told him about the ring's size and cost. The engagement was off. She bought the ring herself.

One night a few months later, when she had just begun to work on her nineteenth film, *The Hairy Ape* (a not very good version of Eugene O'Neill's play, with William Bendix and John Loder), Hayward decided to stop by the Hollywood Canteen. She was a regular hostess, always getting a laugh with her signature line, "Anyone here from Brooklyn?," but also something of a loner, who usually went home alone. This night, however, she accepted an invitation to have coffee with the master of ceremonies, Jess Barker. When he took her home, he tried to kiss her and she slapped his face. "I said over and over I'd never marry an actor," she told friends after her experience with Carroll. "No woman in her right mind would marry an actor. . . . But after I met Jess . . . one thing led to another." By the following spring she was pregnant.

Barker was another one of those good-looking young contract players who would never quite make it. When he met Hayward he had shown some promise in *Government Girl,* with Olivia De Havilland, and was working with Rita Hayworth in *Cover Girl.* Unmarried and twenty-nine, he was eligible for the draft, but a suspicious heartbeat made him 4-F. This embarrassed him, and in an effort to ease his guilt he spent more evenings at the Canteen than most actors did. "It's little enough for me to do," he said.

Barker asked Hayward to marry him three months after that first night at the Canteen, but she hesitated and because of their emerging careers they kept putting off thoughts of marriage. Hayward was in a contract dispute with Paramount—primarily, according to rumor, because they wanted to teach her a lesson for being such "a first-class bitch," as her agent put it. And Harry Cohn at Columbia was planning a big publicity buildup for Barker as one of Hollywood's most eligible bachelors. He was told that marriage would damage him with the bobby-soxer generation. But when Barker said he was thinking of marrying Hayward, Cohn exploded: "Of all the girls in the world, Barker had to get involved with that Hayward bitch."

Another person opposed to the marriage was Hayward's mother, who even tried to persuade ex-agent Medford (whom Hayward had just fired) to find an abortionist. But anyone who knew Hayward knew that if she was pregnant the matter would end in marriage; it did, on July 24, 1944. Then came a brief—very brief—honeymoon at a ranch near Santa Fe, "and within two months," said Linet, "the pregnant bride was seeing her lawyer."

It was a mismatch overcome by passion from the beginning. But the marriage did manage to last for ten years, although it ended in one of the ugliest divorce suits ever to preoccupy Hollywood—and an attempted suicide by Hayward.

=

Gene Tierney and dress designer Oleg Cassini did not meet at the Canteen, but they had one of Hollywood's most tempestuous wartime romances, climaxed by a moving tragedy that was directly related to the Canteen. In 1941 Tierney was a twenty-one-year-old beauty who had signed a contract with 20th Century–Fox after her 1940 Broadway performance in *The Male Animal.* She appeared on track to emerge as a star, with roles in *Hudson's Bay, Tobacco Road,* and *Belle Star,* when she stunned Hollywood, her studio, and her Eastern social-climbing family by marrying a Hollywood dress designer who would have been virtually unknown but for the fact that he was a genuine count with Italian and Russian blood and had been involved in one of New York's most scandalous tabloid stories: his divorce from cough-syrup heiress Merry Fahrney. Both 20th Century and Tierney's family fought the marriage, wondering what such a beautiful woman could see in an unattractive nobody who occasionally designed clothes for some of the studios. (It would be several years before Oleg Cassini became perhaps the first successful designer of moderately priced, off-the-rack dresses.) For a year or so after their marriage, Cassini was blackballed by the studios; at one time he grew so bored playing tennis that he took a five-dollar-a-day job working with the construction crew remodeling his house (which had been bought, of course, by Tierney).

Tierney said that when they first met, she "thought he was the most dangerous-looking character I have ever seen. Not handsome, but dangerous in a seductive way." They both spoke French (she had gone to school in Switzerland) and he was a charmer of the old European school: "To Oleg," Tierney said, "defending a woman's honor—and chasing one—came as a natural instinct." And he fought many a battle (quite a few of which made the tabloids) either in defense of his wife's honor, or of himself, or simply to prove that although he may have been a dress designer he could handle his fists, which he most certainly could.

He could also handle himself verbally at parties and with the media. Louella Parsons, wondering why women found him attractive, wrote that "it must be the mustache," to which Cassini responded by wiring the columnist: "Okay, Louella, you win. I'll shave off mine if you shave off yours."

Whatever he had, the women with whom he was friends included Marilyn Monroe, Lana Turner, Barbara Hutton, Grace Kelly, and Jackie Kennedy.

He and Tierney were married in June 1941, and there were immediate problems. "The strains of my marriage to Cassini would not be long in coming," Tierney said in her autobiography. In his own, Cassini confirmed this: "A lot of frustration was building in me. I was sick of being Mr. Tierney, of not having a career of my own." However, things improved after Cassini went into the service, perhaps because for a while at least he had a significant military career.*

Because of his proficiency in several languages, he volunteered for military intelligence, but heard nothing. Then one day at the 20th Century–Fox commissary, his friend Victor Mature said: "Why don't we join the Coast Guard together?" Mature had his own yacht, *The Bar Bill*, which he could throw into the deal. Besides, he said, "we'll be able to do our bit and stay close to home."

Cassini bought a half interest in the boat. To everyone's surprise, before long, *The Bar Bill* and its crew of eight were patrolling for the Coast Guard off Catalina, despite the fact that the yacht did not have enough power to outrun the explosion from their depth charge if they had to drop one. Cassini spent most of his time belowdecks preparing delicious meals (with their eight-dollar-per-man daily food allowance), while Mature stayed topside developing his tan for shore leaves with Rita Hayworth. They were at sea forty-eight hours, then in port (near Hollywood) for forty-eight.

One night, Cassini went to a party at pianist Arthur Rubinstein's house, where he had an amorous encounter with the wife of a French actor. He arrived home with lipstick smeared on his Coast Guard uniform and shorts, which he hid under the couch before falling fast asleep. He woke the next morning to find Tierney standing over the couch,

---

*In July 1942, Cassini became a U.S. citizen, which among other things cost him his title and made him eligible for the draft.

saying that she wanted him to meet her in town that afternoon—at her lawyer's office. "We're getting a divorce," she said. She had, of course, found the uniform and the lipstick.

Cassini turned on the charm and was a good boy for the rest of the leave; Tierney got over the incident. Besides, according to Cassini, his wife was happy that he was being transferred (as arranged by his mother) to the cavalry, where he would be eligible for officer candidate school (in the Coast Guard, all officers had to be U.S.-born).

Cassini was quite proud of going into the cavalry, toughing it through boot camp and OCS, and he did not mind showing off a little when he was on leave in Hollywood. Once he had an ugly argument with Otto Preminger (who would direct Tierney in *Laura*) over the question of where to open the second front in Europe. Finally, Preminger shouted: "What do you know about it? You're just a soldier!" To which Cassini responded: "What do you know about it? You're just a director."

Another night, he and Gene met Ronald Reagan and his wife, Jane Wyman, at a party at Claudette Colbert's. Cassini was especially proud of his crossed sabers; Captain Reagan, who was wearing the Signal Corps insignia, said: "Oleg, those sabers really do something to me."

When Cassini completed his basic training, Gene, tired of Hollywood and unhappy with the scripts the studio had been offering her, moved to Kansas, determined to become an Army wife. They bought a little house near Fort Riley; Tierney began to decorate it, learned how to cook, and did the laundry. They both said it was one of the happiest periods of their lives. For one thing, Gene was expecting: "Oleg had come home on a furlough from Fort Riley," she wrote in her autobiography, "and said, 'My mother says you won't be here after the war if we don't have a child. So we are going to have one.' "

Tierney also said that just before her husband was to leave for Kansas,

> a friend called and reminded me that I had not appeared at the Hollywood Canteen lately. . . . I felt guilty about that and, except for spells of feeling tired, I had no reason not to go. . . . There was no reason for me to remember meeting a young lady marine at the Canteen among the hundreds of people who had wandered in and out during the evening. And I would not have remembered her, except for the fact that we would meet again many months later. . . .
>
> A few days after I appeared at the Hollywood Canteen, I called my doctor. I was covered with red spots on my face.

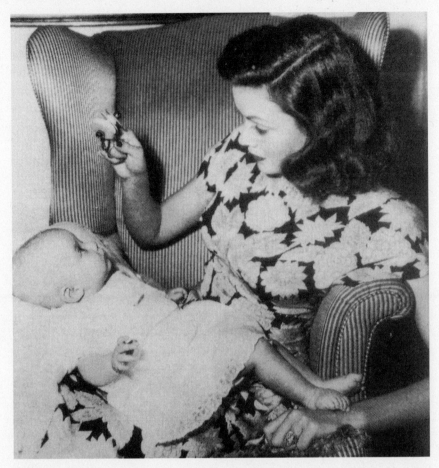

Gene Tierney and her daughter Daria. The Canteen played an unhappy role in this, one of Hollywood's most tragic real-life stories. Simon and Schuster

The spots were German measles. The doctor assured her that the illness would last only a week; it delayed her departure for Fort Riley.

So as to be near her mother, Tierney decided to have the baby at Columbia Hospital in Washington, D.C., Cassini had been given an intelligence assignment and ordered to Norfolk, Virginia, where he saw Sterling Hayden and exchanged Hollywood war stories. Because it was a top secret operation, no one was able to reach him to tell him that his wife had given birth to a premature baby girl, weighing two and a half pounds. Cassini read about it in the Norfolk newspaper.

What he did not learn until he arrived in Washington on emergency leave was that the little girl, Daria, was, as the doctor put it, "not in good shape." Furthermore, said the doctor, "I don't think she'll ever see. I think she is blind."

Cassini felt he had to tell his wife, and it was the "beginning of the agony for us. . . . She seemed to shatter then, she fell apart, and I believe never really managed to put the pieces back together again until many years later. She became hysterical. She cried and cried. . . . I began to think her health was as delicate as the baby's."

According to her autobiography, for at least a year Tierney "told [herself] these things could be corrected later." But when it appeared that Daria was deaf, she went to her doctor with a newspaper article about new findings linking German measles, especially during the first month of pregnancy, with birth defects. The doctor was not encouraging, but he did say that new research was being done on the vision and hearing problems Daria had. Howard Hughes, whom Tierney had dated years before, brought in and paid for an expert (which cost $15,000). But the expert and other doctors said nothing could be done for Daria and advised putting her in an institution for the mentally retarded.

Tierney and Cassini were crushed. It did not help when Tierney took Daria to Pearl Buck, also the mother of a retarded child, for advice; the author of *The Good Earth* said Tierney must come to terms with the situation: "These children often live to old age. The less of a mind, the less one sleeps; the less sleep they need, the more likely they are to live on."

It also did not help when, about a year after Daria was born, Tierney attended a tennis party in Los Angeles:

A young woman approached me, smiled and asked if I recognized her. She said she was in the women's branch of the marines and had met me at the Hollywood Canteen.

I shook my head.

Then she said, "Did you happen to catch the German measles after that night?"

I looked at her, too stunned to speak.

"You know," she went on, "I probably shouldn't tell you this. But almost the whole camp was down with German measles. I broke quarantine to come to the Canteen to meet the stars. Everyone told me I shouldn't, but I just had to go."

And she beamed when she added: "You were my favorite."

Tierney felt there was no point in telling the woman what had happened; she walked away quickly. But, "after that, I didn't care if I was ever again anyone's favorite actress."*

For four years Tierney continued to hope that something might be done, that some new treatment for retarded children would be found. But then she gave up. In fact, she had serious mental problems resulting from the tragedy. "When I think of Gene's illness," Cassini says,

> I think more of Laura, which was her most famous role. It is ironic that through much of the film she played a girl presumed dead who was actually alive; in some ways, Gene was quite the opposite. After Daria's birth, she seemed to die inside. There was a ghostly quality, an evanescence, to both Laura and Gene. Even after Laura is found to be alive, she has a certain mystery, an aura that permeates the film and gives it much of its magic. And Gene? After Daria, there was a distance I never seemed able to bridge. I don't think she was ever truly happy again. She played at happiness, pretending to laugh when the occasion called for it; but it was a role she performed so as not to disappoint or alarm others. This distance was a wound that crippled our marriage.

Tierney agreed. The marriage had been weakened by a number of things, but the strain of coping with a retarded child was unbearable. "Daria was my war effort," said Tierney.

At his own request, Cassini's overseas intelligence assignment was canceled and he was reassigned to Fort Riley. It was a horrible period for both husband and wife. At one point, Cassini seriously considered drowning himself and the baby, but did not have the heart because "Gene was still full of hope for a cure." He also said he wanted to go home "to do what I had once scorned: defend Sunset Boulevard against kamikaze attacks." His health began to fall apart; "I needed to live in order not to die," he said of this time, "and Gene no longer seemed to know how."

Early in 1945, Tierney persuaded a colonel to have Cassini transferred to the Ninth Service Command in Los Angeles, where his main

---

*In his autobiography, Cassini said he did not meet the marine until ten years later, when he went out with "an attractive redhead" who told him about being such a great fan of his wife that she had jumped a measles quarantine to see Tierney at the Hollywood Canteen. He also pointed out that Agatha Christie plotted her 1962 mystery, *The Mirror Crack'd,* around a famous actress who poisons the woman who had given her German measles during her first month of pregnancy.

job was to find dates for the colonel: "Well, Oleg," the colonel would say every morning, "who do we have tonight?"

This colonel was soon replaced by another, who did not like Cassini and had him transferred to Arizona, where he suffered so much from the heat that his eyes became swollen and he could barely see. Then he was transferred to Los Angeles, where he developed an acute case of asthma (why, he was not sure), and finally was discharged from the Army. But when he went back to Hollywood, without his uniform or a job, he quickly found his marriage drifting into the old, pre-war situation, with people often saying, in his hearing, "Look, there goes Gene Tierney's husband."*

The marriage was all the more difficult because Tierney was about to become involved in a now-famous romance. It began one day near the end of the war, while she was filming *Dragonwyck*. Walter Huston read a passage from the Bible and director Joe Mankiewicz called out: "Gene, turn slowly and look into the camera": "I turned and found myself staring into what I thought were the most perfect blue eyes I had ever seen on a man. He was standing near the camera, wearing a navy lieutenant's uniform. He smiled at me. My reaction was right out of a ladies' romance novel. Literally, my heart skipped."

It was the spring of 1946 and the blue-eyed young lieutenant was John F. Kennedy. Soon, these two beautiful people were involved in a serious romance, despite the fact that Kennedy was part of perhaps the most prominent Catholic family in America and Gene would have had to obtain a divorce from Cassini to marry him. But, Cassini says, Tierney insisted that "he'll marry me."

Until one day at lunch, when Kennedy, well into his political career, said rather casually: "You know, Gene, I can never marry you."

That was the end for Gene. They never seriously dated again.

=

As the war went on, Bette Davis, like a middle-aged professor with an eye for the pretty young women in his class, noted that the boys who came to the Canteen "were all much younger and less robust." But she stuck with her Canteen to the end, which was on November 22, 1945. And everyone at the gala closing could agree that it had been a genuine and moving experience for the Hollywood stars who had done their bit. For years they would tell the stories like the one in which Bette Davis

*Tierney and Cassini had another girl, Christina, before they were finally divorced in 1952.

stood beside a blind marine she had escorted to a special room above the stage as he listened to Eddie Cantor telling jokes. Overcome with emotion, Davis started to cry, but a nurse traveling with the wounded marine said: "Shh! Thank God for this place. That's the first laugh from that boy's lips since we left Guadalcanal."

And the time a soldier with a Purple Heart and one battle star on his Pacific Theater ribbon said, after dancing with Deanna Durbin, "Gosh, if I can dance with Deanna Durbin I can dance with the world." It was the first time he had tried to dance with his new artificial legs.

And the boy who would not part with his dog because the dog's mother (which had gone out to the Solomon Islands with the boy) had been killed in an air raid and the boy had promised to take care of the puppy.

And the night Barbara Stanwyck, serving sandwiches, did a double take when Private Harry Righter slammed a nickel on the table where Stanwyck was and yelled, "Hey, Rube!" Righter used to jerk sodas in Brooklyn near where Stanwyck (the former Ruby Stevens) wrapped packages. He would let her have thick malted milks for a nickel.

And the night Marlene Dietrich came, covered in gold paint, straight from the set of *Kismet*. "I had never seen two thousand men screaming in a state of near mass hysteria," said Davis.

And the Christmas Eve when there was a knock on the kitchen door: Bing Crosby and his young sons. They wanted to "help out." For an hour, said Davis, they sang Christmas carols "and there was not a dry eye in the Canteen."

And the Christmas Eve (maybe it was the same one) when Dorothy Lamour dressed up as Santa Claus and no one realized he was a she until she started to take it off.

And there were letters, like the one to Linda Darnell about the night when she counted dancing with 209 G.I.'s: This boy wrote, "I hope you remember me. I'm the one you danced with last Friday at the Canteen, medium height, red hair, nineteen and army uniform."

And the letter from a Filipino soldier, who wrote: "There is more true democracy with all its perfections at the Hollywood Canteen than any other place I have seen."

And this letter: "It was my first Christmas away from home and it didn't seem much like Christmas to me and my buddy. . . . When we left the Canteen that night both of us had a new grip on life and you gave it to us."

Perhaps one young actress summed it up best: "When a soldier going overseas tells me he is honored to meet me, I feel like crying and telling him not to be a fool, but then I realize he wouldn't want me to cry and he'd think I was being rude if I told him he was a fool, so I laugh and we dance and he goes away (I hope) thinking that beneath all the glamour Hollywood's heart is in the right place—which it actually is, only some of us never realized it till now."

It is understandable that Bette Davis would say, "There are few accomplishments in my life that I am sincerely proud of. The Hollywood Canteen is one of them."

TEN

USO 1:
Where the Girls Were

National Archives

It gave me the opportunity of kissing more soldiers than any woman in the world.
—MARLENE DIETRICH

It would be impossible to chronicle completely the activities of the United Service Organizations during the war, even in an entire book. And the USO itself is not much help. Although its fiftieth-anniversary book, *Always Home,* mentions dozens of actors and actresses who participated in USO camp shows at home and abroad during World War II (and later wars), it does not come close to giving us the full picture; when I asked the USO for a complete roster of performers, a spokesperson declined to furnish it.

Always Home does say that the USO produced 428,521 live shows for audiences totaling over 200 million servicemen and servicewomen. Established stars like Al Jolson, Jack Benny, Bing Crosby, Bob Hope, and Marlene Dietrich may have been the most dedicated USO troupers, but there were others—hundreds of them. In many ways, World War II was Hollywood's finest hour. Just about every male star not in the service went on at least one USO tour; among actresses, participation was close to 100 percent. The big stars usually performed free, but lesser-known troupers were given $150 a month and everyone was given $25 a week for out-of-pocket expenses.

(Of course, there was one star who refused to do anything for the cause: Greta Garbo. Orson Welles recounted an incident that took place during the war: "I was having dinner with her and we came out of the restaurant and there was a soldier in uniform without a leg, standing on his crutches with an autograph book, and she refused it. That is how dumb she was! She refused him, yes, in front of my eyes!")

The USO realized that rank had its privileges. In fact, USO actors and actresses wore special uniforms because to be captured in civilian clothes meant possibly being mistaken for a spy. They were also given ranks so they would be treated as officers if captured. When overseas, they worked and lived under conditions often no better than those of the troops they were entertaining. Transportation was usually furnished by the Army or Navy, which meant long, often cold trips in bucket seats on flights that were sometimes more scary and risky than being at the front. There were near misses and crashes; some performers were killed—thirty-seven in all, including the Broadway musical star Tamara Dreisen.* Jane Froman, a popular radio and nightclub singer, was injured in the same crash, which took place near Lisbon in 1943. Froman's USO comeback, after a series of operations on her shattered left knee, was the highlight of a 1952 film about her life, *With a Song in My Heart*, starring Susan Hayward and Rory Calhoun.

When they had enough clout, the stars and producers insisted that the shows were for the enlisted men, not the officers. Once, when putting on a USO show (which included Gypsy Rose Lee, Frank Fay, and Benny Fields) at Fort Monmouth, New Jersey, producer Mike Todd looked out into the audience and noticed that the first fifteen rows were full of officers and local notables. Todd was furious. Told nothing could be done about the situation, he said, "That's what you think!" He refused to put on the show. After about half an hour of audience foot-stamping, the base commander came backstage and asked what the matter was. "This is supposed to be for the Army; that means

---

*The USO also declined to give the names of the USO entertainers who were captured or killed during the war.

enlisted men. This ain't any show for the country club set," said Todd. "If they want it, it'll cost 'em a hundred thousand dollars."

They finally compromised; the Army cleared out all but the first two rows, which were reserved for some brass.

Everyone agreed that the men needed the shows. Kitty Carlisle remembered one she did with Marlene Dietrich. The two were told that the men were "in dire need of entertainment and the opportunity to smell a girl. Why smelling was enough I never figured out."

It wasn't enough, but, like pinups, it was better than nothing. Dietrich knew what the men wanted, and when she went overseas she did not hesitate to give it to them. Well, not all of them.

Although no one could restrain the irrepressible Dietrich, the USO did have to keep its performers from going too far with sexual innuendoes. Gertrude Lawrence, who felt that the men overseas wanted more adult entertainment, was annoyed at the USO for not letting her put on Noël Coward's play *Private Lives*. "Noël never wrote a vulgar line in his entire career," she said. Still, the question of sexy stars cavorting with troops overseas was dynamite—as Lawrence well knew. When entertaining in the South Pacific, she sometimes gave picnics for men she had become friendly with; the photographs would appear in the papers back home. And then letters would come to the men in the South Pacific: "I thought you were out there to fight the Japanese, not to go picknicking with glamour girls like Gertrude Lawrence."

Although the USO and the officers who put on the camp shows urged women performers to resist, the men sometimes got lucky anyway. Gene Tierney's husband, Lieutenant Oleg Cassini, told in his memoirs of the time Donna Reed (whose best-known wartime movie was *See Here, Private Hargrove*) came to Fort Riley, Kansas, on a USO tour. Cassini was assigned to escort Reed and a friend around the post; one night they ended up sleeping in the same room. Cassini went to bed wearing his cavalry boots because his feet were so swollen he could not get them off. Reed's friend (gentlemanly Cassini declined to name her) tried to help, but they were unsuccessful and, he said, became involved in "maneuvers of a different sort. Donna fell asleep but her friend and I continued an exploration of the intricacies of the cavalry uniform. Naturally, with my britches tucked in my boots, I wasn't able to remove them, either . . . An evening that was at once frustrating and creative."

Another soldier who got lucky was little Stanley Clements, who was small enough to play a jockey in a movie, not very good-looking, and not even an officer. He was a private recuperating from pneumonia (lucky for him, because it prevented him from going to Europe with his platoon, which was completely wiped out in the Battle of the Bulge) when the gorgeous blond starlet Gloria Grahame came to Texas with the USO. Gloria had just made her first film—*Blonde Fever*—and had a bit part in the Tracy-Hepburn film *Without Love*. Also, she just loved men. "We don't need a man to support us," she once told her sister. "That we can do for ourselves. We just need a man to entertain us."

But Grahame was in Texas to do the entertaining, and she and Clements were immediately drawn to each other. "We had so much to talk about," said Grahame, that she did not learn on that first meeting that Clements had also worked in films. "I'd never seen him in Hollywood. Then one day he was saying he would be able to take care of me after the war because he had a contract waiting for him. Imagine an actor not telling you right away that he was one, can you? Suddenly it dawned on me: he was the young fellow in *Going My Way*."

He was eighteen and she was nineteen and it was a wartime romance—love, or something, at first sight. The two were married almost immediately in Wichita Falls, Texas, and separated almost immediately, too, after Clements returned to Hollywood and demonstrated his real talents, which were for fighting, gambling, and driving his car through other people's front doors while he was drunk.

Sometimes playing to the men's desire could become tiresome, even drive someone to marriage, as was the case with Paulette Goddard, whose very name would arouse any G.I. who had heard the famous story making the rounds about what she did to director Anatole Litvak when she slipped under the table that night at Ciro's (or was it Litvak under the table, at the Brown Derby?).

Early in 1944, Goddard, now divorced from Charlie Chaplin, was having a relationship with Burgess Meredith. Her most recent film, *Standing Room Only*, was a big hit and she had just been nominated for an Oscar for her role in the war film *So Proudly We Hail*. Feeling on top of the world, so the story goes, she was having too much champagne one night at the El Morocco in New York when someone from Washington asked her: "How would you like to go to China and entertain the troops?" How could Goddard refuse?

Her troupe included actors Keenan Wynn and William Gargan; Goddard's main contribution was a mind-reading act in which she was blindfolded and Gargan put her in a trance. Although she had her USO uniform to wear while traveling, she always wore sexy dresses when she did a show. Knowing what the boys wanted, she gave them—

onstage—as much as she could. Usually she walked on in a tight dress and long gloves; after taking off her gloves in the manner of a stripper, with the men shouting and whistling, she would say, "What's the matter? Haven't you guys ever seen a pair of gloves before?"

As the two-month tour wound through Burma, India, and China, Goddard became known as "Miss Precious Cargo." By the time she returned to California, she was exhausted, as her biographer said, from being "pawed by so many soldiers and told how beautiful she was and propositioned so much." She could hardly wait to return to normal life. She told Anita Loos she was so sick of two months of "double entendres" that when Meredith said at the airport, "Let's get married," Goddard said it "seemed to put a limit on sex once and for all. I let him lead me straight off to the license bureau."

Whether Goddard had any romantic interludes offstage while she was in the China-Burma-India Theater we will probably never know. But we do know that USO shows were conducive to romance and liaisons. The stars were away from home, and the setting was often romantic, especially for the women, who were continually confronted with handsome young men ready to die for their country.

=

Merle Oberon was part of one of the first entertainment troupes to go abroad, early in 1942. Technically, hers was not a USO team, but was sponsored by the War Department. And it cemented her love affair with an RAF pilot.

In a way, the relationship had begun in January 1940, when Oberon came down with the flu. The new sulfa drugs she took for it turned her stunning face into a mass of boils. Her first reaction was horror and hysteria, but three excruciatingly painful and complicated dermabrasion treatments made it possible for her to return to the movies. However, the illness cost her a role in *The Constant Nymph* (which went to Joan Fontaine) and ingrained in her a deep sympathy for anyone who had experienced facial disfigurement.

In the following year she met a young RAF pilot who had experienced far greater disfigurement and suffering than hers. Richard Hillary had been shot down in flames; although he was rescued, "I paid a stiff price" for not wearing goggles and gloves, he said in his book, *The Last Enemy.* Hillary's hands were horribly burned and his face was beyond recognition. But he was pulled from the North Sea and put in the hands of the renowned plastic surgeon Archibald McIndoe, who, on examining Hillary for the first time, said: "Well, you certainly made a thorough job of it, didn't you?" When Hillary asked him when he could fly again, McIndoe said, "The next war."

In time, McIndoe rebuilt Hillary's hands and face, but the pilot was not a pretty sight. People on the street would turn away "closed in as on some dread secret," he would write, or look at him with pity, which at first made him angry. Later, he said, he "was sorry for them. I felt a desire to stop and shake them and say: 'You fools, it's you who should be pitied and not I; for this day I am alive while you are dead.' "

At least one person managed to see some good in what had happened to Hillary: his mother. Once, after reading to him—which she did by the hour while he was still blind—she said, "You should be glad this has to happen to you. Too many people told you how attractive you were and you believed them. You were well on the way to becoming something of a cad. Now you'll find out who your real friends are."

Hillary did. One of the friends was Denise, the fiancée of his closest friend, Peter Pease, an RAF pilot killed at the same time Hillary was shot down. Another was Merle Oberon. After his wounds had healed and his bandages were removed, he convinced the RAF to send him to America to talk to workers in the airplane factories, explaining to them the emotions of the men who flew the planes they were building. But the British Information Service in Washington took one look at him and said the best thing would be for him to keep out of sight. This was a crushing blow, from which he would never recover.

From Washington, Hillary went to New York at perhaps the lowest point since his recovery. He stayed with a friend, publisher Eugene Reynal, who convinced him to start work on a book about his experience in the RAF.* Through Reynal, a friend of Alexander Korda, Hillary was introduced to Korda's wife, Merle Oberon, who was immediately drawn to him. Only the rich, powerful, masculine voice remained of this once handsome, athletic young man; Oberon was not only enchanted by the voice, she was totally sympathetic to his plight as a result of her own experience with facial disfigurement. Oberon's biographers Charles Higham and Roy Mosely unearthed the dramatic and moving story as Tess Michaels, Oberon's secretary, recounted it: "Merle told me she knew he was very much a man still, and she had such a great good heart, that she could breathe her power, her strength into him. It was a beautiful, beautiful thing for her to do."

Soon after she met Hillary, Oberon embarked on probably the most

---

*The book was published in the United States as *Falling Through Space.*

unusual rehabilitation program in the history of World War II. Her husband was in Europe. Oberon asked Michaels to clear her calendar, even of war work, for two weeks. She had what she considered more important war work on her mind. In an apartment in the Ritz Towers, she quite simply restored Hillary's virility. Although Lovat Dickson does not mention Oberon in his biography of Richard Hillary, years later he said: "Merle was just what Richard needed at the time. . . . Their affair was not heavy . . . it was lighthearted, cheerful."

It was a beautifully romantic idyll, but one that could not last. Having been rejected by his government in Washington, Hillary, still in the RAF, had to return to England. Oberon tried to persuade him to stay, but he wanted to rejoin his men. The RAF and his surgeon did not want him to fly, but they could hardly deny him the chance. So he took special training for the injured and was soon flying for the RAF again.

In August 1942, Oberon agreed to take part in a joint operation of the USO and ENSA (the USO's British equivalent: Entertainments, National Service Association) to entertain British and U.S. troops in England. The show included singer Patricia Morison and character actors Allen Jenkins and Frank McHugh. The stars of the show were Oberon and Al Jolson, who had already been on several USO entertainment tours. Oberon was especially anxious to go because her husband was to be knighted for, among other things, *That Hamilton Woman,* and she would be able to stand beside him in Buckingham Palace. She probably also had in mind the possibility of seeing Hillary again.

The trip did not get off to a good start. Oberon biographers have uncovered convincing evidence that Patricia Morison was approached by the FBI and asked to seduce a high-ranking American official to determine if he might have been a German agent. (She refused.) There was also convincing evidence that the Germans were tracking the USO troupe, possibly because they suspected Oberon was working with her husband, who was known to be working for British intelligence. The debarkation of the troupe was kept secret (even to the point of notifying the stars suddenly in the middle of the night that they were to depart and advising them to wear dark, inconspicuous clothes).

The Atlantic crossing was without incident—except for Jolson, who was the last to board the departing plane and immediately made a fool of himself. Looking at his four USO troupe companions, he said icily: "Who the hell are you? I don't need you. I've just been to Alaska on my own and that was good enough for the boys. Why the hell did they send you on this trip?"

The troupe had not been in London long when Oberon told Morison

Al Jolson (below), *Merle Oberon* (at left), *Patricia Morison* (at right), *and an*
unidentified member of their troupe in England on a 1942 joint USO-ENSA tour.
National Archives

there was someone she wanted her to meet. It was Richard Hillary.
Morison recorded her reaction:

> I'm afraid I may have shown my shock at his appearance. There was
> no face. The hands were twisted into claws. But the voice was mag-
> netic and irresistible and the physique was big and impressive. Some-
> thing came through the horrifying twisted flesh: a quality of warmth
> and fineness of character. Merle greeted him with incredible tender-
> ness.

They were having lunch in an old inn. When the RAF pilot left the
table briefly, Oberon told Morison that she and Hillary were going
away for the weekend; she wanted to make him completely happy. By
now, Oberon was apparently falling in love, not just engaged in a soldier's rehabilitation. But she was married to a man about to be knighted
and already being criticized for divorcing his first wife. And Hillary was

in love with a young woman named Mary Booker, to whom he wrote several letters that his biographer, Dickson, says further confirmed that he was "a writer of extraordinary power."

Although she met Hillary again and saw her husband knighted, the USO trip was a disappointment for Oberon, primarily because of Jolson.

Oberon said she could not stand "star behavior." But one night in England she and Morison had a moment of satisfaction when, unrecognized, they ran into a group of G.I.'s and asked them if they had seen the show that night. "Who was on?" one of them asked, and Oberon replied: "Al Jolson." As they moved on, one of the G.I.'s said: "Jesus, I'm glad we missed that."

Despite their dislike for Jolson, the women had to admit that when he blackened his face and sang "My Mammy" and "Swanee," his electrifying energy transfixed everyone. But a break finally came the night Jolson insisted that they perform for the public at the Palladium in London. Oberon said no. They were there to perform for the troops, "not the general public." Jolson was furious and decided to go home. The USO troupe had been scheduled to go to North Africa; that trip was canceled.

They returned home, but not before Oberon became Lady Korda. From then on the troupe called her "Your Ladyship," which she loved. Back in California, Sir Alexander and Lady Korda were immediately promoted to the top of Hollywood society, although their marriage was slowly breaking up. Oberon's husband's title was also useful in that it gave her enough clout even to ward off Harry Cohn's advances when she began making *First Comes Courage* for Columbia.

While she was shooting the film, she heard that Hillary had died, in another fiery plane crash after which both he and his navigator were virtually unrecognizable. There were those who said he had committed suicide, but his biographer argued that Hillary would never have taken his navigator with him.

Oberon was stunned. She quit work on *First Comes Courage* for several days and remained in seclusion, most of the time hysterical. (Very little is known of her love affair with Hillary because a few years later her letters from him were lost in a fire in her home.)

=

Carole Landis and George Murphy wanted to go with the War Department's first entertainment troupe abroad, but they were working on *The Powers Girl*. However, Landis teamed up with comedienne Martha

Raye, veteran actress Kay Francis, and dancer Mitzi Mayfair to go on the second one, which produced not only romance, but a best-selling book—*Four Jills in a Jeep,* by Landis, which was made into a movie starring the four Jills, Phil Silvers, Dick Haymes, and Jimmy Dorsey and His Orchestra.

The Jills left for England in mid-October of 1942, intending to stay five weeks; then ended up spending five months in North Africa as well. And they had some scary moments in airplanes (a B-17 had a forced landing when it caught on fire; another almost ran into the Rock of Gibraltar on a foggy day, and another had to be escorted by Spitfires to and from the front to keep the German JU-88s away).

Kay Francis, the emcee, was a 1930s star whose career probably peaked with 1941's *Charley's Aunt,* after which she began appearing in a string of B pictures, her most recent being *Between Us Girls,* in which she and her screen daughter, Diana Barrymore, had an affair with the same man (Robert Cummings). Carole Landis was the sex object on the tour; she also sang too much, according to Francis. Martha Raye had already arrived as the big-mouth singing comedienne and was about to emerge

Four Jills (and one Joe) in a plane: Kay Francis, Carole Landis, Mitzi Mayfair, Martha Raye, and an unidentified serviceman. Courtesy of the Academy of Motion Picture Arts and Sciences

as the female Bob Hope, who would continue entertaining the troops into the Korean and Vietnam wars; and Mitzi Mayfair was a lively dancer whose film career would consist of one movie—the film version of *Four Jills in a Jeep*.

It was a good team, very popular onstage and off. In Bermuda, two Canadian pilots tried to break into their room, but the Jills were saved by some American G.I.'s. In London, they were quick to learn the peculiar language. The room clerk asked them: "Pardon me, ladies, what time would you like to be knocked up in the morning?" Translation: "When would you like to be awakened?"

Landis and Mayfair quickly attracted some constant suitors: Squadron Leader Joe Walling and B-17 pilot Jim MacVeagh. And eventually Martha Raye met a handsome young lieutenant named Johnny McHugh.

Soon, McHugh was shot down. As for MacVeagh, he did not endear himself to Landis by having Walling call her with the false news that MacVeagh had also been shot down. When Landis began to cry, Walling told her he was just kidding; then MacVeagh came on the line and explained that he just wanted to know if she still cared.

MacVeagh was jealous because Landis had met someone else: Captain Tommy Wallace from Pasadena, California. In her book, Landis said it happened just the way it did on the screen: "I looked up into the steadiest blue eyes I have ever seen . . . and suddenly everything stopped inside me, everything went *boom boom boom crash*. And my knees felt weak."

Ten pages later, Wallace proposed. But it took seventy more pages for them to get married, the delay caused primarily by Landis's concern with how the British press would react and the incredible red tape it took for two Yanks to get married in wartime England. They had a one-night honeymoon just before the Jills were to fly to North Africa. When they parted, Carole was crying and saying how much she would miss him and Wallace said—in fact, *had* to say—"I know it's tough, baby, but it's war!"

However, the troupe was held up at the debarkation point in southern England because of the weather, so Captain Wallace came down for a second honeymoon, which was interrupted all night by friends knocking on their hotel door with strange, trumped-up questions and requests.

When the Jills arrived in Algiers, a colonel said: "I might as well tell you girls that you are not going to like it here. You're not going to like a thing about it"—which was an understatement. They especially didn't like the bombing. And Mayfair was terrified by a man who entered her room, sat down, and stared at her. He did not know English; the only thing he could say was "Me, you pants." He finally left but came back later and repeated the scene—and Mayfair realized that he did not want to get *into* her pants, he simply wanted her pants. He thought they would be a great improvement over his obviously tattered ones. He was so insistent that Mitzi finally gave him the slacks. But she drew the line at the bar of soap he also wanted.

The troupe insisted on going as close to the front as possible to entertain the troops, but the officer in charge of their troupe wouldn't let them go, even after Eisenhower himself gave them the green light. The escort fighters couldn't be spared. Finally Jimmy Doolittle said, "By God, you'll fly and you'll have a fighter escort if I have to fly it myself." When they performed at the front in Algiers, they had a protective umbrella of fighters. "It was a thrilling thought," said Landis, "to know your own fighters were up there to protect you while you were entertaining the kids on the ground."

The show was one of the best they gave on the trip, but the next night it was delayed because of an air raid. They all huddled together in a makeshift shelter. "Kay and Mitzi were lucky," said Landis. "They were wearing their trench coats. I had on my silver fox and Martha was wearing her mink. And we were sitting in three inches of mud."

After the air raid they performed. Landis always knew what the men wanted: When she finished singing she just spread her legs and stretched out her arms—till some G.I. in the rear let out a pathetic groan and said, "I can't stand it." (Which would not have surprised Groucho Marx, who had seen her in action at a USO show in San Diego. "When she came out on stage in that white sheath dinner dress," Groucho said, "there was probably the greatest exhibition of mental masturbation in the history of the military.")

Landis concluded *Four Jills in a Jeep* with the statement "This story has nothing but happy endings." Which was true enough for the book. But she and Captain Tommy Wallace, who was the second of her four husbands, did not live happily ever after. When the shooting of *Four Jills in a Jeep* was completed, Landis went to the Pacific on another USO tour; by this time Wallace had been transferred to the States, and the couple were already learning that the marriage was a mistake. She wrote later that she had warned her husband that "when the war was over and he no longer was a romantic flyer in uniform, but a businessman in civvies . . . I might, at times, appear to overshadow him."

The break came sooner than expected. Wallace was a major in the

Army Air Corps (stationed in the United States) but they still had problems: "I didn't believe," she said, "that in these times a motion picture actress could overshadow a young man who had fought as a pilot overseas." But they were soon divorced.

After the war, Landis had a difficult time reviving her Hollywood career, according to Rex Harrison, in part because she was considered a little too "liberated." And Harrison, who while still married to Lilli Palmer had an affair with Landis in Hollywood and London, thought her wartime experiences contributed to her dwindling reputation.

After the war Landis received some unfortunate publicity when an overzealous fan broke into her dressing room, tried to unzip her costume, and was "unduly familiar." Then, on July 6, 1948, Harrison found her dead in her room. She had overdosed on sleeping pills. The gossip columnists speculated that the disappointing love affair with Harrison had caused her to take her life. Harrison disagreed, saying that the "circumstances" of Landis's life drove her to suicide.

==

For Marlene Dietrich, her USO trip was one long love affair, although she always considered herself just one of the G.I.'s. Long before women joined the ranks of the Army and Navy, Dietrich was there: "Never talk with soldiers," she wrote in her autobiography, "if you want to live a peaceful life without nightmares and bad consciences. Don't talk with us, because we don't need to hear your ridiculous complaints."

She knew what it was like to hear the shells swooshing and the bullets whistling overhead, what it was like to be bombed and strafed in a convoy of trucks, what it was like to have to delouse yourself. And she offered her troops more than entertainment: "I've seen them all; I've loved them all." And she understood them: "Of the soldiers I've met, the G.I.'s were the bravest. Bravery is simple when you're defending your country or hearth. But to be bundled off to a foreign country to fight for 'God knows what,' to lose your eyes, arms, legs, and return home a cripple—that's something quite different."

She did love them, and if she could have she probably would have given that love to all of them. How many she did give it to we will never know, but we do know that she had love affairs with some generals. "All generals are lonely," Dietrich said. "The G.I. can disappear in the bushes with a local girl. Not so the generals. They are protected day and night; eyes follow every one of their movements. . . . They are hopelessly alone."

Both Dietrich and her critics agreed that her career had peaked with

Destry Rides Again and was slowly fading by the time America entered the war in 1941. She was born in Berlin in 1901 and became an American citizen in 1939 after Josef von Sternberg, who first directed her in *The Blue Angel* in Germany, developed her sexy, sultry persona in a series of American films in the 1930s. Dietrich was married and had a daughter, but she was also one of Hollywood's free spirits, involved in numerous affairs with some of Hollywood's most prominent leading men. And, like the boys, whom she felt she was one of, she also liked girls.

By late 1943, Dietrich was at one of the lowest points in her life. Her favorite male lover, the French actor Jean Gabin, had gone home to fight for his country after making two movies (*Moontide* and *The Impostor*) in Hollywood to raise money for the Free French. Her female lover, the screenwriter and feminist Mercedes de Acosta, had gone back to Europe. Dietrich had turned forty and was not getting the roles she once had; in fact, she had agreed to let Orson Welles saw her in half for his magic act in the film *Follow the Boys*. It may have been a low point in her film career, but the scene was filmed in front of a live audience of G.I.'s and she loved it. So, like many a man down on his luck, she decided to join the Army—in this case the USO.

Her first show was at Fort Meade, Maryland, before twelve hundred soldiers. The emcee for her show was a young nightclub entertainer named Danny Thomas, who also worked with her on a mental telepathy act Welles had taught her. But Thomas did more than that: "He taught me everything, how to deal with an audience, how to answer if they shout, how to play to them, how to make them laugh. Above all, he taught me how to talk to them."

When it came time to go overseas, she called a friend who had just come back from a war zone and asked what she should wear. "The most gorgeous dress you can get" was her friend's reply. "These men haven't seen a woman in a long time and you must look as glamorous as you possibly can. Also, be sure to wear a uniform of your own design. The one they give you will make you look and feel terrible."

On her first trip overseas, Dietrich rendezvoused with Jean Gabin in Algiers and they embraced amorously for five minutes in front of hundreds of G.I.'s, who drooled and cheered. The Dietrich show consisted of Thomas, comedian and harmonica player Lynne Mayberry, pianist Jack Snyder, and straight man Milton Frome. Their first show in Algiers was one of the most spectacular in USO history. When a bomb landed near the stage and the power went out, the men yelled: "The show must go on." They had no lights, but, Thomas would recall, "The audience did something incredible. Those thousands of tough, rough guys flashed all of the flashlights they had onto the stage at once. We did the show to the flashlights. They didn't want it to end. And when Marlene took the musical saw she had had since Vienna between her legs and played it, they went completely *insane*! It was the sexiest thing you ever saw! They got down on all fours to look up—into Paradise!"

Thomas's role was to be the bashful clod who hangs back, then retreats as Dietrich slides after him in her sexiest walk, asking him if he would like to try:

> I ran all over the stage [he said], until I fell from exhaustion, hiding under a helmet and calling for air support, which got a big laugh. Marlene said, "You come here, or I will come after you." I buried my head in my coat and she started for me. This was the sexiest possible Marlene, in her skin-tight gown, walking her famous walk, pawing her thighs with each stride. From the crowd there came a moan, reaching a crescendo that shook the ground. Can you imagine— twenty-two thousand men screaming simultaneously?
>
> We never finished the skit. The M.P.'s were afraid the men would storm the stage and try to carry her off. They blocked off the crowd, with submachine guns at the ready.

The Algerian hotel where they stayed was bombed, and Thomas wanted to enter the air-raid shelter, but Dietrich talked him out of it with a rather puzzling remark: "If they hit us they'll get what they deserve."

As the tour continued, Dietrich took her troupe places they were not supposed to be. "We were scared shitless," said Thomas. But Marlene would tell soldiers, even those trying to prevent them from going through a minefield: "Never mind. I am Marlene. I can do anything I like."

She could also get almost anything she wanted, from Cadillacs to seats on planes to extra luggage. "But she always insisted on eating with the boys," said Lieutenant Colonel Robert Armstrong, "instead of the generals." With the generals, she had love affairs.

After North Africa, Dietrich and her company crossed into Italy and, in May 1944, arrived at Cassino, a major Nazi stronghold. They took a wrong turn, got lost, and came within a mile of the fighting, but were finally rescued by a group of Free French soldiers including the actor

Jean-Pierre Aumont. He agreed to help them find their way back to the base but was very worried: "To be responsible for Marlene's capture! In the eyes of the Germans, she was a renegade serving on behalf of the American army and against her own people."

Dietrich and her troupe found their camp, and the officers in charge began to worry about what might happen to her. As they neared Rome, the fighting intensified. But the men insisted they wanted their camp shows at the rear of their front line, and as they moved forward some of the G.I.'s drew large pictures of Dietrich that pointed the way to her camp show base. One night in May, surrounded by a ring of tanks, hundreds of G.I.'s lit the stage with their flashlights, as they had done in Algiers. Said Dietrich, "If they don't like my act, all they have to do is turn off their flashlights."

In June, her troupe went into Rome and sang to the wounded while the fighting was still going on. As she told Leo Lerman for *Vogue*:

I'd always sing "See What the Boys in the Back Room Will Have" first, because that's what they all wanted, and when I'd sing they'd swoon and scream the way bobby-soxers did at Sinatra. It's a sound like wild birds flying, a sound that's wonderful and free. I'd go back to see the wounded they had been bringing in when the show began. In the time it took to do our show, they would have been cleaned up, operated on, and dosed with analgesics, and they would be lying in their beds.

Singing for her German boys also moved her:

They'd come to me and say, "There's some Nazis over there and they're sick. Go and speak German to them, won't you?" I'd go to those young bland-faced Nazis and they'd ask me with tears in their eyes, "Are you the *real* Marlene Dietrich?" All was forgotten, and I'd sing "Lili Marlene" to everyone in that hospital. There was no greater moment in my life.

But Dietrich knew things would never be the same in her country. "The Germany I knew is not there anymore. I don't think of it. I suppose if I did I could never do these tours," she told one reporter when she was back in New York at the completion of her ten-week USO tour.

After helping promote the opening of her film *Kismet*, Dietrich returned to Europe in the fall. By now, according to one biographer, Donald Spoto, she was quite conscious of the legendary persona she was building and ready to exploit and promote it. "Dietrich was a very strong-minded lady," Army press officer Colonel Barney Oldfield told Spoto. "She could be glamorous and she could be earthy. I saw her gnaw on a German sausage like a hungry terrier, but of course she would make a grand entrance that would upstage a reigning queen."

On her second tour she was in London for a while; there she sang for her countrymen in a radio short beamed to Germany. Dietrich always finished the program with a message: Allied boys were on the way to destroy the Third Reich.

After the Allies liberated Paris and started the drive to Berlin, she decided to go to Paris, which became the headquarters of what was by now a one-woman show. As the Allied troops swept into Germany, Dietrich planned to make every effort to find her sister, who was thought to be in Belsen concentration camp, and her mother, who would have been in a concentration camp had she not been the widow of an officer killed in World War I.

It was during this period that Dietrich had an affair with General George Patton. Dietrich was a close friend of Ernest Hemingway, who was in Europe as a journalist. She told him about the affair quite frankly, often sitting on the side of the tub while Hemingway, with whom she never had an affair, bathed. Sometimes Patton would summon her to his quarters; on one occasion, according to Donald Spoto, she fell asleep and he carried her home and spent the night with her. There were those who thought she was having an affair with Eisenhower, not Patton, but when asked about it, she said: "How could I? He was never at the front." Patton gave Marlene two pearl-handled revolvers (one of which she intended to use on herself if she was ever captured).

As Patton started his march across Europe, he personally requested that Dietrich entertain the troops, as close to the front as possible. She seemed afraid of nothing, except "of being unable," she said "to endure this way of living any longer"—and then everyone would say, of course, that "that was an absurd idea for her, to go to war in the first place." She joked about getting killed and amused people with an account of her funeral:

> Douglas Fairbanks, Jr., would appear in naval uniform with a wreath from Queen Elizabeth of England; Gabin would be propped up in

front of the door of the church, a cigarette dangling from the corner of his mouth, refusing to talk to anyone; Gary Cooper would be yawning; James Stewart would be asking whose funeral it was; and Remarque would be at the wrong church.

Whenever she told the story in his presence, Hemingway would always add, "There'll never be such a show; you're immortal, my kraut." Actually, the funeral did not come until almost fifty years later.

Dietrich accompanied Patton across Europe in that miserably cold, dangerous winter of 1944–1945. "Like the rest of us that winter," said Oldfield, "she had to wear long, woolly drop-seat underwear, heavy trousers, and gloves. She ignored the weather and changed into nylon stockings and a sequined evening gown—and in this glamorous outfit she stuck the musical saw between her legs and played for her cheering audience."

Dietrich also learned about the rats that winter: "You're lying on the bare floor in your sleeping bag, the blanket pulled up to your chin, and these creatures run over your face, their paws as cold as death."

And then there was the night she summoned one G.I.—a tall Texan—to her tent and told him, "I have crabs."

The Texan said, "That doesn't bother me."

But Dietrich straightened him out: "What can I do to get rid of them?"

The Texan gave her some delousing powder, told her how to use it, and left, disappointed and angry.

She was also known to walk into the shower area, take a shower with the men, and leave as if nothing had happened. It drove the men wild, of course, and there were those who thought she was not so much a morale booster as a big tease.

In the spring of 1945, during Patton's final push to Berlin, Dietrich stayed behind, to meet another general, James Gavin, and become the official mascot of the Eighty-second Airborne and Gavin's personal pet. "Lili Marlene" became the anthem of the division. One reason, says a Dietrich biographer, that she developed a friendship with Gavin was that under one military plan he was to be the first American general to reach Berlin—and Dietrich wanted to make sure she was in close contact with the soldiers who first entered the city so that she could get news about her mother. Earlier she had located her sister, Elizabeth, at Belsen, but was stunned to learn that Elizabeth was not in fact imprisoned there but, rather, with her husband, Georg Will, was part of a "support group" that worked with the Nazis operating the death camp.

The affair with Gavin ended soon after the war, with Dietrich telling Mitchell Leisen, her director on *Golden Earrings,* that Gavin wanted to marry her, "but I can't be an Army wife." However, the affair had a disastrous impact on Gavin's marriage; two years after the war his wife divorced him. "I could compete with ordinary women," she said, "but when the competition is Marlene Dietrich, what's the use?"

By the time Germany surrendered, in May 1945, Dietrich had returned to New York, telling a reporter: "I'm just a G.I. coming home"—one knocked out by a jaw infection and suffering from frostbite. When she returned to Paris, she learned that one of Gavin's officers, Lieutenant Colonel Albert McCleery, had located her mother, Wilhelmina Dietrich. Mother and daughter had a tearful reunion at the Tempelhof airfield. Wilhemina died in November of that year at the age of sixty-nine; General Gavin's aides arranged for the funeral.

Dietrich entertained the troops for a while in Paris and in occupied Berlin, but gradually the most important experience of her life was coming to an end. Of the war years she said in her autobiography: "My decorations hang on the wall, but they're here only for the children. Normally, fathers receive medals, not mothers. . . . The French medals fill me with great joy. France . . . honored me, a simple American soldier."

＝

Although Ingrid Bergman's love life was less scandalous than Dietrich's, she had her moments. After she finished *Gaslight,* her husband, Dr. Peter Lindstrom, urged her to go on a USO tour to Alaska. He argued that he was putting in long hours in a hospital (he had signed up for the U.S. Army after becoming a citizen, but had not been called because he was a dentist) and that she also ought to be doing something to repay America for all it had done for them. Bergman agreed and was soon on her way to Alaska, missing Christmas of 1943 at home with Peter and their daughter, Pia. She tried to help in any way she could: "The worst part . . . is going around the wards talking. We don't give the whole show but one girl sings and sometimes I sing, sometimes I tell a story. I started to cry the first time, I felt so lost for words," she wrote David O. Selznick.

Christmas Eve she spent with the men: "Four hours without a pause I danced," she wrote Selznick. "I wish you could have seen your reticent Swede in the middle of the room being taught to jitterbug by some nut with 500 boys standing around having the best time they ever had in Alaska."

But she must have spent some time at the officers' club because, according to biographer Laurence Leamer, while she was in Alaska she met Lieutenant General Simon Bolivar "Buck" Buckner and had a love affair with him. They exchanged correspondence long after their Alaska meeting, until Buckner was killed on Okinawa in June 1945.

After Alaska, Bergman returned to Hollywood, made *Spellbound, Saratoga Trunk,* and *The Bells of St. Mary's,* won an Oscar for *Gaslight*—and along the way discovered, finally, that conventional married life with Peter bored her. She could hardly wait for another USO tour, with its promise of romance and adventure—or at the very least the chance to get away from their little home at 1220 Benedict Canyon Drive, two miles from Sunset Boulevard, where she often felt so tense that one night, as she told a future lover, when she came home from work exhausted and little Pia rushed up to greet her, Bergman just slapped the child's face: "I hated myself for it, I felt ashamed, I wanted to hug her to say 'I'm sorry' . . . and I just couldn't."

In June 1945, after Germany had surrendered, Bergman was off to Europe on a USO tour to join Jack Benny and harmonica player Larry Adler. "I am so thrilled I can hardly believe I am on my way," she wrote Selznick. "I can beat almost anyone with my jitterbug and I know samba, rumba, swing, big apple and what have you."

She knew these dances well enough for the dance floor, but not well enough to dance onstage—nor could she sing. And as is often the case with actresses who have no musical or comic talent, she didn't know what to do before an audience. She chose to read from Maxwell Anderson's *Joan of Lorraine;* this did not go over well with the men, who wanted what they usually wanted. At one long dull reading in Kassel, the G.I.'s began waving condoms in the air; Bergman ran offstage in tears. Adler came out on the stage and said the obvious to the G.I.'s: "What a pity you haven't a better use for those."

And it didn't help any that Marlene Dietrich commented, when she and Bergman met for the first time, "Ahhh, now you're coming when the war is over."

Although Bergman could not give the men what they wanted onstage, she did find lovers for herself. Larry Adler played the piano as well as the harmonica; one night Bergman, who had just joined the troupe, came into the room where he was playing the piano for a private party and sat down next to him. Adler did not immediately recognize her. When he finished, she said, "That's nice. What is it?" When Adler said it was original but that he hadn't written it down because he could not write music, she said: "You're very smug, aren't you? You seem to be very proud of your ignorance." That was the beginning of their affair, although the harmonica player–pianist was not the kind of man Bergman was usually attracted to.

Adler told Bergman's biographer Laurence Leamer that she was not exactly his type either.

> Ingrid wasn't fascinating, but you were just dazzled by her beauty. You felt she'd never read a book. She had no interest in world affairs. The one thing I never got her to talk about was her filmmaking in Germany. I think if Ingrid could have made a good picture, she would have made it for the Nazis, for anybody. She was a very dedicated lady. She loved working. And I don't think any individual was as important as her work. I think she needed to show her power over men. She wasn't coquettish or a tease. Ingrid wasn't interested in sex all that much. She did it like a polite girl.

Bergman confessed to Adler that almost without exception, her leading men fell in love with her. In fact, just about everyone she met fell in love with her. One of her first nights in Paris, she received a charming invitation to have dinner with two men she had never heard of. One was *Life* photographer Robert Capa; the other was Irwin Shaw, a young G.I. (who would soon write *The Young Lions,* one of the best novels to come out of the war). She went to dinner and became friends with Capa, who continually wanted to photograph her. Soon, Bergman, Capa, and Adler were a friendly threesome, seen often around Paris—until "one evening," said Adler, "the three of us were in a nightclub in Montparnasse. Ingrid made it clear she wanted me to leave. The next morning she came into my room and said she was sorry. She felt she had let me down. I felt let down. After that I felt a little different. But Capa disappeared and I stayed with her in Paris."

And then there was the day Adler was shot and died in Bergman's arms. Bergman, Adler, and Jack Benny were being driven to Nuremberg in a Mercedes. When they passed a checkpoint without stopping, a nervous young G.I., acting on orders, fired a shot at them. Adler heard the shot, simultaneously felt a sharp blow in the back, and was sure he was mortally wounded. "I began slowly and dramatically to die." But Bergman noted that there was no hole in the back of the seat. The bullet had come close enough, hitting a spring inside the seat cushion; the broken spring hit Adler in the back, hard enough to produce black-and-blue marks. After the incident appeared on the AP wire, Adler received a letter from Buffalo that said, among other things, "Too bad the bullet missed your lousy, yellow Jew spine." Adler ignored it, he said. "Hitler, more than any other factor, made me a confirmed Jew" was his comment.

When the war ended, Bergman did not want to go home, but Adler did. Capa was following his editor's orders, going off on assignments. And Bergman continued the affairs with both of her USO lovers after she returned to Hollywood. Although Adler wrote in his autobiography that he sometimes regretted that he never married her, he said: "I just couldn't face being Mr. Ingrid Bergman." They remained friends to the end of Bergman's life—although at one point she wanted to kill him because he gave an interview to a Swedish reporter who apparently got enough about Bergman to enable him to stretch it a little and write a story about Adler and Bergman headlined I WAS INGRID'S LOVER.

Bergman also saw her other lover when Capa was in Hollywood, and when he wasn't, he wrote her long, passionate letters. But she knew nothing would ever come of that affair. "I cannot marry you," he told her. "I cannot tie myself down. If they say 'Korea tomorrow,' and we're married and we have a child, I won't be able to go to Korea. And that's impossible. I'm not the marrying kind."

Bergman said that was indeed a problem: "He went away and came back again, he went away and came back again, but nothing was ever going to change"—and it didn't until the day in 1954 when he stepped on an enemy land mine, not in Korea but in Vietnam.

———

For most Hollywood actresses, the USO did not mean love affairs with soldiers or fellow performers, just hard work and hardships. They did their duty, and some did a little more. Foreign entertainers like Carmen Miranda, the Brazilian Bombshell (who was actually born near Lisbon), were ready to go anywhere to raise money or entertain the troops. Miranda was never asked to go overseas, but she did go everywhere in the United States; her USO trips contributed to a 1943 physical breakdown. Then when another breakdown threatened, she took a year's leave of absence to try to recover her health, which she never really did. She died in 1955, at the age of forty-six.

Singing star Ethel Merman was pregnant when her new husband, Robert Levitt, a former *New York Journal-American* reporter, was called into the service. Merman knew immediately she was not going to be a good Army wife. At the first Army party she went to, she said "nothing was served but warm martinis," and she hated martinis warm *or* cold. She drank too many of them anyway, and when the general's wife asked her to sing while she was eating her dinner, Merman responded; "Get out of my way, Cuddles, or I'll spit in your eye."

The general's wife took it all right, although she never asked Merman to sing again. But the Army did ask, and she rarely turned them down, even when she was three months pregnant and looked it. "But those army stagehands and electricians lit me beautifully, using a flattering off-pink gelatin. As I swelled and swelled, the spot got smaller and smaller until finally a pin spot lit only my face during the month before the baby came. But obviously the soldiers enjoyed it. Pregnant or not, I was made an honorary top sergeant."

Rosalind Russell was also eager to entertain the troops, but not being a singer or a dancer she had the old problem: "Nobody knew what to do with straight actors." It was George Murphy, Russell said, "who suggested the routine I wound up doing all across the country. He gave me a couple of jokes, advised me to build a Gracie Allen–style act around an invented brother who joins the Army and is a total idiot, does everything wrong. I did, and it worked fine. I'd never thought of myself as a stand-up comic . . . but soldiers are generous audiences."

Russell was married to Frederick Brisson, a Danish-born theatrical producer (in the 1950s he was responsible for *The Pajama Game* and *Damn Yankees*), who had become an American citizen and an Army Air Corps officer. And an incident involving her husband gave Russell one of the best war stories to come out of Hollywood. Brisson and another Dane, Hans Christian Adamson, had been assigned a mission to the South Seas with the famous American flyer Eddie Rickenbacker. At the last minute, Brisson's orders were canceled, but before the mission left California, the Brissons entertained Adamson at dinner. As Russell tells the story in her autobiography:

> During the meal . . . Adamson reached into the pocket where he kept his change and brought out a shiny disc. "Here, Freddie," he said, "I bought this medal for you in the PX." He started to pass the medal across the table in front of me, and my hand shot out and stopped him. "Don't," I said.
>
> Freddie looked shocked. "Rosalind!"
>
> "No, no," I said. "I mean you keep it and you give it to Freddie later on."
>
> Embarrassed, Adamson shrugged. "But I don't believe in what

Freddie believes in. I mean, I don't believe in anything much, and Freddie's religious, and this is the new medal for flyer—"

"Keep it," I said again. "Bring it home to him."

Adamson kept it, and Brisson was very upset. At dawn the next morning, when Adamson called to ask Russell to call his wife on the East Coast and say good-bye to her, Russell said to him: "Hans, you remember that medal you tried to give Freddie last night? Well, nothing's going to happen to you, but if it does, you take that medal out and you hold it in your right hand, and you'll be all right."

The Rickenbacker mission's plane went down in the Pacific and the party was lost at sea for twenty-two days (a moving story told in Rickenbacker's book *Seven Came Through*). Adamson nearly died from diabetes and a broken back, but when Russell finally saw him in the hospital, he raised his right hand, which was completely bandaged, and motioned to the nurse. "You can take this off now."

When the nurse unwrapped the bandage, Adamson's hand was curled into a claw. He pried it open with his other hand, brought out the now all-green medal, and asked: "Can I give it to him now?"

==

For black entertainers, the USO shows were some of the most difficult performances they ever had to do. Hattie McDaniel (Scarlett O'Hara's "mammy" in *GWTW*) traveled to many out-of-the-way black Army camps no one ever heard of, and even gave her rabbit's foot ("I got the part in *Gone With the Wind* because of it") to Lieutenant Commander Gene Markey, screenwriter and producer, to keep on his ship. But these trips to service bases, with their segregated quarters and shows, constantly reminded them that blacks were second-class citizens— especially when the base was south of the Mason-Dixon Line and they could not stay in the same hotel or eat at the same restaurant as their white colleagues.

In the 1940s, most of the black entertainers were not inclined to revolt. But one did. Lena Horne, who, as we have seen, was unhappy at being the token black pinup queen, also raged against the fact that her black brothers were preparing to die for their country but had to endure Jim Crow laws in the Army and Navy. She always had to entertain the white soldiers first and then the blacks, often under the most degrading conditions. Once, at Fort Riley, Kansas, she had to stay overnight to do a separate show for the blacks, an episode she describes in her autobiography. But in the black mess the next morning there was

Lena Horne rebelled at being the token black pinup girl. National Archives

a row of white men up front. "Now, who in the hell are they?" she asked an officer standing next to her.

"They're German prisoners of war," he replied.

Horne stalked off the platform, went to the back of the hall, and sang directly to the black soldiers. But after three songs, she became so choked up she had to leave. And she went directly to the local office of the NAACP, where she found solace with Daisy Bates (who would later work with the Little Rock NAACP chapter when it tried to desegregate the Central High School there). Horne asked how long this sort of thing had been going on. Bates said a long time, but nobody had come out and said anything about it.

"If I said something, do you think anything bad would happen to the soldiers who were there?" Horne asked.

"How could it?" Bates replied.

Horne wired the Hollywood USO that she was quitting, and explaining why. When she returned home she was reprimanded and "the word was very quietly passed," she said, "to keep that big-mouth woman out of the southern camps. So I finished out the war traveling to those camps on my own money, paying my own fares and my own accompanist."

==

Tallulah Bankhead was one of the first to do USO shows and to work at the Stage Door Canteen in New York, where in fact, she claimed to be the first star to dance with a serviceman. She was still on the wagon until the British won the war, although one critic wrote in *PM* that she had consumed a whole bottle of champagne before going onstage for a performance of the original theatrical version of *Dark Victory*. The same critic charged that her USO work was motivated primarily by a desire for publicity.

Of course, the studios did encourage their stars to do USO work because it was good publicity. And the stars knew this, especially the younger, lesser-known ones. Many performers enhanced their film careers on the USO circuit. In fact, June Havoc insists that an act she developed out of her USO camp shows inspired Mike Todd to sign her for the successful Broadway musical *Mexican Hayride*. And the USO shows gave Olivia De Havilland something to do during the time she was not filming, while fighting her landmark case against Warner Bros. that helped break the stranglehold the studios had on the stars.*

No doubt many stars joined the USO, and even went on the "foxhole circuit," as overseas duty was called, for personal or professional reasons, ranging from publicity seeking to image building and opposite-sex chasing. But no one can deny the significant contribution the actors

---

*At the end of a seven-year contract, De Havilland assumed that she was free, only to learn that Warners insisted that she still had six months to go because of six months she had been suspended (without pay). At great risk to her career, De Havilland sued Warner Bros. The judge ruled that a studio could not suspend an employee without pay and add the suspension period to the length of the contract. The court also observed that the studios were guilty of "virtual peonage for employees," holding them in "a life of bondage."

and actresses made with their USO duty. Annabella was a perfect example. After the liberation of Paris in 1944, she offered her services to the USO, primarily with the understanding that she would be sent to Europe. She felt that no matter where she went in Europe, she could fly to Paris for a reunion with her parents. The USO put her in a play, Noël Coward's *Blithe Spirit,* and sent the troupe to Italy, where it was soon sloshing through mud, sleeping in tents, and confronted with wounded men everywhere (all of which infuriated her husband, who was still in the States trying to get overseas).

In Italy—at Naples, Caserta, Rome, and Bologna—Annabella became emotionally caught up in the war, deeply moved by the wounded all around her, but also fulfilled at doing what she could, which she came to realize was quite a bit. She finally managed to arrange a flight to Paris to see her family. On the night she was to leave she had dinner with a young Army surgeon who wept because he had just had to amputate the leg of one of his best friends. But Annabella noticed that when she and some of the others in her troupe did some songs, or danced or told silly jokes, the surgeon began to laugh. At that point Annabella realized: "My God. This USO means something."

ELEVEN

4-Fs, a 1-H, a 2-A, a 4-Z, and a C.O.

The only uniform I was qualified to wear consisted of a plugged hat, red wig, raincoat and baggy pants. The only weapons I could be trusted with were a rubber-bulb horn, a harp, a clarinet and two sleeves' worth of knives. —HARPO MARX

After Pearl Harbor, Helen Hayes's husband, the playwright, screenwriter, and director Charles MacArthur, began to drink heavily. The reason, according to Hayes, was that although the coauthor of *The Front Page* was forty-six, he felt people looked on him as a slacker because he was not in uniform.

"Slacker!" That was the word every male during World War II, no matter how much or how little red blood he had, dreaded. In MacArthur's case, the guilt arose not because he *wanted* to be where the action was, but because "he *had* to be where it was," said Hayes. So he wangled a major's commission and went off to war.

Most men in Hollywood were not as obsessed with being part of the action as MacArthur, but it is fair to say that most who did not go into uniform were miserable. Of course, there were a few who thought people killing each other over territorial rights or resources or over politics was simply dumb. George Sanders, for example, was a pacifist and made no effort to hide how he felt. "The stupidest thing young men can do is throw away their youth," he told David Niven. "They'll never get me. . . . I hold three passports—Russian, American, and British. I shall keep ahead of the sheriff . . . until they order me to do something. Then I shall immediately become a Quaker and if they tell me to drive an ambulance, I shall crash so many, learning how to drive, that they'll send me home."

Before Pearl Harbor, Sanders had said he did not care whether Hitler won or lost, but in 1943, he sent a detailed proposal to Washington for outfitting a fast-moving infantry division with roller skates. Later, he asked Niven in England to give Churchill his idea for attaching a device to the nose of an RAF bomb that sounded the German all-clear signal after it was dropped—which would bring the Germans out of their air-raid shelters. He also felt that the government should "declare love" on a country "in the same pompous way" it declares war. The ministers of war would be ministers of love. We would drop "contraceptive gas bombs," which would cause the enemy to exhaust itself making love. "If God is love," Sanders said, "then love-making must be Godly."

Hollywood's most publicized pacifist was Lew Ayres, who, appropriately, played the young German soldier who was shot reaching out of his trench for a butterfly in the World War I film *All Quiet on the Western Front*. After *All Quiet*, which won him wide acclaim, Ayres drifted into a string of B pictures: "And let me tell you," he said, "the snubs you get sliding down aren't nearly as pleasant as the smiles going up."

Ayres was from Minneapolis, where his father played the cello in the symphony orchestra. He had studied to be a doctor, but also played jazz banjo; a job in Hank Halstead's Orchestra launched his show-business career, which led to a contract with MGM. He quickly became known in Hollywood as someone deeply concerned about religion, philosophy, and the human condition, and he once summed up his own feelings for a reporter:

I have a very simple philosophy. I believe that each man is born with certain limitations and capacities. And it's up to him to find them. A tree bears in its seed the possibility of growing to a maximum height, of spreading to a maximum width, of putting forth a maximum number of leaves. Now, if that tree grows as high, spreads as far and produces as many leaves as it is capable of, it has performed its function as fittingly as it can in the eternal scheme of things. We call that tree beautiful. Then why not the same thing for the lives of men?

In addition, Ayres was a vegetarian. Not exactly your typical Hollywood type. "His intellectual side made me feel a mite inferior," said Ginger Rogers, to whom he was married from 1934 to 1941. "He knew something about everything." And Rogers should have known she was marrying someone in touch with God. On their first date, when Ayres kissed her, Rogers said, "the ground beneath our feet began to move." Ayres said, "You certainly have extraordinary powers to shake a fellow up." So they tried it again, "and the ground under our feet moved again." It was an earthquake.

Ayres was given the going-up smiles again after *Young Doctor Kildare*, the first of a series. But the smiles did not last long. In 1942, he became Hollywood's first conscientious objector and was quoted (by almost everyone who has written a book about Hollywood and the war) as saying "I'll praise the Lord, but I won't pass the ammunition."

In announcing his decision, he prepared a statement for reporters:

Now let us consider war. Is it not strange that no one really wants war, yet few think that life can be successfully or even respectfully lived without it? We all shake our heads sadly over our predicament and then wait for the other fellow to stop it first, each side perhaps eager to be the benevolent victor....

So in my opinion we will never stop wars until we individually cease fighting them and that's what I propose to do. I propose we proclaim a moratorium on all presumed deeds of evil done us, to start afresh by wiping the slate clean and continuing to wipe it clean.... My views have been on file [with the army] for over a year ... and have long been taken for granted by my personal friends.

Furthermore I am, and have been, fully aware of the possible consequences arising from such an action as mine in these emotional times, but against all eventualities I am fortified with an inner conviction that seems to increase proportionately with every obstacle I face. ... This decision is ... the mature result of hours, days, and years of research and reflection.

When drafted, Ayres was sent to the "conshy camp" at Cascade Locks, Oregon. Distributors refused to take his pictures and *The Holly-*

Lew Ayres, shown here leaving Hollywood for a conscientious-objector camp, contributed one of Hollywood's most oft-quoted World War II remarks: "I'll praise the Lord, but I won't pass the ammunition." National Archives

wood Reporter quickly reported that the film industry could not be blamed for Ayres's quirky stand on the war. Full-page newspaper ads denouncing him were published across the land. John Garfield, who was 4-F himself, said: "Lew made us want to show the world he doesn't represent Hollywood."

One surprising defense of Ayres came from ultra conservative Hedda Hopper, who pointed out in her column that "Lew Ayres could have landed a cushy job. . . . It took courage—far greater courage—to do what he did than to wheedle and pull strings to get an officer's uniform." Another conservative who stood up for him was Ronald Reagan's wife, Jane Wyman, who (after the war) became close to Ayres when she and her husband were drifting apart. She found him much easier and more sympathetic to talk to than her husband was.

Ayres was eventually made a medical corpsman. Sent to the South Pacific, he served with courage and distinction, according to the men who knew him. He also turned over his pay to the American Red Cross. And to his surprise, he was treated with respect and allowed to continue his career when he returned to Hollywood, a wiser and somewhat chastened man: "War was more horrible than I had ever imagined it," he said. "Maybe you don't know what a bombed city looks like, or what it feels like to hold a child in your arms while it bleeds to death, or to stand by while kids watch their parents being dumped into mass graves. It got me, and for the first time in my life I understood the callousness of medics around suffering people. They have to be that way."

Hedda Hopper interviewed Ayres and concluded that he was "one of the finest characters in Hollywood." Certainly he stood out in a community that had its share of slackers in dashing uniforms.

But as we have seen, not all the stars who went into uniform were favor-seekers and not all the 4-Fs who remained behind were draft dodgers.

Whether they were or were not slackers, Hollywood stars usually portrayed men of sterling character willing to die for their country, a cause, or the woman they loved. As a rule, any actor not in the service during World War II was either too old or had a legitimate medical reason for being out of the service, although he often looked young and brave and healthy on screen. Being out of uniform was especially difficult for macho actors, whether strong, silent types, like John Wayne and Gary Cooper, or tough guys, like Humphrey Bogart, James Cagney, Pat O'Brien, John Garfield, Edward G. Robinson, and Spencer Tracy.

Tracy was forty-one when the war began, married and a veteran of World War I. He had enlisted in the Navy at the age of seventeen. He did not have to feel guilty about not being in uniform in World War II, but he was constantly heckled by servicemen for being a draft dodger. One night at the fights at the Hollywood Legion Stadium, the heckling was so intense that Tracy had to leave the stadium before the main bout or become part of it.

Pat O'Brien had also been in the Navy in 1917; in fact, he and Tracy were childhood friends and enlisted together. In 1942, O'Brien said, he considered joining again, but his agent told him: "Wake up, Paddy. At your age, even though you might receive a commission, there is a hundred percent chance you'd be relegated to a desk job, probably recruiting in San Diego." His agent convinced him he would be making a more significant contribution entertaining the troops in the USO.

John Garfield, who had been appearing in films since 1933, was under thirty when the war began. Before and after the war he played himself—a tough, cynical, streetwise kid—in such films as *Four Daughters* and *Tortilla Flat*, and a few war films, including *Air Force, The Fallen Sparrow,* and *Destination Tokyo.* He was free to make movies after the United States entered the war because he had a heart murmur. This fact humiliated him to such an extent that he tried to keep his draft status a secret. And in an article for *Theatre Arts,* he described how he felt when he was cheered while entertaining troops in the Caribbean: "I got a thrill that twisted my insides. I got applause before I had done anything to earn it. . . . I know that these men were not made happy because of anything that is part of me. . . . I represented something to them because of the 'star' system."

Or take John Wayne. He was thirty-five, but always looked younger on screen. He had been cast as the hero in numerous B pictures when John Ford brought him out of obscurity to star in the now classic western *Stagecoach.* From then on, through the war, he played a variety of tough screen heroes, sometimes in the saddle, sometimes in uniform. He also played a selfish businessman who sees the light after Pearl Harbor (*Pittsburgh*). Later, of course, both on screen and off, the Duke would emerge as America's most patriotic superhero—and one of the wealthiest. For example, his share of the profits, in addition to his $100,000 salary, from the 1949 film *Sands of Iwo Jima* was $380,000.

But during the war Wayne was very unhappy, although he was legitimately exempt from the draft because of his age, his marriage, and his four children. His biographer Maurice Zolotow said that he tried to enlist, even flying to Washington once to plead with John Ford, now a lieutenant commander in the Navy, to find a slot for him. But he was turned down because of a bad shoulder (and possibly because of all the bad publicity generated by the commissions given out to Hollywood stars and directors).

So Wayne was resigned to fighting our enemies on the screen, in *Flying Tigers, The Fighting Seabees, Back to Bataan,* and *They Were Expendable.*

The last film was most difficult for the Duke. It was to be directed by

Lieutenant Commander Ford (on leave to make the film), from a script by World War I Navy flyer Frank "Sprig" Wead. Lieutenant Robert Montgomery (also on leave to make the film) would play Lieutenant John Bulkeley, the decorated hero of the book *They Were Expendable*. In fact, about the only landlubber connected with the film (about PT boats operating in the Philippines at the beginning of the war) was the Duke, who would portray Lieutenant (junior grade) Robert B. Kelly, second-in-command of the PT squadron.

John Ford was one of Hollywood's authentic World War II heroes; in fact, the story of his wartime experiences would make almost as good a movie as W. L. White's book about the expendable PT boats. After the Normandy landings, which he witnessed with Bulkeley from a PT boat, Ford was temporarily detached from naval duty so that he could go back to Hollywood and make *They Were Expendable*. With the American troops under MacArthur taking heavy casualties as they slowly advanced in the Pacific, the Navy thought that a movie glorifying the heroics of the men fighting out there would provide a big boost for public morale.

Present at the story conference were Ford, Montgomery, Wayne, and Wead. Wead had had a paralyzing accident in San Diego, where he had met Ford. Ford encouraged him to write short stories and screenplays to overcome the boredom of life in a wheelchair. In the 1930s and early 1940s, he had not only written the screenplays for such films as *West Point of the Air, Ceiling Zero, China Clipper, Tail Spin, Dive Bomber,* and *Submarine D-1,* he had also taught himself to walk with crutches. After Pearl Harbor, he reentered the Navy, where he developed the concept of the mini–aircraft carrier. His story was also obviously movie material, and in 1957, John Wayne starred as him in *The Wings of Eagles*.

At the conference, Wead, Ford, and Montgomery were all in uniform. Wayne was wearing gray flannel slacks, a brown sport shirt, and a houndstooth jacket, and was obviously feeling miserable. He said very little, almost appearing to sulk, and was sipping too much from the bottle of Hennessey Ford had brought along for the conference. One thing they discussed was an affair the fictional Kelly had with a naval nurse in a Manila hospital, to be played by Donna Reed. They decided not to use real names in the film—without consulting any of the real-life characters to find out how they felt about their portrayals.

As the conference went on, Wayne became sulkier. The experience was something new for him. The other three men were obviously professional filmmakers and knew what they were doing. But they were also authentic heroes, who were actually in the Navy. Two of them had seen action, and Ford had been wounded. The Duke was a civilian— some had even charged that he was a slacker—but a screen hero of countless gun battles of one kind or another. And in this group, the Duke felt like an A-1 phony.

As Wayne's biographer Zolotow recounts the story, Wayne went to the men's room, where he stayed for such a long time that Ford dismissed Montgomery and Wead. When Wayne came out of the bathroom his eyes were red; he had been crying while running the water loudly, hoping he would not be heard. Ford knew what was wrong and felt sorry for his old friend. But he decided sympathy was not what was called for now: "Listen, you dumb bastard," he said. "Get the hell out of this office. We got a picture to make. We go to Miami for our locations in three weeks. I expect you to be there. And . . . I'm gonna work your ass off. . . . We got to make this in three months or less. We got to get this into release in December. Metro is timing it for December seventh [1945]. Another thing . . . when I ask you to come here for a meeting, I expect you to speak up and let me know how you feel about the story."

Wayne felt fine about the story and was, of course, a great admirer of the three naval officers. He eventually got hold of himself and they made a great movie. When the company was filming on location in Miami, Ford took advantage of a huge brush fire on nearby Key Biscayne to shoot footage for the burning of Manila in his film.

The war was over by the time *They Were Expendable* appeared. *New York Times* critic Bosley Crowther said, "If this film had been released last year—or the year before—it would have been a ringing smash." But it was, and still is, considered one of the finest movies to come out of the war, "an abiding testimony," said critic Howard Barnes, "to the valor that made victory possible."

But the real Kelly and Beulah Greenwalt (the nurse Donna Reed's character was based on) thought it was abiding testimony to libel. They both sued MGM—Kelly for $50,000 and Greenwalt for $400,000. They both won, although they were not awarded as much as they asked for; the courts gave Kelly $3,000 and Greenwalt $250,000.

No doubt Wead's script, Ford's directing, and Montgomery's acting played a big part in creating this great wartime film, but Wayne (who continued fighting the war on screen for years) also played a significant role, which is testimony to the fact that you did not have to be in the war to help justify and explain it to the people who were supporting it. Humphrey Bogart, for example. As Alistair Cooke said, Bogart "proba-

Four old men who seemed a lot younger when they went to war on screen. Clockwise, from top left: *Spencer Tracy (in* Test Pilot*), John Wayne (in* They Were Expendable*), Humphrey Bogart (in* Sahara*), Gary Cooper (in* Sergeant York*).*

bly had no notion, in his endless strolls across the stage drawing rooms of the Twenties, that he was being saved and soured by time to become the romantic, democratic answer to Hitler's new order."

Bogie, however, did not share Wayne's guilt at being out of uniform. He was married and forty-three in 1942, old enough to have seen World War I action as a seventeen-year-old sailor on the troopship U.S.S. *Leviathan*. He even had a scar on his lip (which produced that famous Bogart lisp) to prove that he was in the service, although it had not come from shrapnel, as some Hollywood press releases claimed.

Bogart was not the philosopher Ayres was, but he had his own ideas about war—especially the First World War: "The war was a big joke. Death? What does death mean to a kid of eighteen? The idea of death starts getting to you only when you're older—when you read obituaries of famous people whose accomplishments have touched you, and when people of your own generation die. At eighteen war was great stuff. Paris! French girls! Hot damn!"

He best expressed his attitude about World War II when his friend Raymond Massey announced, right after they finished making *Action in the North Atlantic*, that he was going to Washington to try to join the Marines: "Are you out of your mind?" said Bogart. "At your age, you'd just be a publicity stooge for the Marines. People of our vintage aren't worth a plugged nickel in any Army or Navy in this war no matter what service we had in the last one. Get the ants out of your pants and pay your taxes. That's all you can do in this one."

Like Wayne's, Bogart's main contribution to the war—besides his taxes and his USO camp shows—was made on screen, in *Casablanca*, *Across the Pacific*, *Sahara*, *Passage to Marseille*, and *To Have and Have Not*. *Action in the North Atlantic* was typical.

When they finished the film, Massey was still uncomfortable. He had already offered to serve in the Canadian army. Ignoring Bogart's advice, he in fact went to Washington and offered his services to the Marines. They appeared ready to accept him as an intelligence officer and he was waiting at the Hay Adams House to hear from them when he received a telegram from the Canadian minister of defense: BREATHES THERE A MAN WITH A SOUL SO DEAD WHO NEVER TO HIMSELF HATH SAID THIS IS MY OWN MY NATIVE LAND? PLEASE PHONE ME.

Massey showed the telegram to his Marine recruiting officer, who said: "Of course, you have no alternative." Massey went to Canada, rejoined his old regiment, was commissioned a major and directed to a military tailor who outfitted him properly, and reported to the adjutant general's office, where a major general said: "What the hell are we going to do with you?"

The Canadian army finally found a place for Massey dealing with "recreation, entertainment, and athletics." In typical army fashion, he was given nothing to do with films.

And Bogart was right. An army had nothing for someone of Massey's age who was completely inept at paperwork. There was much more action back on the studio lot in Hollywood.

Massey resigned from the Canadian army after a year, but he had proven his bravery and willingness to serve.

As for Bogart's, his biographer Joe Hyams said:

Bogie was the bravest man I have ever met. And that includes a lot of unknown heroes who were my friends in the South Pacific during World War II. . . . The final test of a man is the way he faces death. Bogie faced death the way he faced life: with courage and dignity as a gentleman.

As every movie fan knows, he died of cancer in 1957.

Three other Hollywood gangsters were too old to be drafted in 1942. George Raft was forty-seven; James Cagney was forty-three; and Edward G. Robinson was almost fifty.

Robinson was Jewish. His persecuted family had migrated from Romania. He did not especially like Britain, so when World War I began, he was actually pro-German because Germany was fighting not only Romania but Russia, which also persecuted the Jews. However, after the sinking of the *Lusitania,* he became anti-German and enlisted as a sailor in 1918. But he said in his autobiography that "I learned more about ships and navigation and the fleet from a picture I made years later—*Destroyer,* with Glenn Ford—than I ever learned at Pelham Bay," where he did his Navy training.

Errol Flynn was never typed as a "tough guy" but in his break-through films, *Captain Blood* and *The Charge of the Light Brigade,* he personified the swashbuckling hero who constantly risked death for any number of noble causes. Although he told columnists that he had tried to join the Canadian air force, he actually did everything to avoid the draft. He was given a deferment to make *Desperate Journey,* about pilots stranded in Germany. Before that he had even risked going to jail by ignoring a draft call, but after his deferment he went to the draft board and took his physical, only to be given far worse news than if he had been classified 1-A. In addition to all his other ailments, including a heart murmur, he had tuberculosis. According to one biographer, Michael Freedman, Flynn was told that he had "perhaps a couple of years to live."

Although he was losing weight and looked terrible both on and off the screen, he made *Desperate Journey,* in which costar Ronald Reagan was supposed to outwit a Gestapo officer who was interrogating him, then beat the Nazi to death. Flynn thought the scene was perfect for him and tried to convince director Raoul Walsh of this. But since Flynn had first appeared with Reagan in *Santa Fe Trail* (when Reagan was relatively unknown), Reagan had emerged as a star (in *Kings Row*) with enough clout to protest about Flynn's move to producer Hal Wallis. Wallis backed Reagan and said the script would not be changed.

Flynn was constantly ridiculed for not being in the service; cynic that he was, he was not bothered much more than was George Sanders. But he had to lie about the fact that he had a legitimate reason for not being in uniform, because he did not want anyone to know that he had tuberculosis. And his public image collapsed completely in 1942, when he was accused by two teenagers of committing statutory rape on them aboard his yacht. Although he was eventually acquitted, the phrase "in like Flynn" now replaced draft-dodging charges across the country.

Meanwhile, Flynn the spy, collaborator, or naïve adventurer—whatever you want to call him—was continuing to fight the war on film. *Edge of Darkness* was about the Nazi occupation of Norway; in *Northern Pursuit,* Flynn plays a Canadian Mountie who stalks a downed Nazi pilot across Canada. The real Flynn collapsed on the set while making the film and was taken to the hospital. There, doctors told him that although he did have TB, if he took care of himself he could live a lot longer than the two years he had been told to expect. To recover, he went to Acapulco. Charles Higham says that FBI files show he was seen there in the company of high-ranking Nazi officers. When Flynn came back to Hollywood he finished *Uncertain Glory,* about a dissolute Frenchman who surrenders to the Nazis to save a hundred hostages, and *Objective, Burma!* which established once and for all that American movie stars, especially Errol Flynn, won the war.

The idea for *Objective, Burma!* began when producer Jerry Wald called writer Alvah Bessie and told him he wanted to make a film about American paratroopers fighting in Burma. Bessie wrote in his autobiography that he mentioned to Wald that there were no American paratroopers in Burma: "So what?" Wald replied. "It's only a moving

Errol Flynn, in battle-torn uniform, on the set of Objective, Burma! National Archives

picture. So look, put some British liaison officers in and stop worrying."

But the liaison officers were not enough; not only did it appear that the Americans captured Burma, *Objective, Burma!* came off as one of the most vicious anti-Japanese films ever made, depicting them as torturing monsters. Screen credits did say that although the actors were American, "they enact experiences common to British, Indian, and Chinese forces." But that, and a similar credit at the end, did not appease the British, who were furious. The film's English release was canceled after one showing; cartoons appeared showing Flynn holding the American flag and standing with one foot on the grave of a British soldier. Months later, when he was presented to King George VI, the monarch asked: "Mr. Flynn, what is this talk that always makes people laugh about you when they mention Burma?"

Flynn replied: "Sir, apparently the picture proved conclusively that I took Burma single-handed."

=

If macho men like Spencer Tracy and John Wayne, and swashbucklers like Errol Flynn, found it difficult being out of uniform during the war, you can imagine the trouble a skinny little crooner like Frank Sinatra had. He "was the most hated man in the Army, Navy, Air Corps and Marine Corps," said author and Marine Corps veteran William Manchester. "In the Pacific we had seen no women at all for two years and there were photographs of Sinatra surrounded by all these enthusiastic girls."

The enthusiastic girls were, of course, the famed bobby-soxers, who swooned every time the singer walked onstage, first with Harry James's orchestra, then with Tommy Dorsey's. After two films (*Las Vegas Nights* and *Ship Ahoy*) in which he appeared as Dorsey's vocalist, Sinatra struck out on his own. By the early forties, he was the first coming of Elvis. When Frankie had his hair cut, the girls would run into the barbershop and go after his shorn locks in the trash. When teenage girls ran away from home, police looked for them in whatever city Frankie was playing; he had to appeal to girls to do their homework after mothers began complaining that their school-age daughters were spending too much time listening to Sinatra radio concerts and records.

Naturally, all this was reported in the press at home and abroad, and the men in uniform—and their parents—began to get annoyed. "Why isn't Sinatra in the service?" the columnists and editorial writers began to ask. He was twenty-seven and married, with one child and another on the way; when he went before his draft board, he was classified 4-F because of a punctured eardrum. THE ARMY SWOONS—SINATRA IS 4-F, said the *New York Post*.

Sinatra was legitimately undraftable, but that didn't satisfy his critics. He was challenged in the media and the bars. After a Sinatra concert in the Hollywood Bowl, with thousands of bobby-soxers shouting "Frankie, we love you," one G.I. was heard to mutter: "I hope they won't forget to flush the bowl."

Then he was reclassified 2-A but the draft board said he was exempt from the service because he was "necessary to the national health," which started a nationwide debate as to whether crooners were essential to the war effort.

Apparently the President thought they were, because he invited Sinatra to the White House when he was seeking the Italian vote in the 1944 campaign. But FDR was immediately criticized for the invitation; Sinatra was not only a civilian, but also had never even gone on a USO tour to entertain the troops. So George Evans, Sinatra's manager, announced that Frankie would tour the nation's service hospitals, then go overseas—despite the fact that there was very real concern about how he would be received abroad.

=

Many movie stars were legitimately 4-F. Gary Cooper was forty; his hip had been improperly set after a youthful auto accident. His first doctor, not knowing it was broken, told him that horseback riding would mend it. So he learned how to ride with a broken hip, developed a distinctive, limping walk—and received 4-F draft status in 1942.

Cary Grant became a U.S. citizen on June 26, 1942, at the age of thirty-eight, and immediately applied for the Air Corps officer candidate school in Miami. He was classified 2-A and informed that he would be called to OCS on September 15. But on December 11, he was reclassified 1-H, a rather peculiar status explained in an RKO memo:

> Washington suggests that they would like to have Cary Grant's name on their list of people who from time to time might do some temporary service. In each instance, if he is called upon, he will have an opportunity to say "yes" or "no" to whatever job is proposed and it is not at all certain that they will call upon him in any case. We understand that the type of work that he might be called upon to do would not be the sort that would require him to drop out of whatever other activities he may be engaged in and the fact that he was doing the work would be publicized.

Either RKO had unusual pull in Washington, or the memo confirms the belief, held by many, that Grant worked for British intelligence during the war.

When Gregory Peck ruptured a disc in his back, it sounded like a firecracker and everyone watching him in Martha Graham's dance class heard it. In fact, it was Graham herself who ruptured it; she was dissatisfied with how far down he had bent his head from a sitting position: "Come on, Gregory, you can do better than that," she said, and put her

Four seemingly healthy young men who had legitimate reasons for not being in the service, although the public was not so sure. Clockwise, from top left: *John Garfield (heart murmur), Gregory Peck (ruptured disc), Peter Lawford (bad arm from childhood accident), Frank Sinatra (punctured eardrum).*

knee on his back and pushed. Years later, when Peck was classified 4-F, his studio issued a statement saying he had injured his back rowing at Berkeley. Of course, the injury did not prevent him from fighting the Nazis in his screen debut, *Days of Glory.*

Apparently back injuries also kept Orson Welles and Dana Andrews out of the Army, permitting Andrews to get his career solidified as the lynch victim in *The Ox-Bow Incident* and the detective in *Laura.*

Like Grant, Ronald Colman was a naturalized U.S. citizen (he was born in England), but at fifty, he was simply too old to be considered for active duty. He had been wounded in France in World War I, fighting for Britain. He had had his swashbuckling, macho days—in *Beau Geste,* the "Bulldog Drummond" series, *Clive of India,* and *If I Were King*—and the studio makeup artists made him look much younger on screen. He did volunteer for the Army (but was turned down) and spent the war selling bonds and making a few movies, the most notable being *Random Harvest,* a World War I drama with Greer Garson.

Another British-born U.S. citizen, Ray Milland, was kept out of uniform by a hand injury, although he did spend some time as an Army civilian flight instructor. But after a long Hollywood career in B pictures, he was able to make his breakthrough movies, *Ministry of Fear* and *The Lost Weekend,* because he was not in the service.

Fred Astaire's draft number was a low 156 but at forty-three, married and with three children, he was never drafted.

Brian Aherne was forty in 1942 but considered himself "reasonably young and active." He carried two draft cards—one from Britain, where he was born, and one from the United States, where he worked—but he was never called by either country. He was asked to tour Army bases to help build morale (usually asking himself, "What am I, an unknown English actor, doing here?"), but by 1943, he said, "I was ashamed to be living a life of ease and comparative luxury at such a time."

Comedian Phil Silvers was 4-F because of his eyes. Bob Hope naturally made a joke out of the whole thing, saying: "I was in class 4-Z, meaning 'coward.' " He also said, "Both Bing and I had been offered commissions as lieutenant commanders in the Navy, but FDR had said, 'No way. I want these people to play for *all* the services.' I guess he didn't want us in the armed forces. After all, he had sworn to protect and defend the United States." Jack Benny, forty-seven in 1941, married and with a child, never heard from his draft board.

Despite the fact that many veteran actors were available, because of either their age or physical disabilities, some studios panicked after

Pearl Harbor and went on a talent search for young males that rivaled the search for Scarlett O'Hara: Lucille Ryman, chief MGM talent scout, said her orders were to "sign up any man who is six feet tall and 4-F. If we signed someone who had no talent, we just used him for background."

Which meant that young men like Jess Barker, Peter Lawford, Sonny Tufts, and Van Johnson were given the big breaks they might never have had without a war, although Barker's heart murmur, in the long run, did not do him much good. He had a few light leading-man parts during the war (in *Government Girl* and *Keep Your Powder Dry*) but after the war he appeared mostly in character roles before drifting out of the movies completely. His main claim to fame was making headlines in his stormy marriage to Susan Hayward.

After Pearl Harbor, Peter Lawford was broke and working as a parking-lot attendant in Palm Beach, Florida. He was handsome, an aspiring actor, and 4-F because of a gruesome accident in his youth: He almost severed his right arm crashing into a glass door at a hotel in Aix-les-Bains where his family was staying. The doctor wanted to amputate to prevent gangrene, but Lawford's mother insisted that he try to save the arm with surgery, which he did.

Born in England, Lawford had already had a role as a child actor in a 1931 British film, *Poor Old Bill,* and a bit part in a 1938 film, *Lord Jeff.* After Pearl Harbor, when he heard that Hollywood was looking for young men, he hitched a ride to California with friends and within a year, after bit parts in several films, had an MGM contract. His break came in a movie called *Pilot No. 5,* when the director decided he would end the film with an anonymous young pilot (Lawford) watching the hero (Franchot Tone) fly off to certain death. As one MGM executive put it, the look on Lawford's face in that one shot caused him to be put under contract to MGM. When Lawford and Louis B. Mayer met to discuss the contract, Mayer said that signing with MGM would be an act of patriotism and that, despite his 4-F classification, the young actor would help to win the war by making morale-building films. According to Lawford's biographer, James Spada, "Peter assured Mayer that he would do his best for MGM and world peace"—which he did in several uplifting wartime films, including *The Immortal Sergeant, Sahara,* and *The White Cliffs of Dover.*

Lawford also spent quite a bit of time explaining why he was not in the Army, which was made all the more difficult by his efforts to hide the deformity of his arm and by the fact that he was a good volleyball player and an avid surfer who helped create the surfing craze of the late 1940s. Despite his modest talent, Lawford went on appearing in films until the mid-1970s.

As did Van Johnson, who was even luckier than Lawford. He had not been called up when, in 1942, while working on his seventh major film, *A Guy Named Joe* (with Spencer Tracy and Irene Dunne), he suffered a life-threatening skull fracture in an automobile accident on Washington Boulevard in Hollywood. It was obvious that Johnson would have to undergo a long recuperation; Louis B. Mayer began looking for a replacement—perhaps John Hodiak, or Lawford. But when Tracy heard that Johnson was to be dumped, he rebelled, saying he would not shoot another scene if MGM did not wait for Johnson to come back. Mayer finally backed down when Tracy agreed to try to be a little nicer to Irene Dunne. He was drinking a lot during this period and was in the habit of unmercifully teasing his costar on the set.

A Guy Named Joe was about a dead World War II pilot (Tracy) coming back to promote a romance between a younger soldier (Johnson) and his girlfriend (Dunne). It was a big hit and made a star out of Van Johnson. Next came *The White Cliffs of Dover* and *Thirty Seconds Over Tokyo*, but Johnson always insisted that Spencer Tracy was responsible for his stardom.

TWELVE

This Is the Army—and the Navy, Coast Guard, Marines, Air Corps, and Signal Corps

The Army'll toughen you up, put some character in that pretty face. When you come back to Columbia, you might be able to carry a picture by yourself, like Gable or Cooper. —HARRY COHN to William Holden

Like those of other Americans in uniform, the military experiences of Hollywood stars differed widely. Some went into the service to exploit their macho image; some were born goldbrickers; some, because they were stars, were given duties that they did not relish or that they thought beneath them; and a great many, to no one's surprise, ended up in the entertainment, morale-building, or propaganda business. Most did their duty and went home to pick up their careers like everyone else. Hence, there was no real "typical" wartime experience for the male Hollywood star.

Perhaps the most untypical of them all was singer Tony Martin's.

When World War II arrived in America, Martin was the model play-boy, an egotistical nightclub singer who had had modest success in a number of pre-war movies (including *Winner Take All, Ziegfeld Girl,* and *The Big Store*) and a string of well-publicized romances, most recently with Lana Turner.

In his autobiography (co-authored with his wife, Cyd Charisse), Martin said he was "railroaded in to 1-A" when he appeared before his draft board. The eye doctor told him, "You're not an ordinary person, Mr. Martin, so I have to be very careful with you"—which meant he had Martin stand very close to the eye chart. Martin passed the draft physical with ease: "It isn't always a good thing to be famous," he said.

Classified 1-A, Martin began campaigning for a commission. He also moved out of his Hollywood residence and went off to Chicago to do ten shows a week at the Chicago Theater and the Chez Paree night-club. Unfortunately, his mail, including a draft notice, was not for-warded, so the FBI called on him to inquire why he was hiding from the draft.

Working through a contact with Lieutenant Commander Maury Aroff, a man–about–Los Angeles whom Martin had known since 1935 and who was now stationed in San Francisco, Martin was able to wan-gle the rank of chief specialist—not a commission, but a high-level enlisted man's rating. His first assignment was recruiting for the Navy in San Francisco: "They figured that if I was there, and the public saw me, I would be something of a come-on and lots of young men would join the V-5 and V-12 programs. . . . As I remember, my only real job was to go out every afternoon and bring a chocolate milkshake back for Commander Walters."

He became friendly with Maury Aroff, who, according to Martin, was not very popular with the Navy brass because he had not attended Annapolis and would not give commissions to favored people, like sons of admirals and the like. But Aroff did give great parties and drove a Cadillac.

Then one day someone told Martin that the Navy was putting the heat on Aroff for his high living. Martin warned Aroff that he had better change his ways, beginning with getting rid of his Cadillac, which he did. Martin had a Studebaker, which the automobile company had given him for a radio guest appearance; he agreed to sell it to Aroff for a $500 war bond. Martin bought an old Chevy, for which he paid $410. Then one day when he was recruiting in Nevada, he read a headline in the local paper. AROFF RELIEVED OF DUTY, MARTIN WARNED BY NAVAL

INTELLIGENCE. The Navy was charging Aroff with accepting a bribe (the Studebaker) to give Martin a commission (which he hadn't done: A chief petty officer is not a commissioned officer). Aroff faced court-martial; Martin was to be a material witness.

Martin was questioned and, he said, pressured by naval intelligence, which reminded him of the Gestapo. "We got the goods on Aroff," one Navy officer said to him. "Are you going to go along with the Navy, or are you going down with this Jew? It's your choice." The interrogators did not know that Martin himself was Jewish. (He had been warned "not to put anything down" when asked about his religion on the form he had to fill out in the Navy.)

Since Martin was not on trial, he did not have a lawyer. The interrogators questioned him until he was so tired he could hardly keep awake; then he was asked to sign a document. "I never did see a transcript of what I signed that day, and that document was never used in Aroff's court-martial," Martin wrote in his autobiography. "I still don't know what I signed and I guess I never will."

Tony Martin was now persona non grata, not only in the Navy, but around the country: "When he appeared on the floor of a nightclub either during the war or after that," said Rudy Vallee, "the father and mother of some boy who had lost his life as a seaman in the Navy would not only refrain from applauding his singing but also might even boo him while he was performing." Thirty years after the war, Martin was still smarting from the affair, convinced he had been given an unfair rap. He never considered the Studebaker a gift and he was never given a commission. Of course, he *was* leading the high life in San Francisco, a fact that was also publicized and was enough, by itself, to anger many parents.

The court-martial dragged on from August through October of 1942, with Martin, the chief witness, denying all the time that he had given Aroff a bribe. He was constantly ribbed by his friends, he lost thirty pounds, and he thought he was going crazy. He was deserted by almost everyone he knew except his mother, and was so down that he began to feel like a criminal until one officer told him he had to fight it, to get hold of himself, to be the old Tony Martin: Strut around a little, get a date, take her to the Top of the Mark. This, Martin did. And he felt better immediately. "From then on I held my head high, I walked like a gentleman, I threw my salutes with the flair of a Cary Grant in the foreign legion" (he was referring, no doubt, to *Beau Geste*).

Aroff was found not guilty, but was forced to resign his commission (he received an honorable discharge). Three days after the trial, Martin was called in to local headquarters and asked to turn in his uniform; he had been found undesirable and unfit for further service in the Navy. He was also told to report to his local draft board within forty-eight hours. TONY MARTIN KICKED OUT OF THE NAVY, said headlines across the country.

Martin went back to Hollywood and hid out, literally, in a hotel until his draft board called him. Then he entered the Army: "Nothing fancy this time . . . Just buck ass private Tony Martin—and they were waiting for me."

His first Army days were spent at Fort MacArthur, near San Pedro, California. Martin was sure the medics jammed the needles a little deeper in his arm and he knew they issued him clothes that were way too large for him—as the issuing lieutenant said, "You deserved it." The lieutenant was sent overseas for his nastiness.

Martin ended up in the Army Air Corps at Shepherd Field, Texas. To sustain him through this period, although he was not a religious man, he "prayed a lot, maybe ten times a day. I repeated the Twenty-third Psalm so often the guys thought I was talking to myself. It was God, prayer, and some sense of survival that got me through all the bullshit."

Martin thought God also helped him with his next assignment. Glenn Miller was forming a big Army band at Yale, and he wanted Martin to be one of his vocalists. "I felt as though I had stumbled into heaven through a side door."

To be part of Miller's band, you had to be an officer. So Martin went to the Air Corps OCS at Miami Beach, graduating in the top third of his class.

The day after he received his gold bar and saw orders indicating that he was on his way to join the new Miller band, "the bottom fell out of my world. An officer came to my quarters. I was told to pack my clothes, I was being shipped out. No commission. No gold bars. And no reason . . ."

But Martin believed that he knews what had happened: As a favor to the Navy, the Army had decided not to promote him.

So buck private Martin was shipped to Goldsboro, North Carolina, where he was assigned to a unit including foul-ups and ex-cons who were being shipped overseas to "some kind of suicide mission." He said the only thing that got him through that train ride to Goldsboro was being befriended by Lieutenant Robert Meservey, who under his stage name, Robert Preston, had just completed *Night Plane from Chungking* before going into the service. Preston consoled Martin with a bottle of scotch.

At Goldsboro, God, through an old friend of Martin's named Jerry Brady—secretary of the Hialeah Park racetrack in Florida—intervened again. Brady's brother happened to be General Francis Brady, commanding officer of the Goldsboro Army base. Brady outlined Martin's case to the general, who called Martin in, looked at his orders, and said: "Obviously somebody in the Pentagon hates you." He canceled the orders sending Martin overseas and assigned him to his headquarters staff, where he produced shows with the camp band, headed by Henry Mancini. "I began to feel like a man again," said Martin.

It was in fact the beginning for Martin of a normal service career. He wanted to do more for the war effort than produce camp shows in the United States, so he went to radar school in Boca Raton, Florida, then decided to go overseas. At a base in Kearns, Utah, he was issued winter clothing, so he figured he was headed for Europe. At Hampton Roads, Virginia, he boarded the U.S.S. *General Mann* and found that his ultimate destination was Bombay.

From here on it was just routine for Radarman First Class Tony Martin. He had a romance with a WAC sergeant, Dorothy Luft, and was in charge of organizing USO and other shows for the China-Burma-India (CBI) Theater. He served with Major Melvyn Douglas, who was also "very controversial" because of his liberal views. This convinced Martin (who could by now be forgiven for a little paranoia) that the CBI was where they sent anyone who was slightly controversial. He also had his share of close calls in airplanes, and came home with war stories—such as the one about the time he and a sergeant were playing gin rummy on a B-24 flying to Burma. Just as the sergeant yelled "Gin!" the pilot dived a thousand feet to avoid some Japanese Zeros. When the plane leveled off the cards were all over the cabin, and Martin said: "Show me!"

He came home with a Bronze Star for his service in the CBI.

Martin's story is a long one, but it is significant, because many people thought that the publicity he received in the court-martial he was involved in early in the war was responsible for much of the public's and the War Department's attitude toward stars in the service. After the Martin experience, the studios had to convince the public that the stars were as eager as anyone to serve their country.

Many people in Washington, especially the President, knew how important they were; even the head of the draft board came to their defense. "The stumbling block," said General Lewis Hershey, "is the failure of the public to appreciate the value of actors. The public is willing to accept certain things, such as work in a war plant, as essential. It fails to accept other things, even though they, too, may be important."

After the Tony Martin escapade, studio publicity departments made every effort to convince the public that movie stars were as eager as anyone else to serve their country and that when a star entered the service he was a model G.I. no matter where he served.

Perhaps excepting Ronald Reagan, the star who received the most publicity for going off to a nonwar was Alan Ladd.

Ladd was born in Hot Springs, Arkansas, in 1913, which made him twenty-nine when he appeared in his first big picture—*This Gun for Hire*, with Veronica Lake. By 1942, Ladd had had bit parts in twenty-seven films, most of them B pictures. Occasionally, he appeared in a major movie—for example, he played a reporter in *Citizen Kane*.

Naturally the public looked to the Alan Ladds of Hollywood to save America: After all, they were playing young hired guns in a country at war. After the Japanese bombed Pearl Harbor, Ladd himself said he could hardly wait to serve—although he managed to hold out for about a year. At first, the Army classified him 4-F because of an early diving accident and pneumonia. However, he finally found a service that would take him: the Air Corps. And his boss, Paramount chief Cecil B. De Mille, was ready to send the hero off to war. De Mille arranged a luncheon for him in Hollywood during which a very modest Ladd, with his best James Stewart demeanor, said: "Like every other guy, I am going into the Army because there's a job to be done. When the job is finished . . . I'll be back."

Ladd's biographer Beverly Linet recounted the reaction:

> He sat down to another standing ovation. It was as if he were headed straight for the Allied Air Force bases in England, where the first round-the-clock bombing of the industrial cities of Essen, Dusseldorf, Solingen and Mulheim had just begun. He was, in fact, bound for Fort MacArthur, just outside of Pedro, California.

But before Fort MacArthur, there was the Lux Radio Theater presentation of *This Gun for Hire* with Joan Blondell. After the program, the band played "Auld Lang Syne" and a spotlight shone on an American flag in the studio. Then De Mille stepped to the microphone and said,

"Tomorrow night at this time the star of this show will be Private Alan Ladd of the United States Army."

For the Paramount publicity department, Ladd now became the model G.I., going off to war; leaving his family (he was married and had two daughters, one born just before he began his military service), a prosperous film career, and a proud studio; and carrying a shaving kit from William Bendix.

From Fort MacArthur, fan magazines reported the usual stories about tough sergeants, how average guys coped with Army life, and how Ladd ached all over from boot camp drills when he went to bed. But of course boot camp was making a man of him. "Since Alan has been in the Army," said *Modern Screen,*

> he is a changed man. He can make a bed as tight and smooth as a snare drum. He can scrub a lovely floor, peel potatoes in artistic style, manipulate the business end of a broom with amazing results, wash clothes without tattletale gray, and rise and shine without a grumble anywhere from four A.M. on.

There was something about Ladd in every monthly issue of *Modern Screen* in 1943. *Photoplay* carried a piece by him on what men in the service said about their girlfriends and wives: "A Soldier's Code for Women." Although he was not on salary while in the Army, the studio gave him two hundred dollars a week to pay four secretaries to handle the fan mail.

When Ladd went home on weekends (as he usually did), he and his wife, Sue, would sit around with their friends Tess and Bill Bendix, while he griped about life in the Army. On one occasion it was just a little much for Bendix, who was 4-F because of asthma but wanted to be in uniform. "C'mon, Laddie. Stop griping," he said, half joking. "You know you're living a plush life down there in San Diego."

That did it! Sue turned on Bendix, and she was *not* kidding: "You're a fine one to talk—considering you're not rushing to join up." As Ladd's biographer reports, Bendix was stunned. Without a word, he got up, left the Ladd house, and walked across the street to his own house. He thought Ladd would come running across the street to apologize, but the apology never came. The Bendixes looked briefly for another house but didn't find one, so the two couples lived across the street from each other, not speaking, for several years.

Shortly after the incident, Ladd was hospitalized for stomach trouble,

then given an honorable discharge because of a double hernia, climax-
ing one of the shortest and best-publicized service careers of World
War II.

=

Rudy Vallee's military career was not as highly publicized as Ladd's or
Martin's, but Vallee felt that the spotlight was on him the entire time
he was in the service—in part, at least, because of the Martin affair.

Vallee was a bandleader and crooner of the late 1920s. His trademark song, "The Vagabond Lover," was also the name of his first
movie. By 1942, he was forty-one, a veteran of many musicals and a
well-established bandleader who was anxious to get a commission and
lead a service band as John Philip Sousa had done in World War I. He
was earning more than $200,000 a year and had a substantial ego; he
decided he deserved a captaincy, as would, he said, any surgeon or doctor who was earning in excess of $75,000.

But, according to Vallee, both he and pianist Eliot Daniel, who had
been with Vallee since 1934, were denied commissions. Vallee had to
go into the Coast Guard as a chief petty officer when he was told that
the draft board was breathing down his neck; this annoyed him because,
he said, his radio program provided jobs for at least 335 people. Once
he was in the Coast Guard, he said he was "almost grateful to Tony
Martin for the fact that I was not a commissioned officer, as being an
enlisted man gave me much more freedom than I would have had were
I wearing a gold braid."

He finally was given his cherished gold braid—two full stripes—
when he was scheduled to lead all the local service bands at a ceremony
for the secretary of the navy in the Hollywood Bowl. It was a proud
moment for Lieutenant Vallee: "I wore a white mess jacket, tuxedo
pants, and the shoulder bars of a lieutenant senior grade."

=

Mickey Rooney did not want a commission. In fact, he did not want to
go into the service at all—primarily, according to biographer, Arthur
Marx, because he believed that his new wife, Ava Gardner, would stray
if left alone. Louis B. Mayer was even more anxious to keep his young
star out of the service. Three years earlier, Rooney had replaced
Shirley Temple as filmland's top moneymaker.

Mayer used every conceivable argument to get the draft board to
classify Rooney 2-A, even arguing that letting Rooney play Andy
Hardy would make it easier to draft the millions of young men headed

into the service. And MGM submitted to the draft board a scene from Rooney's next Andy Hardy movie in which his father, Judge Hardy, explains to Andy's mother why her son would have to go into the Army:

> for the same reason I fought—and my father fought. Perhaps I can best explain it with the words from the first chapter of Genesis: God created man in his own image. But those we're fighting want to create a world in their own image, a world of tyranny, cruelty and slavery. We're not fighting this war for a conquest, Emily, but to make a world that will be safe for our children. We're fighting for tolerance and decency, and for the four freedoms that the President of the United States has so simply stated. It is to make this world safe that our nation has placed it in the hands and hearts of our millions of free men and women. Your son, Andrew, is one of those millions.

Each succeeding Hardy picture, the studio said, "will further this idea, carry Andy, as he grows older, closer to the war, and reveal through Andy and his parents the actual experiences of the young American boy who has taken such a step. The morale of the Hardy family should, and will be the highest type of morale of the American family." MGM also declared that it would cost the studio millions of dollars if Rooney were not permitted to make his next scheduled picture.

In September 1942, at the height of the Tony Martin affair, Rooney was given a three-month extension to make *The Human Comedy*. When the extension was up in December, MGM launched still another effort to keep Mickey out of the service, quoting General Dwight Eisenhower's statement that "motion picture entertainment is as important to the people on the home front as butter and meat."

This effort failed, but by now the studio was getting edgy because the Martin publicity had started the public thinking about coddled movie stars. At the studio's behest, Rooney issued a statement that he was ready to go into the Army or stay home and make films, "whatever the government decides." MGM also decided that Rooney should report to his draft board—which classified him 4-F because of high blood pressure. (He thought this was due to his deteriorating marriage with Gardner.)

This left him free to make *Thousands Cheer, Andy Hardy's Blonde Trouble, Girl Crazy,* and *National Velvet* (with twelve-year-old Elizabeth Taylor). Although Rooney was twenty-three, Andy's "blonde trouble," he says, was of the "Gee whiz, she kissed me" variety: "If the people at Metro had had their way," he says in his autobiography, "I'd have remained a teenager for forty years."

But MGM, the draft board, and the Hardy family could not keep Andy Hardy a teenager forever and neither could Rooney. By early 1943, when he made *Thousands Cheer* (at the age of twenty-two), he knew he was too old and healthy to be out of the Army. He was uncomfortable about his civilian status, even though the camp-show scene at the end of the movie, Mayer said, "will do more for America than ten Mickey Rooneys in uniform."

Rooney knew this was bunkum. He also knew that in the service he could, if nothing else, also produce camp shows; after all, he and Judy Garland had been doing it for years on the screen. Besides, his marriage to Gardner was now over (the last thing she said before leaving him was: "You know, Mick, I'm damn tired of living with a midget") so the question of losing her was moot.

He asked for another draft board medical exam, was reclassified 1-A, and was told to report for Army duty in thirty days. On the last night before he left for the Army, he asked Gardner out to dinner. She accepted, then invited him back to her apartment for a drink and put on a red nightgown; they went to bed. Before he left, he said: "I wanna marry you—again." And she said those famous words of the early 1940s: "Mickey, when you come back, I'll be waiting."

Rooney's first few weeks in the Army were marked by fistfights with other soldiers and Gardner's boyfriends. At Fort Riley, after he was appointed squad leader (for his hard work and marksmanship) one of the soldiers in his squad said: "You lousy fuck, you get to lead just because you been in a movie." The G.I. kept up the hassling until finally, after getting permission from his lieutenant, Rooney took on the G.I. in a bare-knuckles fight, which the lieutenant finally stopped.

A few weeks later, Rooney received a telephone call from Ava asking him to stop writing her. When he asked, "Is there someone else?" she hung up. On his first furlough home, he went to her apartment just as another man was entering it. Rooney whirled him around and challenged him to a fight; it was Howard Hughes. "I was ready to back away," says Rooney, "but then Ava appeared so I had to fight him." They ended up rolling around on the lawn, with Gardner pleading with them both to stop. When they finally did, the three of them consumed two bottles of Dom Pérignon and Mickey left, with Hughes saying, "And Mickey, don't get your ass shot off."

Rooney was shipped to Camp Sibert in Alabama; because of Ava, he was now drinking more than he ever had. Sibert was a chemical-warfare training base but Rooney soon learned that he would have nothing to do with poison gas. The USO, he wrote, was having trouble finding entertainers to go to the front, so the Army was organizing entertaining units of its own. Rooney was assigned to one of these. However, he was in Sibert just long enough to get married—though not to Ava.

He had been asked to accompany his general to Birmingham for a premiere of *National Velvet,* which Rooney had not seen. After the show, a *Birmingham News* reporter told Mickey she had someone she wanted him to meet. The someone turned out to be statuesque (and still-growing) Betty Jane Rase, who was attending the conservatory in Birmingham. She was also Miss Birmingham of 1944. As Rooney recounted this breathtaking moment: " 'Oh, Mr. Rooney,' Miss Rase cooed.

" 'Oh, Miss Birmingham,' I snapped back smartly."

Rooney had an estimated seventeen bourbon-and-branch-waters and then, capping certainly the swiftest wartime courtship in Hollywood, if not in the nation's history, asked Miss Birmingham to marry him. She

Mickey Rooney getting laughs in Europe. National Archives

agreed. Later Rooney said: "I'm lucky I didn't propose to my top sergeant."

Because Betty Jane was a teenager, Rooney had to obtain her parents' consent, which was no problem. Mr. Hollywood and Miss Birmingham were married the following weekend, on September 30, 1944, two days before General Eisenhower launched the Allied attack on the Siegfried Line. They had one day and one night for their honeymoon: "I was charmed with Betty Jane," he said, "with her blonde good looks, her refreshing nature, her Southern drawl. . . . I was happy to have someone to come home to, if I came home."

When Rooney's unit went to France, the problem was not being too close to the front, but staying with it. The Allies were moving so fast across France and into Germany that the entertainers could not keep up with them. "They're never in one place long enough to see a show," said Major Josh Logan, the Broadway producer, now producing for the European theater. His solution was to split the entertainers into three-man teams and give each team a jeep.

Mickey developed a show with three performers—an emcee, who told jokes, a singer (usually male), and at least one musician—which could be staged in a barn. And if Logan is credited with the idea for the "Jeep Show," Mickey Rooney can be credited with developing it and putting on some of the best (for which he was promoted to technical sergeant 3/C) on the western front. "He'd get two hours' sleep," said one of the entertainers who worked with him in Europe, "then go out and put on three or four shows in one day, right up front, where there was real danger of stopping a sniper's bullet." Mickey kept the show going, told the jokes, and did imitations: "God, the troops loved the imitations of their favorite actors," he said. "Gable, both Barrymores, Cagney, Bogart, Edward G. Robinson."

They did seven shows the night before the Allies crossed the Rhine: "Then our guys went off to fight the battle of Remagen about 4:10 A.M. At 4:45 I saw many of the men we'd entertained being brought back in on stretchers, dead or dying." They visited MASH-type units; Rooney tells of meeting one kid who showed him a picture of his girl and was about to have his leg amputated. Rooney said he tried to cheer him up, insisting that the girl would wait for him and that one day he would be as charming as the actor Herbert Marshall, who during his long movie career had been able to disguise the fact that he had lost a leg in World War I. Several years after the war, Rooney said, he ran into the young man in a bar. The ex-soldier told Rooney he had married the girl, they had three children, and he was now an executive at Boeing.

While they were moving around the western front Rooney received a V-mail letter dated November 15, 1944. It was from Betty Jane: "Now, you got another good reason to stay healthy. Ha, Ha." She was six weeks pregnant with the baby who would eventually become Mickey Rooney, Jr.

Rooney senior stayed in Europe, organizing and appearing in shows, until well after the war in the Pacific was over. Summing up his experiences, he said: "I was in the army one year, eight months and twenty-one days. When I left, I was older, wiser and still in one piece. I had one Bronze Star, a good conduct medal, a World War II victory medal, seven bronze campaign buttons on my ETO ribbon and a sharpshooter badge."

=

Like Rooney, Jackie Cooper was an MGM child star whom the studio could not keep from growing up and becoming eligible for the draft. In the 1930s, he was one of the country's biggest child stars as a result of his role in *Skippy* and then in a series of films with Wallace Beery: *The Champ, The Bowery,* and *Treasure Island.*

Cooper was twenty-one at the time of Pearl Harbor. Ever since Robert Montgomery, at one of President Roosevelt's birthday balls, had told him about torpedo boats, he had been eager to join the Navy. But his guardian—his uncle Norman, an agent—and the studio kept discouraging him, until finally, sometime in 1942, he said, "I was ashamed to still be out of uniform." Nevertheless, his uncle managed to get him a draft extension until the end of 1942. Cooper was miserable. "Eventually I wore him [the uncle] down," he said. He joined the Navy V-12 officer training program; by then he had read *They Were Expendable* and was even more fired up to become a torpedo boat officer.

In the Navy program he received the usual star treatment. "I think maybe the only time I really regretted being recognizable was during the war." He got into numerous bar fights when razzed about being a star—and, he said, the Shore Patrol invariably blamed him: "This isn't Hollywood, Cooper. You can't get away with that stuff here."

The V-12 program usually permitted trainees to finish their normal college curriculum, but required that they cram it into two and a half years. Then the trainees went to midshipman school, usually at some major college. Cooper first went to Loyola College in California, then was assigned to Notre Dame, where—actually in 120 days—they made him a "ninety-day wonder."

For Cooper, Notre Dame was an utter disaster, something like "Errol

Flynn Goes to Midshipman School." First, there was the case of the WAVE who locked herself in a South Bend hotel room and threatened to jump out the window because Cooper did not love her. The Shore Patrol finally broke into the room and Cooper was able to coax the WAVE off the window ledge. She was taken away and given some shots; Cooper said he never saw her again. This incident did not make the papers, but word got around; all his mates whistled whenever "The Great Lover" walked by.

However, the next incident did make the press:

SOUTH BEND, Ind., Aug. 5 (AP)—Jackie Cooper, the former child star now in the Navy, has been arrested here and charged with contributing to the delinquency of two teenage girls, aged 15 and 16. The arrest of Cooper and several others followed a drinking brawl on July 22 in a local hotel.

HOLLYWOOD, Calif., Aug. 5 (AP)—June Horne, 25-year-old movie bit player and daughter of director James W. Horne, and fiancée of Jackie Cooper, says she still believes in her fiancé despite his current difficulties.

"He just isn't that kind of boy," Miss Horne said today.

Not only did June Horne stand behind Cooper, she told him she would come to South Bend and marry him immediately if he thought that would help. There was a trial and Cooper was found innocent, but now women would come up to him in restaurants and spit on his uniform because they had a son in Guadalcanal or wherever.

He was dropped from midshipman school and sent to naval boot camp at the Great Lakes Naval Station in Chicago, which he found a breeze in comparison: "I actually enjoyed it." And his luck was about to change. Several thousand miles away, in Hawaii, Claude Thornhill was putting together a band to tour South Pacific military bases. Thornhill had been given the green light to recruit musicians in the Navy. Cooper, a drummer, had once played with him at the Palladium and he figured all the scandalous publicity was what prompted Thornhill to call from Hawaii and ask if Cooper wanted to join him. The band had a drummer, but Thornhill said Cooper could do some drum solos and work up some kind of skit.

Before he left for the South Pacific, Cooper married June Horne: "I think I wanted somebody to miss me in case I never came home." His big band rarely got shot at, even though they dressed in green fatigues and called themselves Thornhill's Raiders. Cooper did witness a Japanese kamikaze attack at Ulithi when the carrier U.S.S. *Randolph* was hit, but perhaps the biggest conflict he witnessed was between Thornhill, who was a chief petty officer, and singer Dennis Day, an ensign who outranked Thornhill, although Thornhill was in charge of the band. Cooper eventually became the full-time drummer in the band and spent almost all of 1945 playing for sailors in the Pacific.

=

The clown Red Skelton was another actor Hollywood managed to keep out of the war for a while. By Pearl Harbor, he was a veteran of several films, including *Whistling in the Dark* and *Lady Be Good*, and star of "The Scrapbook of Satire," a radio program that premiered in October 1941 and came on right after "The Bob Hope Pepsodent Show." By April 1942, Skelton and his "Mean Widdle Kid" saying "I dood it" were so well known that when General Jimmy Doolittle bombed Tokyo, the nation's headlines proclaimed: DOOLITTLE DOOD IT.

The Japanese attack on Pearl Harbor produced a surge of patriotism in Skelton, who rushed home after hearing the news to tell his wife, Edna, that he was joining the Marines. He was twenty-eight, married, and the father of a child, so he would not be drafted. But he wanted to go in anyway, until Mayer convinced him that he would be doing much more for the war effort by staying home to make morale-building movies and entertain the troops in camps shows.

This was a transition period for Skelton during which he was emerging as a star but was still an immature clown. He was making $12,000 a week in 1942, but he spent it immediately—on clothes, two-dollar cigars, and whiskey—and was seeing starlets. When he came home at dawn, he would tell Edna: "You probably won't believe this, Mummy, but I spent the night on Sunset Boulevard waiting for a red light to change."

He was right: She did not believe it. Soon they were separated, and then divorced (on February 17, 1944); although Mummy continued to manage his affairs and dole out money to him, Skelton was ready to marry Muriel Morris, a showgirl he had met while doing *DuBarry Was a Lady*. But at the last minute Morris backed out, wondering why his ex-wife had to manage his affairs. "Either Edna goes or I go," she told Skelton. Muriel went.

No longer married, Skelton had to face his draft board, and there was nothing Mayer could do about it. The comedian passed the Army physical easily, but was not called up for several months. This delay gave him time to appear in the movie *Ziegfeld Follies* doing his now-famous "Guzzler's Gin" skit. (During the filming of *Ziegfeld* it was revealed that Skelton had "borrowed" the "Guzzler's Gin" idea from a comedian named Harry Tugend, who sued and was paid $6,000 for the material.)

"I was the only celebrity to go into the service as a private and come out a private," biographer Arthur Marx quotes Skelton as saying. The trouble with this was that as a private he had to do everything a private was expected to do—like drill and peel potatoes—and as a celebrity comedian he was expected to entertain the troops.

Finally Skelton was shipped to Washington and Lee University in Virginia, where the Army had a school for entertainment specialists. "Actually, I don't think the Army sent Red there to teach him anything," said Hollywood writer-producer Bob Schiller, who was also stationed at W & L. "I think they just wanted to use [him] to entertain the officers there—it was like the brass wanting their own private comedian."

In March 1945, Skelton was assigned to troopship duty, entertaining troops being transported to and from Europe. Before going overseas, he went home to marry Georgia Davis, a gorgeous bit-part actress, who many think actually caused the breakup with Edna. Then he reported to the U.S.S. *General Altman,* aboard which he would perform "Guzzler's Gin" seventeen times a day, seven days a week. This was twenty days before the Germans surrendered. As his biographer says, "It should have been a breeze, like being the social director on a cruise ship. Instead it was a nightmare for Skelton because he was on call twenty-four hours a day as the ship's jester." For the G.I.'s by day and the officers by night, it was "Bring On the Clown." Skelton not only ran out of fresh material (and as a result was booed), he ran out of energy. He finally found refuge in the galley, where a sympathetic mess sergeant let him rest and gave him some homemade booze so he could do his next show. But when the *General Altman* reached Naples, Skelton was on the verge of collapse. He was given shore leave, during which he was asked to do more shows, which brought on a breakdown. Three days after he had arrived in Naples, Skelton was put on a hospital ship—not to entertain the wounded troops and the officers, but to regain his health. This took four months in the Army hospital at Camp Picket, Virginia. Buck private Skelton was given a medical discharge on September 18, 1945.

=

Another Hollywood star who had trouble in the Army was Desi Arnaz, not only because he was a movie star, and married to Lucille Ball, but because of his eye for the ladies, especially blondes. Lucy did not like Desi's being where she could not keep an eye on him. And she had good reason.

After Pearl Harbor, Arnaz resigned his commission in the Cuban army and tried to join the U.S. Navy, only to learn that, as a Cuban citizen, he could not volunteer for the services—although he could be drafted, which he was in May 1943. He was headed for bombardier school when he tore cartilage in his knee playing softball and had to have surgery. After the operation, he could not pass the physical tests required of a bombardier, so, of course, he said, "I was assigned to the infantry."

Arnaz had made four movies, including *Too Many Girls* (costarring with Ball), before he entered the Army, but he was not too well known. It *was* well known, however, that he was married to a movie star. "Naturally," Arnaz said in his autobiography, "all some of those guys could think about was that anyone who came from Hollywood was a glamour boy or a fag or something. I had a few fights and wound up in the compound a couple of times. I also spent a lot of time doing latrine duty and peeling potatoes, but I just couldn't let anybody get away with that shit."

After basic training, his knee was so swollen that he was assigned to limited duty. His first duty was teaching illiterate draftees how to read and write. Then someone in the Army had the bright idea that these boys needed entertainment as much as the G.I.'s in the regular camps. Arnaz was asked to put on some shows for them, but he said no one wanted to come to the camps for illiterates. Lucy rescued him by arranging to have "lots of people"—including herself, Ann Sheridan, Lana Turner, Tommy Dorsey and his band, Mickey Rooney, Lena Horne, and Martha Raye—come to camp.

Then Arnaz was assigned to the psychological section of Birmingham Hospital in the San Fernando Valley, which was being readied to take casualties from the South Pacific. His job was to make the boys, many of them coming directly from the battlefield to the hospital, feel comfortable. He had learned that when they were asked what they wanted most, most of them said immediately: "A cold glass of milk."

So Arnaz gave it to them, served by the item they wanted next most: a pretty young woman. And Lucy supplied the women, bringing out a busload of starlets to serve the men milk and orange juice. Lucy knew this all spelled trouble. Not only were there the milk-and-orange-juice girls, but Desi had also asked her to send out thirty starlets every Tuesday night, for bingo. He figured that with thirty pretty women working the tables, he wouldn't have any trouble getting his patients to come over to the auditorium and play. He was right.

Desi was also enjoying the bingo starlets, but not around the bingo tables. He had been very careful about not getting involved with the nurses at the hospital for fear of a scandal that would hit the papers and get back to Lucy. The Hollywood starlets were different: He could count on them to be discreet. So he had affairs with some of them, assuming that Lucy would never know. However, the gossip columnists found out and so did Lucy. So she began openly dating some of the young actors at the studios, including Peter Lawford and Robert Mitchum, who would soon be joining the service himself.

Then, in September 1944, Lucy filed for divorce. In his autobiography, Arnaz claimed that he could not remember why, but thirty years later, when he asked Lucy to refresh his memory, she said: "You were screwing everybody at Birmingham Hospital . . . the bingo girls, the milk girls, and the worst part of it was that it was me who supplied them to you."

She filed for an interlocutory decree in October, and if Mickey Rooney had the shortest wartime courtship on record, Lucy and Desi had the shortest wartime divorce. It lasted about half a day, according to one biographer: "the shortest in the history of the California courts," Lucy said.

The night before she was going to file for the interlocutory decree, Desi asked Lucy to have dinner; she agreed. After dinner, they returned to their Hollywood apartment and went to bed. "We had a beautiful night," Arnaz said. "The next morning, Lucy was up at seven-thirty and rushing around saying, 'Oh, my God, I'm late.' "

When Arnaz asked where she was going, she said: "I told you, I'm divorcing you this morning. . . . I gotta go through with it. All the newspaper people are down there, I got a new suit and a new hat, I gotta go."

Going out the door, she kissed her husband and said: "I won't say too many nasty things about you. I'll be back as soon as I can." According to Arnaz, she came back and joined him in bed, thereby annulling the interlocutory decree.

Arnaz stayed at the Birmingham Hospital until the war in the Pacific ended. He probably learned more about death and dying there than any Hollywood actor wanted to know, and he certainly was an expert on dying in front of the cameras. In the last movie he made before going into the Army—the highly acclaimed *Bataan,* with George Murphy, Lloyd Nolan, and Robert Taylor—he enjoyed "watching everybody trying to die differently and [seeing] how many ways there are to die when you are shot."

For example, Robert Taylor, handsome hero that he was, did not die in many movies. But according to George Murphy, as the platoon leader sergeant in *Bataan,* he did an Oscar-worthy fade-out. After all of his platoon had been killed and he had buried most of them, and dug his own grave, he picked up a machine gun, aimed it at the hundreds of charging Japanese, and yelled: "Ha, ha! Come and get it! What's the matter with ya? You dirty rotten rats . . . We're here! We'll always be here! C'mon, suckers. . . ."

Taylor's next movie (except for a cameo appearance in *The Youngest Profession,* about autograph seekers) was *Song of Russia,* which was supposed to do for our newest ally what *Mrs. Miniver* did for Britain: inspire young American boys to go out and die for it. The trouble was that Taylor was one of the earliest Hollywood anti-Communists on record. He did not want to do the film. "But," Louis B. Mayer argued, "it's just a boy-girl story set to Tchaikovsky's music, Bob."

But Bob, who played an American conductor who falls in love with a Russian musician (Susan Peters), said, "As far as I can see, it's Commie from beginning to end." He was awaiting his orders to join the Navy and did not want to be part of any "pinko propaganda." "I'd feel more at home playing Jack the Ripper or bleaching my hair and standing by as Shirley Temple's double," he said. He also accused Mayer of delaying his entry into the Navy so he could do the film.

Finally, Mayer brought in Nelson Poynter, head of the Hollywood office of the Office of War Information, who convinced Taylor that the government wanted *Song of Russia.* Taylor agreed to make the film (and it did get MGM in trouble during the anti-Red hysteria of the postwar years). Then Spangler Arlington Brugh (Taylor's real name) was sworn in to the U.S. Navy.

Because he had a civilian pilot's license and 110 hours behind the stick, he was commissioned a lieutenant junior grade, as was customary for civilian pilots, but not, at least at first, assigned to flying. The day he was ordered to report, the actor known as "the man with the perfect profile," whose good looks, bordering on prettiness, made him second only to Clark Gable as Hollywood's leading heartthrob, said "I walked into a barber shop and ordered a butch-cut and came out with about a half-inch of bristle all over my head. I left my own car in the garage and drove down to the Navy base in a beaten-up old station wagon. I figured I had two strikes against me before I came to bat. I was an actor and an officer."

His first CO, who had been tipped off that Taylor was coming, was the only one to recognize him when he reported aboard. But it didn't take his mates long to find out who he really was, especially after he was sent to Livermore, California, to make seventeen training films for the naval air cadets. He tried to get combat duty, but the Navy said he was too old and now, they decided, too valuable an instructor as well.

Taylor was sent to New Orleans to make more films, before finally being assigned to flight instruction. It had been a year since he last flew, so he asked if someone could give him a refresher course—an older pilot, not "one of those twenty-one-year-old kids who'll run all over the base telling everyone I can't do a slow roll." Pilot Tom Purvis, who would become a lifelong friend, described the refresher flight for Taylor's biographer:

"Taylor was nervous the first time we went up together," Purvis said. "He was concerned that I was thinking to myself, 'These handsome Hollywood stars don't take anything seriously except their box-office ratings,' and he was very quiet.

"We got to five thousand feet in an open plane and I said, 'Get ready for a right slow roll.' It was perfect, but when we came out of it Taylor looked like he was going to throw up. I asked him what was wrong."

The roll had bothered Taylor a little, but his real problem was that the three-hundred-dollar cigarette lighter his wife, Barbara Stanwyck, had given him when he went into the Navy, and which he kept in his shirt pocket, was now at the bottom of the Mississippi River. Purvis said: "If you ask me, it's almost funny," but Taylor replied, "You don't know Barbara."

When Stanwyck, who had just been nominated for an Oscar for James M. Cain's *Double Indemnity,* came to New Orleans, Taylor threw a private party for her at the Roosevelt Hotel, but refused all publicity concerning her visit. However, Mayer called from Hollywood and said, "You'd better keep yourself in the public eye, Bob. There's a whole new crop of young guys taking over here and the kids are crazy about them."

Mayer also said it was important to get back to Hollywood as soon as possible. Taylor said he was in no hurry; Mayer replied that he couldn't understand what the Navy was doing to his star. "The next thing you'll want is for me to call you Lieutenant."

"I like that better than being the heartthrob of the nation," Taylor answered.

"If you gave as much of yourself to being a good actor," said Mayer, "as you do to being a good soldier . . . you'd be number one around here instead of number two. . . . So long, Lieutenant."

Taylor's biographer insists that he really preferred the Navy to Hollywood and thought both Mayer and Stanwyck, who also did not believe Taylor really preferred the Navy life, were just "letting their little boy have fun." But when Taylor was out in public it wasn't always that much fun. He was besieged by autograph seekers and, once, by two zany women working as a team—one to distract him while the other cut off his Navy tie.

After this snipping incident, a man called him in his hotel room and said: "I just saw that display in the lobby. That girl had some nerve!"

"Who is this?" Taylor asked.

"Just a man like yourself. Know what I mean?"

"Don't getcha, mac."

"C'mon, you Hollywood men are all the same . . . always expected to be seen with a dame when it's really a man you want. Well, I'm the same as you, Bobby. We talk the same language!"

Taylor said he threw the phone across the room. (However, Stanwyck's biographer Axel Madsen says there might be some truth to the rumors of Taylor's homosexuality.)

Robert Taylor was discharged in November 1945; his most lasting achievement was doing the narration for *The Fighting Lady,* a movie produced by the Navy and 20th Century–Fox. It was voted best documentary in 1944, which is the closest Taylor ever came to an Oscar.

=

Gene Kelly's biggest Navy achievement was also in filmmaking, but his Navy films were unlike any he ever made in Hollywood. By 1944, when he enlisted, Kelly was a star, having had major roles in *For Me and My Gal, DuBarry Was a Lady,* and *Cover Girl.* He hated basic training and was furious when the Navy told him his first assignment was to make a movie. He had been training to fight fascism in Europe and the Pacific, he said, and if he wanted to make movies he would have stayed in Hollywood and made a lot more money than the Navy was paying him.

But in the Navy you do what you're told. Kelly's first film was for personnel suffering from battle fatigue. To prepare for it, he was admitted as a patient to a Navy hospital near Philadelphia. Soon newspapers were carrying stories about Gene Kelly suffering from shell shock and battle fatigue—despite the fact that he had never been overseas.

When this film was completed, he was made a lieutenant junior grade and assigned to the photographic division of the Naval Air Corps. His first assignment there was top secret. As Kelly described it:

> At the time . . . the Japanese were kicking the hell out of us. They had something called Baka bombs which caused so much devastation on our aircraft-carriers that ordinary fire-fighting equipment couldn't put the fire out quickly enough. The result was that men on board those ships were dying most terribly. Admiral King told me he wanted to stage a fake bombing raid in which new fire-fighting equipment would be demonstrated, and that I was to film the results. So about twenty men, eleven of whom were camera operators, were dispatched to a suitable location on the East Coast, together with a tough Irishman who claimed he knew of a foam that could lick the Japanese Baka bombs pretty effectively.

The foam worked, the film convinced Admiral King to send thousands of tons of it to the Pacific, and Kelly became convinced, as his biographer Clive Hirschhorn says, that a camera was as important to the war effort as a gun. And he no longer harbored a grudge at the Navy for not sending him off to fight the Japanese, although he hated it when people came up to him at bond rallies and asked him where he was stationed. When he told them at a photographic unit, they would say something like, "Well, that figures. All you Hollywood guys have an easy setup." He himself no longer felt he had a cushy job and he wished that in boot camp they had taught him less about killing the enemy and more about the camera equipment everyone assumed he knew all about because he was a movie star.

Kelly continued making films for the Navy, including one about the new radar equipment aboard the cruiser *Fall River*, the submarine service, and another about the sinking of the aircraft carrier *Benjamin Franklin* by kamikaze pilots. Near the end of the war, he said, "I was all set to go to Japan with a crew of eleven and with only a camera for a weapon and I was scared to death." But he was saved by the atomic bomb. All in all, Kelly's was a significant naval career, doing what film people were best able to do—make films. Every service needed them.

Melvyn Douglas said his military career was an obvious case of poor casting: "I was too old to be a leading man, even in an Army comedy." And he knew he was going to get the star treatment when he met his slightly drunk sergeant in the orderly room on the first day: "You Douglas?"

"Yes sir, Douglas is my name, sir."

"A fucking movie star, right?"

"Yes sir, a fucking movie star, sir."

"Movie fella," screamed the sergeant, who was not yet thirty, "just remember this! From now on you're just a shit like anyone else."

Not quite. As Douglas said, most of his fellow enlistees were "barely pubescent," while he was one of Hollywood's most popular and sought-after leading men. Any one of the dozens of starlets (and some of the stars) pinned up beside the bunks of the men he was serving with probably would have leaped into bed with Douglas just on the chance that he might pick them to appear in his next movie. No wonder the men envied—and hated—him.

Douglas was forty, but badly wanted to join the Army, in part to clear the political air of questions about his loyalty that arose as a result of all the attacks he and Eleanor Roosevelt had received concerning his appointment to the Office of Civilian Defense. He beat the enlistment cutoff age of thirty-eight by two days because a friend in government alerted him. MGM, said Douglas, "treated me as if I had committed treason by joining the Army." One minor executive said: "Douglas, you've hurt us and you've hurt yourself, too. Think of what you could be making right now."

Douglas had not sought a commission because of the political flak it would have drawn, but he did hope that hard work would earn him the right to an appointment to OCS. Gradually the star treatment subsided as he went successfully through basic training, although occasionally Private Douglas would be called over the loudspeaker to report to some colonel or major, usually to meet the officer's wife. Douglas was, he said, rather pleased at being able to get through basic training at his age. Then he learned that he was being considered for promotion to the rank of captain in the Special Service Branch. When a two-day clearing process turned into a month, he made discreet inquiries and found that he was being investigated by the FBI as "controversial."

So, on May 14, 1943, he wrote Eleanor Roosevelt saying that he had no objection to being investigated but would appreciate a chance to tell his story. Two weeks later he was called before a special board and asked to describe in detail his political activities in numerous liberal causes and his wife's active support of the Roosevelts and the New Deal. A couple of weeks later, Douglas received a letter from Mrs. Roosevelt, who passed on a note she had received from her husband: "Very confidentially, I had this checked up with the War Department and they tell me that, while Military Intelligence did have some feeling about Melvyn Douglas being a Communist or associating with Communists, they have now decided to remove all this from their records."

Douglas also learned from a friend in the Army that military intelligence had bugged his tent one day when his wife visited: "I remember that visit very well," Douglas said later, "and I presume they got an earful."

Douglas finally made captain and, probably for political reasons, was shipped as far away from the political home front as the Army could send him—to Burma, where Americans were involved in building the Ledo Road to supply Chiang Kai-shek's forces in China. Douglas was appointed "theatrical officer," which was considered an important post in the China-Burma-India Theater because the G.I.'s there were more homesick than most. The CBI had what they called a morale problem.

Douglas said that at first he did not think putting on camp shows was really fighting a war. "But after watching G.I.'s standing patiently," he said, "sometimes in mud up to their ankles in the pouring rain, to watch whatever entertainment we could provide, I began to change my mind. The poor guys often began to cry when the pop tunes from home were played. Before we'd been at it two months the mail started rolling in, with comments ranging from simple thank you's to 'This little program was like an oasis in the desert.' "

His worst experience in Burma concerned a show planned around the singer Lily Pons and her husband, conductor André Kostelanetz. They had agreed to come if the Army would assemble a sixty-piece orchestra. Douglas finally managed this feat, after an "organizational marathon," said Douglas, "which eventually included every commanding officer in the CBI . . . and anyone else who could help us trace members of a pre-war symphony orchestra in Calcutta." When Pons and Kostelanetz arrived at the airport they were met by some of the base officers, who told Kostelanetz there was more "brass anxious to meet him." "Never mind the brass," said Kostelanetz, "where are my strings?"

To his satisfaction Douglas had also assembled some strings.

Douglas stayed in the CBI until V-J Day. Early in 1945, he received a stunning "Dear Melvyn" letter. Not that Helen Gahagan Douglas had met someone else and wanted a divorce. No: Rather, she had been elected to Congress and she and the children were now living in Washington—had been living there, in fact, for some time.

=

Before the war, Robert Ryan was a quiet, low-key, modest liberal. His biographer had no idea what prompted him uncharacteristically to enlist in America's foremost fighting machine, the Marines. One friend speculates that the move was professional, that Ryan did it to protect his screen image as a tough Texas Ranger, a Canadian Mountie, or, later, a fighting man in *Bombardier, The Iron Major,* and *Marine Raiders.*

Ryan was thirty-four in January 1944, when he enlisted; his age may have been a factor in his spending his entire Marine tour of duty as a drill instructor at Camp Pendleton in California. But the many wounded and mentally depressed marines he saw coming back from the Pacific had a profound influence on his thinking, moving him irrevocably toward pacifism. He took up abstract painting while at Pendleton; one friend was impressed by the evolution in one of the paintings of "a great agonized face." The friend was not too surprised, on the work's completion, to see that the tortured face was, indeed, Ryan's own.

=

Robert Stack, the future Untouchable, had achieved some fame as "the first boy to kiss Deanna Durbin," which he did at the age of twenty, in *First Love.* But by 1942, he said, "I had played so many flyers in movies that I decided the Navy Air Corps was for me."

The Navy disagreed. Stack could not pass the eye tests even though he was a national champion sharpshooter. But showing more sense than the military usually does in such matters, the Navy made him a gunnery instructor. He served in this slot usefully and honorably until the end of the war. And he came home with his share of scary war stories, such as the time the gunnery crew he was teaching, trying to hit a sleeve towed by a passing plane, shot three holes in their own B-24.

=

If ever there was a model soldier in Hollywood it was Ray Milland, and not because of his military roles in such films as *Wings over Honolulu, Beau Geste,* and *I Wanted Wings.* Like David Niven, he had served in the British Army before World War II—in the Royal Guardsmen, in fact, where he unblinkingly stood guard at Buckingham Palace. But that was long ago (in the 1920s) and in another country. By 1942, he was a veteran Hollywood leading man (he appeared in fifty-two films before making his big breakthrough in *The Lost Weekend* after the war). He had a pilot's license and tried to enlist in the Air Corps after Pearl Harbor, but was turned down because of a tool-shop injury to his left hand. Determined to serve, he finally found a job as a civilian flight instructor at an Arizona base. Eventually he was sent to the Solomon Islands, where he contracted dengue fever. He came home weighing 142 pounds. "I wish I looked that way now," he wrote in his autobiography thirty years later.

=

Unlike Milland, Robert Mitchum was your classic Army cynic, at least to hear him tell it. Which is surprising, because on the screen he played some pretty convincing servicemen, from *Thirty Seconds Over Tokyo* and *The Story of G.I. Joe* in the 1940s to the TV miniseries *The Winds of War* and *War and Remembrance* in the 1980s.

Mitchum had always been something of a rebel. His youth had been spent riding the rails across the country. Hobo life took him from Bridgeport, Connecticut, where he was born in 1917, across the country, and back; convicted of vagrancy, he did a short stint on a Georgia chain gang, from which he managed to escape. By 1939, he was in Hollywood, married, and had vague show-business ambitions. He had already written some poetry; one of his first achievements was an oratorio directed by young Orson Welles and presented at a Hollywood Bowl benefit for European war refugees.

Mitchum then did some writing for nightclub acts until, he said, "I finally figured if a feller was married and there was a war on, then he got himself a lunchbox and really went to work. So I did that. I quit writing and went to work in the Lockheed aircraft plant—and almost wrecked the war effort."

Mitchum says his experience at Lockheed was almost—but not quite—as dreary as his later tour of duty in the Army. But it did have one intriguing aspect: Next to him was a worker named James Dougherty, who was married to an aspiring movie star named Norma Jean Baker. "He used to bring me pinup pictures of his wife and say 'Not bad, eh?' "

Mitchum was nervous as hell about the machine he worked with, but his real problems came when they put him on the night shift. After a while, he found that daylight was affecting his sight and that he was going blind. A doctor confirmed this but said that the blindness was caused by Mitchum's hatred of his work. The doctor said he would write Mitchum a medical release from a job in which he was "frozen." Mitchum protested, but the doctor insisted, so he was once again on the streets looking for work. Then one morning at breakfast, his mother, who was living with him and his wife, said: "Why don't you try and get in the movies? You love acting and if all those other idiots can get away with it, why not you?"

Mitchum said he had no ambition to be a real actor and didn't think he read lines very well, either. But he was big and looked as if he could handle himself in a brawl, which he could. So he decided to look for work as an extra, and found more than that; in fact, he won good parts in such films as *Corvette K-225* and *Aerial Gunner*.

For most of the war, Mitchum had a draft deferment, first because of the Lockheed job and then because he was married and had two children. The draft finally caught up with him in March 1945, but his trouble with the Army started before then. One evening during the shooting of *Thirty Seconds Over Tokyo* on location at Eglin Field Air Force Base in Pensacola, Florida, Mitchum, Van Johnson, Robert Walker, and Steve Brodie were passing the bottle around the barracks when a drunken sergeant came into their room yelling, "Oh, here are the Hollywood fags, all together sucking out of the same bottle." As Brodie told the story:

> With that Mitch came off the deck. He grabbed that son-of-a-bitch and they went fifty feet to the front doors and down six steps before they got outside. Mitch took both doors off the hinges, and when we got to him he was throwing this guy in the air, and when he came down Mitch was clocking him again. It took three of us to stop it. Mitch just came unglued. Word of the fight spread, and about a week later this poor son-of-a-bitch came to apologize. Mitch said he didn't want his apology, but the sergeant said it was a command. Mitch asked him if that meant it wasn't of his own free will, and the sergeant told him his executive officer had ordered him to do it. "Forget it," Mitch said. "Send *him* the next time."

Mitchum also made a conspicuous entrance into the Army. He had been arrested and briefly held in jail, but was released in time for his induction. The fan magazine *Picturegoer*, picking up a studio press release, said that Mitchum had tried to enlist but was rejected because of wounds received in a fight. Mitchum says: "When they took me away, I still had bits of the porch rails under my fingernails."

This was in April 1945, which meant that Mitchum did not have much time in the Army before the war ended. He did his basic training at Camp Roberts in California, then spent the rest of the war at Fort MacArthur as a drill instructor and medical assistant, which he translated later for a TV talk show to "rectal inspector." (Then he asked his host to assist him in a demonstration by dropping his pants.) Still later, in an interview with *Rolling Stone,* he said, "We used to line up nine hundred troops a day, tell them to drop their jeans and spread their cheeks." And still later, he told a *Rolling Stone* reporter that in the Army his job was to look up "the asshole of every G.I. in America."

=

Burgess Meredith, who starred with Mitchum in *The Story of G.I. Joe,* started out with a somewhat different view of the Army. His first assignment at the Santa Ana, California, base was cleaning latrines. Then, suddenly, he was rescued by a call from Katharine Cornell, who wanted him to appear in a revival of *Candida* that was supported by General George C. Marshall because the proceeds were to go to the Army-Navy Relief Fund.

In fact, in his memoir, *So Far, So Good,* Meredith says that he was actually cleaning a latrine when his commanding officer at Santa Ana summoned him to his office and said: "I'm ordered to fly you to New York at once to act in some goddamn play! Some goddamn war, eh, Private Meredith?"

Meredith also remembers opening night in Washington. After the curtain, he was in his dressing room and someone pounded on his door. "Who is it?" he yelled.

"General Marshall. Open up, Private Meredith," came the reply.

Private Meredith opened the door and there, indeed, were General Marshall and Katharine Cornell. Soon they were all dissolved in laughter.

However, Meredith was soon back at Santa Ana and eventually went to Air Corps Intelligence School, graduating as a lieutenant. After graduation, he was sent to London, and in a taped conversation with John Huston, also printed in his memoir, he tells how he made captain: "I was in London, standing in an elevator in the Claridge Hotel, when a four-star general—I think he was in charge of all the supplies in the European Theater—walked in with one of his aides. While we were

Clockwise, from top left:
*Robert Mitchum, who never saw
as much action as he did in* The
Story of G.I. Joe, *but who did
become a rather unique "specialist"; William Holden, who finally
became an officer and after the
war was able, as Harry Cohn
had hoped, to carry a picture by
himself; Alan Ladd, with
William Bendix, whose friendship he lost during the war;
and Robert Taylor, with his wife,
Barbara Stanwyck, whose $300
cigarette lighter he managed to
lose while flying upside down.*

both waiting to go up, he said to me, 'What are you doing as a lieutenant?'

"I answered, 'I'm attached to you, sir.' And, at that he told the aide, 'Make him a captain.' "

His first assignment was to make a film ordered by General Eisenhower, who hoped to offset the main criticisms the British had for American G.I.'s:—i.e., they were "overpaid, oversexed, and over here." The film was supposed to show G.I.'s how to behave in England, and Meredith hit on a brilliant "Let's discover this country together" approach by starting out with his Army superiors asking him to make the film and Meredith following with an aside to the audience: "I don't know why they picked me, I've only been over here a week."

With his camera crew, he took the G.I.'s into British pubs, homes, and offices, letting them know why they should respect British customs and how they were expected to act. It was so successful that he was asked to do another one on France.

But Meredith's best-known war film was one he did not direct: *The Story of G.I. Joe*, in which he played Ernie Pyle. One day in 1944, FDR aide Harry Hopkins called Meredith, who was still in the Air Corps, to say that Pyle wanted Meredith to play him in the movie and that General Marshall was anxious to please Pyle. "Do you want to or don't you want to?" Hopkins bluntly asked.

Meredith said that if he had to give a quick answer, "I certainly did." Within a few hours, his discharge came through, and he was on his way to meet Pyle in Arizona. In Phoenix, Meredith found a strangely anti-war, "spicy tongued fellow" who seemed to be somewhat tired of being venerated by the troops: "If I hear another fucking G.I. say 'fucking' once more, I'll cut my fucking throat," he told Meredith.

Meredith says that he was driving over to the Goldwyn studios to look at the final cut of *The Story of G.I. Joe* when he heard a radio announcer say, ". . . this most beloved friend of the foot-soldier and the most famous war correspondent the country has ever . . ."

Before he heard the name, Meredith turned off the radio. He knew what had happened. He knew it was Ernie Pyle, and he couldn't look at the film that day or for months. "His death so affects me. He was gone for good . . . and I became his shadow."

—

Although William Holden served almost four years in the Army and won an Oscar as the tough, pessimistic prisoner of war in *Stalag 17*, in his real Army career, Holden never came close to a German prisoner-of-war camp—or even to Germany.

William F. Beedle, Jr.—his real name—was the first major married movie star to enlist in the service, on April 21, 1942. His brother was in the Navy Air Corps and Holden was intensely patriotic and anxious to fight for his country. And he did know what a tour of duty in the service would do for his career, because his fan mail had increased dramatically after 1942's *The Fleet's In,* in which he played a dashing young sailor. But it would be unfair to suggest that that was what motivated his enlistment; in fact, Holden was furious at his studio boss, Harry Cohn, for evaluating the effect of an Army career on the Columbia property now known as "Golden Boy" because of his first big hit.

Holden reported to Tarrant Field air base, near Fort Worth, Texas, and was miserable—homesick, missing his new wife, and unable to adjust to the discipline and insensitivity of Army life. At first he could not even sit on the john in the same bathroom with other men, which led to the first and one of the funniest of the many war stories he came home with. Director-writer Garson Kanin, who had met Holden in Hollywood, was also at Tarrant Field. When Holden confessed his problem, Kanin led him to the latrine and directed him to sit down, close his eyes, and think only about what he had to do. After a few minutes, Holden yelled, "Hey, I think it's working"—at which point a young G.I. tapped him on the shoulder and said: "Mr. Holden, could I have your autograph for my mother back home?"

Another time, after being transferred to the Signal Corps base at Fort Monmouth, New Jersey, Holden was talking with fellow actor Richard Webb and failed to salute a passing second lieutenant. When the lieutenant recognized him, he circled Holden a couple of times, looking as if he were inspecting a prize specimen of nerd, and reprimanded him as he told him about the rules for saluting an officer, concluding: "Soldier—don't you forget it."

As Holden and Webb, thoroughly chastened, walked away, Holden said to Webb: "Remember when we were making *I Wanted Wings* at Randolph Field? We had brigadier generals carrying our bags."

As soon as he graduated from Air Corps officers' training school in Miami Beach, Holden was sent back to Tarrant Field as a public relations officer—selling war bonds, making training films, doing radio programs, and so on. In a series of six broadcasts titled "Dear Adolf: Letters to Der Führer," in which fictional letters were read by well-known Americans, Holden was a young soldier who had some thoughts about the girl (probably next door) he would marry. "We'll marry the girl we like," Holden told Hitler, "and the guy who makes a crack about her ancestry had better look out for his teeth."

Holden hated it. This was not his idea of what fighting a war was all about. His misery deepened when his brother, who was flying Hellcats from an aircraft carrier, was shot down in the South Pacific. Holden continued to ask for combat duty but the Army turned him down, feeling that he was more valuable to them making films.

Early in 1945, he was assigned to Fort Roach, the Signal Corps motion picture unit at the Hal Roach Studios in Culver City. When he and Webb, also about to become a "Culver City Commando," as the movie people at Hal Roach were known, reported for duty, they had to stand at attention in the adjutant's office for twenty-five minutes while the adjutant read them the base regulations. When they left the office, Holden muttered: "That son-of-a-bitch."

The son-of-a-bitch was a future President of the United States, Captain Ronald Reagan.

Holden spent the rest of the war uneventfully at Fort Roach, feeling increasingly guilty at never having fought in the war.

=

Probably no one in Hollywood—including Tony Martin, Jackie Cooper, and Frank Sinatra—had more trouble with his wartime experiences than Ronald Reagan did. The difference was that Reagan was a model officer during the war; his troubles came later.

Reagan's problems were fourfold: First, his studio and the fan magazines made every effort to portray him as the model Army officer married to the model wartime wife, Jane Wyman, who was sitting home anxiously worried about her model soldier husband. Second, Wyman was also a movie star, which made him even more susceptible to studio hype. Third, Reagan later ran for governor and President, so the media scrutinized his war record for evidence of favoritism, exaggeration, goldbricking, or high living in his military career. Fourth, Reagan would not listen to Marlene Dietrich, who said of war: "If you haven't seen it, don't talk about it."

When Reagan first entered politics in California, he made it clear that he was not a war hero. Once, when he wrote the *San Francisco Chronicle* in defense of his war record, he mentioned his book *Where's the Rest of Me?* and said, "I devote quite a few pages to my four years in the military and voluntarily made it clear that I never heard a shot fired in anger." Furthermore, like many men who did not see combat, he envied those who did: "We had an almost reverent feeling for the men who did face the enemy."

The fact is, Reagan did what thousands of Americans did: He joined the Reserves and earned a commission, and, when the Army beckoned, his bosses requested a deferment (as thousands of bosses did) on the grounds that he was needed. Anyway, Reagan was not especially anxious to leave his job: "Lew Wasserman [his agent] reminded me of the war that was going on, of Hollywood stars like Jimmy Stewart who had already been drafted and of my own reserve officer status. He said, 'We don't know how much time you have—let's get what we can while we can.' "

But you could get only so much before the new tax laws caught up with you. In fact, according to David Stockman, President Reagan's Office of Management and Budget director, it was Reagan's wartime experience that in 1980 helped campaign adviser Jack Kemp and economists Jude Wanniski and Art Laffer sell candidate Reagan on the benefits of supply-side economics and the evils of high taxes. "I came into big money," Reagan told them, "making pictures during World War Two. You could only make four pictures and then you were in the top bracket [90 percent], so we all quit working after four pictures." (For the record, Reagan never made more than four films in any one year after 1940, although not only because he was avoiding the top tax bracket.)

Before Pearl Harbor, cavalry reserve lieutenant Reagan was left to work at his trade. But after Pearl Harbor a fourth effort to obtain a deferment was rejected because of a "shortage of favorable officers," as the rejecting telegram put it.

When Reagan was called up in April 1942, it was quickly decided that his eyesight disqualified him from active duty. One doctor said, "If you went overseas, you'd shoot a general" (hardly the thing for a future President, especially if the general was named Eisenhower). Another doctor said: "Yes, and you'd miss him."

But the Reagan war mythology began almost on his first day in the Army, which one fan magazine recorded in a story headlined "So Long, Button Nose" and subheaded: "He said it with a grin, she smiled in reply. But when Ronnie went riding off to battle, he left his heart behind him"—with Button Nose, a.k.a. Jane Wyman.

Less than a year later another fan magazine interviewed Wyman for an article titled "My Soldier," which began: "It is nine months now since Ronald Reagan said 'So long, Button Nose' to his wife and baby, and went off to join his regiment. Button Nose the First—Jane Wyman

America's model wartime couple, Jane Wyman and Ronald Reagan, on the cover of Modern Screen, *January 1943.*

to you—has adjusted to the new way of life. . . . Little by little the new pattern of living overlaid the old. Ronnie wasn't around and that was that."

This was all very moving and it did make the millions of women sitting home alone and worrying about their men who were really off to battle feel some kinship, but the fact is that Ronald Reagan never left

California during the war. Much of his time was spent at the Hal Roach Studios and he came home every night. Actually, when Button Nose went off to some southern states to sell war bonds, she was farther away from home than her husband ever went.

His first assignment was as loading officer at Fort Mason, a cavalry base in northern California. He got off to a poor start when he told the commanding officer, Colonel Phillip Booker, "You and I have something in common."

When Booker said, "How's that, Reagan?" the new officer replied: "Well, I understand that you are a graduate of VMI [Virginia Military Institute], and I once played in a picture about VMI called *Brother Rat.*"

"Yes, Reagan, I saw that picture," the colonel replied. "Nothing ever made me so damn mad in my life."

In fact, Colonel Booker, an artillery officer, did not think much of cavalrymen ("I never knew a cavalryman who knew a damn thing"), so he was not too unhappy when Air Corps general George Kenny asked if he had any movie men on his base. Booker had no problem recommending Reagan for the new moviemaking unit at the Hal Roach Studios. When he told Reagan that he was being transferred, the colonel said: "In thirty-four years, this is the first time I've ever seen the Army make sense. This is putting a square peg in a square hole."

The transfer gave Reagan one of his best one-liners of the war. He would always tell the flyboys that "I was physically unfit for the cavalry, but still plenty good for the Air Corps."

Reagan was also good enough for the Hollywood publicity machine and the movie magazines, though they had to play down the fact that he hated to fly—at least according to Patricia Lawford, who in her biography of Peter Lawford said that "the only time Reagan flew during this period was when he went from Los Angeles to Catalina Island on a small plane. The experience was so unpleasant that . . . he never again flew while in the service." But then, he didn't have to, because he didn't go anywhere.

He looked handsome in his Air Corps uniform. He was also married to a popular movie star who was the model girl next door, an Army wife who did all the right things—sold war bonds, entertained the troops at the Canteen, and even made a major contribution to wartime communications. When Army censors said that putting a lot of x's at the end of a letter might be an easy way to send a coded message, Wyman suggested that the girls load up their lips with lipstick and seal their letters with a kiss. The fan magazines showed her writing letters to her own husband in faraway Culver City. As for Reagan, the magazines reported such things as: "Acting is something he did in another life. His mind has no room for that now. Morning or noon, midnight or five o'clock, he's buried deep in the war."

The Reagans also looked like model parents, raising their young daughter, Maureen, and then adopting Michael. (The adoption was also part of the war effort: It was reported that there were many orphans in the world who needed love and attention.) Despite their growing family, they were also referred to as the "constant honeymooners."

The fact is that Ronald Reagan's and Jane Wyman's careers and marriage were significantly affected by the war, as were the careers and marriages of millions of other Americans. When World War II began, Wyman had already made more than twenty films, mostly playing the friend-of-the-heroine in comedies. Her best-known film was probably *Brother Rat;* her breakthrough movie (*The Lost Weekend*) would not come until after the war. Still, she was quite well known and had a legion of fans, probably because many women could identify with her. "I'm queen of the subplots," she said. "I'm the girl who's the second romantic lead. . . . For years I've been the leading lady's confidante, adviser, pal, sister, severest critic."

Reagan had made a few more movies than Wyman, and although he was mostly associated with B pictures he had emerged as something of a hero after *Knute Rockne, All American,* in which he played a Notre Dame star halfback, George Gipp, now known around the world as "the Gipper." And just after he entered the service, *Kings Row* was released. It established an acting reputation for Reagan ("Where's the rest of me?") that would even survive that late-show favorite during his presidency, *Bedtime for Bonzo.*

After *Kings Row,* Reagan was being groomed for stardom while Wyman was still considered the subplot queen. That sort of thing can cause as much of a strain in a marriage as a war. But the war was also slowly but surely pulling them apart, as Reagan became increasingly interested in national and international affairs and less interested in Wyman, who also often disagreed with him about politics.

Like Alan Ladd, he was inundated with fan mail. Although the studio would not give him an allowance to answer it, it did lend his mother $75 a week for a year (eventually to be repaid by Reagan) to answer all the letters from people convinced that their favorite star was off somewhere winning the war.

Regulations said that an air base had to be under the command of a regular flying officer, so Fort Roach was commanded by Paul Mantz, a stunt pilot who was the *only* flying officer on the base. Reagan was assistant public relations and personnel officer, which was a good slot for him because the base was home, at one time or another, to so many actors, including Clark Gable, Burgess Meredith, Alan Ladd, George Montgomery, William Holden, Van Heflin, Arthur Kennedy, and Craig Stevens.

At Fort Roach, there was little reverence for military procedure. In one report, Reagan wrote: "3 A.M. Post attacked by three regiments of Japanese Infantry. Led Cavalry charge and repulsed enemy. Quiet resumed." In another, he noted that Culver City was "a very poor place to make pictures. Recommend entire post be transferred as near as possible to 42nd Street and Broadway, New York City." And once, while watching a column of men smartly marching by to the command of a drill sergeant, Reagan said, loud enough to be heard by the soldiers: "Splendid body of men; with half this many I could conquer MGM."

But the Culver City Commandos had their serious side. The Air Corps motion picture unit at Fort Roach made *Rear Gunner,* starring Burgess Meredith, with Reagan narrating. Reagan's next project was to appear in the joint Warner Bros.–Army film *This Is the Army* (an updated film version of Irving Berlin's World War I musical, *Yip Yip Yaphank*) with a host of Hollywood stars, including George Murphy, who played Ronald Reagan's father, and many soon-to-be-popular songs, the best known being "I Left My Heart at the Stage Door Canteen," and "This Is the Army, Mr. Jones"—"Mr. Jones" being Ronald Reagan.

The critics praised *This Is the Army,* although they ignored Reagan's performance. But Berlin, who apparently thought Reagan was a real soldier, took him aside near the end of the shooting and complimented him on his work: "Young fellow," said Berlin, "you really should give this business some serious consideration when the war is over."

Back at Fort Roach after working on *This Is the Army,* Reagan's unit became involved in photographing a simulated bombing, in Florida, of a mockup of the Peenemünde factories producing V-2 rockets. The films helped the Air Corps devise a bombing plan for these presumably indestructible sites. The Culver City unit also built models of Tokyo and filmed simulated bombing runs, which were shown to pilots and crews before they bombed the actual city. Reagan narrated these films.

On the base, he was a loner, screenwriter Edward Anhalt, who served at Culver City, recalled: "The group in the motion picture unit were jocks or intellectuals. He had no sympathy from the intellectuals. The jocks didn't like him because he . . . didn't drink or chase girls. His main quality was his optimism."

Another Culver City Commando, W. H. Moore, thought he saw Reagan's leadership qualities emerging at the motion picture unit. Reagan would preside at some press briefings "wearing heavy, horn-rimmed glasses. . . . He would get up before the film started and deliver some kind of talk. . . . He did so well I began to see him in the role of politician. He put on weight, his shoulders broadened out, and the boyish air gave way to a stronger, more manly presence. . . . He was Captain Reagan, quite clearly in command."

Reagan said that one incident near the end of the war sowed the seeds of his eventual distaste for bureaucracy and big government. When the government decided to add 250 civilian employees to the base it brought in a 50-person personnel unit, while the *18* members of Reagan's personnel unit handled the 1,300 officers and men on the base. One day when the civilian unit wanted to fire an incompetent secretary, Reagan learned that this was not possible without a trial; the only way to get rid of the woman was to promote her and transfer her to another job. Reagan was appalled. "I didn't realize it," he said later, "but I'd started on a path that was going to lead me a long way from Hollywood" and to the presidential campaign trail, where he would discover the "welfare queen" who drove a Cadillac to pick up her welfare check.

In fact, he would be on that path sooner than he thought. Not long after the run-in with the civil service, he was on his way to Disney Studios to narrate an animated short when, "listening to the car radio, I heard the announcement of a fantastic bomb that had just fallen on Hiroshima." He would soon be out of the Army.

In a sense, Reagan could not really follow Marlene Dietrich's advice to avoid talking about the war, because once he hit the campaign trail, he had to talk about it. Reporters would ask him questions he could not duck, while campaign managers and speechwriters encouraged him to talk about his war record as favorably as possible. And, of course, as every veteran knows (yours truly included), there is a tendency as the years go on to embellish one's war stories. But Reagan did more than embellish; he appeared capable of quite genuinely fusing reality and fiction in his mind and, as time went on, confusing the two. He once told his assistant, Landon Parvin: "Maybe I had seen too many war movies, the heroics [in] which I sometimes confused with real life."

Not only the movies he had seen, but the films he had made and the photographs he had seen informed his tales. For example, Wyman once told *Modern Screen* magazine she had "seen Ronnie's sick face bent over a picture of the small swollen bodies of children starved to death in

Poland." Many, many years later, Reagan told Israeli leader Yitzhak Shamir and Nazi-hunters Simon Wiesenthal and Rabbi Marvin Hier that his concern for Israel dated back to the time when, as a Signal Corps officer, he photographed the Nazi death camps. Could the photo of starving Polish children his wife saw him looking at have been the origin of this bit of history-bending? When challenged, Reagan eventually said he was referring to some "secret film" (actually shown in American theaters in 1945) that he had seen at Fort Roach.

Similarly, in his 1976 primary campaign against Gerald Ford, he said that segregation persisted in the Armed Forces *until Pearl Harbor,* when one black galley hand "cradled a machine gun in his arms ... and stood on the end of a pier blazing away at Japanese airplanes." Segregation was ended "under the leadership of generals like MacArthur and Eisenhower."

Reagan could not accept the fact that segregation persisted in the Armed Forces until President Truman abolished it in 1948. He insisted that the black machine-gunner at Pearl Harbor was real: "I remember the scene. It was very powerful," he told reporter and biographer Lou Cannon. Where did the story come from? There *was* a story about a black galley hand who fired a gun at Pearl Harbor; but where had Reagan seen a picture of him? Author Gary Wills, who researched this incident thoroughly for his book *Reagan's America,* could find no footage of it. Maybe Reagan was thinking of another story he must have heard, about Marine pilot Lieutenant Tyrone Power, who actually grabbed a machine gun at Okinawa and tried unsuccessfully to prevent a bunch of suicidal Japanese from blowing up his plane, *Blithe Spirit.*

But Wills finally decided the President must have recalled a scene from the movie *Air Force,* in which John Garfield cradled a machine gun in his arms and shot a Japanese plane out of the sky. For Reagan, if it happened in the movies, it was real. In his monumental biography *President Reagan: The Role of a Lifetime,* Lou Cannon concluded that Reagan was blessed or cursed with the ability to believe almost any story if it was told sincerely and well. At one Gridiron dinner Reagan was sitting next to columnist Charles McDowell, who is from Lexington, Virginia. McDowell said he told the President he vividly recalled seeing him and Eddie Albert in a drugstore in 1938, when they were on location in Lexington shooting *Brother Rat.* Reagan insisted that he was never in Lexington for the shooting of *Brother Rat;* rather, he said, because McDowell had seen the movie five or six times "that implanted in your head that I was there. You believed it because you wanted to believe it. There's nothing wrong with that. I do it all the time."

Peter Lawford's biographer, Patricia Lawford, cites another perfect example: One of Reagan's favorite war stories concerned a B-17 pilot who had ordered his crew to bail out. All were gone, except for a young wounded gunner who could not move. When the pilot was about to bail out, the boy started to cry, so the pilot remained with the plane, telling the boy: "Never mind, son, we'll ride it down together."

Mrs. Lawford asked: "How could anyone know that was what had happened?" Lars-Erik Nelson, a New York *Daily News* reporter, tracked down the story. The incident did happen—in a 1944 film, *Wing and a Prayer.*

Reagan's longtime aide Lyn Nofziger confirmed this side of his former boss when he said in his memoirs that one of the things Reagan always did best was "convince himself that the truth is what he wants it to be."

In April 1985, a French journalist asked President Reagan if he knew about the *New York Times* report that many of the German SS agents who killed 642 inhabitants of the village of Oradour were buried at the Bitburg cemetery, which he was about to visit. "Yes," replied Reagan. "I know all the bad things that happened in that war. I was in uniform for four years myself."

Ironically, Reagan's war experience seemed to strengthen the fusion between real and unreal in his mind. As he said during the campaign of 1984: "I think the people should understand that three quarters of the defense budget [which he increased by billions of dollars while he was President] pays for pay and salary—or for pay and pension—and then you add to that food and wardrobe."

If you're going to fight wars, you have to have a wardrobe department. MGM did.

—

There was never any confusion in Glenn Miller's mind about the reality of war, although he came out of the same world of make-believe as Reagan did. His orchestra was one of the most popular in the country in the 1940s. They had made two movies—*Sun Valley Serenade* (with a host of stars and a great song, "Chattanooga Choo-Choo") and *Orchestra Wives* (featuring Jackie Gleason, several Hollywood starlets playing the wives, and more great Miller music). The orchestra was riding high when Miller, who was too old to be drafted, suddenly decided he should join the Air Corps: "It is not enough," he said, "for me to sit back and buy bonds. . . . The mere fact that I have had the privilege of exercising the rights to life and work as a free man puts me in the same position as every other man in uniform, for it was the freedom and the democratic way of life we have that enabled me to make strides in the right direction."

Perhaps with premonition, he also said: "I'm going into this war and coming out some kind of hero."

In the service he had hoped to take the Army, Navy, and Marines in the right direction when it came to music—meaning he wanted bands in *every* service that could not only play military music but swing. He was frustrated by the military bureaucracy, but the Air Corps eventually permitted him to create one of the great bands of the 1940s, picked from some of the top musicians who were already in the service or whom he persuaded to join. From his own band, there was first trumpeter Zeke Zarchy, arranger Jerry Gray, bassist Trigger Albert, and trombonist Jim Priddy; from Benny Goodman's band, pianist Mel Powell and trumpeter Steve Steck; from Artie Shaw's, trumpeter Bernie Privin and sax player Hank Freeman; from Harry James's, saxist Chuck Gentry; from Tommy Dorsey's, guitarist Carmen Mastren; from Will Bradley's, clarinetist Peanuts Hucko; from Vaughan Monroe's big band, trumpeter Bobby Nichols; from Jan Savitt's, two saxophonists, Jack Ferrier and Gabe Gelinas; the great drummer Ray McKinley, a personal friend of Miller's; and vocalist Johnny Desmond.

There were also first-rate musicians from various symphony orchestras and recording studios who could swing as well as play marches. Miller's was some band, although its organizer would continue to meet resistance from a few military men who were still playing music for the last war. "We played those Sousa marches pretty straight in the last war and we did all right," one officer said to Miller.

"Tell me, Major," Captain Miller replied, "are you still flying the same planes you flew in the last war, too?"

The Miller Air Corps Band's most famous song was not a Sousa march but a swinging, marching arrangement of W. C. Handy's "St. Louis Blues," first suggested by Ray McKinley. Other Air Corps marching tunes included "Blues in the Night" and "The Jersey Bounce." And Miller did not hesitate to speak heresy when talking about traditional Army band music. "We've got to keep pace with the soldiers. . . . There's no question about it—anybody can improve on Sousa."

In the spring of 1944, the huge band was ordered to England— twenty string players, five trumpets, four trombones, one French horn, six reeds, two drummers, two pianists, two bassists, a guitarist, three arrangers, and five singers. (They were a tremendous hit, as anyone who was in England during the buildup before the landing in Nor-

Glenn Miller leads his big Army Air Corps Band during World War II. American Forces Network Alumni Association

mandy will remember.) And Miller's chance to become a World War II hero came immediately. Although some of his men wanted to take it easy for a couple of days after their first night in London, Miller wanted to move on and play a concert for the RAF at Bedford. His wish prevailed, the band moved to Bedford, and that night a V-rocket hit the quarters the band had left behind in London, completely demolishing the place. One of Miller's associates, Don Haynes, attributed their missing the bomb to the "Miller luck," which, he said, had been working for a couple of years.

This ultimate big band continued playing in England for almost a year. Miller said the greatest sound produced at his concerts was "thousands of G.I.'s reacting with an earsplitting, almost hysterical yell after each number."

However, he was still having problems with the military brass. He had agreed to do some BBC broadcasts in addition to his concerts over the American Armed Forces radio, but a BBC executive said listeners were complaining that in outlying areas they could only hear the louder passages; therefore, he said to Miller, "you must keep your volume constant at all times."

Miller could not believe what he was hearing. When the executive confirmed it, he canceled his BBC broadcasts, an act that inspired one BBC official to hurl at him that by now old chestnut about Americans: "You're overpaid, overfed, oversexed, and over here."

Although Miller, who hated to fly, usually flew with his band to concerts around England, he began to cut back on his flying when his plane almost landed on top of a B-17 taking off at Hendon Airdrome. But after the liberation of Paris, he began getting impatient to take his orchestra to France; when the orders were finally given, Haynes made plans to fly over to Paris to arrange for the band's arrival. Miller, anxious to get going (and telling Cecil Madden, a BBC producer, that he had promised to attend a reception in Paris), decided to go in Haynes's place and make the arrangements. He found a colonel, Norman F. Baesell, who was flying over in the personal plane of some general. In the afternoon of December 15, 1944, Miller, Baesell, and the pilot, Flight Officer F. O. Morgan, were ready to fly from a small airstrip at Twinwood Farm to Paris. Just before they took off, Haynes said to Miller: "Happy landings and good luck. I'll see you in Paris tomorrow."

Miller, who was visibly uneasy about flying in the foggy, drizzly weather of that afternoon, replied: "Thanks, Haynesie. We may need it."

They did, but the Miller luck had finally run out. Three days later, Haynes brought the band over to Paris only to find that Miller had not yet arrived. His plane and its passengers were never seen or heard from again. There were many theories about what happened to them, but biographer George T. Simon investigated them all and concluded that the original theory was the valid one. The small plane had simply iced up and gone down in the English Channel.

The band had planned to stay on the Continent six weeks, but it was so popular it stayed six months. Jerry Gray took over the big band, Ray McKinley organized a dance band, and Powell headed a small jazz group. "Next to a letter from home," General Jimmy Doolittle once told Glenn Miller, "your organization is the greatest morale-builder in the ETO."

USO 2:
They Also Served Who Acted Tough, Read Shakespeare, Did Tricks, Sang, Danced, and Told Jokes

The closer we got to enemy fire, the louder the laughter. If it started getting hysterical, I knew it was time to dive for a foxhole. —BOB HOPE

The USO was the obvious way for actors not in the service to make a contribution to the war effort. But many veteran actors did not know exactly what to do up there onstage, in front of a lot of men in uniform. It was especially difficult for the macho guys who were usually viewed by their fans as being as tough and manly off the screen as on. Bob Hope could tell jokes, Al Jolson could sing, Harpo Marx could play the harp, and Charles Laughton could read from the Bible or Shakespeare. But what could Humphrey Bogart do? The USO finally decided the best thing was for him to be himself.

When Humphrey Bogart, accompanied by his wife, Mayo Methot, a former actress and singer, went overseas with the USO in December

1943, he was best known to the G.I.'s as the ultimate tough guy—he usually played a gangster. Maybe he was even tougher when he played the good guy—for example, Sam Spade in *The Maltese Falcon.* The kind of guy to whom one young woman, who had been through three hundred air raids in London, wrote saying she always wished he was there with her in the shelter because he was so tough and cool. Or the kind of guy who, when he walked up to a bunch of G.I.'s in North Africa to bum a cigarette, would be asked: "How're your boys doing?"—meaning a couple of Hollywood gangsters the G.I. knew were in trouble with the law. And Axis Sally, the Tokyo Rose of Europe, said in one of her German radio broadcasts: "Hello suckers! What do red-blooded Yanks think about Hollywood sending over a phony movie gangster killer to show you guys how to be tough?"

Actually, Bogart would see quite a bit of fighting overseas—but most of it was between him and Mayo. Sometimes he fought with someone in a camp bar who wanted him to prove how tough he was. On their last night in Hollywood before leaving for New York, he and Mayo had a good scrap at the Cock 'n' Bull on Sunset Boulevard, and Peter Lorre predicted that Mayo would "come back with a Purple Heart and a black eye." She naturally thought Bogey would be taking North Africa single-handed, despite the fact that the Allies had invaded it more than a year earlier and the beaches were long since secure. But at "21" in New York, she envisioned Bogart going ashore with shells falling all around his landing craft. And she wanted to be with him. "I love that son-of-a-bitch so much! If they're going to get him, they're going to get me."

Sometimes he would also have trouble getting her. One night in Oran, she locked him out of her room and he began to break the door down, when a colonel appeared and demanded that Bogart, who was in his USO uniform, give his name, rank, and serial number.

Bogart yelled back: "Got no name, rank, and serial number, and you can go to hell!"

The next day, when asked to apologize, he said: "I didn't mean to insult the uniform, I just meant to insult you."

Onstage, the Bogarts were not really much of an act. They traveled with two New York entertainers, Don Cumming and Ralph Hark, and called themselves "The Filthy Four." Mayo sang a few songs, including her trademark, "Embraceable You," and Bogart did some sloppy card tricks but mostly recited lines from his movies and poked fun at himself about being so tough. "Now, everybody stay where you are, see," he might start off. "We'll have a little music, see? And some laughs. And then I'll tell you what I'm really over here for—to get a new mob. The draft took all my best rod men. Anybody want to get in on the racket?"

When a G.I. asked him how he could fire thirty shots from a six-shot revolver, Bogart replied: "Shhhhhhh. That's it, kid, that's my secret weapon. It's gonna win the war." Then he'd say, "I'm gonna let you in on the real inside dope. You want to know where you're going next? Well, I gotta be cagey about this, but you remember I made a picture called *Casablanca*? And where did you guys go after that? Uh-huh. Well, I just finished one called *Passage to Marseille*. Get it? Don't tell anybody."

Some of Bogart's best performances, however, took place offstage. Biographer Joe Hyams tells the story of the time Bogart was in Caserta having a couple of drinks with columnist Ernie Pyle and director John Huston. There were a few battle-hardened men at the bar. Suddenly one of them tossed Bogart a machine gun, saying, "Okay, tough guy, show us just how tough you really are."

In his best Duke Mantee manner, Bogart grabbed the machine gun, yelled, "Thanks, pal, this is it," and fired several rounds at the wall, coming close to Huston and Pyle. Then he tossed the gun back to the G.I., saying "Sorry, pal, I didn't know it was loaded."

Another time, some paratroopers insisted on teaching him how to hit the ground in a parachute jump, saying he might have to do it some-time in a movie. After learning how, Bogey, with a few drinks in him, leaped off the bar, shouting "Geronimo!"—and knocked himself out.

Although the Filthy Four visited towns that had been shelled just the day before their arrival, they were never bombed. But Bogart's USO experience was real enough—and so were the fights with Mayo.

The marriage was almost on the rocks; and his next war movie would be *To Have and Have Not,* with a newcomer: Lauren Bacall. "I don't know how it happened," wrote Bacall. "It was almost impercepti-ble. It was about three weeks into the picture—the end of the day—I had one more shot. I was sitting at the dressing table in the portable dressing room combing my hair and Bogey came in to bid me good night. He was standing behind me—we were joking as usual—when suddenly he leaned over, put his hand under my chin, and . . ." Bogey, as only he could do it, took a worn matchbook out of his pocket and asked Bacall to write her telephone number on the back. He was forty-four and married; she was nineteen; the rest is Hollywood history.

Humphrey Bogart did not see much action with the enemy when he went to North Africa in 1944, but he had a few skirmishes with his wife, Mayo Methot. Edward G. Robinson said, "I never pretended to be anything but Little Caesar," when he entertained troops in France. National Archives

=

Edward G. Robinson was one of the first entertainers to follow the troops into France after D-Day. In places like Saint-Lô and Caen he entertained, "never pretend[ing] to be anything but Little Caesar." With the help of Jack Benny, Milton Berle, and George Burns, he worked out a routine, about which he said, "It embarrassed me every time I did it, but they loved it."

> Pipe down, you mugs, or I'll let you have it. Waddaya hear—from the mob?
>
> *(Holds out the violin case)*
>
> I suppose you guys think there's a fiddle in this case. Who do you think I am, Jascha Heifetz? That's what the USO Committee thought when they sent me over. I had to promise 'em I was going to play a little long-hair music, like maybe the finish of the Unfinished Symphony. . . .
>
> *(Case flops open, revealing a submachine gun)*
>
> But how can you play Beethoven on a Chicago typewriter? This is the kid himself talking—Little Caesar. Remember? You'd better remember, because anybody who don't will find himself at the bottom of the East River with his feet in a cake of cement! I ain't kidding, neither. . . . Everything is jake until I get to thinking about all the shooting that's going on in the world and Little Caesar ain't in on it, and I get awful lonely, awful heartsick. So I goes back to the draft board, sticks my roscoe in the doctor's ribs, and says, "Doc, if you say I'm 4-F again, I'll drill you fulla holes!" So what do you think he says? "5-F!"

Sometimes a Hollywood tough guy did not feel comfortable playing tough in front of soldiers; he would try to work up a song-and-dance routine, with mixed results. But for one celluloid gangster of the 1930s it was easy. By 1944, James Cagney had starred as George M. Cohan in *Yankee Doodle Dandy,* so when he went to England with the USO in 1944 it was as Cohan, not as the gangster of *Public Enemy.* When he met reporters in England (after a frightening trip over on the troopship *Mauretania,* with submarine alerts and the captain telling them that there was not enough life-saving gear on board for everyone) he said he was just there "to dance a few jigs, sing a few songs, say hello to the boys, and that's all."

He had worked up a routine on the history of dance styles, ending with Fred Astaire, the highlight being one of his own numbers from

Yankee Doodle Dandy. In one of the first shows, Cagney became a little winded and a G.I. yelled: "Hey, Jim, you're getting old."

Cagney, who was forty-five, agreed but asked the young G.I. to come up onstage. "I'll tell you what I'll do," Cagney said. "I'm going to have the piano player begin and I'll start dancing. All you've got to do is hop from one foot to another, eight times on each foot, in time with the music."

The G.I. agreed. Before Cagney was through the first chorus the kid was ready to collapse and his fellow soldiers were jeering him.

=

Pat O'Brien was a tough guy, but he rarely played a gangster. He was usually a priest (*Angels with Dirty Faces*), a coach (*Knute Rockne, All American*), a tough soldier (*Marine Raiders, The Iron Major, Secret Command*), or a G-man (*Public Enemy's Wife*) who brought the gangster in or gunned him down. But an even tougher role was to play for the G.I.'s, so when O'Brien went overseas, he developed a little Irish song and dance, told a few jokes, and then got out of the way for the showgirls. He had tours of duty in the Caribbean and South Pacific, which the USO told him "was a great place for a pleasure cruise." Actually, O'Brien says, his troupe ended up in steaming jungles with cannibals near their camps: "We were lucky, it was Lent," he said.

Spencer Tracy was another 1930s tough guy, sometimes good, sometimes bad. But his best roles were men of forthright honesty and integrity—as in *Captains Courageous* and *Boys Town.* He was really too old for the service, but was unhappy about not being in uniform and did not think selling bonds on the radio was enough. Pat O'Brien suggested he go on a USO tour, but Tracy didn't know what he could do. And he did not want to just go out, shake hands, and joke with the boys. John Garfield once persuaded him to do this at the Hollywood Canteen and Tracy was visibly uncomfortable.

Lionel Barrymore asked what was wrong with singing for the troops. Tracy said he couldn't sing a note, to which Barrymore replied, "That's why I'd pay money to hear you try."

So Tracy worked up his own version of "Pistol Packin' Mama," and went on a USO tour just to get it "off his conscience." The tour produced a few happy moments for him in Hawaii when he discovered the troops did not mind that he was not Betty Grable. A young marine told him: "Gee, Mr. Tracy, I'll bet you could really act if you tried."

However, Tracy did not really like the road trips. On another long, dreary journey to Alaska in 1944, he was grounded by bad weather in

Seattle. After a few days of sitting in a hotel room, he simply quit and came home—and his USO career was over. "Once is enough," he said. Spencer Tracy's main contribution to the war effort was three films: *A Guy Named Joe, The Seventh Cross,* and *Thirty Seconds Over Tokyo.*

As we have seen, John Garfield was one of the most dedicated proponents of the idea that actors and actresses had an obligation to entertain the troops. Early in the war, he wrote an article on this subject for *Theater Arts* which virtually established the wartime credo for actors:

> Remember the romantic character who had wanderlust in his eye, and nothing much in his head? He just wanted to enjoy life with no cares or responsibilities. For years he's been popping up in magazine stories, circulating library novels and in the productions of Hollywood and Broadway. I got to know him well.
>
> But now, this fellow is as dated as a cup of coffee with three lumps of sugar. There's too much work to be done. The lovable bum is no longer lovable. He doesn't justify his existence. And you don't do it by simply holding down a job, or by earning money, or by paying taxes—or even by buying war bonds. You've got to find more ways than these to take care of your responsibilities to the war effort—until the government solves the problem for you.

In the spring of 1944, when his picture *Pride of the Marines* was delayed, Garfield went to Italy with a USO group billed as "The Flying Showboat." It consisted of Garfield; actor Eddie Foy, Jr., who was making something of a career out of playing his own father (in, for example, *Lillian Russell, Yankee Doodle Dandy,* and *Wilson*); two starlets, Olga Klein and Sheila Roberts; and actress Jean Darling, who had appeared in a number of the early, silent "Our Gang" comedies and would later play Carrie Pipperidge in the original Broadway production of *Carousel.*

En route to Europe, Garfield stopped in Washington to attend the President's Birthday Ball. Waiting to be introduced to FDR, he kept thinking, "Little East Side boy going to meet the President." When he reached the President, Roosevelt took his hand and said, "John Garfield—hear you're going overseas."

"Yes, Mr. President," Garfield repied.

"Well, I hope you have as good a time as I did," Roosevelt said, no doubt referring to the Tehran Conference in late 1943, when he met Stalin for the first time. The cordiality and compromise at that meeting made it perhaps the high point of the Soviet-Western relationship.

Exactly what the Flying Showboat did other than the usual song-

and-dance routine and nostalgic hometown jokes is not clear, but the troupe was apparently a big hit. Quite a few acts were performed under fire, mostly in Italy, where the fighting was still intense. One of Garfield's best routines was about seeing a sign all over Italy reading "Al Ricovero," wondering who would be running for office in these times, and then discovering *"ricovero"* meant "shelter." (Incidentally, he spent quite a bit of his time in shelters. People who traveled with him said Garfield was quite obviously scared during air raids and did not mind showing it. The one consolation, he said, was to find colonels and other soldiers just as scared.)

Once, at the Army's request, the troupe was driven through the night in utmost secrecy to entertain Yugoslavian guerillas. They arrived at two A.M. and an hour before dawn gave their show. What intrigued Garfield about the performance was that the guerillas needed an interpreter for everything, except when the performers mentioned a Hollywood star. Then they just clapped like mad.*

On the way back to the United States, the troupe did a show in Casablanca. "It looks like Beverly Hills," said Garfield, "but smells bad." All in all the trip was rewarding for Garfield. "You can't imagine how wonderful those guys are until you see 'em and live with 'em," he said.

===

George Raft had come to Hollywood with the reputation of being the next Rudolph Valentino. But after flipping that coin all through *Scarface,* he was tabbed as a gangster. He never really shed this persona, in part because of his past. He grew up in Hell's Kitchen, where he was a boxer and a hoofer with close ties to the mob. For a while he was known as the world's fastest Charleston dancer.

Raft was nearly fifty at the beginning of World War II, though, so his professional dancing days were behind him. His contribution to the war effort was a show he called "The Calvacade of Sports," which consisted of a traveling band of boxers who put on bouts, usually refereed by Raft, at Army and Navy bases. "It only stood me about $50,000," he said. "Next to what I gave my mother, spending this gave me the most satisfaction. . . . The kids were fighting for me."

---

*In the 1950s, when Garfield was under investigation by the House Un-American Activities Committee, this episode was held against him as suggesting he was pro-Communist.

=

Another actor who first established his reputation as a gangster was Paul Muni (*Scarface, The Shame of the Nation,* and *I Am a Fugitive from a Chain Gang*). However, unlike Raft, Muni went on to establish himself as one of Hollywood's "genius" actors—and as the deliverer of one of the most succinct appraisals of Hollywood on record. When asked how many actors there were in the Screen Actors Guild, he replied, "I'd say about one in every hundred."

Muni did not feel comfortable entertaining troops, although he did visit hospitals to talk to the wounded, and his one live appearance—in a sketch with swimmer Esther Williams—was received with roaring approval at the Santa Ana air base. (When asked whether Williams had talent, he replied "Wet yes, dry no.") But, he said, "I'm not a stand-up comic like Bob Hope or a stand-up sex symbol like Carole Landis."

Muni, a Jew, came to America from Eastern Europe with his parents when he was seven. He was a dedicated anti-Nazi, who felt his best effort for the war would be an anti-Nazi movie. He kept looking for one until he found a script, based on the Russian play *Pobyeda,* about a Soviet paratrooper who held seven German prisoners underground in a town occupied by the Nazis. The film was called *Counter-Attack* and the acting by Muni and the seven German prisoners was as authentic as anything done during the war. One of the German actors, Harro Meller, was actually an ex-Nazi officer; and one night he was arrested on Hollywood Boulevard wearing storm-trooper boots and striding along as you would expect any good Nazi to do. Although *Counter-Attack* received rave reviews, it was released eight days after V-E Day, so Muni's contribution to the war effort was minimal.

=

John Wayne and Gary Cooper were typed not as gangsters but as film-land's toughest cowboys and bravest soldiers, so it was especially awkward for them to be out of uniform. It was also difficult for them to go out and do live entertainment for the troops. Bogart and Robinson could get away with mocking gangsters, but it was impossible for Wayne and Cooper to go onstage and mock soldiers and almost as difficult to mock cowboys, since so many G.I.'s came from the West and identified with them.

Wayne's biographer Maurice Zolotow said Wayne went to the war zone many times with USO groups, but was "always . . . hesitant to publicize both his rejection by the service and his USO appearances." Cooper, like his friend Spencer Tracy, was not keen to do a USO tour, but Tracy talked him into it. "Go on and do it. It's really sort of fun." So Cooper agreed to go on a five-week tour of New Guinea with a group that included Una Merkel (veteran of that immortal barroom brawl with Marlene Dietrich in *Destry Rides Again*), Phyllis Brooks, best known as a B picture leading lady, and accordionist Andy Arcari.

Cooper insisted he would not sing, but Tracy said he had to, and sing he did. In fact, because he was a terrible ad-libber and not very funny (except when mocking himself), he did quite a bit of singing such sillies as "Pistol Packin' Mama" and "Mairzy Doats." But it was possible to be so bad even the troops didn't like you. The tour was close to a total disaster for Cooper until someone suggested that he give Lou Gehrig's farewell speech as a New York Yankee. (Cooper had appeared as Gehrig in *The Pride of the Yankees.*) He could not remember the speech, but a G.I. who could wrote it down for him. Whenever he gave it, a hush fell over the entire audience.

It was the most popular thing Cooper did—except on one USO tour after returning to the States, when he kissed a WAVE at Hunter College in Manhattan. Three thousand WAVEs in the audience swooned.

Reluctant or not, Cooper later said his trip to the South Pacific was one of the most moving experiences in his life: "Those kids'll be sitting out on a muddy hillside waiting for hours for the show to start. It can rain like hell, but they wouldn't think of moving an inch until it's over. Under those conditions, you rise above yourself and give it everything you've got."

=

Cary Grant fans did not expect the handsome master of light comedy and romance to win the war in the trenches, and neither did the Army. After it classified him 1-H, expecting him to be on call for special services but not enlist full-time, Grant made it known that he would do anything the Army or USO wanted him to do. He also released a statement saying that he did not want publicity: "The business of working for one's country should be done without such fanfare, and with the dignity it so rightly deserves. I therefore have no intention of mixing the two."

In addition to raising money for the United War Relief and British War Relief (work for which he was awarded the King's Medal by George VI), Grant went on some entertainment tours, usually passing up the big headline shows in favor of small, out-of-the-way camps. Perhaps this was because he really did not know what to do onstage. Although he began his career in the 1920s in England as a song-and-dance man and juggler, that did not seem appropriate in the 1940s for the smooth debonair man with the light quips and a talent for winning and breaking hearts. So mostly what Grant did on the circuit was simply talk to the men about Hollywood and making movies.

=

Unlike the many male actors who felt uncomfortable in front of live audiences, Charles Laughton loved to perform for the troops. What he liked best, as his biographer Simon Callow stresses, was to communicate what he had learned and was learning as he progressed through life. Laughton "had neither politics nor philosophy," said Callow, but he had a most vivid appreciation of beauty and the rightness of things. He would read from the Gettysburg Address, Shakespeare, and the Bible, although at first the G.I.'s protested the latter. "They did not want to hear anything from a dull book," he said. "The Bible was not dull to me and I had to prove to them that it was not dull. I used every trick I had learned and they liked it and asked for more."

Laughton had begun his USO work by reading innocuous things, mostly in hospitals, but one day he tried something serious and the response was immediate: "They started to talk about their own problems—being in bombers over Germany or in foxholes, or how they felt after they had been maimed." Literature, Laughton found, "was a great help to them because other people in centuries gone and in the present had had all the experiences there were to be had and the G.I.'s felt they were not alone."

When he began to go on USO tours and face large audiences, Laughton had a similar reaction: "We all do the same things together," he said, "laugh, or wonder, or pity—and we all feel good and safe because the people around us are the same as we are."

Although he brought books with him to a performance as props, he had memorized almost everything he intended to say and he didn't just "read" from great literature. There would be one-liners, anecdotes, and rambling introductions, all after a dramatic entrance (as described here by Callow):

It started with him shambling onto the platform in an overcoat from which, balefully eyeing the audience, he would remove books, one by one, making a pile out of them. Then the overcoat would come off to reveal him attired much as he would be in the street, i.e., shabbily. He'd chuckle: "Here we are again—an actor and an audience . . .", and he'd be off with the first reading, after which, "I'll tell you a story," he'd suddenly say, and it might be a four-line gag about a little boy he spoke to in Athens, Ohio, or it might be an anecdote about Henry Moore.

Laughton perhaps agreed with the British charlady in one of his anecdotes who, when another charlady said: "Isn't this a bloody awful war?" replied: "Ohhh, I don't know. It's better than no war at all."

=

As a child, Orson Welles had shown considerable talent for poetry, painting, cartooning, acting, playing the piano, and magic. By 1943, after *Citizen Kane, The Magnificent Ambersons,* and *Journey into Fear,* he was one of Hollywood's best-known personalities. He had no trouble getting up on a stage and mesmerizing his audience. For the G.I.'s, he chose his favorite hobby, magic. He organized a thirty-minute "Wonder Show," in which he was aided from time to time by Rita Hayworth, Joseph Cotten, Agnes Moorehead, Marlene Dietrich, and Jean Gabin. For one stunt he had G.I.'s tie Cotten inside a sack, put him in a trunk, which they also tied up, and then, at Welles's instruction, tie up the trunk again—as Cotten emerged from the back of the auditorium, arriving on stage to help the soldiers untie him. In another act he hypnotized a chicken.

This was at a time when Welles was breaking off his relationship with actress Dolores Del Rio and conducting an increasingly open affair with the nation's new young sex symbol, Rita Hayworth—who, Hollywood and the press assumed, was engaged to seaman Victor Mature, on a Coast Guard cutter in the Atlantic. Word began to spread that in a forthcoming "Wonder Show" act, Welles would saw Rita in half, which prompted Mature to comment: "A hell of a way to woo a girl." But when sawing time came, it was Dietrich, not Hayworth, whom Welles sawed in half. This was primarily because Harry Cohn, Hayworth's boss at Columbia, threatened to sue if she submitted to Welles's saw. Later, after Welles and Hayworth were married, a condensed version of the "Wonder Show," featuring him and Dietrich, was included in the film *Follow the Boys.* So the spectacle of Marlene Dietrich being sawed in two by Orson Welles was immortalized on film.

=

Except for the women who played up to what the men really missed away from home, the most popular entertainers during the war were the comedians and the song-and-dance men. Joe E. Brown, whose own son was killed during the war, became the first Hollywood actor to perform at a frontline base after the war began. That was in Alaska in 1942. He developed a joke that would become his signature and, in one form or another, was copied by other overseas entertainers. It also demonstrated how corny you could be in front of such a homesick audience and get away with it. Brown would point to a G.I. and say: "You. Where did you come from?" When the boy answered—no matter what the city—Brown would respond: "You mean you admit it?" And everyone would laugh.

The comedians were loved because of what men at war have known for centuries: that you need some laughter to get through. Beneath the toughness and bravado was genuine sadness, which the sensitive Harpo Marx noted on several of his USO tours. He would look at the sea of young faces fixed on him and marvel that they could even crack a smile. He saw them not as soldiers, "but as the kids they had been just ten or fifteen years ago, hoping that Daddy would keep on playing and making funny faces and bedtime would never come. I couldn't help thinking that when bedtime finally came for some of these kids, it would be a nightmare followed by an eternity's sleep. No explosion of applause was powerful enough to erase that awful reality."

Harpo never went overseas, but traveled for four years and 200,000 miles across the United States, playing in front of a half million men for the USO. In the old days on the circuit, he said, you would ask a vaudeville comedian leaving a town what the audience was like, and he would say: "Typical Boston audience," or "They haven't changed in Pittsburgh." But in the USO you didn't have to ask:

> They were the same in Boston and Pittsburgh as they were in San Diego, Wichita Falls and Newport News. They were terrific. They were always ready to explode. All you had to do to light the fuse was walk onstage. From that moment on, they were yours. You could do anything—play "Nola" on your teeth, imitate Dorothy Lamour, tell a joke about the WACs, or juggle a stack of tin plates—and the house went off like an arsenal full of TNT.

When you had a really great gag, the audience did indeed explode. Once, Harpo was playing in the outdoor courtyard of a hospital in California, according to his autobiography. There was a large audience before him but also hundreds of patients looking down from their rooms. They could see Harpo and also the hospital fountain, a replica of the Manneken-Pis, the famous Brussels statue of a naked little boy urinating.

Harpo began his harp concert by playing "Annie Laurie" very softly, but the splashing of the fountain obviously annoyed him. Finally he stopped the music, turned to the statue, put his finger to his lips, and shook his head. Slowly the little boy stopped peeing (Harpo had conferred with the hospital maintenance man before the concert) and the audience went wild. The people in the courtyard had to duck crutches and other flying objects hurled from the hospital windows by men who were convulsed with laughter. Nobody heard the rest of "Annie Laurie," not even Harpo.

=

Brian Aherne longed to be a comedian when he went on his one-man USO show. He was fairly well known—perhaps better known than he thought—as a tweedy, pipe-smoking British leading man who had been appearing on screen in the United States since 1933, most notably in *Juarez* and *My Sister Eileen*.

At Fort Benning, the commanding general eyed him suspiciously and said: "I shall be glad if you will explain to me what you are doing here."

Aherne tried to explain but did not satisfy the general, who replied: "Entertaining the boys is not my business. My duty is to train these very young men to kill or be killed. I have exactly eleven weeks in which to do it. All I want to know is, Can you help me?"

Aherne said probably not; all he hoped to do was "bring a comforting presence and a kindly word to those kids, many of whom must be frightened and lonely." The general was not entirely convinced, but indicated he would give Aherne a chance.

And then Aherne's panic really set in: "Oh, for an hour with Jack Benny's gag man," he said in his autobiography, cursing Hollywood for not supplying him "with a word of material." But, "I needn't have worried. The moment I mentioned my name, the boys greeted me with surprise and pleasure. I was astonished to find they all knew me." And they seemed to enjoy his "talk with the boys," as he put it in his autobiography.

Unlike Aherne, Phil Silvers had USO experience of a sort: He had played the sergeant in the film version of Carole Landis's *Four Jills in a Jeep*. So it was not surprising that Frank Sinatra asked Silvers (who was on his honeymoon with Jo-Carroll Dennison, Miss America of 1942) to put together a show for him.

Silvers agreed to cut short his honeymoon to organize Sinatra's tour because he was aware his buddy had a real problem. He could hardly introduce the Bobby Sox King with the usual "And here he is, the idol of America's youth!" The G.I.'s would probably have thrown C-rations at them. (Silvers was not worried about himself because, he felt, his thick glasses made his own 4-F rating obvious.) He finally came up with this approach, outlined in his autobiography, *The Laugh Is on Me:*

I suggested to Frank that he be presented as the underdog of the show. I would open with a few well-aimed Army jokes—food, the draft, civilian clothes. Then Frank wanders on, casually. Jokes about Frank: "I know there's a food shortage but this is ridiculous. . . . He weighed twelve pounds when he was born and he's been losing weight ever since." Frank asks if he can sing. We go into my singing lesson bit. I shape his tones, slap his cheeks, browbeat him, convince him he can't sing at all. Then my clarinet bit, for which Frank goes into the audience and heckles me. By this time, I figured the men would be demanding, *"Let Sinatra sing!"* The soldiers had been under-dogs so long, I was sure they would love this underdog.

They eventually did, but for a while Silvers and Sinatra were not sure how the show would go. For one thing, they went to Europe in May 1945 and were naturally criticized for not arriving until the war there was over. Sinatra insisted on going before the G.I.'s in his best civilian clothes, including freshly shined shoes. When the Army learned that the Silvers-Sinatra skit called for the singer to go out into the audience, they wanted to send two MPs with him, but Sinatra said no. And pretty soon, according to Silvers, "he had those audiences in the palm of his skinny hand." When Sinatra asked for requests, the soldiers always screamed "Nancy with the Smiling Face," which Sinatra had made popular over the Armed Forces Radio Network (and for which Silvers had written the lyrics—"the only lyric I ever wrote").

When they were in Rome, Silvers said, Sinatra wanted to have an audience with the pope. Sinatra arranged this through Myron Taylor, the American ambassador to the Vatican. Apparently the pope did not pay much attention to Sinatra once he learned he was not an opera singer, but when Silvers asked the pope to bless some rosary beads for Bing Crosby, he was quite pleased and threw in an extra pair of beads for Mrs. Crosby. After the audience, Sinatra said to Silvers, "You creepy bum. I get you in to see the pope and you're plugging Crosby." (Silvers couldn't win; later, when he gave the beads to Crosby, saying the "last hand that touched them was the Pope's," Crosby said, "Everything's a gag.")

=

You would expect a Bing Crosby tour of the European bases to be different from a Sinatra tour, and it was. In the first place, when Crosby went abroad in 1940, he was married and had four highly publicized sons. He also went over two months after D-Day, doing quite a few shows in France and Germany and trying to keep up with the advancing General Patton.

Hope and Crosby had already started their friendly rivalry in the first *Road* movie—*Road to Singapore*—and Crosby was an established singing star of "stage, screen, and radio," as they used to say in the 1930s. In 1942, he and Fred Astaire appeared in *Holiday Inn*—which, among other things, introduced one of the war's most nostalgic, tear-jerking songs, perhaps the most popular song ever to come from a Hollywood movie. When its composer, Irving Berlin, introduced it to the film's cast, he said: "I have an amusing little number here."

The amusing little number was "White Christmas," which, Berlin later said, because of the war "took on a meaning I never intended. It became a peace song."

Crosby concurred: "So many young people were away and they'd hear this song at that time of the year and it would really affect them. I sang it many times in Europe in the field for the soldiers. They'd holler for it; they'd demand it and I'd sing it and they'd all cry." But Crosby would probably have gotten a laugh, at least when he began the song, if he had sung Berlin's verse, which alludes to a snowless Christmas in Beverly Hills.

When Crosby went to England, everyone recognized him immediately with his pipe, open shirt, and a variety of hats, from porkpie to G.I. cap or helmet, depending on the occasion and whether they were in the war zone. "My little company," as he called his USO troupe, consisted of comedian Joe De Rita, musicians Earl Baxter and Buck Harris, singer Jeannie Darrell, and dancer Darlene Garner. Despite some hairy incidents in Europe, after they left England, Crosby apparently made the whole experience seem like a real-life *Road to Berlin*. "He ad-libbed us clear across France," said Garner and Darrell. Typical Crosby quips: When a British woman he met on the street asked him to sing, he said: "I only sing in Berkeley Square." And, when a German scout plane flew overhead while he was giving a show in France, he looked up and said: "Oh-h-h. I thought it was the stork again."

Crosby's biggest problem in England was the large crowds he attracted. They made everyone nervous because it was the period when the buzz bombs, or "doodlebugs," were coming over regularly. Bing was continually having to promise to sing only if the crowd agreed to disperse immediately. "Pennies from Heaven" was one of his favorite crowd-dispersing songs. One show he recorded for broadcast to the troops in Europe had to be held back because there were so many explosions in the background; the British Army was afraid that it would destroy the troops' morale to have to listen to bombs possibly falling on their loved ones back home.

When he reached France, Crosby often set off with just a jeep driver, trying to bring some of that Crosby cool to the men in the front lines. The troops were moving so fast that they would often get ahead of their lines of communication. Crosby's driver told biographer Charles Thompson that "the advice was that if you don't see our telephone lines, turn around and come back." On one trip, when the driver noticed suddenly that in a little town the American lines had disappeared, they made a quick about-face and retreated. That evening, when Crosby was having dinner with top American brass in France, he mentioned the name of the little town he and his driver had been in that morning. One general walked across the room to a map, looked at it, and said, "We haven't taken that yet. It's still in German hands."

"Well, we had it for a few minutes this morning," said Crosby.

Crosby found that in France he was not as well known as he was in England. And to no one's surprise, not being recognized did pique him a little. "At first, it's a relief to be where nobody knows you," he told one movie writer, "no jams, no autographs, just rolling along with the rest of 'em. But finally it gets downright embarrassing."

＝

Fred Astaire had flown across the Channel with Crosby on both men's first trip to the front lines. And they remembered the flight well because their pilot appeared to be about seventeen years old and it had not been long since Glenn Miller's disappearance.

Entertaining the troops was nothing new for Astaire. He did it with his sister Adele in New York in 1917, after their Broadway debut in the musical *Over the Top*. By the 1920s, the Astaires were popular in London and on Broadway, but their act broke up after Adele married Lord Charles Cavendish. Astaire went to Hollywood for a screen test, which resulted in the now-famous (though very likely apocryphal) appraisal: "Can't act. Slightly bald. Can dance a little." The appraiser might as well have added, "Can't sing much either." But it didn't matter. After the public saw Astaire dance, first with Joan Crawford in *Dancing Lady* and then with Ginger Rogers in *Flying Down to Rio,* he was launched. He had a six-year partnership with Rogers and also appeared with just about every talented female dancer to emerge in Hollywood, including Rita Hayworth, Eleanor Powell, Cyd Charisse, and Judy Garland.

Astaire could hardly believe the reality of war. "They've unbelievable guts," he said about the men at the front. "They go back in there time and time again to hit the Germans. It's something impossible to forget."

When they let him, he would dance near enough to the front to hear the gunfire. Just before the Battle of the Bulge, he and Dinah Shore were pinned down for nearly twelve hours, most of the time in a muddy ditch. Astaire would dance on anything, but he usually carried his own six-foot-by-twelve-foot mat in case the stage was inadequate. The G.I.'s liked to see him dance, but what they really wanted was to hear what it was like to dance with all those lovely Hollywood stars. ("Just fine," said Astaire, always the gentleman.) In hospitals, he would leap from beds; in barracks he'd jump on and off tables, just as he did in the movies. In one show, he was so intense the taps on his shoes flew into the audience and he could not resist quipping: "It's more dangerous on the front row with me dancing than it is on the front line."

Then on one historic day in September 1944, he put on the first concert at the famous Olympia Music Hall since the liberation of Paris. There were two thousand American troops in the audience and hundreds of French people, who besieged him after the show with cries of "Vive Monsieur Astaire!"

=

Of all the song-and-dance men who entertained at the front during the war, perhaps the most legendary was Al Jolson. After a sparkling career in vaudeville, Jolson made history in 1927, when he starred in Hollywood's first talking feature, *The Jazz Singer.* In the 1930s he appeared in a number of successful films, but by *Swanee River* in 1939, his career was going downhill fast. He was fifty-five when the Japanese attacked Pearl Harbor, and his telephone call that day to Stephen Early, FDR's press secretary, was not his first offer to sing for the troops. As early as New Year's Day, 1941, a little over three months after the passage of the Selective Training and Service Act, he had written Early offering— for free—to organize a committee for entertaining the troops.

The USO was quick to take Jolson up on his offer. Less than two months after Pearl Harbor he was singing before soldiers stationed at the Jacksonville air station in Florida. When the audience roared, Jolson asked the men, "Do you really mean it? And if you do, may I come back?"

The key words were "come back"—something the jazz singer, who had not had a responsive live audience in ten years, could not help but think about. The thought intensified when his tour of southern military bases packed in sixty thousand G.I.'s in two weeks. Then Jolson went to Washington to plead that he be sent overseas; the War Department authorized a trip to Alaska, a Special Services uniform, and officer's status.

But in Alaska, Jolson ran into the old problem: The boys didn't want to see a middle-aged jazz singer in blackface; they wanted the girls. In fact, there had been rumors that Dorothy Lamour or Lana Turner was on the way. Jolson met the problem head-on, with a few jokes: "Gypsy Rose Lee was gonna be here with us, but due to circumstances beyond our control, she couldn't make it. She'd already been signed to appear on the bare-asspirin program." He went on, the jokes getting a little dirtier and the laughter louder; then there were jokes about Hitler and Hirohito and home, until finally the men were ready for some songs. "I almost wore the knees out of my pants singing 'Mammy,' " he said.

And Al Jolson found a new audience, even though it was captive. "You either stay and listen to me," Jolson joked, "or get buried in a hundred feet of snow. You've got noplace else to go."

This audience was not always easy to reach. "It became necessary," he said, "for us to give shows in foxholes, gun emplacements, dugouts, to construction groups on military roads; in fact, any place where two or more soldiers were gathered together, it automatically became a Winter Garden for me and I gave a show. Imagine carting the piano to these locations. Sometimes it was by truck, once on a sidecar and once on a mule pack."

Obviously the G.I.'s had to appreciate anyone who would go to that much trouble to entertain them. But Jolson, like Benny and Hope, didn't care if the laughter and applause came easy; he loved them. He also genuinely loved the boys, and once, when a young soldier told him how homesick he was for Dixie—"thutty miles t'other side of Bummingham, Alabama"—Jolson stopped to see the kid's mother the next time he was near Birmingham. And when another boy asked him to call his mother, Jolson said: "I'll do better than that. I'll take her out to dinner. What's her name?"

When he asked for more names, about fifteen hundred were shouted back. He wrote down several and called them all. One person who knew Jolson in the World War II days remembers him sitting in his suite at the Sherry Netherland in New York and making one phone call after another to relatives and girlfriends of the boys he had entertained overseas.

After Jolson returned to New York from Alaska, he went on a three-week tour to Trinidad, where one of the regimental hostesses said, "Your coming here is quite the most wonderful thing that has ever happened to us." Then he was ready for his European tour with Merle Oberon, Patricia Morison, Allen Jenkins, and Frank McHugh.

Perhaps it is understandable that he was upset to see there would be others in the show. So far he had been a one-man act, accompanied only by his pianist, Marty Fried, or later Harry Akst.* He was beginning to think that the comeback kid, Al Jolson, was the biggest thing that ever happened to the U.S. military. When he finally left the English USO tour, he told reporters: "I just feel I can do better on my own." He was telling the truth.

There should be no mistake about the fact that Jolson was one of the most dedicated troop entertainers of World War II. He went everywhere, including some of the toughest, dirtiest outposts in Africa. After one trip he came down with malaria. He loved making the boys a little happier. And he did make a remarkable comeback as a result of the war. One of the reasons he returned from England was to appear in a new CBS radio program, "The Colgate Show Starring Al Jolson." Shortly after that, Harry Cohn's brother, Jack, approached him about Columbia making a picture based on his life and inspired, in part, by the success of *Yankee Doodle Dandy.* A deal was finally worked out; Jolson would get a share of the profits but not star in the film. (The leading role eventually went to Larry Parks, although Jolson's voice was dubbed in singing his classic songs.)

After the thirteen-week "Colgate Show" was over, Jolson and Akst went to North Africa, where Jolson delivered one of his most memorable "messages"—a kick in the rear (at Mamie Eisenhower's request) to General Eisenhower for not writing more often. But when they returned to the States, Jolson was feeling low, despite his comeback and movie contract. When Akst, who had just called his wife to tell them

---

*Jolson and Fried parted when Fried sued Jolson for back pay after Jolson had gotten him a draft exemption so that he could accompany Jolson on his USO tours.

they were back, heard Jolson sobbing, he asked why. "You've got someone to come back to," Jolson replied. "Who've I got? Not a soul in the
world cares whether I live or die."

But on his next USO tour, the entertainer—not the soldiers—got
lucky. In May 1944, after Jolson appeared on the "Philco Radio Hall of
Fame Show" in New York, he and Akst started back to California, touring the South on what Jolson called the Purple Heart circuit, hospitals
full of wounded G.I.'s. At White Sulphur Springs, Arkansas, they went a
little out of their way to play at the Eastman Annex in Hot Springs.
The story goes that a twenty-year-old woman, Erle Galbraith, asked
Jolson for his autograph after he sang at the Annex. But according to
Jolson biographer Herbert Goldman, she insists she did no such thing:
"With my upbringing? In the South?" Rather it was Jolson who asked a
general he was getting some additional gas ration stamps from to introduce him to the pretty young X-ray technician in civilian clothes who
had stood watching him all during his performance. And on being
introduced, Galbraith says, the fifty-eight-year-old actor used one of
the oldest Hollywood lines in the book: "He asked me if I wanted to go
into the movies."

Galbraith said nothing and they soon parted as Jolson and Akst drove
off to Corpus Christi, Texas. But Jolson could not get Erle Galbraith
out of his mind. He obtained her address from a general he knew at the
hospital where she worked and then asked Akst to write her a letter.
Akst refused: "You can make a damn fool of yourself if you want to, but
I won't help you do it." So Jolson called the hotel secretary and, following up on his opening gambit, dictated a note that said he was a Columbia producer and wondered whether she would come to Hollywood for
a screen test.

A few days later, Jolson received a call from a lawyer who said he
represented one of the finest old families in Arkansas—the Galbraiths.
When he met with Jolson, the lawyer said he wanted to verify
Columbia's interest in Erle Galbraith as a potential actress. He suggested to Jolson that "it would be most unfortunate if you were throw-
ing a curve." Jolson assured the lawyer that there were no ulterior
motives involved and that Erle should come for her test. She did, claim-
ing later that she had no acting ambition or talent, "but who could resist
the chance for a wonderful vacation?"

Jolson met her at the station with a platoon of Columbia executives,
all of whom had the same reaction when she stepped off the train: She
was just as beautiful as Jolson had proclaimed. Responding to Jolson's
query, "How have you been?" she replied: "Mistah Jolson, I've been just

fine." Harry Cohn, who hated southern accents, went through the roof
when he heard her speak.

The screen test confirmed what everyone at Columbia knew. Galbraith was beautiful enough to be a star but did not have the voice for
it. She was given a six-month, hundred-dollar-a-week contract and was
used in a couple of films (including 1945's *A Thousand and One Nights*).
When her Columbia contract expired, Jolson found her a few extra
parts at 20th Century–Fox; gradually, a romance developed. But before
Jolson could ask Mr. Galbraith for his daughter's hand, he took off with
Akst on another tour of the Purple Heart circuit. This ended with Jolson in the hospital, being operated on for a spot on his lung. Erle was
one of his first visitors and the only one who could draw him out of a
deep depression. He was sure he would never sing again.

While Jolson was in the hospital, Harry Cohn and two Columbia
producers working on *The Jolson Story* visited him. When Cohn walked
in the room he asked Jolson, "You gonna die?" Jolson (loaded with
painkillers) responded by leaping out of bed and singing—apparently
enough to convince Cohn he was all right. But a few weeks later, Cohn
told his two aides, "This guy's gonna die."

But he didn't. On one of Galbraith's visits, Jolson asked her to marry
him, and then later joked: "I was quite floored by that southern drawl.
But I had only to take one look at that kisser, that little face, and those
big dark eyes. I knew with a dialect like that she would never stand a
chance on the screen, though. So I thought I'd better marry the poor
kid."

Erle's father did not think it was so funny. When Jolson wrote him
asking for permission, Mr. Galbraith replied that he had never been so
insulted in his whole life. "You are old enough to be my daughter's
father."

True enough. But, Galbraith said, "I can twirl Dad around my finger"—and she went back to Hot Springs to do just that. She and Jolson
were married on March 23, 1945, less than a year after the day the
pretty little X-ray technician in Arkansas met the famous singer from
Hollywood.

It was the classic marriage of sugar daddy and young, appreciative
girl. The Jolsons adopted a six-month-old boy, naming him Asa Albert,
and settled down in what Erle called the "perfect home" (it had
belonged to Don Ameche). Erle remained at Jolson's side for the rest of
his life.

Meanwhile a much weaker Jolson had developed a "new voice,"
which he tried out as a guest on Milton Berle's radio show. "I'm not too

strong now, but they've promised me when I'm feeling better they'll let me go to Tokyo. . . . And there I'll sing 'Mammy.' "

He never did go, although he did have a second comeback. He went on singing for soldiers until he died of a heart attack in 1951, after returning from a USO tour during the Korean War.

=

Although soldiers loved to hear songs that reminded them of home or of their loved ones, the comedians who could make them laugh probably did them the most good. As John Steinbeck said in one of his *New York Herald Tribune* columns applauding Bob Hope: "He gets laughter wherever he goes from men who need laughter."

It was sometimes too easy to get a laugh. "Nobody was half as good as the G.I. audiences made him look," said Harpo Marx. "For this reason a lot of young comics, dancers, and vocalists I knew became established. They made it big doing camp shows. They made it too big. When the war was over they didn't know, or had forgotten, how much hard work it took to win over a club full of drunks or to impress producers and casting directors."

On the other hand, Edward G. Robinson did not think the comedians had it that easy. A stand-up routine during a war, he said, "is the single hardest performance in the world to give—all alone on the stage in front of thousands of men who may be dead the next day."

Before he was drafted in 1944, Red Skelton did three thousand camp shows. Groucho Marx, with his painted eyebrows and mustache, was a great favorite, stalking back and forth across the stage with his slouching walk, uttering one quip after another. There was the one about his famous Uncle Gridley, who was unemployed after Admiral Dewey said: "You may fire Gridley when you are ready"; the same uncle, while on watch, "fell asleep in a sixteen-inch gun and he was dishonorably discharged."

Another favorite was Jimmy Durante, the singer-comedian whose big nose was so important to his career that it was insured for $1 million by Lloyd's of London. "Schnozzola" had been a Broadway-Hollywood star through most of the 1930s, but by the end of the decade his career was slipping badly. Like Jolson, he revived it during the war by entertaining the troops, and if there was a turning point in his comeback it came on his radio show during Christmas of 1942, when he introduced a nonexistent character named Umbriago. Durante became so beloved that G.I.'s voted him the person they would most like to live next door to (except June Allyson, of course). Paratroopers were known to yell,

"Umbriago!" when they jumped; marines sometimes shouted, "Umbriago, that's my boy," when they charged onto a beach. Durante told Ed Sullivan that one of his most moving experiences during the war came when he entertained at a hospital on Staten Island. Two lieutenants, each of whom had lost an arm, sat side by side on a bed—applauding Durante with their remaining hands. And a woman wrote Durante about her son, who had just died at Iwo Jima. His buddy had told her that the boy died with a smile on his face and yelling, "Umbriago!"

One of the most popular USO comedians was Jack Benny. By World War II, America knew him as the star of *Charley's Aunt, To Be or Not to Be,* and *George Washington Slept Here.* He was also one of the country's favorite radio comedians. Like Hope, Benny had begun entertaining at Army camps long before Pearl Harbor. And, like Hope, he loved the loud and easy laughter they always heard at the camps. The two men often argued about which one was the bigger ham. It was an argument neither could ever win, although Benny's biographer, Irving Fine, suggests that someone once gave the nod to Benny with the remark: "Every time he opens the refrigerator and the light goes on, he does a five-minute monologue."

Both Jack Benny and Larry Adler were veterans of the foxhole circuit by the time they joined Ingrid Bergman in Europe in the spring of 1945. In the summer of 1943, they had gone on a nine-week tour through North Africa, Egypt, and Italy, accompanied by singer Wini Shaw, British actress Anna Lee, and pianist Jack Synder. They called their C-47 cargo plane "Five Jerks to Cairo"—an allusion to the Billy Wilder film *Five Graves to Cairo.* (The C-47's pilot eventually married Anna Lee.)

Once, when the troupe was flying from Kano to Lagos, Nigeria, a military base sent an urgent message to land. The base's strip was too small for the plane, which overshot the runway and landed on its nose. When the performers learned that the only reason the base had ordered the plane to land was so the men could see Jack Benny, Adler was furious and refused to perform. Benny, never passing up a chance to give one of his monologues, naturally put on a show.

Adler, a harmonica player, was also an excellent writer and very good at comedy. In fact, Benny thought Adler was the funniest man in the world and wanted the harmonica player to write for him, especially after the parody of a popular song from *Oklahoma!* they worked up for Iran (they once did a show there when the temperature was 110 degrees—in the morning.):

Oh, what a hell of a morning
Hundred and ten in the shade.
Oh, what a hell of a mor-ning
Even too hot to get
Oh, much too hot to get
It's much too hot to get . . .

Adler declined Benny's invitation to write for his shows when they returned to the States, although he enjoyed being a writer. He bought a Hermes typewriter and pretended he was another Ernie Pyle—not a gag writer. In fact, he was pretty good as a poor man's Ernie Pyle; while he was overseas he did a column for the Chicago *Sun* as well as some radio programs. Often he made his editors and producers squirm, as when he reported riding in a car that struck a pedestrian near Cairo: An officer who was also in the car said, "I hope we killed him." Adler said this was a little rough. The officer explained, "If he's wounded we have to take care of him for life. If he's killed, we make a payment to his family and, bingo, that's it."

Then there was the time he interviewed a pilot who had definite ideas about how to deal with an enemy pilot: "And if he bails out do I just sit by and let him land? What for? To give him a chance to try to kill me again? No sir, I say you kill the enemy and stuff the rules."

When he was writing for *Collier's,* he gave his rules for doing a show, which included no segregation and no preferential seating for officers. Four officers wrote from the South Pacific explaining why seats had to be reserved for officers; later he learned that all four officers were killed before his responding letter arrived.

Although the Five Jerks were never too far from the fighting, they never had any bombs dropped near them or any shots fired at them— except one night in North Africa, returning to quarters after a show, when a nervous young sentry fired a shot because the driver of their car did not give the proper signal. When they had satisfied the sentry and were proceeding on their way, a black cat crossed the road in front of them. Benny said: "*Now* he tells us."

After leaving Cairo for Tehran, the C-47 ran into a heavy sandstorm. When the pilot told Adler that the plane was running low on fuel and he could not raise anyone on the radio, Adler was so scared that, although not religious, he started praying—for which he was immediately embarrassed. "Take it back, you son-of-a-bitch," he said to himself. "If you're going to die, do it honestly."

Benny was a very mild man but he could be caustic. Once, in Benghazi, Libya, he was greeted by a lieutenant obviously from the South. As reported by Benny, the exchange went something like this:

"Hi, Mistuh Benny. Ah'm comin' to see your show t'night. You all got Rochester with you?"

"No," I said.

"Well, I sho am disappointed. You cain't have much of a show without that Rochester. He's just about the funniest damn coon in the world."

I didn't think it was my place to get into a discussion with him about his racist language, so I merely said, "Well, I hope we'll put on a nice show even without Rochester." I was there to bring our men a little time out for laughter—they sure needed any relief at all, with the monotony and the unbearable heat.

But this fool wasn't satisfied. "Seems to me, Mistuh Benny, without Rochester, you ain't got no show."

"You really love Rochester, don't you?" I said. "You love him that much, huh? Well, let me ask you something. Would you walk into this canteen and sit down with him and eat with him at the same table?"

His expression got nasty. "Well, sir, ah come from a part of the country where we don't sit down with nigras."

"I thought so, young man, and that's why I didn't bring Rochester on this trip. I didn't want him to be embarrassed and humiliated by ignorant folks like you. You say you love Rochester. You'll walk ten miles to see him perform. But you won't sit down at the same table and drink a glass of Coca-Cola with him. You make me sick."

I walked out of that canteen.

Benny called his 1943 USO tour "the most thrilling and memorable trip I have ever had in my life." He loved the response he almost always got from the G.I.'s, and it didn't make any difference to him that they would laugh at anything.

In fact, all he had to do was comment on being thirty-nine forever or being a skinflint, or tell a joke like "I don't know how much liquor Phil Harris [the orchestra leader on his radio show] drinks but you can name any patent medicine and he'll tell you how much alcohol it contains," and his G.I. audiences would break up.

After a few months back on a normal diet, Benny was ready to go again. In the summer of 1944, he and Adler went to the South Pacific, accompanied by singer Martha Tilton, actress Carole Landis, and the Army Air Corps Band. When they arrived at Christmas Island the boys head a big sign ready: "WELCOME FRED ALLEN"—Benny's archrival. They waited for his reaction. He let out a big laugh and said it was the funniest thing he had ever seen.

Landis didn't let the men down either; she knew what they wanted. She stepped off the plane wearing a loose-fitting halter that barely concealed her breasts. As she bowed lower and lower, the boys started yelling and screaming. Then Adler stepped forward and took Paulette Goddard's "gloves" quip into the stratosphere on the laughter scale: "Anyone would think you fellows had never seen a mouth-organ player before."

Another surefire laugh-getter for Benny, along with his ancient Maxwell and his manservant, Rochester, was his violin playing. In one skit (used years later on television), in the middle of his performance with Martha Tilton he picks up a violin and starts playing. On cue, a straight man labeled "General MacArthur" gets up from the audience and starts to leave and two Japanese soldiers sneak onto the stage and promise to surrender if Jack will only stop playing.

Both Benny and Adler found the real General MacArthur insufferable and neither wanted to attend a cocktail party given by his staff. They flipped a coin, Adler lost, and his instincts were right. It was mostly drunken generals and one sober colonel, who accompanied Adler. The tone of the party was set by one drunken general from Texas, who said he had just heard a great poem:

> Roses are red, violets are blue
> Said Eleanor to Franklin, "How long must I stay in
>   the White House with you?"
> Said Franklin to Eleanor,
>   "You kiss the niggers, I'll kiss the Jews,
> We'll stay in the White House as long as we choose."

When Adler was about to explode, a colonel cautioned him, saying any one of these generals had the power to send him home or put him in jail. "I shut up," Adler said in his autobiography, "and I still regret having done so."

The following year, right after Germany had surrendered, Benny, Adler, and Tilton went to Europe, where, as we have seen, they were joined by Ingrid Bergman, with whom Adler began a romance. Benny's most memorable experience in Europe was the time he and Adler went to see General Eisenhower. The purpose of the visit was to obtain Ike's permission for Benny and his troupe to visit Berlin, which was off limits to civilians. There is some confusion as to how they obtained their meeting with the top Allied commander. Adler said Kay Summersby (who was rumored to be having an affair with Ike, although the rumors never appeared in print) arranged it, whereas Benny recalls that General Patton arranged the interview.

At any rate, they were allotted ten minutes, and although Ike appeared disappointed that Bergman did not come along, he invited the men to stay for coffee and a chat. When the possibility of running for President came up, Eisenhower said: "Bad business. Of course I'm aware of it but why don't people read their history? It's never worked, that a military man has made a good president. I'm a graduate of West Point and I'm trained to take my orders from a civilian commander-in-chief. I know they're talking about me running but I'll have nothing to do with it."

When they arrived in Berlin they ran into director Billy Wilder, who went with Benny and his troupe to Nuremberg, where they planned to do a big show on July 4, 1945. Wilder especially wanted to see the platform where Hitler had made his first speech about Nazism. There were at least forty thousand G.I.'s in the audience, all laughing and shouting at Benny. After the show, Wilder and Benny had to urinate, so they went up to Hitler's platform at the top of the stadium. When they stepped onto the historic spot they were ankle-deep in urine. Hundreds of G.I.'s had had the same idea.

Benny was in a state of shock most of the time he was in Germany. "Like so many American Jews," he said, "I had the special pang of knowing that but for the grace of God and my father's emigration, I could have been one of the victims of Dachau or Buchenwald or Auschwitz." Benny was a tireless traveler of the foxhole circuit: "No other trouper," Leo Rosten wrote in *Look* magazine, "with the exception of Robert Hope, was as generous of his time or profligate of his energy."

You could write a book about Bob Hope's World War II travels—in fact, Hope himself has written three books wholly or partly about his trying to win the war with jokes: *I Never Left Home, Have Tux Will Travel,* and *Don't Shoot, It's Only Me.* His first trip out of the country to entertain the troops was in the summer of 1942. He says he agreed to go if he could take Frances Langford along, "figuring they would never send a girl if it wasn't completely safe—and she wouldn't go if it wasn't." That was before he realized that Langford "happily went places that a guy like me could get killed."

They let him take Frances as well as comedian Jerry Colonna and guitar player Tony Romano, and although there was no shooting in

Jack Benny (at the piano), like Bob Hope (shown here with Jerry Colonna), loved the fact that G.I.'s would laugh at almost anything he said or did. National Archives

Alaska, the only practical way to get there was by plane and there was always bad weather. It was Hope who insisted on making a night flight from Cordova, Alaska, to Anchorage in what turned out to be a record sleet storm. To make matters worse, their radio went out. As they approached Anchorage, there were mountain peaks all around and "we couldn't even see our propellers."

But after one near miss with another plane and putting on their parachutes and Mae West life jackets because the twenty-year-old captain was about to order everyone to bail out before they hit a mountain, they saw the landing field. The plane they had narrowly missed was a United Airlines plane. Its pilot reported them to the tower, which ordered all searchlights in the area turned on.

No doubt Hope was as scared as anyone on the plane, but like any great artist, he made art out of experience. Such trips produced not only white knuckles but good jokes. He said "I knew it was an old plane when I saw the pilot ... wearing goggles and a scarf." And "Never did so many men think so seriously about getting down on their knees without even one pair of dice.... Even the automatic pilot bailed out."

Such frights did not deter Hope and his gang from following the troops wherever they went. By 1943, American soldiers were fighting in North Africa, and that's where Hope felt he ought to be: "I didn't feel quite right about only playing Army camps safely in the U.S." He also did not feel right about the "packaged entertainment" sent to the troops in the form of radio shows or movies, "while the entertainers were safe at home. You had to go to *them* to be truly appreciated. I was determined to be appreciated even if it killed me."

The troops not only appreciated him, they loved him. And every new base or country gave him more material. In London, he said, one of the most important things he did was explain to the men the insignia of the British junior officers: "They're little round discs sort of like beehives and the English call them pips.... The girls in the WAAFs wear the same insignia.... I was out with a gal who told me she was a lieutenant and she had two pips."

As he tells it in *Don't Shoot*, his show would start something like this: "Well, here I am in good old Jolly. You know, England—that's the place Churchill visits when he leaves America.... Here in England, everything is strange. Everybody drives on the wrong side of the street. Just like California." Then, before he introduced his first song or skit, out would come a series of rapid-fire gags. Commenting on the raid on Tokyo by James Doolittle (whom Hope would later call "the only man George C. Scott is required to salute"), Hope quipped: "Once when

Doolittle's tail gunner yelled 'Zeros at eleven o'clock!' Doolittle replied, 'What are you worried about? It's only eight-thirty.' "

After a few weeks in London, Hope and his troupe were off to North Africa (where the mosquitoes "are so big they have to use landing strips") and more jokes, good and bad. But it didn't make any difference how funny the jokes were, the men at war loved remembrances from home. Hope began to make a little history of his own as the war's only "legend," as *Time,* which put Hope on its cover, called him.

> It sprang up swiftly, telepathically, among U.S. servicemen in Britain this summer, traveling faster than even whirlwind Hope himself, then flew ahead of him to North Africa and Sicily, growing larger as it went. Like most legends, it represents measurable qualities in a kind of mystical blend. Hope was funny, treating hordes of soldiers to roars of laughter. He was friendly—ate with servicemen, drank with them, read their doggerel, listened to their songs. He was indefatigable, running himself ragged with five, six, seven shows a day. He was figurative—the straight link with home, the radio voice that for years had filled the living room and that in foreign parts called up its image. Hence boys whom Hope might entertain for an hour awaited him for weeks. And when he came, anonymous guys who had no other recognition felt personally remembered.

In his column, Ernie Pyle wrote a "testimony" for Hollywood to believe, "no matter what narrow escape story Bob tells when he gets back":

> I was in two different cities with [the Hope troupe] during air raids and I will testify that they were horrifying raids. It isn't often that a bomb falls close enough that you can hear it whistle. But when you can hear a whole stick of them whistling at once, then it's time to get weak all over and start sweating. The Hope troupe can now describe that ghastly sound.

As war correspondent John Steinbeck wrote in *The New York Herald Tribune:*

> When the time for recognition of service in wartime comes to be considered, Bob Hope should be high on the list. This man drives himself and is driven. It is impossible to see how he can do so much, can cover so much ground, can work so hard and can be so effective. . . .
>
> Hope does four, sometimes five shows a day. In some camps the

men must come in shifts because they can't all hear him at the same time. Then he jumps into a car and rushes to the next post. Because he broadcasts, and because everyone listens to each broadcast, he can't use the same show more than a few times. . . .

Hope takes his shows all over, not only to the big camps. You hear the same thing in little groups on special duty. "Bob Hope is coming Thursday." They know weeks in advance that he's coming. It would be a terrible thing if he didn't show up.

Just how much the men wanted Hope was demonstrated at a show Hope gave near Bizerte, Tunisia, to an audience of 7,500 soldiers, sailors, and WACs. Some G.I.'s pulled a gag on him. Hope had just given his opening line—"The fog was so thick in London one night, the anti-aircraft shot down three submarines"—when a tank burst through the audience and came toward the stage. (Hope later quipped that he had never seen a critic driving a Sherman tank before.) He was ready to jump off the platform when the tank stopped right in front of him. A G.I. wearing a crash helmet and carrying a folding chair got out, sat the chair down in front of his tank, and said: "Okay, make me laugh!"

Which Hope did, of course, with his usual volley of one-liners—and a song: "*Tanks* for the Memories."

But he couldn't make them all laugh. The hardest show he ever did in his life, he said, was at a hospital for a group of about five hundred advanced cases of battle fatigue. "We got very few laughs," he recalled, and those they did get came "from individuals to whom a phrase or line or word that wasn't really a joke at all, for some private reason would seem funny."

It was groups such as these, and his reaction to all the men who had seen action, that gave Hope his obsession with entertaining the troops. He had told *Time* that "when the war ends, it'll be an awful letdown"; back in California he immediately missed all the guys and gals left at the front. "We knew we were going to have to go back to them."

He was uncomfortable back home, especially after *Time* had called him "'first in the hearts of the servicemen.' People started to look at me like I was Mount Rushmore." He wondered why he got more attention than other entertainers, including those in his own group. "They took the same chances and worked just as hard as the boss." But being on the cover of *Time* embarrassed him (he quipped that it was not true that he had the cover story tattooed on his chest and engraved on his shaving mirror).

D-Day, June 6, 1944, was the date of Hope's last Pepsodent radio show of the season. For that night he forgot the one-liners; he and his writers put together a speech heard by 35 million people—as many as or more than heard one of the President's Fireside Chats:

> You thought of the hundreds of thousands of kids you'd seen in camps the past two or three years . . . the kids who scream and whistle when they hear a gag and a song. And now you could see all of them again . . . in four thousand ships on the English Channel, tumbling out of thousands of planes over Normandy and the occupied Coast . . . in countless landing barges crashing the Nazi gate and going on through to do a job that's the job of all of us. . . . We knew we'd wake up one morning and have to meet it face to face, the world in which America has invested everything these thirty long months . . . the effort of millions of Americans building planes and weapons . . . the shipyards and the men who took the stuff across . . . little kids buying War Stamps, and housewives straining bacon grease . . . farmers working around the clock . . . millions of young men sweating it out in camps, and fighting the battles that paved the way for this morning.

Hope knew that to be a legend you had to keep working at it; by the summer of 1944, just after D-Day, his gypsies, as he called them, were ready for a tour of the South Pacific and new gag material.

One of their first stops was Eniwetok, where Hope said that when Langford and a new dancer, Patti Thomas, got off the plane, "the G.I.'s whistled so much they blew three planes off the runway."

He said it was a great feeling to bring laughter to men in places where "the only thing breaking the monotony was finding a new fungus growing on you"—like Pavuvu, where they entertained fifteen thousand men who were in training for the invasion of Peleliu; 40 percent of those never came home. A few months later, Hope was visiting a hospital in Oakland, California, when one G.I. yelled, "Pavuvu!" "He didn't have to say anything else," reported Hope. "I just went over and shook his hand." It turned out that all the men on the ward were veterans of Peleliu, and Hope left the hospital in tears.

On a trip from Brisbane to Sydney, Australia, they had another scary plane incident when their Flying Boat "feathered" a prop (it stopped) and went into a dive. The pilot ordered the passengers to jettison everything they could. The plane had to make a forced landing on a small lake near Laurieton. The Aussies who rescued them asked: "I say there, do you chaps have any American cigarettes?"

In Laurieton, they put on a show for the Australian troops. It laid an egg: "American Army jokes meant nothing to them," Hope said. He thought the Aussies got even by never radioing anyone that Hope's party had landed near the town, which meant that for three days the plane was listed as missing.

But soon they were back among friendly G.I.'s at Hollandia, New Guinea, where one of them would get a bigger laugh than Hope ever did. One moonlit night, after Frances Langford started singing "I'm in the Mood for Love," some guy stood up and yelled: "You've come to the right place, baby." Some G.I.'s who were there that night may still be laughing.

When Hope returned from the South Pacific, he was in the States only a few months before he was ready to go back to Europe. "When I get home these days," he said, "my kids think I've been booked there on a personal appearance tour."

It was after V-E Day, so Hope was worried that his troupe (which now included singer Gale Robbins in place of Langford, and accordionist Ruth Denas) and his jokes would no longer bring the enthusiastic response they used to. The troupe did its first show in London's Albert Hall; Hope said that "after the first laugh, I stopped being nervous. More than ever now, our group represented home to them, the one place in the world they wanted to be. . . . A lot of the laughter was homesickness . . . but I'll take 'em any way I can get 'em."

He found that war jokes had become "nostalgia" and that he could get laughs by telling the guys and gals how it used to be. He did notice that the wolf whistles were not as enthusiastic as they had been in the South Pacific—but then, he realized, the G.I.'s back from Europe had had a chance to meet some English girls.

Hope was also invited to be one of the first to visit Hitler's Berlin underground bunker, where the German dictator had killed himself and his girlfriend, Eva Braun. They drove through a bombed-out section of Berlin. Hope later said it "looked like the South Bronx after a rock concert." The bunker itself "was a shambles, furniture scattered around as if the last tenant had just gotten a divorce and his ex-wife had tried to take the rugs with her." Hope came away with two souvenirs— a toilet handle and a huge Nazi flag—which he obtained by giving the Russian guards a couple of packs of cigarettes, "the first postwar Russian trade pact," he said.

For the men Hope was entertaining, the war, which was probably his finest hour, was over. But for him, the jokes were just beginning—not only for the men who were stationed in Europe during the Cold War but for the ones who would fight in Korea, Vietnam, and Iraq. Since

World War II, anywhere in the world you found American fighting men and women, you would find Hope. When a G.I. in Tunisia called him a draft dodger and asked, "Why aren't you in uniform?" Hope was the only comedian in the world who could reply: "Don't you know there's a war on? A guy could get hurt."

FOURTEEN

The End

"The war's all over but the shooting."
—SAMUEL GOLDWYN

The year 1945 will long be remembered; within it are the dates of many of the most memorable events of World War II: the Yalta Conference (February 4–12); the execution of Benito Mussolini (April 28); the death of Adolf Hitler (April 30); the creation of the United Nations in San Francisco (April–June); V-E Day and the end of the Thousand-Year Reich after only twenty-two years (May 8); the dropping of the atomic bomb on Hiroshima (August 6); and V-J Day (August 14). And, of course, early in the year (April 12), there was the death of President Roosevelt and the abrupt succession to the presidency of Harry S Truman.

Many Republicans in Hollywood, as elsewhere across the nation, hated Roosevelt and perhaps took his death with silent satisfaction: At last, "that man in the White House" was gone. Sterling Hayden, who was in France when a sergeant, crying, brought him the news, thought there would be more than silent satisfaction for some. He thought of "all the Bel Airs and Hamptons. I thought of a club car called 'Assassination Special.' There will," he told the sergeant, "be a high old time in some circles."

Most actors and actresses, however, were stunned by the President's death. Orson Welles had campaigned for FDR in 1944 and it was Welles who had suggested to the President that he turn Republican attacks on his dog, Fala, into a joke. After FDR's famous Fala speech (in which he said he did not mind Republican attacks on himself, but Fala resented the attacks and had "not been the same dog since") he asked Welles how he did as a public speaker. Was his timing right? Welles said he did just fine. When Roosevelt died, Welles gave a eulogy heard across the country, and his love of FDR was understandable; the President had once told Welles that they were "the two best actors in the world."

Bob Hope also loved him. "He was the greatest audience I ever worked for. . . . Roosevelt laughed so loud I wanted to sign him up for my radio audience. . . . He would roar . . . and tilt that long cigarette holder upward. The whole audience would turn to watch him. Each time the cigarette lighter tilted, they laughed automatically."

FDR could also occasionally tell a pretty good joke himself; for example, the one about the marine on Guadalcanal who couldn't find any Japanese. His CO told him to go to the top of a hill and yell, "To hell with Hirohito!" But when he did, a Japanese soldier answered, "To hell with Roosevelt!" And the marine said: "Just my luck. I can't shoot a fellow Republican."

So, FDR probably would have laughed at Groucho Marx's quip after his death. Groucho was appearing on Dinah Shore's weekly radio show, "Bird's Eye Open House," which was canceled the night of Roosevelt's death. But Groucho was paid his $3,000 anyway. The next week was Roosevelt's funeral, so the show was canceled again, and again Groucho was paid. "I thought to myself, There are not enough people dying."

Evelyn Keyes spoke for most of Hollywood's younger generation when she said Roosevelt was "the first man, the only man I had ever voted for; the President who had been in office the major part of my life. . . . How could we all go on without him?"

We had to go on with Harry Truman, "history's monstrous typographical error," said screenwriter James M. Cain. Sadly, Roosevelt did not live to see the death of Hitler and the defeat of Germany, although he died knowing the Nazis were through. On V-E Day, Lucille Ball and

Desi Arnaz led a Hollywood Canteen conga line that wiggled out the door and down Cahuenga Boulevard. Joe Pasternak called Marlene Dietrich to remind her of her promise to go to bed with him when Hitler was dead, and she said, "Hitler is alive and well and living in Argentina." And when the United Nations was created in San Francisco, Louis Dolivert, a Free French activist married to the actress Beatrice Straight, seriously considered proposing Orson Welles as secretary-general. He argued that the United Nations should be an organization of people, not governments, and that its leader should not be a politician or a diplomat but someone known around the world as the symbol of boldness and youth. Welles said he knew about Dolivert's plan but never took it seriously: "I was terribly flattered that people were talking about it," he later said, but "I wasn't very keen about it. I was in on the founding of the thing and at the founding it was apparent to me that all the limitations we know now were inherent in it." If Welles really saw what would eventually happen to the United Nations, he truly missed his calling.

But the war had aroused Welles's political instincts; he exercised them in life, on the radio, and in films. *The Stranger,* for instance, concerned the persistence of fascism after the war. He also thought of running for the Senate, as Citizen Kane's model, William Randolph Hearst, had done. He was talked out of doing so by Alan Cranston (then a powerful Democratic leader in Sacramento) because, said Welles, "he wanted to be Senator" himself. And, like Hearst, Welles dreamed of being President someday: "It might be a possible future," he said. But he felt that his marriage to an actress would be detrimental to a political career, and this feeling played a big part in his eventual separation from Rita Hayworth.

Roosevelt's death had completely killed the project Lieutenant Commander Douglas Fairbanks, Jr., was working on in naval intelligence, a plan to try to overthrow Hirohito and the Tojo military clique with a coup d'état involving the Dowager Empress. Roosevelt had shown some interest in the idea, but what Fairbanks and others planning the coup did not know was that the government was working on something else, which would bring the Pacific war to a speedy conclusion—and it was *not* the bat plan. (Someone had the idea of extracting bats from the Carlsbad Caverns in New Mexico, where there were supposed to be thirty million of the creatures, outfitting them with little incendiary bombs, and dropping them over Japan's industrial area around Osaka Bay, where the bats would do their natural thing: roost in the roofs, attics, and lofts of the homes and factories in the industrial area. Then the little bombs would ignite and completely destroy Japan's war-making industry. The government seriously explored this idea, especially after six bats accidentally burned down an auxiliary air base in New Mexico.)

Lieutenant Tim Holt, a bit-part actor who had appeared in *The Magnificent Ambersons* and would later work with Humphrey Bogart in *The Treasure of the Sierra Madre*, was involved in the bat project as a flight bombardier, and Bing Crosby was approached to invest in the company that would make the containers for the little bat bombs. (Crosby declined the offer, but it inspired the rumor, after the first A-bomb had been dropped, that one of his companies had made the containers.) Zeppo Marx *did* found a company that made coupling devices, including the clamping mechanism that carried the A-bombs to Japan.

The bomb did not surprise director Alfred Hitchcock. In 1944, he was considering the plot gimmick—or McGuffin, as he called it—that would require Ingrid Bergman to marry a German in order to spy on him (as she did with Claude Rains in *Notorious*). Hitchcock decided that his McGuffin would be uranium hidden in wine bottles in the cellar. When David Selznick asked him, "What's all this about uranium in wine bottles?" Hitchcock said that uranium "was an unstable element, just like the world, and that everybody knew it was rare. It seemed to me that . . . someday somebody would make a bomb out of it." The FBI heard about the plot of *Notorious* and investigated Hitchcock, who would later claim that he anticipated the A-bomb.

Truman's decision to drop the bomb on Hiroshima jolted the stars—as it did the rest of the world—except Commander (he had been promoted) Fairbanks. He was on leave when his mother called him and said: "Douglas, did you listen to the radio this morning?"

"No," Fairbanks replied.

"They've just dropped some new bomb on Japan," his mother said.

"Oh, just another big blockbuster, I expect," her son in naval intelligence replied. "The papers always have to write something sensational. Take no notice."

The Japanese, however, knew it was not just another blockbuster and almost immediately surrendered. Bob Hope says:

I was in the Nuremberg Stadium watching the G.I. Olympics in a rainstorm, when they announced over the loudspeaker system that Japan had offered to surrender. It was a moment I'll never forget. That whole stadium full of guys seemed to rise twenty-five feet in the air. Nothing in my life had prepared me for that experience. The

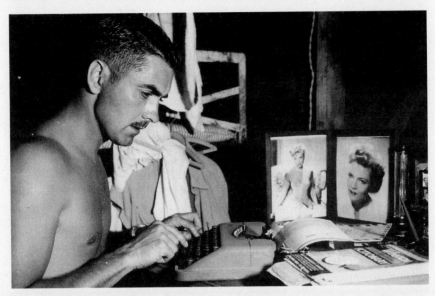

Tyrone Power, after seeing some of the first photographs of the devastated Hiroshima, wrote from the South Pacific that "the human mind cannot grasp" the power of the new atomic bomb. National Archives

cheering, the shouting, even the crying. Thousands of men who knew at that one moment they were going to live. There were no questions, no doubts.

He said the A-bomb changed history and "eventually made the Cold War a joke"—at least for Bob Hope.

Tyrone Power, still on Saipan in the Pacific, wrote his friend Watson Webb of the impact on him of some of the photographs taken after the first bomb was dropped:

It is not just the immediate effect that it is going to have on the Japs, and the war in general . . . but the effect it is going to have on us all for the rest of our lives. For as surely as I sit here writing to you this morning . . . our whole lives have changed. . . . Even if I were allowed to tell you what it was like, I doubt whether I could. It actually defies description. There are no words in our poor vocabulary, at present, to draw an adequate picture of it. The human mind cannot grasp it.

After V-J Day, Power flew two cargo flights to Japan and wrote Annabella that he knew the Japanese "hate us. You can feel it in the air. You can see it on their faces, when they pass you on the street."

Ingrid Bergman was in Paris when she heard the news of the Japanese surrender. She leaped out of the jeep in which she and her lover, Bob Capa, were riding, and said, "I'm going to throw myself at somebody and kiss him."

"Which one?" asked Capa as Bergman ran into the Champs-Elysées. It did not take her long to pick out a G.I. and give him a long kiss, which he returned with interest. One wonders whether he is still alive—and whether he remembers.

Unlike most of her colleagues, Bergman was not anxious to leave Europe. "She did not want to go home," said Larry Adler. "She didn't want to go back to California. In New York she tried to get me to stay a few days. Then she wanted to take the slowest plane back to Los Angeles." It was not Hollywood, but a bad marriage, to which Bergman did not want to go home.

Essentially, Hollywood actors and actresses—with a few notable exceptions—reacted to the end of the war as the rest of the country did. But those exceptions help to set Hollywood apart from your average town. When the war in Europe ended, Paul Muni was seized with the idea of filming a biography of Alfred Nobel, the Swedish munitions manufacturer who spent his life making explosives that would kill people but left his fortune to be devoted to the pursuit of peace. Having found every book he could on Nobel, Muni retreated to his home to see if he could develop a screen treatment. During his isolation he came to question why any sane person would ever want to become an actor, although he was fully aware, he said, that "I am unhappy if I am not working."

He finally decided it was Freud he ought to be doing a biography of, but went on with his research (eventually buying an option on Herta E. Pauli's biography, *Alfred Nobel,* and approaching every studio in Hollywood looking for a producer. But they turned him down: No one was interested in peace, they said).

However, John Wayne, of all people, was stricken with a brief case of peace fever, advocating love-not-war in one of his first postwar movies, *Angel and the Badman,* which he also produced. The angel was the dark-haired beauty Gail Russell, who persuaded the badman to hang up his gun. (The angel, in reality, died tragically of alcoholism at the age of thirty-six.)

Louis B. Mayer also made a movie out of his reaction to the end of the war. After a second bomb was dropped on a Japanese city—Nagasaki—Mayer decided to make a movie about the A-bomb. The result was *The Beginning or the End.*

And for Ginger Rogers, the end of the war meant that she finally got the Noguchi bust she had commissioned before Pearl Harbor. The sculptor had finished it while he was interned.

Gene Kelly, still in the Navy in July 1945 and en route to the far Pacific for what he thought would be the last major battle of the war, thought: "Well, this is it. We're not going to start the invasion of Japan. But I was stopped in Hawaii and brought back to San Francisco, and the number of days between the first and second bomb was sort of a drunken nightmare to me, as I sat waiting to see what was going to happen next." Before being discharged he returned to the Anacostia naval base near Washington, D.C., where he edited a film about the destruction of the aircraft carrier *Benjamin Franklin* by kamikaze.

As James M. Cain said, in Hollywood the war "impacted on nine hundred guys separately and differently." Most of them reacted in character. Clark Gable found that losing Carole Lombard and seeing combat had sapped his ambition and made moviemaking seem like sissy stuff—which it was, of course, compared to being shot at at thirty thousand feet. His first postwar movie was *Adventure*, with Greer Garson. Gable found the whole experience of making this film tiresome and annoying, especially the publicity line "Gable's back and Garson's got him." He did not like Garson, did not really want to be "back," and did not want to be "got" by any woman. He was also miserable during the shooting of the film, often shaking on the set. David Niven (who was not in the film but was close to Gable after the war) attributed this trembling to Dexedrine. Gable took amphetamines to fight a weight problem caused by the excessive drinking he had started doing after Carole's death and had continued in the service and after the war.

When Jimmy Stewart came home on the *Queen Elizabeth*, his agent-producer, Leland Hayward, arranged a big party for him at the St. Regis Hotel in New York, but Stewart was late because he insisted on remaining at the ship awhile: "I want to stay until a few of my boys come ashore."

"The wait grew longer and longer," said Hayward later. He finally asked Stewart, "How many are there?"

"I guess a couple of hundred," Stewart replied. He was shaking hands with and saying good-bye to all of them.

Stewart came back to Hollywood a real hero but did not want to be one. He refused a ticker-tape parade ("Thousands of men in uniform did far more meaningful things and got small or no recognition for it") and an invitation to run for governor of Pennsylvania ("It's only in pictures that I make a good officeholder. . . . I talk much too slowly for a politician") and insisted on an "anti-hero" clause in his contract preventing the studio from promoting him as a "war hero."

He also should have included an anti-fishing clause. *Life* did a photo story on Stewart's homecoming; the *Life* photographer, Peter Stackpole, decided he wanted a picture of Stewart fishing on his favorite lake in his Pennsylvania hometown. According to Henry Fonda (who, to judge by his autobiography, may have been just a tad jealous of all the attention Stewart was given when he came home), Stewart agreed to pose as Stackpole wanted, even though he had never fished before. He and Stackpole ended up in a boat on the lake, and on one of his first attempts to cast, Stewart hooked a big one—a *Life* photographer, "right under the eyebrow. . . . Jim told me that story during lunch at '21,' " said Fonda, "and I practically slid under the table."

The contract just discussed was with the new independent studio Liberty Films, which had been established by George Stevens, William Wyler, and Frank Capra. Stewart's first postwar film, *It's a Wonderful Life,* put to rest the gossip that the war had probably ruined his acting career. There were also stories going around that James Stewart was so disillusioned with acting that he wanted to leave the business, but "that is plain nonsense," Stewart said.

Tyrone Power's homecoming was more in the classic tradition. It took place in November 1945, in Portland, Oregon. He was returning on the U.S.S. *Marvin McIntyre,* and Annabella—through "friends," as she put it—had found this out and had come to meet him, much to Power's surprise. When he finally saw her on the dock, he raced to her and embraced her and kissed her so hard one soldier yelled, "Take it easy, Jesse!" (Power had played Jesse James, to Henry Fonda's Frank James, in 1939.) Power said: "It was the top moment I've ever lived. . . . It was as though you'd died and gone to hell and then you come back and there was an angel holding open the door of heaven you'd ceased to believe existed at all."

Mickey Rooney also kissed his new wife, Betty Jane, when he came home, but when he did, horror of horrors, he found that although he had not grown an inch, she had—several, in fact: "At seventeen," he wrote in his autobiography, "she had been only a couple of inches taller than I. Now . . . all dolled up in her high heels, she seemed to tower over me by almost a foot."

Betty Jane also became pregnant again, at the same time Rooney discovered that they had little in common. She did not like his friends—"not even my very oldest and best," he said. Rooney was having trouble trying to revive his movie career, and they were fighting all the time, until finally, three months pregnant, Betty Jane simply went home to Mother. Rooney said that was "the best idea" she had had in a long time—and it was over.

Then there were the surprise homecomings: "Five o'clock one morning," said Wayne Morris's wife, Patricia, "the bell awakened me from a sound sleep. I flew to the door—and found Wayne standing there. . . . I forgot how unglamorous I was . . . and he didn't seem to notice." Morris was toasted at numerous cocktail and dinner parties. But he never gained the stardom that had been hoped for him, drifting into westerns and good-pal roles for most of the rest of his career, which was not long. In 1959, at the invitation of his uncle David, Morris was watching naval air maneuvers aboard the aircraft carrier U.S.S. *Bonhomme Richard* when he suffered a heart attack and died, at the age of forty-five.

The homecoming of Melvyn Douglas, who had served in the China-Burma-India Theater with Tony Martin, actually took place in Washington. When he arrived at the Capitol he told the page "to inform Representative Douglas that Major Douglas is outside waiting." They had a tearful reunion. Years later, he learned that Marine major Paul Douglas (soon to become a United States senator) arrived at the Capitol a few hours after Army major Melvyn Douglas and told the same page to "inform Representative Douglas [*his* wife, Congresswoman Emily Taft Douglas] that Major Douglas was outside waiting." The page called the Capitol police, and only the arrival of Congresswoman Emily Douglas prevented her husband from being taken off to jail.

Tony Martin did not have a girlfriend waiting to kiss him when he came home from the war (although he did renew his old friendship with Rita Hayworth on New Year's Eve, 1945; before long, he said, "I was in love again"). But he vividly remembered getting a call from the judge advocate who handled the Navy's case against him. The judge advocate said he was in California for a few days and "we should get together for a drink."

"Fine," said Martin, and they set a date. Martin said: "I went over to his hotel—and hit him in the mouth and left. It was one of the most satisfying moments in my life."

Martin said that returning to his profession was every bit as hard as he thought it would be. "I wasn't just an ordinary honorably discharged serviceman," he said. "It was more as though I were a convict out on bail."

The war had a lasting impact on several stars, especially the ones who had gone into the service. Robert Ryan's friends, as well as his biographer, Franklin Jarlett, agree that the actor was profoundly affected by his service in the Marine Corps, which no doubt influenced his decision to become active in SANE (the National Committee for a Sane Nuclear Policy) and the American Civil Liberties Union. As a summation of his feelings about the war, Ryan hung in his home his painting of "the great agonized face."

William Holden, too, was seriously disturbed by the war, primarily because of the guilt he felt at not being in combat while his brother, a Navy pilot, was killed. He did not work for eleven months after the war, but when he did he quickly proved, as Harry Cohn had hoped, that he could carry a movie. He had two successes in 1950, *Sunset Boulevard* and *Born Yesterday,* although he had considerable help from Gloria Swanson in the first and Judy Holliday in the second.

Jackie Cooper concluded in his autobiography, *Please Don't Shoot My Dog:* "I think the war probably saved me. . . . I would [otherwise] be a drunk and total loss today."

Gary Cooper thought he had been too serious during the war and felt an urge to get away for a while, an urge he never satisfied.

Harpo Marx wrote in his memoirs: "At the end of the war we enlarged our house. We threw out the butler, disconnected the buzzer on the dining room floor and got rid of the rest of the Beverly Hills nonsense. . . . The next thing we threw out . . . was Dr. Spock."

Gene Kelly felt that he had neglected his daughter, Kerry, during the conflict; he has regretted this the rest of his life.

Laurence Olivier said: "The war kept us from being sucked into Hollywood." One of his friends thought the impact of the war on him was "profound. . . . He was a completely different man."

Sterling Hayden was also different. Evelyn Keyes said that after the war, all he wanted to do was "hang around my apartment and read the *Communist Manifesto* aloud to me." (The war—and husband Charles Vidor—also aroused Keyes's passion for liberal politics.)

And it was during the war that Mary Astor began to wonder, "What's so damned important about being an actress?" She said: "I saw my little world, insulated, self-absorbed, limited. And all the twenty years of hard work seemed sour and futile."

The war was the most profound experience of Marlene Dietrich's life. It made her hate Hollywood and moviemaking more than ever. "When we returned to the United States at the end of the war," she said, "we were greeted with stupid remarks. We were not allowed in restaurants without wearing ties, no matter how many medals a paratrooper wore on his chest. . . . My hatred of 'carefree' Americans dates from this time." But there was also the need to make some money, so with great foreboding and reluctance, Dietrich returned to Hollywood, where many thought she was washed up despite her emergence as the legendary Marlene of the Battle for Europe. However, Dietrich did make several Hollywood movies after the war, beginning with *Golden Earrings*. And soon she rose to greater heights in one-woman shows in which she played the persona she had created during the war.

The war also had a significant effect on Ronald Reagan. Captain Reagan was still in uniform when he heard the news of an atomic bomb dropped on Hiroshima. He was on his way to the Disney studios to narrate an animated film and he realized it was the beginning of his new, issue-oriented career. From now on, he would be more aware of national and international affairs: "I was blindly and busily joining every organization I could find that would guarantee to save the world—including the Republican Party."

Reagan also became somewhat paranoiac and avidly anti-Communist. He began keeping guns by his bedside and was convinced that the Communists planned to take over the motion picture industry, not for the money but for a "world-wide propaganda base." He was an FBI informer and president of the Screen Actors Guild. But he was a simplistic anti-Communist of the kind who believed that if you were not openly anti-Communist, you must be pro-Communist. Jane Wyman, a conservative and a Republican, could not go that far. They argued politics all the time, although Reagan did not pay much attention to "the little woman." In December 1947, she told a reporter: "There is no use in lying. I'm not the happiest girl in the world. It's nothing that happened recently, it's an accumulation of things that have been coming on for a long time."

By 1948, Reagan, without Jane, had embarked on his own special film career: the road to Washington.

For others, the main impact of the war was to help start them on the road to stardom. In one way or another, it gave several actresses and actors their big break. Judy Holliday's first notable film role was in *Something for the Boys* (which also introduced Perry Como to the movies). She played a Rosie the Riveter type in a defense plant and had one line: Raising her welder's mask, she said, "I once knew a girl who got carborundum in her teeth and it turned her into a radio receiver set." This was followed by *Winged Victory*, another war film, and then *Adam's Rib*. Her career was given a temporary setback when Darryl F. Zanuck, in his first interview with her, explained the star system and how it made her his property. When he tried to force his newly acquired property onto the casting couch, she screamed: "These belong to you, too, Mr. Zanuck," and threw her falsies at him. However, by now her persona as the perfect smart, dumb blonde was well enough known that she was offered a part in the new Broadway play *Born Yesterday.*

Lucille Ball also played a Rosie the Riveter part in *Meet the People.* It was not a breakthrough role, but one biographer says it foreshadowed her role as Lucy in the television series that was not too far in the future.

Eve Arden was making *My Reputation* (becoming the first woman to appear in bed with her on-screen husband *without* obeying the Hays Office by keeping one foot on the floor) when she noticed several different girls wandering around the lot wearing Russian uniforms. She learned that they were auditioning for a part in a war film called *The Doughgirls* (with Ann Sheridan, Jane Wyman, and Alexis Smith) and tried out for the part even though she was told that Jack Warner would not give the part to anyone not under contract to Warner Bros. But Arden's screen test was so funny that Warner signed her to what she called "the only kind of contract I wanted to sign"—two pictures a year, an option on a third, and the right to do Broadway shows and radio. Television's future "Our Miss Brooks" was on her way.

Jane Wyman and Ronald Reagan, both members of the Screen Actors Guild, argued politics after the war until their marriage broke up. Here, a SAG meeting in 1946. From left: Edward Arnold, Walter Pidgeon, Wyman, Dick Powell, Robert Montgomery (president), George Murphy, Reagan, Alexis Smith, Robert Taylor, and Gene Kelly. Screen Actors Guild

As we have seen, Veronica Lake's career was launched with considerable assistance from a publicity photograph taken for the wartime film *I Wanted Wings;* and it was the G.I.'s coming home still in love with the *Life* photo of Rita Hayworth that helped turn the postwar *Gilda* into the film that established Hayworth forever as one of America's preeminent sex goddesses. Carmen Miranda attributed her popularity as the "Queen of the Samba" to the effort to win friends in Latin America during the war; her career began a quick decline afterward, when the nation—and movie audiences—became indifferent to our good neighbors to the south.

There is little doubt that Elizabeth Taylor would have made it into the movies somewhere, sometime, but the war played a role in bringing her from England (where her American parents operated an art gallery) to America. When war was declared in 1939, the Taylors wanted to get their two children out of Europe, so they came back to America and opened a gallery in Los Angeles. Young Elizabeth spent a lot of time at the gallery, and one day a woman named Andrea Berens, an admirer of the paintings of Augustus John (several of which Elizabeth's father had brought with him from London), came by the gallery. While Berens was looking at the John paintings, ten-year-old Elizabeth wandered into the room. Berens was so struck by her pure beauty that she said, "Cheever must see this child."

Cheever Cowdin, Berens's fiancé, was chairman of the board of directors of Universal Pictures. He was invited to tea that Sunday by the Taylors, and after Elizabeth had shown him her doll collection, he urged her to come by the studio for a screen test. In those days everyone was looking for another Shirley Temple or Deanna Durbin; Cowdin quickly signed the girl to a contract with Universal.

It was partly because of the war that Taylor got the part that helped establish her as a child star. One night in 1942, her father, an air-raid warden, was walking with another warden, Sam Marx, an MGM producer who was working on the first Lassie movie, *Lassie Come Home.* No doubt with daughter Elizabeth in the back of his mind, Taylor asked Marx what was new with Lassie (known later in Hollywood as "Greer Garson in furs").* Sam Marx said that the actress playing the girl who frees Lassie so she can make the long trip home was too tall for Roddy McDowall, so they were looking for another girl. Taylor mentioned his daughter, her contract with Universal, and the fact that she was smaller

---

*Lassie was played by a male, a circumstance that, Groucho Marx always said, made people suspicious of Hollywood.

than Roddy McDowall. Elizabeth was invited to do a screen test, and, as Marx recalls it: "We had five other girls whom we were considering. We practically had selected one because I didn't expect much from Elizabeth. But the moment she entered there was a complete eclipse of all the others. She was stunning, dazzling. Her voice was charming and she had no self-consciousness whatsoever. We gave her a test, and when we looked at it the next day, we knew we had a find."

=

Mamie Van Doren was nine when her mother and father moved to Los Angeles to work in defense plants. Mamie was struck by the glamour of Hollywood and knew she wanted to be a movie star from the moment she arrived, but especially after she went to watch the stars coming to a big party at the Mocambo. One of the first to arrive was Mae West: "Clad in twinkling silver sequins," said Mamie, "her pale blonde hair encircling her head like a halo, she was escorted by an entourage of half a dozen tanned and beautiful well-built men. If a genie had suddenly appeared, I would have gladly traded anything I had to be just like her."

Miss Van Doren had plenty, and she said in her autobiography that "If you are young, healthy, energetic and possessed of the normal set of biological urges, the casting couch also can be fun with the right person." Inevitably, she went into films and became known as "the poor man's Marilyn Monroe," appearing in such films as *The Second Greatest Sex, Sex Kittens Go to College,* and *The Private Lives of Adam and Eve.*

=

Shelley Winters was appearing on Broadway in *Rosalinda,* an English version of *Die Fledermaus.* She had a small part, that of Fiji, and near the beginning of the second act she was supposed to greet the Prince, played by Oscar Karlweis, and Adela, played by a young soprano whose name Winters could not remember by the time she wrote her autobiography but whose boyfriend was in the Army. Winters vividly recalled that it was wartime: This was the first time she had had her name on Broadway in lights—and the lights were dimmed because of blackout regulations. When, one night, the Prince and Adela did not appear, Shelley repeated her four lines a couple of times and then, as everyone in the cast and the orchestra began to panic:

I proceeded to improvise a five-minute monologue about the conditions in Vienna at the turn of the century. Including the traffic problems. It began to take on the sensation of a nightmare in slow motion . . . what the hell did I know about Vienna in the 1900s, especially its traffic problems? . . . The audience was in hysterics. But it seemed as though I were out there for hours, floating around the stage, staying in character and carrying on about my love for the Prince and Viennese society.

Just as Winters was ready to suggest the audience could go home, the Prince and Adela appeared. Karlweis said: "I'm sorry we're late, Fiji, but the emperor had one of his parades and it delayed us." Fiji responded, "See, I knew it was the traffic."

After the show, who should appear backstage but Columbia's Harry Cohn, insisting that Winters come to his New York studio and do a screen test—performing any kind of monologue as long as it was as funny as the one she had just done onstage to save *Rosalinda*. Winters did Dorothy Parker's short story "The Waltz," and signed a seven-year contract with Columbia.

The reason the Prince and Adela had not appeared onstage was that Adela had failed to hear the cue call. She was sitting in her tights in her third-floor dressing room, totally absorbed in the letter she was writing to her boyfriend in the Army. Thus Shelley Winters's own version of *A Star Is Born*.

=

The male actors, of course, were more affected by the war. It was not just the young unknowns, like Peter Lawford and Van Johnson, who got the breaks; many established actors fortunate enough to be able to stay home also emerged into the limelight. After *Mrs. Miniver*, Walter Pidgeon was a star and continued to be one during the war, with so many actors in the service. But when the war was over and the Gables and the Stewarts returned, Pidgeon began to slip back into his usual role as a comfortable pipe-smoking British gentleman, playing second fiddle to actresses like Greer Garson, then character parts.

Gregory Peck's first movie was *Days of Glory*, in which Russians fight Nazis. Although it did not make him a star, it did establish him as an accomplished actor. One studio head who saw the film and was impressed by Peck's performance was Darryl Zanuck, who picked him to play the priest in *The Keys of the Kingdom*. That role led to Peck's first Oscar nomination and a long career in Hollywood.

Gary Cooper had been making films since 1928, but it was his role in *Sergeant York*, for which he won an Oscar, that established him as an

When Mickey Rooney came home from the Army, he found that his wartime bride, Betty Jane Rase, had grown several inches. Shelley Winters (wearing her wartime husband's wings) holds her Columbia contract. A letter to a boy in the Army helped launch a new star.

Walt Davis

actor. And *Casablanca* did for Humphrey Bogart what *York* had done for Cooper, not only confirming his acting ability but establishing him as a romantic leading man.

John Wayne became a leading man during the war and a star warrior on the screen, primarily because of the absence of so many leading men. After Wayne's brief fling with peace in *Angel and the Badman,* John Ford decided that Wayne was such a great screen warrior that they should continue fighting wars on film for many years.

Gary Merrill's thirty-three-year movie career, of which the highlight was *All About Eve* (not just for his performance but because he married the film's leading lady, Bette Davis), started with the Broadway production of *This Is the Army,* which led to a part in the movie *Winged Victory.* Both productions used real soldiers; Merrill was in the Army—at Camp Upton (near Yaphank, Long Island), the camp that inspired Irving Berlin's World War I stage musical, *Yip Yip Yaphank.* In 1942, the Army decided to do a World War II version of the show, and Merrill was among the first of the real soldiers recruited for it. *Yip Yip Yaphank* was later made into a movie, in which Merrill did not appear (but Ronald Reagan did, and so did George Murphy, who played Reagan's father).

The war definitely hurt Ronald Reagan's career. By 1954, he was playing Las Vegas with a quartet, "The Continentals," and saying Hollywood was a "truly sick industry." He was happy to take a job as host on General Electric's weekly TV series, "Death Valley Days," which led to his touring the GE plants and giving upbeat, anti-big-government talks. He also made occasional movies, the most notable being *Bedtime for Bonzo* and *Hellcats of the Navy. Hellcats* was his next-to-last film and the only one in which he costarred with Nancy Davis. (Johnny Carson once quipped that White House orders were that there were "only two reasons to wake up President Reagan in the middle of the night: One is World War III; the other is if *Hellcats of the Navy* turns up on the late show.") *Hellcats* contains this something less than immortal exchange between Davis and Reagan:

NANCY: What are you going to do after the war?
RONNIE: I told you a hundred times.
NANCY: I want to hear it once more.
RONNIE: I'm going into the surplus business. I'm gonna buy up all the old mines and sell 'em to the man in the moon.
NANCY: But there's no water on the moon!

RONNIE: How do you know so much about the moon?

NANCY: I know a lot about it. I spend all my time looking at it when you're away.

＝

The year 1945 was a turning point for Hollywood. America's returning veterans, probably still smitten with all those girls pinned over their bunks and the ones they had drooled over in the USO shows, had also been thoroughly exposed to movies and movie stars while in the service. After the war, they obviously wanted more: In 1946 more people went to movies than in any other year in Hollywood's history.

By the end of the war, with all the returning servicemen who had seen not only death and Gay Paree but also London, Rome, Berlin, and Tokyo—and sex in the raw—realism would be the order of the day. The prudish, cautious Hays Office was rapidly losing its power. Billy Wilder had bought James M. Cain's *Double Indemnity,* and MGM took Cain's *The Postman Always Rings Twice* out of mothballs, where it had been since 1932. No longer were adultery and conspiracy to murder your husband taboo subjects. And Hollywood was ready for other forbidden topics—alcoholism (*The Lost Weekend*), anti-Semitism (*Gentleman's Agreement*), and mental illness (*The Snake Pit*).

As for the star warriors of World War II, Sir Cedric Hardwicke said, quoting that old chestnut about actors, "Let them be well used; for they are the abstracts and brief chronicles of the time; after your death you were better have a bad epitaph than their ill report while you live."

No one can argue that actors were not well used during the war, and not just as fund-raisers and troop entertainers. Their screen portrayals of the Nazis will probably live on forever, and beginning with the baby boomers, most generations to come will have their view of our erstwhile enemies shaped by the films now available on television and in video rental stores. Considering reports from time to time that there still exists a small Nazi movement in Germany, perhaps our actors and their "ill report," continually reminding future generations how evil this kind of authoritarian movement can be, will turn out to provide one of Hollywood's most significant contributions to freedom. You might argue that these films do not accurately depict our former enemies, but for those of us who remember what actually happened, it is hard to imagine how anyone could exaggerate the evils of Adolf Hitler and the Nazi movement.

Epitaph

I came to Hollywood because I had no place else to go. —AUDIE MURPHY, who went *To Hell and Back* twice, once in Europe and once in Hollywood

---

Tony Randall was twenty-one at the time of Pearl Harbor and was just beginning his stage career when the Army called him: "I was gone four years," he said. "Eli Wallach was gone six. When we came back from the Army, we were no longer kids. We had to start all over again . . . rather late in life. The war screwed up my generation."

Not all of it, although for these young aspiring actors there were no deferments to make movies and no cushy assignments to work on Signal Corps films. On the other hand, many of the aspiring actors who went into the service were given opportunities to prove what they could do. Melvin Kaminsky of the Bronx, soon to change his name to Mel Brooks, had such a case of patriotic fever in his senior year in high school that, according to his biographer, you would have thought "the Wehrmacht might have been massing for an attack on Ebbets Field." Kaminsky enlisted in the Army, saved Ebbets Field, and along the way learned, both in Europe and at Fort Dix, New Jersey, that he could make the troops laugh. Sid Caesar had a similar opportunity in the Coast Guard when, with two other Coast Guardsmen, he produced his first comedy skit, "Six On, Twelve Off," based on his service's watch duty for guarding a pier.

Stand-up comic Danny Thomas attributed to the war the warm reception he got from the audience and the press on his first night at Chicago's Martinique. After a leaden opening, in which he announced Italy's surrender that day, he said he also wanted to pay tribute to our Allies by singing a little song the Russians were singing in the streets of Stalingrad: "Berchtesgaden Choo-Choo," sung to the tune of "Chattanooga Choo-Choo."

Sammy Davis, Jr., had left his post as a drummer in the Will Mastin Trio (with his father and uncle) and enlisted in the Army immediately after Pearl Harbor. The taxi ride to Times Square to enlist was a montage of every war movie he had ever seen: "I was marching with thousands of men singing 'You're a Grand Old Flag.' Pat O'Brien was my captain and Spencer Tracy was the chaplain. . . . Between 125th and 42nd streets I won my wings in the Air Force and I saw myself zooming off on dangerous missions bombing enemy ships and dog-fighting with Zeros."*

But Davis soon found that the Army was a little different from the way it was portrayed in Hollywood—especially for blacks. On his first day in camp, he approached a PFC sitting on the barracks steps and said, "Excuse me, buddy, I'm a little lost. Can you tell me where 202 is?"

The PFC pointed toward 202, saying: "And I'm not your buddy, you black bastard." It was Davis's first Army experience with the ugly anti-black feeling existing in parts of the country. He soon found that when he started dancing, the attitude toward him would often change, although some of the rednecks would try to make him dance faster and faster, hitting him in the stomach and saying, "Didn't you hear me say 'faster,' Sambo?" which invariably led to another fight.

Davis nevertheless learned that "my talent was my weapon, the

---

*But he had an "athlete's heart," which prevented him from being sent overseas. (He lost his eye in a 1954 automobile accident, after he was already launched on a successful recording and television career. His nose was broken twice in barrack-room fights.)

power, the way for me to fight"—a lesson that stayed with him all the way to Broadway and Hollywood, where in 1956 he appeared, respectively, onstage in *Mr. Wonderful* and on screen in *The Benny Goodman Story.*

The war usually had an impact even on the future stars who had had no chance to display their talents in the service or who, at the time, had no thought of an acting career. Lee Marvin, the son of a New York advertising executive and a fashion writer, had no intention of being an actor when he joined the Marines in 1942. He was invalided out after twice escaping death in the Pacific. "There are two prominent parts of your body in view of the enemy when you flatten out—your head and your ass," he told his biographer, Donald Zec. "If you present one, you get shot in the head. If you raise the other you get shot in the ass. I got shot in the ass."

After Marvin came out of the hospital and returned to civilian life, he held several odd jobs before becoming an actor. It took him six years to reach Hollywood. And he learned one important lesson in the Marines: "Life is every man for himself. You can't ever let your guard down and the most useless word in the world is 'Help.' " How many films have we seen, from *The Dirty Dozen* to *The Big Red One,* in which Marvin acted out his credo on the screen?

Before the war, Burt Lancaster was an acrobat; whenever he was in Hollywood he would look for work. But he was told that, despite his good looks, the studios were not interested in anyone who did not have professional acting experience. In the Army he went to North Africa and learned how to be a top sergeant the hard way. After discharge in 1945, he was in an elevator in New York when he noticed someone looking at him in a rather strange way. The man was Jack Mahlor, a Broadway associate producer; he was seeking someone to play a top sergeant in a play, *A Sound of Hunting.* Lancaster has been playing top sergeants, gangsters, cowboys, and other assorted tough guys ever since.

Marlon Brando and Sidney Poitier both learned quite a bit about acting during their war years—Brando (who was 4-F because he was nearsighted and had a football-damaged knee) because he wanted to be in the Army, and Poitier because he wanted out of the Army (in which he had enlisted at the age of sixteen, lying about his age). Brando's expulsion from Shattuck Military Academy (for smoking, the school said) had humiliated him. It also enraged his father, who decided that the service might make a man of Marlon. So almost everywhere Brando went during the war, he pretended to be a military veteran with a bad knee. He put on a good enough act to inspire passengers on a train to

Milwaukee to pay his fare after he insisted that, as a wounded veteran, he should be able to ride free.

Poitier had enlisted because "it would get me off the streets." But once in, he decided he wanted out. So, risking a court-martial, he feigned insanity; then, when threatened with shock treatment, he told the truth and was eventually discharged.

Later, progressing from amateur to professional acting, both men won Oscars—Brando for *On the Waterfront* and *The Godfather* and Poitier for *Lilies of the Field.*

Jack Lemmon learned how to be a real Ensign Pulver in the Navy. When he graduated from the Harvard naval program, the captain congratulated him, saying: "You have the lowest marks of any officer ever commissioned by the ROTC." Lemmon's first assignment was to report to the aircraft carrier U.S.S *Lake Champlain,* where he launched a naval career designed, his biographer Don Widener said, to "convince the Navy he was ill-suited for any war-like duty." It didn't matter much, because the *Lake Champlain* was in the process of being decommissioned after having brought thousands of troops home from Europe after V-E Day. And through a series of comic maneuvers, making one mistake after another, Ensign Lemmon was given the best possible fitness report and rewarded with cushy desk jobs, first in Washington, then in Boston, until the war was over. There was probably no one in Hollywood better prepared to play Ensign Pulver in *Mister Roberts,* for which Lemmon won an Oscar as best supporting actor.

Having been the intercollegiate wrestling champion at St. Lawrence University, Kirk Douglas did not need the service to "make a man out of him." Already on Broadway at the time of Pearl Harbor, he felt "a wave of patriotism and a wave of Jewishness. . . . I wanted to fight, to drop bombs on them." He joined the Navy, was sent to midshipman school at Notre Dame, then was assigned to Patrol Craft 1139. He says he liked being on a sub chaser: "It was fun, like playacting." But the "playacting" became real enough when PC 1139 sighted a Japanese submarine and dropped its depth charges: One of the charges exploded too soon, injuring Douglas and putting him in the naval hospital in San Diego for five months. He was given a medical discharge in 1944 and resumed his Broadway career. That took him to Hollywood in 1946 for his first film role, in *The Strange Love of Martha Ivers* with Barbara Stanwyck.

Charlton Heston knew he wanted to be an actor even before he signed up as a drama and speech student at Northwestern University. But at nineteen, he enlisted in the Air Corps, where he learned how to operate the radio on a B-25. He had a brief career in early TV before he played a jilted ex-G.I. in his first professional film, *Dark City.*

Steve McQueen enlisted in the Marines when he was seventeen, and was discharged at the age of twenty with no idea what he wanted to do. But like a lot of young men, he took the chance given him by the G.I. Bill to go to school. He accepted an invitation to study at the Neighborhood Playhouse in New York, eventually replacing Ben Gazzara in the 1955 Broadway production *A Hatful of Rain.* He made it to Hollywood in 1956 to begin his film career with a small part in *Somebody Up There Likes Me.*

The G.I. Bill also played a part in Paul Newman's film career. He had no thought of being an actor until he went back to Kenyon College on the G.I. Bill after serving three years in the Navy, mostly as a radioman-gunner on Navy torpedo planes. He apparently saw little action at Okinawa or Guam, but at Kenyon he found action one night in a barroom brawl that put him in jail and off the football team. With plenty of time on his hands, he started reading for a play and found that he liked acting because it was one way of getting attention. His first Broadway success, *Picnic,* led to a film contract with Warner Bros.

The war and the G.I. Bill also played a major role in Tony Curtis's becoming an actor. He enlisted in the Navy before graduating from high school and as a young recruit visited the Hollywood Canteen, falling in love with films and the city. In the Navy, he was assigned to the submarine U.S.S. *Dragonette;* for a long stretch the crewmen had only one film to watch—*Gunga Din,* starring Cary Grant. The men cut the sound and began acting out the roles themselves. Curtis played Grant, developing a case of hero worship. Injured while helping to load torpedoes, he was medically discharged, and attended New York City's Dramatic Workshop on the G.I. Bill. His film career took off after his role in *The Sweet Smell of Success.*

Of all the young stars to show up in Hollywood after World War II, no one could say that the war had more of an impact on his career than Audie Murphy. Murphy, from a sharecropping family in Texas, enlisted in the Army in 1942, at the age of eighteen. In France, from August 15, 1944, to January 26, 1945, he won three of the highest decorations awarded to an American serviceman—to go with the two medals he had already won in Italy. His platoon, as part of the Seventh Army under General Alexander Patch, had landed at St. Tropez and Cavalaire (in a move originally designed to protect the flank of the Allied troops that had landed at Normandy the previous month). The various accounts of what happened (including Murphy's own, given in

his book, *To Hell and Back*) are confusing, but somehow in one engagement he did manage to kill 240 Germans and stop six German tanks
while concealed in an out-of-commission tank destroyer that was leak-
ing gas and in danger of blowing itself up—as indeed it did after Murphy left it. In the process he uttered one of the great quotes to come out
of the war. When his battalion headquarters, which with Murphy's
direction was firing at the German tanks, asked: "How close are the
Germans?" Murphy replied: "Hold the line. I'll let you talk to them."

The Army brought Murphy home and put the handsome but baby-
faced twenty-one-year-old who had killed 240 "Krauts" to work glorifying an Army career, which led to a *Life* cover story. In Hollywood,
Jimmy Cagney, who with his brother William had just started his own
company and had a pretty good case of patriotism himself, was
impressed: "I saw Audie's picture on the cover of *Life* magazine and said
to myself, There is a typical American soldier . . . assurance and poise
without aggressiveness." My God, he might even be another Jimmy
Stewart!

Murphy accepted an offer from Cagney to come to California. "I
don't care anything about Hollywood," Murphy said. "I just want to
make some money and then come back to Dallas and live." He signed a
contract with the Cagney company for $150 a week and agreed to go to
acting school. But Murphy really didn't think he would do well in Hollywood: "Acting is day-dreaming. As an actor, I make a good stunt
man"—especially riding horses and shooting guns, which meant that
inevitably he would become a movie cowboy. But not for a while.

Cagney made no movie with Murphy, although the war hero was
lent to Paramount for a bit part in *Beyond Glory*, a story about a West
Point captain (Alan Ladd) court-martialed for misconduct. Murphy had
only eight words to speak—"seven more than I could handle," he said.

After an MGM screen test, which he failed miserably, the word
around town was that Murphy "would get lost in Hollywood," as
William Cagney put it. At the same time, Murphy was experiencing
another Hollywood trauma. His girlfriend, Jean Peters, whom he had
met at the Actors' Laboratory, threw him over for a tall, pasty-faced
forty-year-old who wore tennis shoes and drove a beat-up Chevrolet.
His name was Howard Hughes. Murphy eventually married an aspiring
young actress named Wanda Hendrix and a few years later Hughes
married Peters.

Down and out in Hollywood with no one encouraging him but Hendrix, Murphy was living in a body-building gym owned by one of his

admirers. He felt it was too late to go back into the Army, and his acting ability was far from promising. But at this point, his career was more or less taken over by one of Hedda Hopper's reporters, David McClure.

McClure had been in Europe in the Signal Corps during the war and not only knew of Murphy's heroics, but envied him. He had wanted to be an infantryman, but was denied his wish because of poor eyesight. Then one day "Spec" McClure was having a conversation with an actor named Harry Morgan, who said, "They can call me a Communist if they like, but when our most decorated soldier has to sleep in a gymnasium, I think that's awful."

McClure agreed. He arranged to meet Murphy, liked him, and decided to take over the rehabilitation of his career. "Audie was somebody worth fighting for. I was determined to get him a break in Hollywood."

Which McClure did, by calling a director who was shooting a film called *Texas, Brooklyn and Heaven,* and asking: "How the hell can you make a movie about Texas without Audie Murphy?" This brought Murphy a bit part in the film. Then McClure got him a part in *Bad Boy,* in which the all-American hero was cast as a criminal (although he was turned into a good boy at the end).

Murphy also aggravated his problems by reminding his directors that he had "no talent"—not that they needed reminding. But *Bad Boy* was good box office, so Universal decided to put Murphy in another film, *The Kid from Texas,* which launched his Hollywood career as king of the B westerns.

While Murphy was working on *The Kid from Texas,* McClure had another brainstorm. He would ghostwrite Murphy's autobiography, hoping to produce a best-seller that would further Murphy's movie career.

To Hell and Back was an instant best-seller and helped inspire Universal to make two more quick westerns starring Murphy: *Kansas Raiders* and *Sierra.* Then McClure heard that MGM was making *The Red Badge of Courage,* based on Stephen Crane's Civil War novel, which McClure had already spotted as a possible Murphy vehicle and had urged him to read. "If you get the lead it should make a star out of you," he said.

The director of *The Red Badge of Courage* was John Huston. When McClure called him to suggest he use Murphy in the cast, Huston said MGM wanted a star, not a B-picture western actor. But according to *New Yorker* writer Lillian Ross, who wrote a book about the making of the film, Huston thought Murphy was like a "great horse. . . . He vibrates.... They just don't see Audie the way I do.... Why, in the war he'd go out of his way to find Germans to kill. He's a gentle little killer."

MGM, still insisting on a star, overruled Huston, so Hedda Hopper went to work on its chief of production, Dore Schary, threatening to criticize the company in her column for not using America's greatest war hero in one of the greatest war stories ever told by an American. Schary gave in. Hopper reported in her column that "for a change, we'll have a real soldier playing a real soldier on the screen." (MGM also decided to have a real wartime cartoonist—Bill Mauldin—play a soldier on the screen.)

The Red Badge of Courage was a disaster from the first Hollywood previews until the last box office receipts were counted. Critics praised Murphy's performance, but because the movie was not a success, it did not do for him what *Champion* did for another ex-serviceman, Kirk Douglas.

Despite the acclaim for his acting, a discouraged Murphy went back to what he did best (making westerns*) until at the height of the Korean War someone had the bright idea that *To Hell and Back* would make a hell of a movie—if only Murphy could play the lead! Hollywood was not sure.

By now, Murphy had been typecast; his marriage to Wanda Hendrix had long ago disintegrated; and he was known around town as a high-stakes gambler and womanizer. McClure said he "seduced more girls than any man I ever knew—with the possible exception of Errol Flynn." Murphy was also telling press interviewers things that prompted reporters to smile and say, "I can't print that," to which Murphy replied, "If I can't tell the truth, what's the use of talking?"

But Universal finally decided that no one but Audie Murphy could play Audie Murphy. Murphy said it was the first time anyone "fought an honest war and then came back and played himself doing it." He also hoped *To Hell and Back* would be the first picture to "show the infantry like it really was."

However, the film was a great disappointment to him. The military scenes were real enough, in part because the Army put the Forty-

---

*Murphy's movies included *The Cimarron Kid* and *Duel at Silver Creek* (1952); *Gunsmoke, Columns South*, and *Tumbleweed* (1953); *Ride Clear of Diablo* and *Drums Across the River* (1954); and *Destry* (1955). The only difference among these westerns, said Murphy, was that "they changed the horse."

fourth Infantry Division at Hollywood's disposal. But (in McClure's opinion) the producer, Aaron Rosenberg, portrayed Murphy as a cross between John Wayne and Abraham Lincoln. The final result was so embarrassing to Murphy that he felt "disloyal to those who were . . . buried out there in Europe."

Still, *To Hell and Back* made $10 million (Murphy's share was $400,000), becoming the biggest hit in Universal's history, even bigger than *The Glenn Miller Story*. Naturally, there would be a sequel: *The Way Back*, about Murphy's problems returning to civilian life and trying to make it in Hollywood. Several writers, including McClure, were put to work on this project. One came up with a story line in which "Audie had to rid himself of all his war neuroses by reliving the war in *To Hell and Back*." Murphy said no to that, so then the writers decided he would find salvation by saving McClure from being a drunkard, which McClure was not. This time it was McClure who said no—and threatened to sue.

Murphy and McClure were then asked to prepare a script, but Murphy balked at going into his personal life, which had been in turmoil for some time. His marriage to Hendrix had lasted only a year and his second marriage (to Pamela Archer) was also in trouble, primarily because of Murphy's instability and womanizing. Said McClure, "Murphy was still a sick boy. . . . I had no idea whether he would ever get well. So I refused to put a happy ending on the script"—and *The Way Back* was put away.

The fact was that Audie Murphy had not really come back from hell; he was only in a new one, one made up of his immaturity, the big money he spent on toys and gambling, and beautiful, tempting women, who were naturally attracted to a handsome young (he never seemed to age until the last couple of years of his life) war hero–movie star. But in the last analysis, hell was boredom.

So Murphy continued fighting his personal demons and going bankrupt while making B pictures or appearing in small roles in major films, until his last movie—appropriately titled *A Time for Dying*. His biographer believes that what Murphy suffered from was the illness later called post-traumatic stress disorder. He had fought his way through it to a partial recovery, and had partially resolved his financial crisis. He died (at forty-six) on his way to Martinsville, Virginia, to help persuade a company called Telestar Leisure Investments to invest in a Martinsville company that built prefab housing (in which Murphy had an interest). He was flying in a small plane with four other passengers when they hit bad weather approaching Martinsville. They tried to land at Roanoke, but flew into a mountain about twenty miles from the airport.

As Bill Mauldin said, "After cutting a swath through the Wehrmacht" Murphy tried "to do the same thing in Hollywood." Hollywood made a big movie about that swath he cut through the German army, but could not figure out how to film his Hollywood years. Perhaps Murphy's most enduring epitaph was uttered by Gregory Peck in a film about the Korean War, *Pork Chop Hill.* Trying to discourage a young soldier about to risk his life for some unworthy objective, Peck says to the boy: "Who the hell do you think you are—Audie Murphy?"

Sources and Bibliography

This book is based on secondary, not primary, sources. Despite the fact that some of the stars whose wartime experiences are portrayed in this book are still alive, I decided early on there would be no interviewing. As Otto Friedrich says in the foreword to *City of Nets,* his book about Hollywood in the 1940s: "No more interviews. Surely there is no one of importance in Hollywood, dead or alive, who has not been interrogated over and over again. And in no other field of history, not in Hitler's Berlin or Roosevelt's Washington, have so many interviews grown into so many ghost-written autobiographies"—to say nothing of the many excellent memoirs and Hollywood biographies to appear in recent years. In fact, in the case of several stars, there are available an autobiography and several biographies.

Also, I chose not to clutter the book with footnotes or endnotes citing the source for every statement made about a star. Most of these war stories came from the following biographies, memoirs, magazine profiles, and collections of biographies. And if, after consulting these sources, you cannot find the source of some story or fact offered here, please write me care of Random House, 201 E. 50th St., New York, N.Y. 10022 and I will cite the source for you. The books are listed alphabetically under the name of the star to whom the book is devoted.

ABBOTT, BUD, AND LOU COSTELLO. Costello, Chris. *Lou's on First.* New York: St. Martin's Press, 1981.
———. Thomas, Bob. *Bud and Lou.* New York: Lippincott, 1977.
ADLER, LARRY. Adler, Larry. *It Ain't Necessarily So.* New York: Grove Press, 1984.
AHERNE, BRIAN. Aherne, Brian. *A Proper Job.* Boston: Houghton Mifflin, 1969.

ALBERT, EDDIE. Parish, James R., and William T. Leonard. *Hollywood Players: The Thirties*. New Rochelle, N.Y.: Arlington House, 1976.

ALLEN, FRED. Allen, Fred. *Much Ado About Me*. New York: Little, Brown, 1956.

———. Taylor, Robert. *Fred Allen*. New York: Little, Brown, 1989.

ALLEN, GRACIE. Burns, George. *Gracie*. New York: Penguin, 1988.

ALLYSON, JUNE. Leighton, Frances Spatz. *June Allyson*. New York: Putnam, 1982.

ANDREWS, DANA. Parish, James Robert. *Hollywood Reliables*. New Rochelle, N.Y.: Arlington House, 1980.

ARDEN, EVE. Arden, Eve. *Three Phases of Eve*. New York: St. Martin's Press, 1985.

ARNAZ, DESI. Arnaz, Desi. *A Book*. New York: Warner, 1976.

———. Harris, Warren G. *Lucy and Desi*. New York: Simon and Schuster, 1991.

ASTAIRE, FRED. Thomas, Bob. *Astaire*. New York: St. Martin's Press, 1984.

———. Freedland, Michael. *Fred Astaire*. Portland, Ore.: W. P. Allen, 1976.

ASTOR, MARY. Astor, Mary. *My Story*. New York: Doubleday, 1959.

———. Astor, Mary. *A Life on Film*. New York: Delacorte, 1971.

AYRES, LEW. Shipman, David. *The Great Movie Stars: The Golden Years*. New York: Hill & Wang, 1979.

BACALL, LAUREN. Bacall, Lauren. *By Myself*. New York: Knopf, 1978.

BALL, LUCILLE. Harris, Warren G. *Lucy and Desi*. New York: Simon and Schuster, 1991.

———. Higham, Charles. *Lucy*. New York: St. Martin's Press, 1986.

———. Morella, Joe, and Edward Z. Epstein. *Forever Lucy*. Lyle Stuart, 1986.

BANKHEAD, TALLULAH. Bankhead, Tallulah. *Tallulah*. New York: Harpers, 1952.

———. Israel, Lee. *Miss Tallulah Bankhead*. New York: Putnam, 1972.

BENNY, JACK. Benny, Jack, with Joan Benny. *Sunday Nights at Seven*. New York: Warner, 1990.

———. Benny, Mary Livingston, and Hilliard Marks. *Jack Benny*. New York: Doubleday, 1978.

———. Fine, Irving A. *Jack Benny*. New York: Putnam, 1976.

BERGMAN, INGRID. Bergman, Ingrid. *My Story*. New York: Delacorte, 1980.

———. Leamer, Laurence. *As Time Goes By*. New York: Harper and Row, 1986.

BERLE, MILTON. Berle, Milton. *An Autobiography*. New York: Delacorte, 1974.

BOGART, HUMPHREY. Benchley, Nathaniel. *Humphrey Bogart.* New York: Little, Brown, 1975.

———. Gehman, Richard. *Bogart.* New York: Fawcett, 1965.

———. Hyams, Joe. *Bogie.* New York: New American Library, 1966.

BOYER, CHARLES. Swindell, Larry. *Charles Boyer.* New York: Doubleday, 1983.

BRANDO, MARLON. Thomas, Bob. *Marlon.* New York: Random House, 1973.

BRYNNER, YUL. Brynner, Rock. *Yul.* New York: Simon and Schuster, 1989.

CAESAR, SID. Caesar, Sid. *Where Have I Been?* New York: Crown, 1982.

CAGNEY, JAMES. Cagney, James. *Cagney by Cagney.* New York: Doubleday; 1976.

———. Offen, Ron. *Cagney.* Chicago: Henry Regnery, 1972.

———. Warren, Doug. *Cagney.* New York: St. Martin's Press, 1983.

CAIN, JAMES M. Hoopes, Roy. *Cain.* New York: Holt, Rinehart & Winston, 1982.

CANTOR, EDDIE. Cantor, Eddie. *Take My Life.* New York: Doubleday, 1957.

———. Cantor, Eddie. *The Way I See It.* Englewood Cliffs, N.J.: Prentice-Hall, 1959.

CARLISLE, KITTY. Hart, Kitty Carlisle. *Kitty.* New York: Doubleday, 1988.

CASSINI, OLEG. Cassini, Oleg. *In My Own Fashion.* New York: Simon and Schuster, 1987.

CHAPLIN, CHARLES. Chaplin, Charles. *An Autobiography.* New York: Simon and Schuster, 1964.

———. Robinson, David. *Chaplin.* New York: McGraw-Hill, 1985.

CHARISSE, CYD. Charisse, Cyd. *The Two of Us.* New York: Mason Charter, 1976.

CHEVALIER, MAURICE. Chevalier, Maurice. *With Love.* New York: Little, Brown, 1960.

———. Freedland, Michael. *Maurice Chevalier.* New York: William Morrow, 1981.

CLIFT, MONTGOMERY. Bosworth, Patricia. *Montgomery Clift.* New York: Harcourt Brace Jovanovich, 1978.

———. LaGuardia, Robert. *Monty.* New York: Arbor House, 1977.

COHN, HARRY. Thomas, Bob. *King Cohn.* New York: Putnam, 1967.

COLBERT, CLAUDETTE. Quirk, Lawrence J. *Claudette Colbert.* New York: Crown, 1985.

COLMAN, RONALD. Colman, Juliet Benita. *Ronald Colman.* New York: William Morrow, 1975.

———. Smith, R. Dixon. *Ronald Colman, Gentleman of the Cinema.* Jefferson, N.C.: McFarland, 1991.

COOPER, GARY. Arce, Hector. *Gary Cooper.* New York: William Morrow, 1979.

———. Carpozi, George, Jr. *The Gary Cooper Story.* New Rochelle, N.Y.: Arlington House, 1970.

———. Swindell, Larry. *The Last Hero.* New York: Doubleday, 1980.

COOPER, JACKIE. Cooper, Jackie. *Please Don't Shoot My Dog.* New York: William Morrow, 1981.

COTTEN, JOSEPH. Cotten, Joseph. *Vanity Will Get You Somewhere.* San Francisco: Mercury House; 1987.

CRAWFORD, JOAN. Considine, Shaun. *Bette and Joan.* New York: Dell, 1989.

———. Crawford, Christina. *Mommie Dearest.* New York: William Morrow, 1978.

———. Crawford, Joan. *My Way of Life.* New York: Simon and Schuster, 1971.

———. Thomas, Bob. *Joan Crawford.* New York: Simon and Schuster, 1978.

CROSBY, BING. Shepherd, Donald, and Robert F. Slatzer. *Bing Crosby.* New York: St. Martin's Press, 1981.

———. Thompson, Charles. *Bing.* New York: David McKay, 1976.

DANTINE, HELMUT. Hamilton, Sara. *Photoplay,* "Important Import," November 1943.

DARNELL, LINDA. Davis, Ronald L. *Hollywood Beauty.* Norman, Okla.: University of Oklahoma, 1991.

DAVIES, MARION. Davies, Marion. *The Times We Had.* Indianapolis: Bobbs-Merrill, 1975.

———. Guiles, Fred Lawrence. *Marion Davies.* New York: McGraw-Hill, 1972.

DAVIS, BETTE. Considine, Shaun. *Bette and Joan.* New York: Dell, 1989.

———. Davis, Bette. *This 'n' That.* New York: Putnam, 1987.

———. Higham, Charles. *Bette.* New York: Macmillan, 1981.

———. Hyman, B. D. *My Mother's Keeper.* New York: William Morrow, 1985.

———. Leaming, Barbara F. *Bette Davis.* New York: Simon and Schuster, 1992.

———. Spada, James. *More Than a Woman.* New York: Bantam, 1993.

———. Stone, Whitney. *Mother Goddam.* New York: Hawthorn, 1974.

DAVIS, SAMMY, JR. Davis, Sammy, Jr. *Why Me?* New York: Farrar, Straus & Giroux, 1989.

———. Davis, Sammy, Jr. *Yes I Can.* New York: Farrar, Straus & Giroux, 1965.

DE CARLO, YVONNE. De Carlo, Yvonne. *Yvonne.* New York: St. Martin's Press, 1987.

DIETRICH, MARLENE. Bach, Steven. *Marlene Dietrich.* New York: William Morrow, 1992.

————. Dietrich, Marlene. *Marlene Dietrich's ABC.* New York: Doubleday, 1961.

————. Dietrich, Marlene. *Marlene.* New York: Weidenfeld & Nicolson, 1989.

————. Frewin, Leslie. *Dietrich.* New York: Stein & Day, 1967.

————. Higham, Charles. *Marlene.* New York: W. W. Norton, 1977.

————. Spoto, Donald. *Blue Angel.* New York: Doubleday, 1992.

DISNEY, WALT. Schickel, Richard. *The Disney Version.* New York: Simon and Schuster, 1968.

————. Thomas, Bob. *Walt Disney.* New York: Simon and Schuster, 1976.

DOUGLAS, HELEN GAHAGAN. Douglas, Helen Gahagan. *A Full Life.* New York: Doubleday, 1982.

DOUGLAS, KIRK. Douglas, Kirk. *The Ragman's Son.* New York: Simon and Schuster, 1988.

————. Munn, Michael. *Kirk Douglas.* New York: St. Martin's Press, 1985.

DOUGLAS, MELVYN. Douglas, Melvyn. *See You at the Movies.* Lanham, Md.: University Press of America, 1986.

DURANTE, JIMMY. Fowler, Gene. *Schnozzola.* New York: Viking, 1951.

————. Robbins, Jhan. *Inka Dinka Doo.* New York: Paragon House, 1991.

FAIRBANKS, DOUGLAS, JR. Connell, Brian. *Knight Errant.* New York: Doubleday, 1955.

————. Fairbanks, Douglas, Jr. *Salad Days.* New York: Doubleday, 1988.

————. Fairbanks, Douglas, Jr. *A Hell of a War.* New York: St. Martin's Press, 1993.

FARMER, FRANCES. Farmer, Frances. *Will There Really Be a Morning?* New York: Little Brown, 1972.

FLYNN, ERROL. Flynn, Errol. *My Wicked, Wicked Ways.* New York: Putnam, 1959.

————. Freedland, Michael. *The Two Lives of Errol Flynn.* New York: William Morrow, 1979.

————. Higham, Charles. *The Untold Story.* New York: Doubleday, 1980.

————. Thomas, Tony. *The Spy Who Never Was.* Secaucus, N.J.: Citadel, 1990.

————. Wiles, Buster. *My Days with Errol Flynn.* Santa Monica, Calif.: Roundtable, 1988.

FONDA, HENRY. Fonda, Henry, as told to Howard Teichmann. *My Life.* New York: New American Library, 1981.

FONTAINE, JOAN. Fontaine, Joan. *No Bed of Roses.* New York: William Morrow, 1978.

FORD, JOHN. Sinclair, Andrew. *John Ford.* New York: Dial Press, 1979.

GABLE, CLARK. Tornabene, Lyn. *Long Live the King.* New York: Putnam, 1976.

GABOR, ZSA ZSA. Gabor, Zsa Zsa, as told to Gerold Frank. *Zsa Zsa Gabor.* London: Barker, 1960.

———. Gabor, Zsa Zsa, as told to Wendy Leigh. *One Lifetime Is Not Enough.* New York: Delacorte, 1991.

GARBO, GRETA. Gronowicz, Antoni. *Garbo.* New York: Simon and Schuster, 1990.

GARDNER, AVA. Gardner, Ava. *Ava.* New York: Bantam, 1990.

GARFIELD, JOHN. Swindell, Larry. *Body and Soul.* New York: William Morrow, 1975.

GARLAND, JUDY. Edwards, Anne. *Judy Garland.* New York: Simon and Schuster, 1974.

———. Frank, Gerold. *Judy.* New York: Harper & Row, 1975.

———. Shipman, David. *The Secret Life of an American Legend.* New York: Hyperion, 1993.

GARNER, JAMES. Strait, Raymond. *James Garner.* New York: St. Martin's Press, 1985.

GARNETT, TAY. Garnett, Tay. *Light Your Torches and Pull Up Your Tights.* New Rochelle, N.Y.: Arlington House, 1973.

GODDARD, PAULETTE. Morella, Joe, and Edward Z. Epstein. *Paulette.* New York: St. Martin's Press, 1985.

GOLDWYN, SAM. Berg, A. Scott. *Goldwyn.* New York: Knopf, 1989.

———. Marx, Arthur. *Goldwyn.* New York: W. W. Norton, 1976.

GRABLE, BETTY. Pastos, Spero. *Pinup.* New York: Putnam, 1986.

GRAHAME, GLORIA. Curcio, Vincent. *Suicide Blonde.* New York: William Morrow, 1989.

GRANGER, STEWART. Granger, Stewart. *Sparks Fly Upward.* London: Granada, 1981.

GRANT, CARY. Harris, Warren G. *Cary Grant.* New York: Doubleday, 1987.

———. Higham, Charles, and Roy Mosley. *Cary Grant.* New York: Harcourt Brace Jovanovich, 1989.

———. Nelson, Nancy. *Evenings with Cary Grant.* New York: William Morrow, 1991.

———. Wansell, Geoffrey. *Haunted Idol.* New York: William Morrow, 1984.

GREENSTREET, SYDNEY, AND PETER LORRE. Sennett, Ted. *Masters of Menace.* New York: E. P. Dutton, 1979.

HARDWICKE, CEDRIC. Hardwicke, Cedric. *A Victorian in Orbit.* Garden City, N.Y.: Doubleday, 1961.

HAVOC, JUNE. Havoc, June. *More Havoc.* New York: Harper & Row, 1980.

HAYDEN, STERLING. Hayden, Sterling. *Wanderer.* New York: Knopf, 1963.

HAYWARD, SUSAN. LaGuardia, Robert, and Gene Arceri. *Red.* New York: Macmillan, 1985.

———. Linet, Beverly. *Susan Hayward.* New York: Atheneum, 1980.

HAYWORTH, RITA. Kobal, John. *Rita Hayworth.* New York: W. W. Norton, 1978.

HEPBURN, KATHARINE. Carey, Gary. *Katherine Hepburn.* New York: Pocket Books, 1975.

———. Edwards, Anne. *A Remarkable Woman.* New York: William Morrow, 1985.

———. Freedland, Michael. *Katharine Hepburn.* London: W. H. Allen, 1984.

———. Hepburn, Katharine. *Me.* New York: Knopf, 1991.

———. Higham, Charles. *Kate.* New York: W. W. Norton, 1975.

HESTON, CHARLTON. Crowther, Bruce. *Charlton Heston.* London: Columbus Books, 1986.

———. Munn, Michael. *Charlton Heston.* New York: St. Martin's Press, 1986.

HITCHCOCK, ALFRED. Spoto, Donald. *The Dark Side of Genius.* New York: Little, Brown, 1983.

HOLDEN, WILLIAM. Thomas, Bob. *Golden Boy.* New York: St. Martin's Press, 1983.

HOLLIDAY, JUDY. Carey, Gary. *Judy Holliday.* New York: Seaview Books, 1982.

———. Holtzman, Will. *Judy Holliday.* New York: Putnam, 1982.

HOPE, BOB. Faith, William Robert. *Bob Hope.* New York: Putnam, 1982.

———. Hope, Bob. *I Never Left Home.* New York: Simon and Schuster, 1944.

———. Hope, Bob, as told to Pete Martin. *Have Tux Will Travel.* New York: Simon and Schuster, 1954.

———. Hope, Bob, as told to Pete Martin. *The Last Christmas Show.* Garden City, N.Y.: Doubleday, 1974.

———. Hope, Bob. *Don't Shoot, It's Only Me.* New York: Putnam, 1990.

———. Marx, Arthur. *The Secret Life of Bob Hope.* New York: Barricade Books, 1993.

———. *Time,* "Hope For Humanity" (cover story). September 20, 1943.

HORNE, LENA. Haskins, James. *Lena.* New York: Stein & Day, 1984.

———. Horne, Lena. *Lena.* New York: Limelight, 1986.

HOWARD, LESLIE. Howard, Leslie Ruth. *A Quite Remarkable Father.* New York: Harcourt Brace, 1959.

———. Howard, Ronald. *In Search of My Father.* New York: St. Martin's Press, 1981.

HUDSON, ROCK. Hudson, Rock, and Sara Davidson. *Rock Hudson: His Own Story.* New York: William Morrow, 1986.

HUGHES, HOWARD. Dietrich, Noah. *Howard.* New York: Fawcett, 1972.
———. Drosnin, Michael. *Citizen Hughes.* New York: Holt, Rinehart, & Winston, 1985.
HUSTON, JOHN. Huston, John. *An Open Book.* New York: Knopf, 1980.
JOHNSON, VAN. Beecher, Elizabeth. *Van Johnson.* Racine, Wisc.: Whitman, 1947.
JOLSON, AL. Freedland, Michael. *Jolson.* New York: Stein & Day, 1972.
———. Goldman, Herbert G. *Jolson.* New York: Oxford University Press, 1988.
KELLY, GENE. Hirschhorn, Clive. *Gene Kelly.* New York: St. Martin's Press, 1985.
KEYES, EVELYN. Keyes, Evelyn. *Scarlett O'Hara's Younger Sister.* Secaucus, N.J.: Stuart, 1977.
KORDA, ALEXANDER. Korda, Michael. *Charmed Lives.* New York: Random House, 1979.
———. Kulik, Karol. *Alexander Korda.* New Rochelle, N.Y.: Arlington House, 1975.
LADD, ALAN. Linet, Beverly. *Ladd.* New York: Arbor House, 1979.
LAHR, BERT. Lahr, John. *Notes on a Cowardly Lion.* New York: Knopf, 1969.
LAKE, VERONICA. Lake, Veronica. *Veronica.* New York: Citadel Press, 1971.
LAMARR, HEDY. Lamarr, Hedy. *Ecstasy and Me.* New York: Fawcett, 1967.
LAMOUR, DOROTHY. Lamour, Dorothy, as told to Dick McInnes. *My Side of the Road.* Englewood Cliffs, N.J.: Prentice-Hall, 1980.
LANCASTER, BURT. Clinch, Minty. *Burt Lancaster.* New York: Stein & Day, 1984.
———. Windeler, Robert. *Burt Lancaster.* New York: St. Martin's Press, 1984.
LANCHESTER, ELSA. Lanchester, Elsa. *Elsa Lanchester Herself.* New York: St. Martin's Press, 1983.
LANDIS, CAROLE. Landis, Carole. *Four Jills in a Jeep.* New York: Random House, 1944.
———. Landis, Carole. *Photoplay,* "Don't Marry a Stranger," April 1945.
LAUGHTON, CHARLES. Callow, Simon. *Charles Laughton.* New York: Grove Press, 1987.
———. Higham, Charles. *Charles Laughton.* New York: Doubleday, 1987.
LAUREL, STAN, AND OLIVER HARDY. Skretvedt, Randy. *Laurel and Hardy.* Beverly Hills: Moonstone Press, 1987.
LAWFORD, PETER. Lawford, Patricia. *The Peter Lawford Story.* New York: Carroll & Graf, 1988.
———. Spada, James. *Peter Lawford.* New York: Bantam, 1991.
LEIGH, VIVIEN. Edwards, Anne. *Vivien Leigh.* New York: Simon and Schuster, 1977.

————. Vickers, Hugo. *Vivien Leigh.* New York: Little, Brown, 1988.

LEMMON, JACK. Widener, Don. *Lemmon.* New York: Macmillan, 1975.

LOMBARD, CAROLE. Swindell, Larry. *Screwball.* New York: William Morrow, 1975.

LOOS, ANITA. Loos, Anita. *A Girl Like I.* New York: Viking, 1966.

LOY, MYRNA. Loy, Myrna, with James Kotsilibas-Davis. *Myrna Loy.* London: Bloomsbury, 1987.

MACDONALD, JEANETTE. Parish, James Robert. *The Jeanette MacDonald Story;* New York: Mason Charter, 1976.

MARTIN, TONY. Martin, Tony, and Cyd Charisse. *The Two of Us.* New York: Mason Charter, 1976.

MARVIN, LEE. Zec, Donald. *Marvin.* New York: St. Martin's Press, 1980.

MARX, GROUCHO. Arce, Hector. *Groucho.* New York: Putnam, 1979.

————. Chandler, Charlotte. *Hello, I Must Be Going.* New York: Doubleday, 1978.

————. Marx, Groucho. *Letters.* New York: Simon and Schuster, 1967.

MARX, HARPO. Marx, Harpo, with Rowland Barber. *Harpo Speaks.* New York: Freeway Press, 1974.

MARX BROTHERS. Crichton, Kyle. *The Marx Brothers.* Doubleday, 1950.

MASSEY, RAYMOND. Massey, Raymond. *A Hundred Different Lives.* New York: Little, Brown, 1979.

————. Massey, Raymond. *When I Was Young.* New York: Little, Brown, 1976.

MCDANIEL, HATTIE. Jackson, Carlton. *Hattie.* Lanham, Md.: Madison, 1990.

MENJOU, ADOLPHE. Menjou, Adolphe. *It Took Nine Tailors.* New York: Whittlesey House, 1948.

MEREDITH, BURGESS. Meredith, Burgess. *So Far, So Good,* New York: Little, Brown, 1944.

————. Parish, James Robert, and William T. Leonard. *Hollywood Players: The Thirties.* New Rochelle, N.Y.: Arlington House, 1976.

MERMAN, ETHEL. Merman, Ethel, with George Eels. *Merman.* New York: Simon and Schuster, 1978.

MERRILL, GARY. Merrill, Gary. *Bette, Rita and the Rest of My Life.* Augusta, Maine: Lance Tapley, 1988.

MILLAND, RAY. Milland, Ray. *Wide Eyed in Babylon.* New York: William Morrow, 1974.

MILLER, ANN. Miller, Ann, with Norma Lee Browning. *Miller's High Life.* New York: Doubleday, 1972.

MILLER, GLENN. Simon, George T. *Glenn Miller and His Orchestra.* New York: Thomas Y. Crowell, 1974.

MIRANDA, CARMEN. Gil-Montero, Martha. *Brazilian Bombshell.* New York: Donald I. Fine, 1989.

MITCHUM, ROBERT. Downing, David. *Robert Mitchum.* London: W. H. Allen, 1985.

———. Eels, George. *Robert Mitchum.* New York: Franklin Watts, 1984.

———. Tomkies, Mike. *The Robert Mitchum Story.* Chicago: Henry Regnery, 1972.

MONROE, MARILYN. Guiles, Fred Lawrence. *Norma Jean.* New York: McGraw-Hill, 1969.

———. Jordan, Ted. *My Secret Life with Marilyn Monroe.* New York: Penguin, 1989.

———. Summers, Anthony. *Goddess.* New York: Macmillan, 1985.

MONTGOMERY, ROBERT. Parish, James Robert, and Don E. Stanke. *The Debonairs.* New Rochelle, N.Y.: Arlington House, 1975.

MORRIS, WAYNE. Bruce, Jon. *Silver Screen,* "Hats Off to Wayne," May 1946.

———. Morris, Mrs. Wayne. *Photoplay,* "My Husband Is Home," April 1945.

———. Parish, James Robert, and William T. Leonard. *Hollywood Players: The Thirties.* New Rochelle, N.Y.: Arlington House, 1976.

MUNI, PAUL. Lawrence, Jerome. *Actor.* New York: Putnam, 1974.

MURPHY, AUDIE. Whiting, Charles. *Hero.* Chelsea, Mich.: Scarborough House, 1990.

NEWMAN, PAUL. Kerbel, Michael. *Paul Newman.* New York: Pyramid, 1974.

NIVEN, DAVID. Morley, Sheridan. *The Other Side of the Moon.* New York: Harper & Row, 1985.

———. Niven, David. *The Moon Is a Balloon.* New York: Putnam, 1972.

———. Niven, David. *Bring On the Empty Horses.* New York: Putnam, 1975.

OBERON, MERLE. Higham, Charles, and Roy Mosley. *Princess Merle.* New York: Coward-McCann, 1983.

O'BRIEN, PAT. O'Brien, Pat. *The Wind at My Back.* Garden City, N.Y.: Doubleday, 1964.

———. Parish, James Robert. *Hollywood Reliables.* New Rochelle, N.Y.: Arlington House, 1980.

OLIVIER, LAURENCE. Holden, Anthony. *Laurence Olivier.* New York: Atheneum, 1988.

———. Kiernan, Thomas. *Sir Larry.* New York: Times Books, 1991.

———. Olivier, Laurence. *Confessions of an Actor.* New York: Simon and Schuster, 1982.

———. Spoto, Donald. *Laurence Olivier.* New York: HarperCollins, 1992.

PECK, GREGORY. Freedland, Michael. *Gregory Peck.* New York: William Morrow, 1980.

PICKFORD, MARY. Eyman, Scott. *Mary Pickford.* New York: Donald I. Fine, 1990.

PIDGEON, WALTER. Parish, James Robert. *Hollywood Reliables*. New Rochelle, N.Y.: Arlington House, 1980.

POITIER, SIDNEY. Poitier, Sidney. *This Life*. New York: Knopf, 1980.

POWELL, WILLIAM. Francisco, Charles. *Gentleman: The William Powell Story*. New York: St. Martin's Press, 1985.

POWER, TYRONE. Arce, Hector. *The Secret Life of Tyrone Power*. New York: William Morrow, 1979.

———. Guiles, Fred Lawrence. *Tyrone Power*. New York: Doubleday, 1979.

RAFT, GEORGE. Yablonsky, Lewis. *George Raft*. New York: McGraw-Hill, 1974.

RATHBONE, BASIL. Rathbone, Basil. *In and Out of Character*. Garden City, N.Y.: Doubleday, 1962.

RAYMOND, GENE. Parish, James Robert, and William T. Leonard. *Hollywood Players: The Thirties*. New Rochelle, N.Y.: Arlington House, 1976.

REAGAN, RONALD. Edwards, Anne. *Early Reagan*. New York: William Morrow, 1987.

———. Reagan, Ronald. *Where's the Rest of Me?* New York: Karz, 1965.

———. Reagan, Ronald. *Sincerely, Ronald Reagan*. Ottawa, Ill.: Green Hill, 1976.

———. Reagan, Ronald. *An American Life*. New York: Simon and Schuster, 1980.

———. Wills, Garry. *Reagan's America*. New York: Doubleday, 1987.

ROBINSON, EDWARD G. Robinson, Edward G. *All My Yesterdays*. New York: Hawthorn, 1973.

ROGERS, GINGER. Rogers, Ginger. *Ginger, My Story*. New York: Harper-Collins, 1991.

ROGERS, ROY, AND DALE EVANS. Rogers, Roy, and Dale Evans. *The Story of Roy Rogers and Dale Evans*. Waco, Tex.: Word Books, 1979.

ROONEY, MICKEY. Marx, Arthur. *The Nine Lives of Mickey Rooney*. New York: Stein & Day, 1986.

———. Rooney, Mickey. *Life Is Too Short*. New York: Villard, 1991.

RUSSELL, JANE. Russell, Jane. *Jane Russell*. New York: Franklin Watts, 1985.

RUSSELL, ROSALIND. Russell, Rosalind. *Life Is a Banquet*. New York: Random House, 1977.

RYAN, ROBERT. Jarlett, Franklin. *Robert Ryan*. Jefferson, N.C.: McFarland, 1990.

SANDERS, GEORGE. Sanders, George. *Memoirs of a Professional Cad*. New York: Putnam, 1972.

———. Vanderbeets, Richard. *George Sanders*. Lanham, Md.: Madison, 1990.

SHEARER, NORMA. Lambert, Gavin. *Norma Shearer*. New York: Knopf, 1990.

————. Quirk, Lawrence J. *Norma Shearer.* New York: St. Martin's Press, 1988.

SILVERS, PHIL. Silvers, Phil. *The Laugh Is on Me.* Englewood Cliffs, N.J.: Prentice-Hall, 1973.

SINATRA, FRANK. Kelley, Kitty. *His Way.* New York: Bantam, 1986.

————. Wilson, Earl. *Sinatra.* New York: Macmillan, 1976.

SKELTON, RED. Marx, Arthur. *Red Skelton.* New York: Dutton, 1979.

STACK, ROBERT. Stack, Robert. *Shooting Straight.* New York: Macmillan, 1980.

STANWYCK, BARBARA. Diorio, Al. *Barbara Stanwyck.* New York: Coward-McCann, 1983.

————. Madsen, Axel. *Stanwyck.* New York: HarperCollins, 1994.

STEWART, JAMES. Eyles, Allen. *James Stewart.* New York: Stein & Day, 1984.

————. Robbins, Jhan. *Everybody's Man.* New York: Putnam, 1985.

SWANSON, GLORIA. Swanson, Gloria. *Swanson on Swanson.* New York: Random House, 1980.

TAYLOR, ELIZABETH. Kelley, Kitty. *Elizabeth Taylor.* New York: Simon and Schuster, 1981.

————. Sheppard, Dick. *Elizabeth.* New York: Harper & Row, 1974.

TAYLOR, ROBERT. Wayne, Jane Ellen. *Robert Taylor.* New York: St. Martin's Press, 1973.

TEMPLE, SHIRLEY. Black, Shirley Temple. *Child Star.* New York: McGraw-Hill, 1988.

————. Edwards, Anne. *Shirley Temple: American Princess.* New York: William Morrow, 1988.

THOMAS, DANNY. Thomas, Danny. *Make Room for Danny.* New York: Putnam, 1991.

TIERNEY, GENE. Tierney, Gene. *Self-Portrait.* New York: Wyden Books, 1979.

TODD, MICHAEL. Cohn, Art. *The Nine Lives of Michael Todd.* New York: Random House, 1958.

TRACY, SPENCER. Davidson, Bill. *Spencer Tracy.* New York: Dutton, 1987.

TURNER, LANA. Morella, Joe, and Edward Z. Epstein. *Lana.* Secaucus, N.J.: Citadel Press, 1971.

————. Turner, Lana. *Lana.* New York: Dutton, 1982.

VALLEE, RUDY. Vallee, Rudy. *Let the Chips Fall.* Harrisburg, Pa.: Stackpole Books, 1975.

VAN DOREN, MAMIE. Van Doren, Mamie, with Art Aveilhe. *Playing the Field.* New York: Putnam, 1987.

WAYNE, JOHN. Ramer, Jean. *Duke: The Real Story of John Wayne.* New York: Charter, 1973.

————. Shepherd, Donald, and Robert Slatzer. *Duke.* New York: Zebra, 1985.

————. Wayne, John. *America: Why I Love Her.* New York: Ballantine, 1979.

————. Zolotow, Maurice. *Shooting Star.* New York: Simon and Schuster, 1974.

WELLES, ORSON. Leamings, Barbara. *Orson Welles.* New York: Viking, 1985.

WEST, MAE. Eels, George, and Stanley Musgrove. *Mae West.* New York: William Morrow, 1982.

————. West, Mae. *Goodness Had Nothing to Do with It.* New York: Manor Books, 1976.

WINTERS, SHELLEY. Winters, Shelley. *Shelley.* New York: William Morrow, 1980.

WRAY, FAY. Wray, Fay. *On the Other Hand.* New York: St. Martin's Press, 1989.

WYMAN, JANE. Morella, Joe, and Edward Z. Epstein. *Jane Wyman.* New York: Delacorte, 1985.

YOUNG, GIG. Parish, James Robert. *Hollywood Reliables.* New Rochelle, N.Y.: Arlington House, 1980.

YOUNG, LORETTA. Morella, Joe, and Edward Z. Epstein. *Loretta Young.* New York: Delacorte, 1985.

YOUNG, ROBERT. Parish, James Robert. *Hollywood Reliables.* New Rochelle, N.Y.: Arlington House, 1980.

These sources were also especially helpful:

Coffey, Frank. *Always Home.* McLean, Va.: Brassey's, 1991.

Dick, Bernard F. *The Star-Spangled Screen.* Lexington: University Press of Kentucky, 1985.

Eastman, John. *Retakes.* New York: Ballantine, 1981.

Friedrich, Otto. *City of Nets.* New York: Harper & Row, 1986.

Hoopes, Roy. *Americans Remember the Homefront.* Spring Valley, N.Y.: Hawthorn, 1977.

Katz, Ephraim. *The Film Encyclopedia.* New York: Crowell, 1979.

Koppes, Clayton, R., and Gregory D. Black. *Hollywood Goes to War.* Berkeley: University of California Press, 1987.

Lingeman, Richard R. *Don't You Know There's a War On?* New York: Putnam, 1970.

Maltin, Leonard. *Movie and Video Guide 1993.* New York: Signet, 1992.

The New York Times Directory of Film. New York: Arno Press, 1974.

Parrish, Thomas, ed. *The Simon and Schuster Encyclopedia of World War II.* New York: Simon and Schuster, 1978.

Simon, George T. *The Big Bands.* New York: Macmillan, 1967.

ABOUT THE AUTHOR

ROY HOOPES, the Washington bureau chief of *Modern Maturity* magazine and the author of several books, including biographies of James M. Cain and Ralph Ingersoll and an oral history of the World War II home front, has been a film buff all his life. Born in Salt Lake City, he lives with his wife, Cora, near their two sons, Spencer and Tom, and their families, in the Maryland suburbs of Washington, D.C., and in Dewey Beach, Delaware.

ABOUT THE TYPE

The text of this book was set in Janson, a typeface designed in about 1690 by Nicholas Kis, a Hungarian in Amsterdam. In 1919 the matrices became the property of the Stempel Foundry in Frankfurt. Janson is an old-style book face of excellent clarity and sharpness. Its serifs are concave and splayed; the contrast between thick and thin strokes is marked.